"Lives Full of Struggle and Triumph"

New Perspectives on the History of the South

Florida A&M University, Tallahassee
Florida Atlantic University, Boca Raton
Florida Gulf Coast University, Ft. Myers
Florida International University, Miami
Florida State University, Tallahassee
University of Central Florida, Orlando
University of Florida, Gainesville
University of North Florida, Jacksonville
University of South Florida, Tampa
University of West Florida, Pensacola

New Perspectives on the History of the South
Edited by John David Smith

"Lives Full of Struggle and Triumph"

Southern Women, Their Institutions,
and Their Communities

Edited by Bruce L. Clayton and John A. Salmond

Foreword by John David Smith, Series Editor

University Press of Florida

Gainesville/Tallahassee/Tampa/Boca Raton
Pensacola/Orlando/Miami/Jacksonville/Ft. Myers

08 07 06 05 04 03   6 5 4 3 2 1

Library of Congress Cataloging-in-Publication Data
Lives full of struggle and triumph: Southern women, their
institutions, and their communities / edited by Bruce L. Clayton
and John A. Salmond; foreword by John David Smith.
p. cm. — (New perspectives on the history of the South)
Includes bibliographical references and index.
ISBN 0-8130-2675-X (cloth: alk. paper)
1. Women—Southern States—History—Sources. 2. Women—
Southern States—Social conditions. 3. Women—Confederate States
of America—History—Sources. 4. Segregation—Southern States—
History. 5. Southern States—History—Sources. 6. Southern States—
Social life and customs. I. Clayton, Bruce. II. Salmond, John A.
III. Series.
HQ1438.S63L58 2003
305.4'0975—dc22   2003057916

The University Press of Florida is the scholarly publishing agency
for the State University System of Florida, comprising Florida A&M
University, Florida Atlantic University, Florida Gulf Coast University,
Florida International University, Florida State University, University
of Central Florida, University of Florida, University of North Florida,
University of South Florida, and University of West Florida.

University Press of Florida
15 Northwest 15th Street
Gainesville, FL 32611-2079
http://www.upf.com

Contents

Foreword

As historian Anne Firor Scott notes in her introduction to *"Lives Full of Struggle and Triumph,"* the field of southern women's history remained in its infancy until the 1960s. For example, women's history received no historiographical essay and a total of only three page references in Arthur S. Link and Rembert W. Patrick's *Writing Southern History* (1965), the influential guide to southern historical scholarship of that era. Twenty-two years later, however, Scott and Jacqueline Dowd Hall contributed a fifty-six-page historiographical essay, "Women in the South," to *Interpreting Southern History* (1987), edited by John B. Boles and Evelyn Thomas Nolen. In the intervening years scholars had transformed southern women's history into a major subspecialty within the fields of both southern and women's history. Scott observes correctly that today only a book-length treatment could assess adequately the burgeoning corpus of scholarship on southern women's history.

Fourteen of the leading historians in this vibrant and exciting field have contributed chapters to Bruce Clayton and John Salmond's splendid *"Lives Full of Struggle and Triumph."* In keeping with the best recent work, the authors position southern women—black and white, affluent, middle class, and poor—at the center of social change and institution- and community-building over the course of the southern past. Readers will find the essays original, well researched, engagingly written, and timely. In general, they underscore the role of gender in constructing politics, economics, religion, education—in short, every institution in the South's colorful past. More specifically, the essays illustrate clearly the agency that southern women always have held but that has largely been ignored or undervalued by traditional historical analyses.

Three chapters focus on marriage, and another addresses education in the Old South. Examining the marriage of William Byrd II and Lucy Parke Byrd, Paula A. Treckel concludes that "Lucy was unwilling to yield to her husband's authority, and her desire for true intimacy within their marriage was in direct conflict with her husband's need for power and control."

Giselle Roberts analyzes the evolution of Sarah Morgan from Louisiana belle to South Carolina journalist and wife. In her newspaper work, Morgan "offered readers an ideal; a vision in which women's work outside the home was accepted as a valued contribution to the domestic ideal, and one that rebuilt a single, adult woman's identity rather than destroying it." According to Warren Ellem, Blanche Butler Ames, wife of Mississippi governor Adelbert Ames, "belonged with neither the politically active women visible in reform movements nor those women who accepted traditional definitions of their roles." Anya Jabour concludes that the female academy of the Old South "offered southern daughters an alternative to an identity based on family connections: a sense of self anchored in female community."

The Civil War era broadly conceived provides the context for three other chapters. Focusing on the role of women on the Confederate home front in Edgefield District, South Carolina, Orville Vernon Burton notes that they "found that the exigencies of the Civil War enabled them to make a more substantial and active contribution to community life" and, subsequently, "these women envisioned a broader, more active position for themselves in the social and political life of the South." Barbara E. Mattick writes that while the history of the Catholic nuns of St. Augustine, Florida, "shows that the strong anti-Catholicism associated with the North in the 1850s had little hold in the South," their pedagogy was "consistent with the prevailing values and prescribed behaviors for American women." In her analysis of the first two decades of the history of the United Daughters of the Confederacy, Karen L. Cox explains that the Daughters "reaffirmed the region's conservative traditions, even as they expanded woman's sphere."

The remaining seven essays examine southern women in the segregation era. Glenn Feldman concludes that in the 1920s, women of the Alabama Ku Klux Klan "shaped the order, its ideology, its goals, and the implementation of its program . . . in important ways." Examining how southern women viewed Eleanor Roosevelt, Pamela Tyler finds that "Southern women's views of this First Lady were inextricably bound up with their opinions about the aspects of southern life in which Mrs. Roosevelt interested herself." Sarah Hart Brown rescues from oblivion Esther Cooper Jackson, a leader of the Southern Negro Youth Congress and editor of *Freedomways*. Kathi Kern tells the story of Thelma McGee, a black Mississippian who triumphed over all manner of adversity to become a schoolteacher and to retain her family's homestead.

Catherine Fosl analyzes the contributions of Anne McCarty Braden, a Kentucky white patrician; the "mere mention of her name pumped adrenaline into the veins of segregationists in the Cold-War South." Elizabeth Jacoway investigates Arkansan Vivion Brewer, president of the Women's Emergency Committee to Open Our Schools, an organization that "became the moral and political force by which Little Rock was brought to its collective senses" during the school desegregation crisis, 1958–60. In the book's final chapter, Michelle Haberland uses the Vanity Fair apparel factory in Jackson, Alabama, as a window to view the unionization, desegregation, and politicalization of the women who worked in the plant from its founding in 1939 until the 1980s.

Collectively, the essays in *"Lives Full of Struggle and Triumph"* suggest the breadth, depth, and high quality of the recent explosion of research in southern women's history. Just as women's history has become a major field for all historians, southern women's history plays an essential role in unraveling the complex history of race, class, and gender relations in the American South.

John David Smith
Series Editor

Preface

The genesis of this book occurred at a meeting of the Southern Historical Association. We had just heard two excellent papers, one by an established scholar, one by a graduate student. What they had in common, though widely divergent in period and subject matter, was that they both explored the way two groups of women, one in the immediate post–Civil War years, one in the years after World War II, had created institutions through which they hoped to alter the course of their lives, and by extension, that of the communities in which they lived. For some time now, we have been convinced that women's history, whether done by men or women, has exhibited not just solid research and analysis, but a welcomed and invigorating vitality. We concluded that these two papers deserved a wider audience. Thus was born the notion of producing a volume of essays written by a blend of experienced scholars and young historians, spanning the sweep of the history of southern women from the colonial period to the late twentieth century, but each directed in a specific way to the theme of this book's subtitle, *Southern Women, Their Institutions, and Their Communities*. Widely variegated as they might be, each essay would be concerned with change, either with the institutions that women created in order to effect change, as in Elizabeth Jacoway's piece; those within which they worked in order to shift their direction, as in the piece by Michelle Haberland; or those they wished to change, including that of marriage. Some of the essays deal with social change on the broadest of scales, others with the intimate details of personal life. Most also chronicle how such changes impacted on the networks and the communities in which these women worked and lived. They cover, therefore, a wide spectrum, but the themes of change—social, personal and institutional, and community—are the unifiers.

These essays are grouped in four parts. In the first, "The Private World," those by Paula Treckel, Warren Ellem, and Giselle Roberts, deal with change in that most private of institutions, marriage; the fourth essay deals with the education of white women in the antebellum South, before the Civil War changed their lives forever. The three remaining parts all in some way concern women and the key public events of the day, the larger questions or defining eras of southern history. Part 2, for example, has the Civil War as its subject matter. Vernon Burton explores how the lives of women in a single South Carolina county changed as a result of the climactic struggle. Barbara Mattick, too, deals with a particular group, the Catholic nuns of St. Augustine, whose institution faced new challenges as a result of the war, while Karen Cox details the creation of the United Daughters of the Confederacy, an institution dedicated to shaping and preserving historical memory of the Lost Cause. The essays in part 3 both deal with the South during the era of segregation, and with the vastly differing experiences of white and black women in that time. Part 4, "The Era of Social Change," is the longest in this book as its agencies and individuals, white and black, joined in the task of challenging the racial caste system that had for so long dominated their region. For Esther Jackson it was the Southern Negro Youth Congress and the Communist Party, for Anne Braden, the Southern Conference Educational Fund, and for the unsung women workers at the Vanity Fair mill, their International Ladies Garment Workers Union local. But again, the linkage among these institutions was the great public issue of civil rights and the quickening drive to free all southerners once and for all from the blight of segregation.

Of course, to divide these essays in this way is, inevitably, to make some rather arbitrary choices, as many could easily fit into more than one part. Kathi Kern's gentle, perceptive piece about Thelma McGee's girlhood in the Mississippi Delta, with its emphasis on the sustaining power of community, could well fit in part 1. Yet McGee's life, eventually and inevitably, intersects with the great changes sweeping the South in the 1960s. She became part of the change-making institutions, hence our rationale for including her story in the final part. Similarly, though Warren Ellem's essay is about the relationship between Adelbert Ames and his wife, Blanche, its backdrop is the central event of southern history, the Civil War and its aftermath, and so it could have been placed in part 2. Nevertheless, we believe our organizational principles have an inherent logic. More importantly, we also believe that these essays reflect the exciting world of southern women's history and constitute, in the welcome words of one of our anonymous referees, "a splendid sampler of the very latest and best in scholarship on southern women."

The editors wish also to thank Ms. Heather Wilkie of La Trobe University and Ms. Alison Gardiner of Allegheny College for their work in turning marked copy into readable prose.

Bruce Clayton
John Salmond

Introduction

ANNE FIROR SCOTT

Southern white women have long been romanticized in myth, legend, and fiction. Black women, too, have been the subject of myths, though of a quite different kind. And in both cases the myths have tended to fill the vacuum left because hardly anyone paid any attention to women's history, to the varieties of women's experience, or to change over time. It was as if the world were composed only of men, or at least as if only men made history.

Even when a handful of daring pioneers began to write the history of southern women in the 1920s, their work—though often excellent—did not make its way into the consciousness of the overwhelmingly male historical establishment or into what we might call the mind of the reading public for a very long time. So recent has been serious scholarship on the subject that of the six pioneers who were living when I joined their company in 1962, I knew five, all of whom welcomed an addition to their number and gave me as much help as they could.

Historians interested in the sociology of knowledge will find a fertile study in the rapid growth of women's history in the twentieth century. While it is difficult to identify underlying causes for any major intellectual shift, some things are clear. First, the nineteenth century had witnessed extraordinary changes in the level of education and in the political involvement of both middle-class and working-class American women. One manifestation of that activism was a good deal of writing about women, much of it encompassing their history, but even at a time when most respected American historians were amateurs, the women's historical writing did not elicit the attention granted their male contemporaries. Nor did any of the women writers have anything like the resources that made possible the work of a Francis Parkman or a Henry Adams.

The nineteenth-century pattern of women's history written to support or in response to women's political activism continued for a very long time. One has only to think, for example, of the six-volume *History of*

Woman Suffrage or Mary Beard's *Women's Work in the Municipalities,* both of which are now seen as useful primary sources. Mary Beard was a transition figure: Working with her husband, Charles, she had a good understanding of the historian's task. Even so her book is not carefully documented.

After Beard the first serious scholarship dealing with women's past dealt with southern women. Oddly enough this initial work came from a graduate student at the University of Wisconsin who had grown up in Baltimore. No one now knows what inspired a young woman named Virginia Gearhart to select "The Southern Woman 1840–1860" as her dissertation topic. Working without models in a place far from the primary sources, she exercised impressive ingenuity in digging for evidence and in the process began to use types of data that would be belatedly discovered by the historical establishment years later. Some of the questions she raised still await a curious scholar. The wonder is not that her dissertation was not always first rate, but rather that it existed at all.

Because the University of Wisconsin required Ph.D. graduates to publish something from their dissertations in order to retrieve a hundred-dollar deposit, she wrote an article and sent it to the *South Atlantic Quarterly.* That journal, published at Duke University, has the distinction of having published three of what are now seen as pioneering articles in southern women's history.[1]

After Gearhart (who shortly married and became Virginia Gray) came the important works of Julia Spruill, Guion Johnson, Eleanor Boatwright, Marjorie Mendenhall, and Elizabeth Taylor. Excellent as was much of their work, only Taylor, younger than the others, ever made her way into the historical establishment. Virginia Gray became an archivist. Eleanor Boatwright committed suicide before she could write the book she had contemplated; Marjorie Mendenhall suffered from severe depression and died from a mistaken drug. Julia Spruill became a Christian Science reader and did dedicated service as the wife of an academic. Guion Johnson was in her eighties when she was finally recognized as a first-rate social historian and received the recognition she had deserved for half a century. Most of her adult life she worked as a volunteer in the interest of women and for the rights of African Americans.

Except for Elizabeth Taylor, who continued against the advice of her mentors and colleagues to work on woman suffrage in the South, there was very little visible work in southern women's history in the 1940s and 1950s beyond a master's essay here and there or an ephemeral article.

Then, in the social upheaval of the 1960s a reawakened feminism began to stir among young women and among some older ones as well. One consequence was a sudden jump in the numbers of women applying for graduate study, among them a good many who were intent upon learning more about women who had preceded them. At the same time a handful of traditionally trained academic women began to turn their attention to the history of their own sex. In 1961 the Southern Historical Association invited a paper on post–Civil War southern women, and a year later that paper was published in the *South Atlantic Quarterly*.[2] It was as if someone had dynamited a mountain. By the 1970s the avalanche was underway.

At first came a trickle of writings, followed by a flood of articles, conference papers, lectures, books, graduate and undergraduate courses—so many that by now even the most dedicated scholar is easily overwhelmed. We commiserate with each other. "Have you read . . .?" And "It's on my shelf" or "I heard her give a paper, but has she written a book?" And so on. The Southern Association for Women Historians has provided a new venue in which scholars can try out their ideas, debate their concepts, present their research. It would be a brave person who tried now to do the kind of overview that Jacquelyn Dowd Hall and I undertook in the middle of the 1980s.[3]

Of course, the history of southern women is a subset of several larger fields: to wit the social history of the South, women's history worldwide, American women's history. In all of these areas new ideas are percolating. Some may be passing fancies; others may fundamentally change the way history is written. Inevitably work on southern women is being shaped by these currents of thought.

The decades after 1960 witnessed not only an expansion in the quantity of scholarly work but also many new directions, including subjects and concepts that might have startled the pioneers. (It is amusing and a little scary to imagine Julia Spruill confronted with an essay on William Byrd's sexual fantasies.) I share the wry feelings the late C. Vann Woodward expressed in the preface to a new book on southern politics, when he wrote:

> Here is a book filled with splendid examples of the way history has
> come to be written at the end of the twentieth century: whereas the
> writer of the preface began his writing back toward its beginning—in
> the 1930s . . . Fashions change, and over the next six decades so to
> some extent did his writing, but that does not make him a precursor
> or inspirer of the new school.[4]

In the 1960s, when I began, history was still written much as it had been in the 1930s. Like Woodward I often feel, reading contemporary work, that the ground has shifted under my feet. But some changes I do understand and many I welcome and have been influenced by. History being written now has been changed by the introduction of new subjects, new ways of viewing traditional subjects, and new kinds of attention to race, class, and gender, which are seen not as stable entities, but as concepts that are socially constructed. There is also a great deal of emphasis upon the agency of groups earlier treated as subjects rather than as creators of their own life experience.

Here is my own idiosyncratic list of some of the significant changes that have come about since I first began to write about southern women:

- *The availability of sources.* Materials dealing with women, once hard to identify, can now be found on microfilm and on the Internet so that much work that once required travel can now be conducted in one's own study. As so much new data become available new questions can be asked. Once the problem was how to find material about women; now the problem is how to choose among the vast quantities available and how to evaluate what is before us. Among the broadened sources is the systematic use of oral history.

- *Narrowing focus.* The early work often encompassed large numbers of years or whole categories of experience as well as wide reaches of geography. Scholars are now more likely to focus on one community, one family, one person, one organization, one limited period or place. The more we learn, the less confident can any one scholar feel that she or he can encompass everything. One example of this trend has been the growth in community studies following the lead of Suzanne Lebsock in her *Free Women of Petersburg,* for which she examined every extant legal record.[5] Useful as this narrowing focus has been, problems sometimes arise from too much generalization from small examples.

- *The search for what lies beneath the surface.* The need to be aware that beneath the perceived "facts" of any historical situation there may be forces, conscious or unconscious, shaping behavior is far from new: one thinks of Marx, Spengler, Toynbee, Freud, Turner, and a host of others. In recent years this insight, more common among those writing grand theory, has become part of the historian's tool kit, and to it we owe important insights and interpretations that have enriched our understanding and provided new tools for the analyst.

The difficulty comes when enthusiasts, embracing their insights with devotion, ask more of them than they can support. Historians writing about the distant past are sometimes tempted to assert with assurance what was in the hearts and minds or even in the unconsciousness of people when primary sources, in the nature of things, offer little support for such interpretations. Some humility is in order, and the concept itself should logically lead us to ask what drives *us* to ask and to seek to answer the questions we have chosen? What will future historians say about our time that we have not had the wit to discern?

- *Post-emancipation studies.* In the early studies antebellum women tended to overshadow all else. For white as well as black women the years after 1865 were mostly unexplored. That has begun to change with splendid work on the years after 1865. Glenda Gilmore, Laura Edwards, Leslie Schwalm, and Elsa Barkley Brown are among the pacesetters. There are many more at work who are beginning to publish.

- *African-American women are now examined from their own perspective* rather than, as they were for so long, from the records and perceptions of whites. For many decades all we knew about slave women came from records of their masters or from an occasional abolitionist-inspired memoir. The scholarship of slavery has changed dramatically with the work of such scholars as Allen Kulikoff, Deborah Gray White, Brenda Stevenson, and Marli Weiner. Similarly a group of outstanding historians such as Darlene Clark Hine, Elsa Barkley Brown, and Tera Hunter are identifying and using primary sources to rewrite the history of black women in the years after emancipation. The very important and much overlooked work of black women in the civil rights movement is now being carefully studied by scholars such as Chana Lee, and by many of the authors gathered in Darlene Clark Hine's sixteen volumes of black women's history.

- *A search for the roots of southern "identity"* has led to a good deal of focus on women, especially on those who promoted the ideology of the Lost Cause. Karen Cox, Fitzhugh Brundage, Joan Johnson, and Nancy MacLean have come to this subject in different ways. Jacquelyn Hall's work on Katharine Du Pre Lumpkin examines the subject from the other side: How does one transform a southern identity?

• *Labor history has blossomed,* along with the recognition that after the Civil War mill women made up an increasing part of the female population and that middle-class women were in a minority. Here again Hall and her students have been in the forefront. Scholars such as Mary Frederickson, John Salmond, and Tera Hunter have helped to open this field.

• *The emergence of "gender" as a tool of analysis.* As long as most history was written as if the world were inhabited only by men, no one worried about the importance of gender in shaping politics, economics, religion, education, and so on. As soon as the history of women began to flourish, men began to complain that "You can't understand women without understanding men." An opposite point—that to understand men and their activities at any time one needed to know what women were doing—would have been appropriate for two thousand years or more. Odd as it is that the concept only appeared when women were made part of the historical enterprise, it is an important addition. Kathleen Brown's work on the intertwining of ideas about gender, race, and class in early colonial Virginia provides a good example of just how useful the concept can be.

• *Women studies and cultural studies have multiplied rapidly in colleges and universities.* Both intend to be interdisciplinary, however that word is defined. One result has been intensified attention to what historians can learn from other disciplines. Another is the fairly rapid adoption of terms and concepts from other fields. Scholars interested in trying to integrate the findings of various fields have developed and enriched feminist theory.

• *A renewed interest in women and politics.* One significant change in which historians of women have taken the lead is a broader definition of the "political." Another is finding women active in politics long before they had the right to vote—as Elizabeth Varon discovered in antebellum Virginia. Stephanie McCurry has done a great deal to expand our understanding of antebellum political culture with a focus on the yeoman farmer and what she calls the politics of the household, as has Elsa Barkley Brown for the later period. The uses women have made of voluntary associations as a tool for political action have been explored by many scholars since the point was made in *The Southern Lady* in 1970.

- *Men are now writing women's history.* Some male historians are learning to make use of women's documents in their analysis of subjects hitherto treated as solely male. Clarence Mohr's work on the breakup of slavery in Georgia is a good example. More recently Edward Ayers has shown that southern history can be written that takes full account of both women and men. Collaboration between male and female scholars appears to be developing, to the benefit of all concerned.

The essays in this volume illustrate some of these trends. Some also contribute to ongoing debates. Did the Civil War change southern women? This subject has been debated for many years, without resolution. Giselle Roberts' essay on Sarah Morgan provides yet another striking example of the way the war wrought a fundamental change in one woman's life, a change that led her to undertake things which she would not have thought of doing before the war. Warren Ellem's essay drives one more stake into the heart of the all-too-simple view that politics in the South was exclusively a male domain. Karen Cox's essay on the United Daughters of the Confederacy offers a complex analysis of that institution and provides another piece for the emerging picture of the Lost Cause.

Glenn Feldman sheds new light on the complex part women played not only in creating the second Ku Klux Klan but also as objects of Klan violence. Pamela Tyler makes ingenious use of attitudes toward Eleanor Roosevelt to add to our understanding of the varieties of twentieth-century southern women. Sarah Hart Brown has written the biography of an important black woman civil rights leader. Elizabeth Jacoway's essay adds to the mounting body of evidence that middle-class white women in many parts of the South took up civil rights when their children's schooling seemed to be at risk. Catherine Fosl goes one step further to describe a true native-born southern radical. Together these essays, taken with those by Paula Treckel, Anya Jabour, Orville Vernon Burton, Barbara Mattick, Kathi Kern, and Michelle Haberland, add another piece to the developing historiography of southern women. And so the generations follow one another. In each we argue, debate, discuss with our contemporaries and our predecessors, and, in the process, learn. No one, taking an overview, can be other than impressed at how far we have come in a few decades. The editors of this volume are to be congratulated on taking another step in this exciting process.

Notes

1. See Anne Firor Scott, ed. *Unheard Voices: The First Historians of Southern Women* (Charlottesville, 1992) for the complete story of the pioneers.

2. Anne Firor Scott, "The New Woman in the New South," *South Atlantic Quarterly* 62 (autumn 1962): 471–83

3. Anne Firor Scott and Jacquelyn Dowd Hall, "Women in the South," in John Boles and Evelyn Nolen, *Interpreting Southern History: Historiographical Essays in Honor of S. W. Higginbotham* (Baton Rouge, 1987), 454-509. A measure of the change is the fact that an earlier bibliographical volume, published in 1963, had contained three references to women's history, two of which were footnotes. The 1987 essay was fifty pages and we had to limit ourselves carefully to stay within the space allowed. Such an essay now would no doubt yield a book.

4. Jane Dailey, Glenda Elizabeth Gilmore, and Bryant Simon, *Jumpin' Jim Crow: Southern Politics from Civil War to Civil Rights* (Princeton, 2000), xi.

5. In citing specific books and scholars I am simply searching for relevant *examples*. This is not a bibliographical essay, and there are so many alternate examples that naming them all would lead to long catalogs. I cite work that has had the most influence on my own thinking. Each reader will have his or her own list.

I

The Private World

1

"The Empire of My Heart"

The Marriage of William Byrd II and Lucy Parke Byrd

PAULA A. TRECKEL

The month was unusually cold, noted William Byrd II in his diary on July 30, 1710, "indeed the coldest that ever was known in [Virginia]." Could the weather, he wondered, have caused the fever and headaches suffered by his people? Thank God none had died. On that chilly day he also "read a sermon in Dr. Tillotson and then took a little [nap]." In the afternoon Byrd had a "little quarrel" with his wife, Lucy, but "reconciled" their dispute "with a flourish. Then she read a sermon in Dr. Tillotson to me. It is to be observed," he recorded, "that the flourish was performed on the billiard table." After eating fish for dinner and reading a little Latin, Byrd and his wife "took a walk about the plantation." That evening, although he "neglected to say [his] prayers," he enjoyed "good health, good thoughts, and good humor, thanks be to God."[1]

Most students of early American history are familiar with William Byrd II, the "great American gentleman," whose secret, coded diaries reveal the daily life of a member of Virginia's eighteenth-century planter elite. These journals have given generations of historians insights into the Chesapeake's changing economy, master-slave relations on early Tidewater plantations, and the development of plantation society and culture in the colonial South.[2]

Byrd's remarkable candor in recording his most personal activities—the most infamous is his account of giving his wife a "flourish" on the billiard table—also provides a glimpse into the private world of a Virginia gentleman. In recent years, biographer Kenneth A. Lockridge used the diaries to psychoanalyze Byrd and to trace his self-conscious struggle to construct an independent identity as a man and as an American. Historians Michael Zuckerman and Daniel Blake Smith also studied the diaries to shed light on familial mores in the eighteenth-century South. They argue that Byrd blurred the distinction between his public and domestic worlds and created a community, a web of relationships, in the region he ruled.[3]

In addition to providing insights into individual development and the establishment of community in the Chesapeake, William Byrd's diaries give the modern reader an interior view of marriage and gender relations among the Virginia gentry during an important transitional period in American history. The journal entries illuminate Byrd's tempestuous relationship with his first wife, Lucy Parke Byrd, and reveal how at least one gentry couple struggled to reconcile their often conflicting notions of men's and women's proper roles in the colony's emerging plantation economy. The Byrds' stormy marriage was filled with tensions over power and intimacy, authority and love, reason and passion. The couple's slaves often found themselves the innocent victims of the Byrds' battles in the eighteenth-century war between the sexes.

The transformation of the Chesapeake economy from the seventeenth to the eighteenth century prompted modifications in the region's social structure. Although the concept of the patriarchal family was one that most English colonists brought with them to North America in the seventeenth century, harsh reality prevented them from realizing their ideal in Virginia. Because mortality was high and life expectancy low, family life was extremely fragile there. Men seldom lived long enough to assert their accustomed authority over their wives and children; labor shortages throughout most of the century meant that women often helped their husbands supply their families' basic needs. Wives who outlived their spouses were, of necessity, granted greater legal rights and responsibilities than their counterparts in northern colonies, where family life was more stable.[4]

By the end of the century, demographic conditions improved, however, and it was possible for men and women to organize their families' lives in more familiar ways. Because men lived longer, they were able to assume their traditional role as household heads, directing the lives and organizing the labor of their wives and children. As the planters prospered, they began to invest in slave labor. Women whose husbands could afford slaves to work in their tobacco fields were free to devote themselves to bearing and rearing children and to their domestic tasks. A hierarchy based on race, class, and gender emerged in the early eighteenth century, and Virginia's affluent and aspiring planters looked to the mother country for refined models of behavior and family organization.[5]

Yet, even as Chesapeake planters were finally able to replicate the patriarchal family that had long been their ideal, a new paradigm of family life emerged in England with the potential for softening the severity of men's authority and tempering its extremes. Emphasizing conjugal felicity and filial affection, this new English concept of family was a response to, and refuge from, a world transformed by commerce and beset by social change. It provided its members with a sense of order in their lives. England's men and women of the gentry class, concerned by what they saw as a decline in public virtue and breakdown in community, viewed the domestic circle as a "sanctuary of comfort and protection" from worldly influences.[6] The English family, they thought, was the last, best hope to preserve and internalize their culture's values. This new family model emphasized the complementary nature of women's and men's roles and encouraged affection between husband and wife, parents and children. Although the man was still the head of the family, the woman, it was asserted, was the heart of the home; women's selfless love had the power to tame men's harsh passions and bring harmony to the domestic sphere.

This new ideal of family was a paradox for Englishwomen, however. They were told their real "freedom" rested in their subjugation to their husbands; their authority came through submission to their husbands' will. Only by completely subordinating themselves to their spouses did women have "power" to control them. The reward for their submission, obedience, and humility was security, protection, and happiness. These ideas about families, marriage, and men's and women's proper behavior provide the background for understanding the clash of wills between William and Lucy Byrd in early eighteenth-century Virginia.[7]

William Byrd II was the son of Indian trader, public official, and planter William Byrd and his wife, Mary Horsmanden Filmer Byrd. Born in 1674, he was seven years old when his ambitious father sent him to England to receive a gentleman's education and to learn firsthand the ways of the aristocracy. After attending Felsted Grammar School in Essex, he served an apprenticeship in the Netherlands with his father's commercial agents and later entered the Middle Temple to study law. The young William also developed friendships with members of the aristocracy, who elected him to membership in the Royal Society in 1696. Although Byrd spent most of his formative years in England and considered himself an Englishman, his colonial birth marked him as an outsider and both thwarted his efforts to marry into the aristocracy and limited his political potential. Finally, in 1705 he returned to Virginia to claim his sizable inheritance after his father's death.[8]

The Chesapeake Byrd confronted when he returned to Westover, his estate on the James River in Charles City County, was a far cry from the England he had left behind, and he found it difficult to adjust to the isolation of his colonial home. To assuage his loneliness and increase his prospects, he began courting Lucy Parke. The beautiful younger daughter of Colonel Daniel Parke II and his wife, Jane Ludwell Parke, Lucy lived with her mother and her sister, Frances, at Queen's Creek in York County, near Williamsburg.[9] Lucy's mother was the daughter of a prominent Virginia family. Her father was an ambitious, unscrupulous planter who had served in the House of Burgesses and on the governor's council. Parke's violent temper and reputation as a womanizer humiliated his wife and quite likely embarrassed his daughters; he lived openly with his mistress and fathered a son who was reared, at his insistence, by his wife. In 1697 Parke left his wife in charge of his estates and traveled back to England, where he joined the army, became aide-de-camp to the duke of Marlborough, and brought Queen Anne news of the Allied victory at Blenheim. On March 29, 1705, as reward for his military exploits, Parke was appointed governor of the Leeward Islands.[10]

Before he departed England for the Caribbean, Parke received a letter from his long-suffering wife informing him that she was resigning as manager of his Virginia properties. His complaints about the plantation's lack of profits made her "wonder how you think we live [e]sp[e]cially you that have lived so like A man of quoallety al your life: and know so wel how A gentelwoman should live." Jane Ludwell Parke also expressed frank concern about her daughters' marriage prospects. Frances, she reminded her husband, was "wanting but to months of entering In to hir 20: year: the younger [Lucy] wel gon In hir eighttenth." Because Parke forbade them to entertain callers in their Queen's Creek home, they had few suitors. Jane Parke had done her best to educate her girls, to provide them with dancing lessons, and to teach them French, but the only new clothing they had was one outfit each. Lest her husband become irate over the expense, she explained: "[T]his is what I could not avoid doeing for them: to have them look toalerable like other Peepell."[11]

William Byrd thought a connection with Daniel Parke, one of the few native-born Americans ever appointed governor of a British colony, could further his own political ambitions. To that end, Virginia's most eligible bachelor sought permission to court Parke's daughter Lucy. "Since my arrival in this country I have had the honour to be acquainted with your daughters," he wrote his prospective father-in-law, "and was infinitely surpriz'd to find young ladys with their accomplishments in Virginia. This surprize was soon improv'd into a passion for the youngest for whom I have all the respect and tenderness in the world." William was interested in Lucy's dowry as well as her beauty. He discussed his financial status, because marriage was first and foremost an economic proposition in this era, and remarked, "I dont question but my fortune may be sufficient to make her happy, especially after it has been assisted by your bounty." Impressed, Parke agreed to the match and promised £1,000 as a marriage settlement.[12]

William used the refined language and sophisticated manner of an English gentleman to woo Lucy. Recycling words he had employed before in his failed courtship of an Irish heiress and aping the literary conceits of the learned men he admired, he addressed Lucy as his "Fidelia" and styled himself "Veramour." Was she faithful to him? Was his love for her true? Or was William simply giving lip service to the new notion that affection should exist between husband and wife? "May angels guard my dearest Fidelia and deliver her safe to my arms at our next meeting," he wrote, "and sure they wont refuse their protection to a creature so pure and charming, that it would be easy for them to mistake her for one of themselves." "Fidelia," he swore, "possess[ed] the empire of my heart," and he longed to be hers forever.[13]

What did nineteen-year-old Lucy Parke think of these effusive letters from her thirty-two-year-old suitor? Surely she was flattered, perhaps even awed, by the attentions of this mature, wealthy man, but did she respond in kind? Was she seduced by his attentiveness and urbane language or confused by his use of classical imagery and his flights of romantic allegory? Did she believe his profession that she had conquered the empire of his heart? Certainly Lucy's upbringing and education were provincial, far removed from the customs of the sophisticated English aristocrats whom William emulated. But her father's exploits and the Parke family's public humiliation may well have made her wise beyond her years, more knowledgeable than most young women her age of the ways of men and the world.

William Byrd had much to offer his "Fidelia." Undeniably the home he could provide was more stable and financially secure than the one in which she was reared. Was she seeking a strong, assertive, older man to care for her as her father had not? A gentleman of property and standing, respected and esteemed by his peers? A man ruled by cool reason rather than the hot passions and violence that governed her father's behavior? A man she could trust to be discreet in his indiscretions? Undoubtedly Lucy considered all of these things when she accepted William's proposal of marriage.

Did Lucy Parke love William Byrd, this man who vowed his eternal love for her? Did she believe that theirs would be a union bound by love, intimacy, and mutual esteem, a far cry from that of her parents? Although mutual affection became more important in mate selection as the century progressed, many elite couples in England and the colonies continued to base their marriages primarily on economic considerations. "I know it is the desire of all young people to be married," Daniel Parke dryly commented to his daughter, "and though very few are as happy after marriage as before, yet every one is willing to make the experiment at their own expense." Certainly Lucy and her sister knew that the choice of a husband was the most important decision in their lives; their father counseled them to "Consider who you marry is the greatest concern to you in the world."[14]

On May 4, 1706, at the Parkes' Queen's Creek plantation, William Byrd wed Lucy Parke on the same day Frances Parke married John Custis IV.[15] The Byrds' marriage, which lasted a decade, was a volatile, yet loving, union. The couple's quarrels and passionate reconciliations are recounted in the first extant volume of William's diary, which begins in 1709, three years after they wed and nearly two years after their daughter Evelyn's birth. The Byrds' marital difficulties were the consequence of their differing views of men's and women's proper roles. Their conflicts were also exaggerated by William's insecurities and exacerbated by the differences in their ages. A mature man, set in his ways, he envisioned himself as the patriarch of Westover, benevolently ruling over his lands and his household of family members, servants, and slaves. Clearly he thought he could mold his young wife—her thoughts, her actions, her appearance—to his liking. But Lucy had other ideas. As William struggled self-consciously to construct his identity as an English planter-patriarch, Lucy resisted his authoritarian, arbitrary ways. She demanded greater closeness and affection in their marriage and found it difficult to submit to his will. Her desire for intimacy threatened his need for authority and control. Could he surrender the "empire of [his] heart" to her and still be master of all in his domain? Could he share his deepest thoughts and fears with her, yet demand her submission to his will? In other words, the Byrds' marital difficulties centered on the age-old conundrum: Does loving someone place you in his or her power, or give you power over him or her? It is also possible that the Byrds' battle of wills and their attempts to resolve their problems reflected some of the fundamental conflicts inherent in the new model of English family life so eagerly embraced by the gentry in the eighteenth-century Chesapeake.[15]

Lucy Parke Byrd's attitudes toward her role as a woman, a wife, and a plantation mistress, and her ideas about marriage as revealed in her husband's diary, also illuminate white women's role in the emerging plantation culture of the region. A charming, passionate woman who appears to have cared deeply for her husband, Lucy expressed her feelings openly; her laughter and sparkling personality enlivened and enriched William's life. Lucy's laughter, however, could quickly change to tears of sorrow. Her frustration with her husband, a consequence of her desire for greater intimacy and an unwillingness to submit to his will, sometimes resulted in expressions of rage. Sadly, she vented her anger not only on him but also on those doubly marked by their race and gender—the female slaves who served her family.

Was Lucy emotionally unstable, as many historians have concluded? Was she a "willful woman" of "Bad Disposition" or merely "fiery and free spirited"? Was she "spoiled and temperamental," or a loving, affectionate woman who simply refused to yield to her husband's authority, who balked at his despotic administration of their household and challenged his decisions? Or was her passionate expression of her feelings simply a reflection of the belief that women were naturally more emotional than men— a view held by most in the early eighteenth century?[16]

The daughter of a tyrannical man who humiliated his obedient, compliant wife, Lucy often refused to emulate her mother by passively acquiescing to her demanding husband. Instead, she fought back. In doing so, she both embraced and violated notions of womanhood espoused by English family reformers and admired by William; although her actions were often ruled by her heart, not her head, Lucy refused to submit to her husband as women were instructed to do. What did William make of his passionate young wife who challenged his decisions, disagreed with his pronouncements, and refused to behave in the manner of a genteel Englishwoman? It must not have taken him long to see that his hope of creating a domestic patriarchy at Westover would never be realized.[17]

To William, Lucy's emotional nature was emblematic of feminine weakness. His belief that men were naturally superior to women was typical of his day. It is likely he shared the sentiments of George Savile, marquis of Halifax, author of "The Lady's New-Year's-Gift, or Advice to a Daughter," who insisted that

> There is Inequality in the Sexes, and that for the better Oeconomy of the World, the Men, who were to be the Law Givers, had the better share of Reason bestow'd upon them; by which means your Sex is the better prepar'd for the Compliance that is necessary for the better performance of those Duties which seem to be most properly assign'd to it. . . . We are made of differing Tempers, that our Defects may the better be Mutually Supplied: Your Sex wanteth our Reason for your Conduct, and our Strength for your Protection; Ours wanteth your Gentleness to soften and to entertain us.[18]

Men were rational beings, ruled by reason; women were governed by their emotions. "Female passions," wrote William Byrd, "require to be managed sometimes, to confine them within bounds and keep them, like a high-mettled horse, from runing away with their owner." Like most Enlightenment thinkers, he believed it was men's responsibility to rein in women's passions: The head must always rule the heart. Extremes in behavior must always be avoided; moderation, balance, and restraint were the edicts that governed Byrd's life. These were values expressed in John Tillotson's *Sermons Preach'd Upon Several Occasions* and Richard Allestree's *Whole Duty of Man*, works in the library at Westover.[19]

Just as Byrd derived his model of gentlemanly behavior from these prescriptive works, he also probably read such guides as *The Ladies Calling*, also by Allestree, to provide insight into the behavior of women and their appropriate roles. The "final authority on the nature and duties of women" for more than a century, *The Ladies Calling* extolled the distinctly "feminine" virtues of modesty, meekness, compassion, affability, and piety.[20]

"Modesty," Allestree proclaimed, "[is] the most indispensable requisite of a woman; a thing so essential and naturall to the Sex, that every the least declination from it, is a proportionable receding from Womanhood." Meekness, too, was required because God had placed women in a position inferior to men. Women, however, were more compassionate than men, for, it was asserted, they had more tender natures. Affability was always expected of them because they were spared, by virtue of their sex, the cares and worries assumed by men.[21]

A wife's chief responsibility was obedience to her husband—by virtue of her marriage vows and because it was ordained by God. She must protect her husband's reputation as her own and guard against jealousy. If her husband proved unfaithful, she should, according to Allestree, view this infidelity as a trial by God for some sin she might have committed. She must submit to it and not reproach her husband for his actions. "[T]he breaches of Wedlock will never be cemented by Storms and loud Out-cries," Allestree warned. "Many men have bin made worse, but scarce any better by it: for guilt covets nothing more then an opportunity of recrimi-nating; and where the Husband can accuse the Wive's bitterness, he thinks he needs no other apology for his own Lust."[22]

Certainly Lucy's mother, silently submitting to her husband's flagrant infidelity, was the model of this philosophy. When Daniel Parke returned from England in 1692 with his mistress—he introduced her to the coun-tryside as his "Cousin Brown"—Jane Parke welcomed her into their home. When "Cousin Brown" gave birth to a son shortly after her arrival in the colony, Jane quietly assumed responsibility for raising her husband's ille-gitimate child, christened Julius Caesar Parke. What did Lucy and her sis-ter think of their father's blatant adultery? Did they witness any "Storms and loud Out-cries" in the privacy of their home or share their mother's bitterness at their father's behavior? Perhaps Lucy learned firsthand the value of Allestree's advice. Turning a blind eye to a husband's unfaithful-ness was a way of dulling the pain of his betrayal.[23]

Allestree also urged his female reader to be a good "huswife," skilled in all domestic tasks. As manager of her husband's household, she must "not wast . . . and embezle [his] Estate, but . . . confine her Expences within such limits as that can easily admit." She must be expert in "the well-guiding of the House" and must demand truth, fidelity, diligence, and industry of her servants. While overseeing the household, however, she must always re-member that her authority was subordinate to her husband's.[24]

Lucy Parke was probably familiar with this genteel idea of a gentle-woman's proper role. Her sphere, she had been taught, was the household, and she was responsible for its management. Lucy and her sister, Frances, were trained in needlework and cookery and had been taught all manner of housewifely accomplishments by their mother. It was considered unneces-sary for them to receive a formal education; women who desired the same education as men were seen as defying their femininity. The Parke sisters most likely received only the most rudimentary schooling in reading, writing, and mathematics, although Jane Parke thought it important that her daughters receive tutoring in French and dancing to render them agreeable to prospective mates. Having watched her mother struggle to administer her father's estates and make them profitable, Lucy was probably content to leave such matters to her husband and turn all of her attention to her domestic tasks.[25]

William, on the other hand, was loathe to delegate management of their household to his wife. Jealous of his authority, he did not even trust Lucy to "guide the house," and this interference was a cause of many quarrels in their marriage. Many of the couple's most violent arguments erupted not when she challenged his authority in his sphere but when he trespassed into what she clearly deemed her arena—the day-to-day operation of their home. All who dwelled on William's plantations, he believed, were his to command; all were members of his "family"—his wife, his children, his servants, his slaves. As he later explained, "I have a large family of my own. . . . Like one of the patriarchs, I have my flocks and my herds, my bondmen, and bond-women. . . . I must take care to keep all my people to their duty, to set all the springs in motion, and to make every one draw his equal share to carry the machine forward. But then tis an amusement in this silent country."[26]

Viewing all the residents of his plantations as his subordinates, Byrd blurred the distinctions among them—distinctions based on race, gender, and class. Indeed, within the universe of his household he rarely conferred higher rank or priority of place on his wife and children. In his diaries he referred to Lucy as "my wife" and his children as "my son" and "my daughter." He seldom identified them by their given names, as he often did his house slaves. The words he used in reference to them underscored their relationship to him; William's choice of terms betrayed his belief that all at Westover revolved around him. In viewing his wife as his possession, subordinate to him, he jeopardized her position within their household.[27]

Although in theory the planter-patriarch reigned supreme over his entire plantation, most Chesapeake planters delegated the day-to-day operation of the "great house" and supervision of household servants or slaves to their wives. William Byrd, however, was clearly reluctant to do so. Resentful of any encroachment on what he deemed his purview, he repeatedly criticized Lucy "for not minding her business," and his diary is a veritable litany of complaints. He reproached her for serving "new beef" before the old, "contrary to good management"; she improperly mended his shoes; he complained that she did not prepare his dish of stewed cherries correctly; he found fault with the cleanliness of their daughter's nursery; she did not govern her servants well.[28]

William was especially angry when Lucy spent his money unwisely.

Women's emergence as conspicuous consumers of their husbands' wealth was, ironically, a consequence of the new conception of the genteel English family. Charged with making houses into homes, women embellished the domestic sphere in which they were increasingly confined. In doing so they helped fuel the commercial revolution that transformed England into a nation of shopkeepers. Women also became avid consumers of fashion as a means of self-expression and a way of demonstrating their husbands' ability to pay. William Byrd, however, clearly shared Allestree's belief that a good wife should live within her husband's means, and a major quarrel ensued when William received "an invoice of things sent [for from England] by my wife which are enough to make a man mad." When the ship's captain delivered goods ordered by Lucy "to an extravagant value," William was "out of humor very much." In the end, he "made an invoice of the things my wife could spare to be sold." Lucy, understandably, "was in tears about her cargo," but a year later the argument was renewed. "[My] wife and I had a terrible quarrel about the things she had come in but at length she submitted because she was in the wrong," he noted. "For my part I kept my temper very well."[29]

Reared in a household where money was tight and deprived of fine things during her childhood, Lucy probably hoped her wealthy husband would indulge her taste for silks and satins. Did she resent William's management of their finances? Were her self-indulgent shopping sprees a form of rebellion against his tightfistedness? Money was another emblem of a husband's power, and William controlled the purse strings at Westover. Lucy, on the other hand, had witnessed her mother's management of the family's accounts and knew such oversight was something women could do. Although Lucy's extravagance challenged her husband's authority, in the end she submitted to his will.[30]

In criticizing Lucy for her spendthrift ways and domestic failings, William demonstrated his rule not only over the plantation as a whole, but over her as well. His standards, and only his, prevailed at Westover. One major source of contention was the couple's control of the labor and behavior of their chattels. Lucy had been well instructed by her parents in the treatment of her slaves. Daniel Parke taught his daughters to "Be Calm and Obligeing to all the servants, and when you speak doe it mildly Even to the poorest slave." He also warned them that "if any of the Servants committ small faults yt are of no consequence, doe you hide them. If you understand of any great faults they commit, acquaint yr mother, but doe not aggravate the fault." When William reproved Lucy in front of their servants and slaves, however, he undermined her authority over them and made it more difficult for her to control them. Lucy's problems managing her house slaves illustrate the damaging effect of her husband's relentless criticism.[31]

Lucy could be a cruel mistress. William disapprovingly recorded in 1710 that she "caused little Jenny to be burned with a hot iron." Later he reported a more disturbing incident: "In the evening my wife and little Jenny had a great quarrel in which my wife got the worst but at last by the help of the family Jenny was overcome and soundly whipped." Clearly Jenny refused to obey her mistress and fought back. That Lucy "got the worst" of their battle and had to be rescued by other slaves did not bode well for her authority over them, but the most violent confrontation between mistress and slave was yet to come.[32]

"I had a terrible quarrel with my wife concerning Jenny that I took away from her when she was beating her with the tongs," William recalled. "She lifted up her hands to strike me but forbore to do it. She gave me abundance of bad words and endeavored to strangle herself, but I believe in jest only. However after acting a mad woman a long time she was passive again."[33]

Again and again Jenny was the object of Lucy's wrath. Why? It was unusual for Lucy, or William for that matter, personally to correct the servants; ordinarily the Byrds ordered their punishment by others. Did Lucy believe that Jenny was her husband's mistress? Although William gives no evidence that she was, we cannot know what Lucy suspected. Was a clash of personalities between Jenny and Lucy perhaps to blame for their friction? Did Jenny's saucy behavior provoke her mistress's persecution? Or did Lucy project her rage against her husband onto her slave, a convenient, ever-present scapegoat? Female slaves, doubly marked by their race and gender as inferiors in a world ruled by white men, were especially vulnerable to abuse. In William's chilling account of their battle, Lucy wanted to strike him but directed her anger against herself instead. Because of this graphic expression of frustration, William called her "mad"—a word describing someone either angry (which Lucy clearly was) or mentally unbalanced. Eventually Lucy regained her composure and, as William says "was passive again," a woman's proper state, in his view.

William understood that Lucy's ill-treatment of their slaves was her way of flouting his authority and an attempt to demonstrate her own. "My wife and I had a terrible quarrel about whipping Eugene while Mr. [Robert]

Mumford was there," he recalled. "[S]he had a mind to show her authority before company but I would not suffer it, which she took very ill." Not only did Lucy trespass on her husband's prerogative by publicly punishing his personal slave, but she also abused those in her command in a futile attempt to win recognition of her authority over them. She and her slaves knew that William was the ultimate ruler of the household, and her mistreatment of them further proved her powerlessness.[34]

Lucy also had her favorites among the Byrd family slaves. Anaka, her maid, probably came to Westover with Lucy when she married. Fond of drink, Anaka often stole from her master's supply. Lucy was more forgiving than her husband, who related he was "out of humor with my wife for trusting Anaka with rum to steal when she was so given to drinking." He whipped the slave for stealing his ale but later "forgave Anaka, on my wife's and sister's persuasion."[35]

Both William and his wife vented their anger with each other on their defenseless slaves. William recorded that "my wife caused Prue to be whipped violently notwithstanding I desired not, which provoked me to have Anaka whipped likewise who had deserved it much more, on which my wife flew into such a passion that she hoped she would be revenged of me." William saw Anaka as Lucy's surrogate; whipping her was his way of punishing Lucy for her disobedience. He was so angered by his wife that even when she "came to ask my pardon and I forgave her in my heart," he "resent[ed], that she might be the more sorry for her folly."[36]

Only rarely did Lucy invade William's sphere at Westover, but when she did, she felt his wrath. In the rambling house he inherited from his father, the intensely private man found sanctuary in the library, filled with books he imported from England and the Continent. There he retreated each morning to read works in French, Dutch, Hebrew, Latin, and Greek, settle accounts, and write in his diary. Behind his library's locked doors, William was transported from the cultural wilderness, the "silent country" of the Chesapeake, to other, far richer worlds. There he explored ancient Greece and Rome and toured the great cultures of Europe, Asia, and Africa. His exceptional library included books on travel, medicine, agriculture, and the arts, as well as classical works on law and politics. A connoisseur of books, William Byrd over the course of his lifetime amassed the largest and finest private library in colonial America.[37]

In this private space Lucy was an unwelcome intruder. William often refused to let her borrow his books and was angry when she moved his personal papers. In locking Lucy out of his library, William shut her out of an important part of his life and revealed his fear of the emotional intimacy of marriage.[38]

Lucy was persistent. Again and again she reached out to her husband. William, however, insisted on limiting and controlling his wife's access to the world of ideas that so delighted him. Although he owned a copy of Mary Astell's *Serious Proposal to the Ladies*, in which the author championed women's intellect, it is doubtful that William supported Astell's radical goal of equal education for women. More likely he agreed with Astell's argument that women's education made them better wives and mothers. To that end, he would decide what it was his young wife should know; he would mold her mind so that she would be his ideal companion. William quite likely applauded Richard Steele when the latter admonished his female readers to "learn in silence of your Husbands and spiritual Guides, read good Books, pray often, and speak little." Was it, then, at William's insistence that Lucy read aloud to him from John Tillotson's *Sermons Preach'd Upon Several Occasions* after the couple made love? Did he give Lucy Marcus Aurelius's *Meditations* in an effort to instill her with virtue? And did he subscribe to the *Tatler*, a periodical that reinforced women's subordinate, dependent position, for his wife's moral edification?[39]

Even as he controlled Lucy's access to the written word, William mocked his wife's lack of education. He laughed at her when she chastised him for speaking Latin with a visiting minister and excluded her from their conversation. It was bad manners, she cried. But it was more than that. He was just as furious when he caught her on the stairs listening to his conversations. William understood knowledge was a source of his superiority and would not, could not, share its riches, or his innermost thoughts, with his wife who loved him. What did he fear? That she would discover he was not the man she thought him to be?[40]

William Byrd's obsessive need to control his wife even extended to Lucy's appearance. As the couple prepared to travel to Williamsburg for the lieutenant governor's ball, William took issue with her decision to pluck her eyebrows. Proud of Lucy's beauty and aware of the impression she made on Virginia's powerful elite, he wanted her appearance to be exactly right. Her beauty and refined behavior were emblems of his position in the colony; she was an extension of him. "My wife and I quarreled about her pulling her brows. She threatened she would not go to Williamsburg if she might not pull them; I refused, however, and got the better of her," he smugly noted, "and maintained my authority." Lucy's presence at the so-

cial event of the year was important to her husband, and William was doubly honored when Lieutenant Governor Alexander Spotswood asked Lucy
to be his partner in opening the ball. Although her husband's will prevailed, Lucy's threat showed she understood her value to him.[41]

In disputing William's command throughout their marriage, Lucy
threatened his manhood. William's anxieties about authority, his sense of
inadequacy, and his doubts about his masculinity probably originated in
his youth. It has been suggested that in order to curb his apprehensions
and gain some control over his life, William obsessively followed a health
regime based on regular sexual relations, proper diet, and exercise. Yet he
also used sex to control and dominate his wife. His method of resolving
disagreements and reconciling their quarrels was to "roger" Lucy or give
her a "flourish." Subscribing to the sexual etiquette of the day in which
men were the pursuers and women the pursued, William was, by his account, always the initiator and Lucy the passive but willing object of his
desire. He took great pride in listing the variety of places they coupled—
the billiard table, the trestle—and in noting when he performed "with
vigor." Significantly, William also "rogered" Lucy more than once in his
library, his domain, surrounded by the many volumes filled with the
knowledge that empowered him and was denied to her.[42]

It is likely William was a selfish lover. He noted having intercourse with
his wife throughout her pregnancies, sometimes only days before she was
delivered, and even when she felt ill or was indisposed. Their activities
probably compromised her pregnancies and may even have precipitated
her miscarriages. Only twice in the four years of his diary does he mention
that he gave Lucy pleasure. In one of these instances, he observed, "I gave
my wife a powerful flourish and gave her great ecstasy and refreshment."
Was she always his willing partner? Perhaps Lucy understood that sexual
union was the only way her husband knew to demonstrate his love for her.
Realizing that their lovemaking was the only way she could achieve the
kind of intimacy she desired with her husband, she willingly submitted to
his overtures.[43]

The tone of William's diaries is one of cool detachment, curiously devoid of emotion. His entries on his infant son's death, his daughter's near-
fatal illness, and Lucy's miscarriages seem almost cruelly indifferent to the
modern reader. It may well be, however, that William's journal was his way
of taming his turbulent feelings; through writing he acquired the emotional detachment he longed for and struggled to achieve.[44]

Like many men of his time, William was unfaithful to his wife. He occasionally "committed uncleanness" while in Williamsburg and recorded his transgressions with servants or prostitutes in his diary. He sometimes stole a kiss from a "Negro girl" or "made . . . good sport" with an Indian, but on most occasions he expressed remorse for his actions. Although Lucy suspected his infidelity, it is likely that she followed Allestree's advice and her mother's example and did not directly reproach her husband for his faithlessness. Growing up with her father's adultery and reared with her illegitimate brother, Lucy probably expected such behavior from men. Perhaps she had observed that in the calculus of marriage "a philandering husband abroad means greater wifely power at home."[45]

When William flirted with a neighbor's wife in Lucy's presence, however, she was justifiably upset. "I played at [r—m] with Mrs. [Mary] Chiswell and kissed her on the bed till she was angry and my wife also was uneasy about it, and cried as soon as the company was gone," William recalled. Later, he "neglected to say my prayers, which I should not have done, because I ought to beg pardon for the lust I had for another man's wife." What made this episode so disturbing to Lucy was its public nature; her husband humiliated her before their friends. Although William regretted his actions, it was not because he had embarrassed his wife. Rather, he had stepped over the line of acceptable behavior for a gentleman. His public flirtation challenged Charles Chiswell's authority over his wife and jeopardized a friendship.[46]

When William rebuffed Lucy's attempts at marital intimacy and asserted his authority over her, she turned to her sister, Frances, and a network of other women for support. The separation of men's and women's worlds, a consequence of their changing economic and social roles, led to the emotional estrangement of the sexes in the eighteenth-century Chesapeake, even as spousal affection was idealized. Women's domestic duties bound them to their homes, while men's responsibilities often took them into the larger world. Relatively isolated on plantations, mothers and daughters enjoyed close relationships, and sisters were often best friends. After her mother's death in 1708, Lucy confided in her sister and enjoyed the company of her female neighbors. The opportunity to visit their circle of friends was a much-anticipated break from plantation routine for southern women. Women's friendships were also reinforced by their domesticity and strengthened by the shared experiences of pregnancy and childbirth. Female friends and neighbors assisted Lucy during her confinements and comforted her when she suffered miscarriages.[47]

In an age when a woman's worth was measured by her ability to bear and rear children, Lucy's difficult pregnancies were a source of worry and self-doubt. When she shared her fears with her husband, however, he did not know how to console her. "[M]y wife . . . was melancholy for her misfortunes and wished herself a freak," he recalled, "for which I rebuked her." But a rebuke was not what Lucy sought from her husband; William was emotionally incapable of providing her with the loving reassurance that she required. Consequently, Lucy turned to those with whom she shared the common bond of gender to meet her emotional needs.[48]

Lucy's closest friend was Mary Jeffreys Dunn, the wife of a local minister. When Dunn's husband beat her and threatened to kill her, William offered her refuge at Westover. During her year-long residence there she became Lucy's confidante and constant companion. Although initially William welcomed her into his family, he soon regretted his hospitality. He came to view Dunn as a "Devil" whose purpose was to "infect" his wife with her ill humor. William feared that "if [she] tarry with us much longer my wife and I, who us'd to be envy'd for a happy couple, shall very probably come to extremitys." Just how had Dunn accomplished this alienation? "What with seasonable flattery, and humouring all my wives foibles, and easeing of some of her domestique troubles, she has gain'd so intire an ascendant over her that she draws her into her interests even against mine," William complained. Dunn "preacht up a very dangerous doctrine, that in case a husband dont allow his wife mony enough, she may pick his pocket . . . to do her self justice, of which she is to be her own judge." She encouraged Lucy's defiance and "bred very unpleasant controversys betwixt me & my wife." In addition to usurping his authority over his wife, Dunn appropriated William's command of his servants and slaves. "I will be master of my family," he thundered, "in spight of all the weak politiques practic'd to abuse my good nature."[49]

Was Mary Dunn so evil, or did William exaggerate the threat she posed to his marriage? Always uncomfortable with his emotions and insecure in his command, he was jealous of this rival for his wife's affection. Lucy no longer confided in him or joined him in long, private walks around the plantation. Instead, she entrusted Dunn with her confidences and strolled with her. He blamed Dunn for his wife's defection and wanted Lucy to choose—him or Dunn. William voyaged to England at the height of their marital difficulties, either to jolt his wife into realizing their marriage was at risk or to flee a problem he was emotionally unable to resolve. Although Dunn's support gave Lucy comfort and the strength to defy her authoritarian husband, Lucy's love of William won out over their friendship, and the

Byrds reconciled. But the couple's entanglement with Mary Dunn shows just how complex and competitive marital vows and the bonds of female friendship could be in the eighteenth-century South.[50]

The marriage of Lucy Parke Byrd and William Byrd II survived their many battles and passionate reconciliations, and William anticipated a long and happy life with his engaging wife. Colonial matters required that he travel to England in 1715, but he urged his wife to join him when he realized his return to Westover would be delayed. Following the birth of their daughter, Wilhelmina, Lucy set sail for England. Their loving reunion was tragically cut short by Lucy's sudden death from smallpox in November 1716. William was overwhelmed with grief and blamed himself for her death. "I little expected that I should be forced to tell you the very melancholy news of my dear Lucy's death," he wrote his brother-in-law, John Custis. "Gracious God what pains did she take to make a voyage hither to seek a grave." Her death was punishment, he thought, for his pride in her beauty and accomplishments. "No stranger ever met with more respect in a strange country than she had done here, from many persons of distinction, who all pronounced her an honor to Virginia."[51]

Lucy's death stunned William. He had never permitted himself to acknowledge how much he loved and depended on his infuriating, passionate, spirited wife. Just as her reception in England was a reflection on him, he saw her death as punishment for his faults—his pride in her, his vanity. She was an extension of him in death as in life. Her death was a form of abandonment, and in mourning her he grieved for a lost part of himself.

Although William eventually remarried, his second wife, Maria Taylor Byrd, was far more conventional than his first. An English heiress, she understood the rules that governed English society and the relationship between husbands and wives, and was comfortable with them. Unlike Lucy, she did not trespass on William's prerogative, challenge his authority, or defy his will. An excellent housewife, a successful mother, Maria was the epitome of the genteel, submissive English lady William had always wanted Lucy to emulate. Her manners were impeccable: she could be relied upon not to listen in on his private conversations or borrow books from his library. But Maria was not a woman he gave a "flourish" to on the billiard table or "rogered" in the library. She lacked the passion and emotion of Lucy, the light and love of William's life. Instead, the placid Maria was the model mistress to complement William's ideal gentleman-planter. She brought calm, order, and discipline to his household and his life.[52]

One has to wonder if William Byrd, having finally gotten what he wanted—a docile, compliant, obedient wife to suit his cultivated estates—was happy. Or did he miss free-spirited, defiant, exciting Lucy who never gave up her efforts to defy his authority and achieve true intimacy with him? In their ongoing battle of wills was she finally the victor? Did she, in the end, truly conquer the "empire of [his] heart"?

Lucy Parke Byrd's marriage to William Byrd II occurred during a transitional moment in the history of Virginia. As the Chesapeake was transformed into a plantation-based economy dependent on slave labor, women's and men's roles began to change. Aspiring gentlemen-planters such as Byrd tried to create a hierarchy of race, class, and gender in the region. These self-styled gentlemen-planters wielded great authority over all in their domain—their wives, their children, their servants, and their slaves. During the earliest years, however, their domestic patriarchies were sometimes imperfectly wrought, and the planters' power and authority were challenged by the women with whom they shared their lives.

The plantation mistress, modeled after the English gentlewoman, had a particular role to play within the region. Neither master nor slave, she was dependent on both for her status. Her authority was derived from the men of her household yet required her willingness to submit to their will. Some planters' wives, such as Lucy Parke Byrd, uneasily embraced the new ideal of conformable womanhood emerging in the Chesapeake and the corresponding separation of spheres, and alienation of affections, that it engendered. Lucy was unwilling to yield to her husband's authority, and her desire for true intimacy within their marriage was in direct conflict with her husband's need for power and control. These issues were central to the couple's marital difficulties and their battle for the empire of William Byrd's heart.

Although played out in the setting of the eighteenth-century Chesapeake, the drama of the Byrds' marriage—their struggle to reconcile their emotional needs with their conflicting ideals of family life—is curiously contemporary. It provides us with a poignant reminder that the men and women of the past were, after all, only human.

Notes

The editors thank the editors of the *Virginia Magazine of History and Biography* for permission to republish this essay.

1. Louis B. Wright and Marion Tinling, eds., *The Secret Diary of William Byrd of Westover, 1709–1712* (July 30, 1710; Richmond, 1941), 210–1.

2. Louis B. Wright and Marion Tinling, eds., *The Great American Gentleman: William Byrd of Westover in Virginia: His Secret Diary for the Years 1709–1712* (New York, 1963); Louis B. Wright, *The First Gentlemen of Virginia: Intellectual Qualities of the Early Colonial Ruling Class* (San Marino, Calif., 1940), 312–47. For a description of the three surviving diaries, see Kenneth A. Lockridge, *The Diary, and Life, of William Byrd II of Virginia, 1674–1744* (Chapel Hill, 1987), 1–12. On the development of the Chesapeake plantation economy, see Allan Kulikoff, *Tobacco and Slaves: The Development of Southern Cultures in the Chesapeake, 1680–1800* (Chapel Hill, 1986). On the emergence of social networks in the region, see Daniel Blake Smith, *Inside the Great House: Planter Family Life in Eighteenth-Century Chesapeake Society* (Ithaca, N.Y., 1980).

3. Lockridge, *Diary, and Life, of Byrd;* Michael Zuckerman, "William Byrd's Family," *Perspectives in American History* 12 (1979): 255–311; Smith, *Inside the Great House,* 199–204.

4. On the status of women in the seventeenth-century Chesapeake, see Lois Green Carr and Lorena S. Walsh, "The Planter's Wife: The Experience of White Women in Seventeenth-Century Maryland," *William and Mary Quarterly* (hereafter cited as *WMQ*), 3d ser., 34 (1977): 542–71; Lorena S. Walsh, "'Till Death Us Do Part': Marriage and Family in Seventeenth-Century Maryland," in *The Chesapeake in the Seventeenth Century: Essays on Anglo-American Society,* ed. Thad W. Tate and David L. Ammerman, Original Essays Series (Chapel Hill, 1979), 126–52; and Daniel Blake Smith, "Mortality and Family in the Colonial Chesapeake," *Journal of Interdisciplinary History* 8 (1978): 403–27.

5. This transformation of Virginia's economy is outlined in Kulikoff, *Tobacco and Slaves,* 23–44. On women's changing status, see Lorena S. Walsh, "The Experiences and Status of Women in the Chesapeake, 1750–1775," in *The Web of Southern Social Relations: Women, Family, and Education,* ed. Walter J. Fraser, Jr., R. Frank Saunders, Jr., and Jon L. Wakelyn (Athens, Ga., 1985), 1–18; and Russell R. Menard, "From Servants to Slaves: The Transformation of the Chesapeake Labor System," *Southern Studies* 16 (1977): 355–90. On women's legal rights in the southern colonies, see Marylynn Salmon, *Women and the Law of Property in Early America* (Chapel Hill, 1986).

6. John Dwyer, *Virtuous Discourse: Sensibility and Community in Late Eighteenth-Century Scotland* (Edinburgh, Scotland, 1987), 111.

7. On the rise of the affectionate family among the gentry in eighteenth-century England, see Lawrence Stone, *The Family, Sex, and Marriage in England, 1500–1800* (New York, 1977), 221–480. Stone asserts that it was this affectionate, domesticated family that gave rise to individualism. See also Dwyer, *Virtuous Discourse,* 95–140. Gordon S. Wood, *The Radicalism of the American Revolution* (New York, 1992), 145–57, discusses how the breakdown of patriarchal absolutism in the home gave rise to a spirit of independence in the American colonies. For an overview of changes in the American family during the colonial period, see Daniel Blake Smith, "The

Study of the Family in Early America: Trends, Problems, and Prospects," *WMQ*, 3d ser., 39 (1982): 3–28. On parent-child relationships in this new genteel, affectionate family, see Philip Greven, *The Protestant Temperament: Patterns of Child-Rearing, Religious Experience, and the Self in Early America* (New York, 1977) 265–331. On women's "freedom through subjection" within the new family, see Sarah Emily Newton, "'An Ornament to Her Sex': Rhetorics of Persuasion in Early American Conduct Literature for Women and the Eighteenth Century American Seduction Novel" (Ph.D. diss., University of California, Davis, 1976), 29–31.

8. For a short sketch of Byrd's life and career as a writer, see Robert Bain, "William Byrd of Westover (1674–1744)," in *Fifty Southern Writers Before 1900: A Bio-Bibliographical Sourcebook*, ed. Robert Bain and Joseph M. Flora (Westport, Conn., 1987), 55–74.

9. Byrd had voyaged to Virginia for a short visit in 1696 and while there was elected to the House of Burgesses, but he returned to London the next year. On early plantation houses of the Chesapeake, see Darrett B. Rutman and Anita H. Rutman, *A Place in Time: Middlesex County, Virginia, 1650–1750* (New York, 1984), 66–9; and Gloria L. Main, *Tobacco Colony: Life in Early Maryland, 1650–1720* (Princeton, 1982), 140–50, 160. Nancy Ehrich Martin, "Lucy Parke Byrd: Inside the *Diary* and Out" (M.A. thesis, University of Rochester, 1994).

10. Carrying a political conflict with Commissary James Blair into the nave of Bruton Parish Church, Parke assaulted the commissary's wife before the entire congregation. He also horsewhipped Lieutenant Governor Francis Nicholson in a dispute at a meeting of the College of William and Mary's board. See Marion Tinling, ed., *The Correspondence of the Three William Byrds of Westover, Virginia, 1684–1776*, 2 vols. Virginia Historical Society Documents, 12, 13 (Charlottesville, 1977), 1:252–3 n. 1; and Louis B. Wright and Marion Tinling, eds., *William Byrd of Virginia: The London Diary (1717-1721) and Other Writings* (New York, 1958), 16–17. For a complete study of Parke's unsavory activities, see Helen Hill Miller, *Colonel Parke of Virginia: "The Greatest Hector in the Town"* (Chapel Hill, 1989), 69–161.

11. Jane Ludwell Parke to Daniel Parke II, July 12, 1705, Custis Family Papers, 1683–1858, Virginia Historical Society, Richmond.

12. William Byrd II to "Seignor Fanforini" (Daniel Parke II), [ca. 1705–6], in Tinling, *Byrd Correspondence*, 1:256–7. See also Miller, *Colonel Parke of Virginia*, 166. William Byrd never received Lucy's promised dowry; it was listed among Parker's debts after his death, according to Pierre Marambaud, *William Byrd of Westover 1674-1744* (Charlottesville, Virginia, 1971), 27.

13. William Byrd II to "Fidelia" (Lucy Parke), February 4, 1705/6, in Tinling, *Byrd Correspondence*, 1:258. Byrd learned these techniques in his unsuccessful courtship of Lady Elizabeth Cromwell, an Irish heiress, who played "Facetia" to his "Veramour." On Byrd's failed wooing, see Lockridge, *Diary, and Life, of Byrd*, 34–39; and Tinling, *Byrd Correspondence*, 1:195; and the letters from William Byrd II to Lady Elizabeth Cromwell, 216–9 (June 12, 1703), 221–44 (July 3, 20, 27, August 5,

25, September 4, 11, 18, 1703). On Byrd's recycling of courtship language and names, see Bain, "William Byrd of Westover," 57. On courtship rituals of later southern planters, see Steven M. Stowe, *Intimacy and Power in the Old South: Ritual in the Lives of the Planters* (Baltimore, 1987), chap. 2, esp. 51–67.

14. Daniel Parke II to Frances Parke (later Custis), 1702, in *Recollections and Private Memoirs of Washington, by His Adopted Son . . .*, by George Washington Parke Custis, ed. Mary Anna Randolph, Custis Lee, and Benson J. Lossing (New York, 1860), 24. Daniel Parke allowed his daughters the right to refuse suitors and agreed to the marriage of his daughter Frances to John Custis IV only "if my daughter likes him." See Daniel Parke II to John Custis III, August 25, 1705, in ibid., 16.

Catherine Clinton discusses the rituals of courtship in the antebellum South in *The Plantation Mistress: Woman's World in the Old South* (New York, 1982), chap. 4.

15. Jo Zuppan, "John Custis of Williamsburg, 1678–1749," *Virginia Magazine of History and Biography* (hereafter cited as *VMHB*) 90 (1982): 177. Daniel Parke was not enthusiastic about Frances's match with John Custis; see Miller, *Colonel Parke of Virginia*, 168.

16. Lockridge, *Diary, and Life, of Byrd*, 66; Wright and Tinling, *London Diary*, 17; Zuckerman, "William Byrd's Family," 269; Marambaud, *William Byrd*, 27.

17. Most biographers accept Byrd's characterization of his wife. Wright and Tinling remark, "If he is telling the truth about her shortcomings, [Lucy] would have been a trial to any man, for she was a petulant, undisciplined, and spoiled girl who knew little or nothing about household management" (Wright and Tinling, *Secret Diary*, xx). They also point to Frances and John Custis's marital problems that led to their taking steps to implement a formal separation as evidence of mental instability in the Parke family; see ibid., x–xi, xiv, xx; and Lockridge, *Diary, and Life, of Byrd*, 66. For a definition of "domestic patriarchalism," see Elizabeth Fox-Genovese, "Placing Women's History in History," *New Left Review* 133 (1982): 22–24; and Kulikoff, *Tobacco and Slaves*, 166–7.

18. George Savile, "The Lady's New-Year's-Gift, or Advice to a Daughter," 1688, in *The Complete Works of George Savile, First Marquess of Halifax*, ed. Walter Raleigh (Oxford, UK, 1912), 8. Byrd owned a copy of Halifax's *Miscellanies* (London, 1700), which contained "The Lady's New-Year's-Gift." See Kevin Jon Hayes, "William Byrd's Library" (Ph.D. diss., University of Delaware, 1991), 304.

19. William Byrd II to Anne Taylor Otway, June 30, 1736, in Tinling, *Byrd Correspondence*, 2:483. Kenneth Lockridge asserts that William Byrd constructed his sense of self from guides such as these; see Lockridge, *Diary, and Life, of Byrd*, 20–5. Hayes, "Byrd's Library," 430–31, 435, 492, indicates that Byrd owned these works and others like them.

20. On prescriptive literature for seventeenth- and eighteenth-century colonial women, see Julia Cherry Spruill, *Women's Life and Work in the Southern Colonies* (New York, 1972), 213–4. Mary Sumner Benson, *Women in Eighteenth Century*

America: A Study of Opinion and Social Usage (Port Washington, N.Y., 1966), 16–8, cites Allestree and Halifax as two of the most influential authors of the day. Newton, "'An Ornament to Her Sex,'" 26–56, discusses how authors manipulated their female readers to embody the ideas they prescribed. Kathryn Shevelow, "Fathers and Daughters: Women as Readers of the *Tatler,*" in *Gender and Reading: Essays on Readers, Texts, and Contexts,* ed. Elizabeth A. Flynn and Patrocinio P. Schweickart (Baltimore, Md., 1986), 107–23, explores how Halifax used paternal authority to reinforce his message in "Advice to a Daughter."

21. Richard Allestree, *The Ladies Calling In Two Parts . . .,* 5th ed. (Oxford, UK, 1677), 16 (on modesty), 33 (on meekness), 75–7 (on compassion and affability).

22. Ibid., 191 (on a wife's obedience), 192 (on protecting her husband's reputation), 181–4 (on coping with his infidelity; quotation on 184).

23. Daniel Parke was not alone in his behavior. Many men in England openly kept mistresses, according to John Evelyn, who remarked: "The Impudence of both sex, being now become so greate & universal, Persons of all ranks, keeping their Courtesans so publickly, that the King had lately directed a Letter to the Bishops, to order their Cleargy to preach against that sin" (quoted in Miller, *Colonel Parke of Virginia,* 70). Parke's behavior, however, had little effect on his political ambitions in Virginia.

24. Allestree, *The Ladies Calling,* 194–5 (on managing his estate), 223–4 (on "the well-guiding of the House"), 229 (on managing the servants).

25. Daniel Blake Smith notes that throughout the eighteenth century, women's literacy rate lagged far behind that of men in Virginia. Smith, *Inside the Great House,* 62. For more information on women's education in the early Chesapeake, see Spruill, *Women's Life and Work in the Southern Colonies,* 185–207.

26. William Byrd II to Charles Boyle, Earl of Orrery, July 5, 1726, in Tinling, *Byrd Correspondence,* 1:355.

27. In his diary Byrd often referred to his house servants by name, but perhaps he did so because he had many slaves but only one wife and one daughter. For a discussion of Byrd's definition of "family," see Zuckerman, "William Byrd's Family," 274–6.

28. Wright and Tinling, *Secret Diary,* 18 (April 7, 1709), 19 (April 9, 1709), 43 (June 4, 1709), 137 (February 2, 1710), 216 (August 12, 1710), 543 (June 13, 1712).

29. The role of women as consumers in the eighteenth-century English economy is discussed in G. J Barker-Benfield, *The Culture of Sensibility: Sex and Society in Eighteenth-Century Britain* (Chicago, 1992), 154–214. On women's fashions as a reflection of their husbands' status in eighteenth-century Virginia, see Kathleen M. Brown, *Good Wives, Nasty Wenches, and Anxious Patriarchs: Gender, Race, and Power in Colonial Virginia* (Chapel Hill, 1996), 272–3. Wright and Tinling, *Secret Diary,* 48 (June 14, 15, 1709), 202 (July 9, 1710).

30. The Byrds' battle of wills even erupted at the gaming table. William needed to win to maintain his superiority over his wife; Lucy wanted to prove her skill at cards and challenge her husband's authority. Their contests often led to passionate argu-

ments. Lucy was especially angry when William cheated her in order to win (Wright and Tinling, *Secret Diary*, 75 [August 27, 1709], 135 [January 28, 1710], 254 [November 6, 1710]).

31. Daniel Parke II to Frances Parke (later Custis), October 20, 1697, in Custis, *Recollections and Private Memoirs*, 15n.

32. Wright and Tinling, *Secret Diary*, 205 (July 15, 1710), 307 (February 27, 1711).

33. Ibid., 494 (March 2, 1712).

34. Ibid., 462 (December 31, 1711). The violence directed at slaves by nineteenth-century plantation mistresses is discussed by Catherine Clinton, "Caught in the Web of the Big House: Women and Slavery," in Fraser, Saunders, and Wakelyn, *The Web of Southern Social Relations*, 27–32; and Elizabeth Fox-Genovese, *Within the Plantation Household: Black and White Women of the Old South* (Chapel Hill, 1988), 308–16. On how Lucy projected her anger at her husband onto her female slaves, see Brown, *Good Wives, Nasty Wenches, and Anxious Patriarchs*, 326, 361.

35. Wright and Tinling, *Secret Diary*, 42 (June 2, 1709). On an earlier occasion Anaka drank her master's decanter of rum and replaced the spirits with water, hoping he would overlook her crime. Unfortunately, she was caught and whipped, ibid., 22 (April 17, 1709). Anaka, together with Evelyn Byrd's nurse and Prue, another slave, apparently broke into the cellar and stole strong beer, cider, and wine. An angry Byrd "turned Nurse away upon it and punished Anaka" and later "caused Prue to be whipped severely." Lucy Byrd and Mary Duke's support of Anaka was validated when Byrd later discovered that his overseer had lost the cellar key and entered through a window. After that, "because he had not the key the door was left open and anybody went in and stole the beer and wine &c," ibid., 337 (April 30, 1711), 338 (May 1, 1711).

36. Wright and Tinling, *Secret Diary*, 533 (May 22, 1712). For another example, see ibid., 583 (September 12, 1712). Lockridge opines that William Byrd objected to Lucy's treatment of her slaves because it was performed irrationally and threatened his own power over them. Byrd was not opposed to the idea of punishment of slaves and often had them whipped by his overseer (Lockridge, *Diary, and Life, of Byrd*, 68).

37. Lockridge believes Byrd encoded his diaries to protect his thoughts from his wife's prying eyes. Lockridge, *Diary, and Life, of Byrd*, 48–9. Susan Manning discusses how Byrd jealously guarded his hours in his library and how his writings were his way of ordering his life (Susan Manning, "Industry and Idleness in Colonial Virginia: A New Approach to William Byrd II," *Journal of American Studies* 28 (1994): 179.

38. Wright and Tinling, *Secret Diary*, 461 (December 30, 1711).

39. Richard Steele, *The Ladies Library* (London, 1714), 39–40; Newton, "'An Ornament to Her Sex,'" 46–7. Reading lists for young women in the eighteenth century often included Tillotson's *Sermons*, which inculcated the proper piety in their female readers and reinforced women's subordinate role. An eight-volume set

of *The Emperor Marcus Aurelius Antoninus, His Conversation with Himself . . .*, translated into English in 1701 and bearing the ownership signature of Lucy Byrd, is attributed to the Byrd library. On the *Tatler* and the didactic tradition that reinforced the submission of women while it exploited them as an audience, see Shevelow, "Fathers and Daughters," 107–10. On Byrd's ownership of copies of the *Tatler*, see Hayes, "Byrd's Library," xx.

40. Wright and Tinling, *Secret Diary*, 105 (November 11, 1709), 18 (April 8, 1709).

41. Ibid., 296–7 (February 6, 1711); Brown, *Good Wives, Nasty Wenches, and Anxious Patriarchs*, 319. For a comment on the early eighteenth-century fashion of plucking eyebrows and hairlines, see Wayne Craven, "Virginia Portraits: Iconography, Style, and Social Context," *VMHB* 92 (1984): 206. On the significance of Lucy's being asked to open the ball with Spotswood, see Cynthia A. Kierner, "Genteel Balls and Republican Parades: Gender and Early Southern Civic Rituals, 1677–1826," *VMHB* 104 (1996): 190.

42. Lockridge discusses Byrd's sexual anxieties and his misogyny in his revealing analysis of the commonplace book William kept after Lucy's death. See Kenneth A. Lockridge, *On the Sources of Patriarchal Rage: The Commonplace Books of William Byrd and Thomas Jefferson and the Gendering of Power in the Eighteenth Century*, The History of Emotions Series (New York, 1992), chaps. 1–2, 4; and Lockridge, *Diary, and Life, of Byrd*, 29, 67. Wright and Tinling, *Secret Diary*, 209 (July 26, 1710), 214 (August 6, 1710), 275 (December 21, 1710), 293 (January 28, 1711), 541 (June 7, 1712), 543 (June 12, 1712), 570 (August 14, 1712), 583 (September 12, 1712).

43. Wright and Tinling, *Secret Diary*, 337 (April 30, 1711). Michael Zuckerman sees Byrd as an emotionally remote man, isolated from his wife. Byrd's "expressions of fond concern were almost wholly dissociated from his notations of sexual relations with her. On only four occasions in nearly four years did he enter an expression of compassion or affection for her on the same day that he recorded intercourse with her." According to Zuckerman, Byrd's mentions of their sexual activities made up only 7.1 percent of his references to his wife. Zuckerman, "William Byrd's Family," 270 n. 31, and 271 nn. 32, 33). See also Brown, *Good Wives, Nasty Wenches, and Anxious Patriarchs*, 330–1.

44. For an insightful account of Byrd's emotional detachment from his family, see Zuckerman, "William Byrd's Family," 255–311. Zuckerman attributes Byrd's "elemental emotional insufficiency" to a premodern sensibility regarding family life versus the life of the larger community and distinguishes between his behavior in Virginia and in England.

45. Wright and Tinling, *Secret Diary*, 90 (October 6, 1709), 247 (October 23, 1710), 250 (October 29, 1710), 425 (October 20, 1711). Typical is the entry in which he reported drinking and gambling while in Williamsburg, then retiring to his rooms, where "I committed uncleanness, for which I humbly beg God Almighty's pardon" (ibid., 442 [November 23, 1711]). Newton, "'An Ornament to Her Sex,'" 96.

46. Wright and Tinling, *Secret Diary*, 101 (November 2, 1709). While running

the dividing line in 1728, Byrd criticized his fellow commissioners for breaking "the Rules of Hospitality, by several gross Freedoms they offer'd to take with our Landlord's Sister . . . I was the more concern'd at this unhandsome Behaviour, because the People were extremely Civil to us, & deserv'd a better Treatment" (William Byrd, *Histories of the Dividing Line Betwixt Virginia and North Carolina*, ed. William K. Boyd [New York, 1967], 53 [March 9, 1728]).

47. By William's account, Lucy suffered at least two, possibly three, miscarriages over a four-year period. Many of her difficulties may be attributed to complications from malarial infection. She and William lost their nine-month-old son, Parke, and nearly lost their daughter, Evelyn, to the disease. Evelyn was born on June 16, 1707. Parke was born on September 6, 1709, and died on June 3, 1710 (Wright and Tinling, *Secret Diary*, 79–80, 186–7). Lucy's miscarriages and other pregnancy-related illnesses are noted by William in ibid., 31 (May 7, 1709), 38 (May 21, 1709), 64 (July 27, 1709), 65 (July 30, 1709), 78 (September 3, 1709), 79 (September 5, 1709), 108 (November 18, 1709), 142 (February 14, 1710), 239 (October 4, 1710), 309 (March 4, 1711), 342 (May 10, 1711), 347 (May 20, 1711), 350 (May 26, 1711), 352 (May 31, 1711), 364–7 (June 23–30, 1711). On female friendship in the plantation South, see Smith, *Inside the Great House*, 73–9; and Brown, *Good Wives, Nasty Wenches, and Anxious Patriarchs*, 302–3.

48. Wright and Tinling, *Secret Diary*, 302 (February 16, 1711).

49. Byrd reported: "My wife told me of the misfortunes of Mrs. Dunn—that her husband had beat her, and that she had complained to Mr. Gee of it, who made Mr. Dunn swear that he would never beat her again; that he threatened to kill her and abused her extremely and told her he would go from her. I was sorry to hear it and told my wife if he did go from her she might come here," ibid., 322 (March 31, 1711). William Byrd II to "Dunella" (Mary Jeffreys Dunn), [1711–15?], in Tinling, *Byrd Correspondence*, 1:275–9.

50. Lockridge asserts that William left Lucy over her dependence on Dunn; Lockridge, *Patriarchal Rage*, 21–2.

51. William Byrd II to John Custis IV, December 13, 1716, in Custis, *Recollections and Private Memoirs*, 32–3.

52. In England following Lucy's death, William gave vent to his misogyny. Perhaps his anger and fear of women grew out of his sense of his wife's "abandonment" and his awareness of his emotional dependence upon her. On the intensification of William's misogyny following Lucy's death, see Lockridge, *Patriarchal Rage*, 6–45. On Byrd's marriage to Maria Taylor, see Tinling, *Byrd Correspondence*, 1:196; Lockridge, *Diary, and Life, of Byrd*, 121; and Marambaud, *William Byrd*, 44–7. On William Byrd's role in the "refinement" of Virginia in the eighteenth century, see Richard L. Bushman, *The Refinement of America: Persons, Houses, Cities* (New York, 1992), 100, 113.

2

The New Andromeda

Sarah Morgan and the Post–Civil War Domestic Ideal

GISELLE ROBERTS

In April 1862, twenty-year-old Sarah Morgan peered anxiously from the window of her home on Church Street in Baton Rouge, Louisiana. For three days, rumors had been circulating that the Union army was preparing to shell the city. While "nothing [could] be heard positively," reports indicated that the Confederate gunboat defending Baton Rouge had been sunk by the enemy, who were organizing en masse to "take possession" of the city. "There is no word in the English language which can express the state in which we are all now [in], and have been for the last three days," Sarah wrote excitedly. "I believe that I am one of the most self possessed in my small circle of acquaintance, and yet, I feel such a craving for news . . . that I believe I am as crazy as the rest, and it is all humbug when they tell me I am cool."[1]

Realizing that they "had best be prepared for anything," Sarah gathered together a "running bag" filled with a host of essential items as well as many sentimental keepsakes. "My treasure bag being tied around my waist as a bustle, a sack on my arm with a few necessary trifles and a few *un*necessary ones—I had not the heart to leave the prayer books father gave us—carving knife and pistol safe, I stood ready for instant flight," she wrote. "My papers I piled on the bed, ready to burn, with matches lying on them."[2]

On this occasion, the Yankees did not arrive. Sarah's reprieve, however, was short-lived, and in the following days she came to the realization that her childhood home would have to be abandoned for safer quarters. As Sarah reflected on the likely fate of her rosewood furniture, the elegant parlor, and the pleasant balcony where she had often sat strumming her guitar, precious memories came flooding back. In this home she had received the news of her brother's death in a duel. In her bedroom, she had spent many nights crying over his loss. Months later, in the parlor, Sarah had kissed her father, Judge Thomas Gibbes Morgan, as he lay on his deathbed. She had also bid farewell to her soldier brothers, Gibbes and George, as they set out to defend the Confederate cause. "O my dear Home!" she sighed as she watched for the Yankees. "How can I help but cry at leaving you forever? For if this fight occurs, never again shall I pass the threshold of this house where we have been so happy and sad, the scene of joyous meeting and mournful partings, the place where we greeted each other with glad shouts after ever so short a parting, the place where Harry and Father kissed us goodbye and never came back again!"[3]

For Sarah Morgan, and for all southerners, the household stood at the center of their antebellum world. It defined identity by reflecting status according to race, class, gender, and age. It set out reciprocal obligations between masters and slaves, husbands and wives, and parents and children. It defined the tasks and responsibilities allotted to different members of the household, and regulated the expression of power through this organizational structure. For southern women, the household was also infused with ideas about womanhood and was inextricably tied to the feminine ideal. It was the site of mothering and morality, a "haven from the outside world" where women could extend guidance and care to their kin.[4]

When Sarah Morgan lost her home during the Federal invasion of Baton Rouge, she lost the foundation upon which she had built her identity as an elite young lady. Stripped of the security of her Church Street life and set adrift in a world "turned upside down," Sarah regarded her homelessness as an assault on her femininity. "O my home, my home!" she lamented. "I could learn to be a woman there, and a true one, too. Who will teach me now?" Inhabiting a sparsely furnished, one-bedroom apartment in Clinton, Louisiana, Sarah viewed her prospects with trepidation. "I look forward to my future life with a shudder," she confided in her diary in July 1862. "Why, if all father has left us is lost forever, if we are to be pennyless, as well as homeless, I'll work for my living. How I wonder? I will teach! I know I am not capable, but I can do my best. I would rather die than be dependent, I would rather die than teach. There now, you know what I feel! Teaching, before dependence, death before teaching. My soul revolts from the drudgery." War had indeed "reshuffled the deck" of the southern hierarchy, leaving Sarah to navigate her way through a daunting and unfamiliar social landscape where status and gentility could no longer be assumed, but rather were notions to which to cling.[5]

The American Civil War changed Sarah Morgan's life forever. The extent to which the war can be regarded as a "watershed" for elite women has preoccupied historians, particularly since the publication of Anne Firor Scott's pioneering work on the southern lady. She, together with an earlier generation of scholars, argued that the Civil War "provided a springboard" from which women leaped into a world "heretofore reserved for men." Recent scholarship has revised this interpretation and suggests that the wartime experiences of elite southern women led them to "invent new selves designed in large measure to resist change" rather than to embrace it. While these historians have often emphasized the ways in which post-war life fostered women's involvement in the social reform movement, they conclude that "everything had changed, and nothing had changed." In the postbellum South, ladies may have entered the "public arena," but they continued to cling to the preexisting racial and class hierarchy as they looked for ways to assert their status in a world without wealth or slaves.[6]

While the scholarly debate has centered on the watershed aspect of the war, historians have only just begun to examine how elite women invented "new selves" in the postwar period. Much of this recent academic work has centered on an analysis of the ways in which domesticity emerged as a site for the reconstruction of the elite southern identity. LeeAnn Whites contends that that the reassertion of a conservative model of femininity was inextricably tied to the resurrection of elite southern masculinity. In order to rebuild their demoralized soldiers, women subordinated themselves within the domestic sphere to become the "last legitimate terrain of domination" for their men. By doing so, women's sense of self became firmly attached to their domestic and familial role. Laura Edwards provides a variation on this theme, arguing that elite southern women fashioned an ideal of domesticity as a mechanism through which to assert their status. By attending to the needs of their husbands and children, "putting well-prepared meals on the table, banishing dirt and dust, selecting tasteful interior decorations, and maintaining a cheerful, supportive atmosphere," southern ladies were able to reconstruct their identities as "worthy women." Further, they would distinguish themselves from African American and poor white women.[7]

As Edwards has noted, the domestic reconstruction of elite white womanhood was most successfully achieved through marriage, which usually facilitated the establishment of a new household and granted women the status of wife and mistress. In this environment, wives could attend to their homes and children, while exercising deference and submission toward their husbands. By centering their analysis on married women, scholars have paid far less attention to the postwar experiences of other women. This essay will examine the life of one single, adult woman, who rebuilt her elite identity through employment. Trapped as an unwelcome guest in her brother's household, Sarah Morgan used her secret career as a writer to free herself from the shackles of dependence. While her work provided her with the means to attain a home of her own, it also forced Sarah to grapple with her understanding of the single woman's place in the postwar community in which the antebellum ideals of marriage, submission, and gentility were often pitted against women's employment and independence.

Sarah Morgan spent her girlhood in training for a world that was lost with the coming of war. Born in New Orleans, Louisiana, on February 28, 1842, Sarah was the seventh child of Judge Thomas Gibbes Morgan and Sarah Hunt Fowler. Thomas, born in New Jersey in 1799, had moved to Baton Rouge in the 1820s to pursue a career in law. After the death of his first wife, he met Sarah, a Northern-born woman who had been raised by her guardian, George Mather, on his sugar plantation in St. James Parish, Louisiana. The couple married in 1830 and moved to the "Crescent City," where Thomas worked as a collector for the Port of New Orleans, and Sarah tended to the needs of their eight children.

In 1850, the family relocated to Baton Rouge, where Thomas served as a district attorney and, later, a district judge. The Morgans became well-known, highly respected members of the community, often described by locals as the "proud Morgans," or the "aristocrats of Baton Rouge."[8] Like most professionals in the city, their life was comfortable and genteel, not opulent. Thomas, Sarah, and the children occupied a handsome double-story home on Church Street with wide galleries that provided some relief from the oppressive Louisiana summers. Like most of their neighbors, the Morgans were also slaveholders, owning eight slaves who worked as domestic servants.[9]

The landscape of Baton Rouge and its surrounds provided the backdrop for Sarah's socialization in the edicts of the southern tradition. Her girlhood, like that of most elite young women, furnished Sarah with training that would later allow her to fulfill the important duties associated with marriage and motherhood. Under the tutelage of her mother, sisters, and a collection of female relatives and friends, Sarah was instructed on temperament, piety, fashion, social graces, and manners. After "ten short months of schooling," she spent her days at the family home studying French and the classics, playing her guitar, and enjoying the company of family and friends. Socialized within a world dominated by family, household, and community, Sarah was also educated on the complexities and nuances of the southern hierarchy, which used race, class, and gender to construct relationships and identities. Elite white men such as Thomas Gibbes Morgan dominated this hierarchy by governing politics, business, familial relationships, and the household. The Morgan family's slaves were relegated to positions of legal, economic, and social inferiority.[10]

Sarah Morgan enjoyed her privileges, but like her mother and sisters, she too was bound to respect the head of household, whose position as master, husband, and father reinforced his power and authority. In a society governed by reciprocal obligations, women deferred to men and received protection and respectability in return. Sarah, like most women, accepted her place. She supported the notion of reciprocity, citing her parents' marriage as successful, in part, because of their ability to fulfill their designated roles. "I want to think all marriages as happy, all husbands as indulgent and kind, all wives as mild and submissive as father and mother," she wrote in May 1862, "I look for no more beautiful model." As a young lady, Sarah revered the image of her father as the benevolent patriarch, and looked for these qualities in a husband. "My lord and master . . . [must be] the one that, after God, I shall most venerate and respect," she declared. "Woe be to me, if I could feel superior to him for an instant!"[11]

The Civil War destroyed much that had governed Sarah's world. In November 1861, her father died after a severe asthma attack. In May 1862, the Morgan women lost their home and almost all of their possessions in their flight from Baton Rouge. In November, Sarah was thrown from a horse and spent months incapacitated by a back injury. Some doctors speculated that she might never walk again, but under the care of General Albert Carter and her sister-in-law, Lydia, Sarah made a partial recovery at the Carter plantation in East Feliciana Parish. The Federal invasion of Port Hudson in July 1863, however, forced the Morgan women to make a final desperate exodus to occupied New Orleans, where they joined the household of Sarah's half-brother and Unionist sympathizer Judge Philip Hicky Morgan. It was in his home that she received news of the death of her brothers Gibbes and George in February 1864. "Dead! dead! Both dead!" Sarah cried upon hearing the news. "O my brothers! What have we lived for except you? We who would so gladly have laid down our lives for yours, are left desolate to mourn over all we loved and hoped for, weak and helpless; while you, so strong, noble, and brave, have gone before us without a murmur. God knows best. But it is hard—O so hard!"[12]

Confederate defeat brought little relief to a devastated family. Sarah lost her home, possessions, and slaves: everything that had previously defined her status and her membership in Louisiana's urban elite. War had also robbed Sarah of her intended life as a young southern lady, forcing her to become a woman without the beaux and balls that characterized a belle's rite of passage.[13] Without an independent fortune, Sarah spent the late 1860s as a dependent in the household of her half-brother. In 1872, she, her mother, and her nephew, Howell, moved to South Carolina to make their home with Sarah's younger brother, James. A midshipman in the Confederate States Navy, James had just returned from Egypt, where he had served as a captain in the Egyptian army. Upon his arrival in South Carolina, he purchased Hampton plantation on the Congaree River just four miles below Columbia. The property, spanning several thousand acres, contained a new house and a "huge barn capable of stabling a hundred animals."[14]

Sarah and her mother moved to South Carolina with the intention of making "Jimmy's" new house a home. The domestic arrangements seemed perfect from the outset. With the arrival of his mother and sister, James was able to devote his complete attention to planting cotton: rebuilding his masculinity through hard work that would later translate into "earned wealth." In turn, the Morgan women were finally allowed to take charge of their own household, giving them a sense of autonomy that they had not enjoyed since their antebellum days in Baton Rouge. As mistresses of Hampton, Sarah and her mother were able to create a happy, inviting home, cooking, cleaning, and providing James and Howell with the love and moral guidance that only women could bestow. "This is my path in life," Sarah had once commented, "the adopted mother of some orphaned child, and the housekeeper at the hearth of some widowed, or bachelor brother."[15]

James Morgan's marriage to Gabriella Burroughs in early 1873, however, threw Sarah's congenial domestic arrangements into disarray. The new "Mrs. Morgan" was eager to be the commanding mistress of Hampton, and did not take kindly to the presence or the well-meaning advice of the "former managers." Within weeks of her arrival, Gabriella took charge, and Sarah and her mother found themselves relegated to the position of unwanted guests. The Morgan women experienced a demoralizing shift in their understanding of their own dependence. Sarah and Mrs. Morgan had regarded their domestic arrangements as reciprocal: They submitted to James, worked within his household, and received protection and respectability in return. As "unwanted" and "useless" guests, the Morgan women were unable to fulfill their end of the reciprocal arrangement, or to participate in the fulfillment of the domestic ideal. No longer regarded as contributing members of the household, Sarah and her mother were cast into the role of economic dependents, who were compelled to live off James and Gabriella's charity to survive.[16]

This new arrangement was intolerable to Sarah, who had once vowed that she would "rather die than be dependent."[17] Depressed and discouraged by her sister-in-law's efforts to evict her from Hampton, Sarah turned to Francis Warrington Dawson for assistance. A wartime friend of James and the editor of the *Charleston News,* Frank had fallen in love with Sarah in January 1873, less than six weeks after the death of his wife. Writing on mourning paper from the Broad Street offices of the *News,* Frank regarded Sarah as his salvation: a "guardian angel" whose morality and "strong right hand" led him to "betterment." "You can bring anything from me," he declared, "more, at least, than [any] other mortal can, and I, under your hand, were capable of harmonies of usefulness which no other touch can waken. You are the complement of my life; its crown and completeness, and so, time shall show."[18] But Sarah remained dubious about the constancy of Frank's love or the propriety of his lavish attentions, dismissing his overtures as nothing more than a passionate but fleeting "winter romance." Thirty-year-old Sarah refused to consider marriage to a recent widower as an appropriate resolution to her personal unhappiness.[19]

Frank was aware of Sarah's plight, and when he visited Hampton in late January, he made her a business proposal. The couple had often talked about political issues, and in one conversation, Sarah had likened the fate of the white people of Louisiana to that of Andromeda, a Greek mythological figure who had been chained to a rock by her father and left to be devoured by a sea monster. Frank was suitably impressed by Sarah's analogy, and implored her to write an editorial for his newspaper. Sarah initially refused, but was eventually won over by the editor's insistence. "Very well, Captain Dawson, but I shall make my own conditions," she explained. "I shall write that for you exactly as I spoke it, but I refuse to take the trouble to re-read it because I don't consider it worth it. As I finish each page, I shall throw it away—on the floor. If you choose to go down on your knees to pick up the pages, that's your own affair—only since nobody is to know I have written it, on getting back to your office, you shall recopy the whole in your handwriting and destroy my original so it shall be thought you wrote it yourself."[20]

Frank consented, and "The New Andromeda" appeared in the *News* on March 5, 1873. "This is indeed inauguration day," Frank wrote to Sarah on the eve of her debut, "the inauguration for you, let us pray, of a new career—one for which you have full capacity and in which you will do even more good for others than for yourself."[21] The event marked a turning point in Sarah's life. At Hampton, she too had become an Andromeda. Sarah's new position at the *News*—where she was contracted to write one social article and two general pieces per week—provided her with an income, allowing her to reclaim power over her future and her identity as an elite southern woman. She kept her newspaper work an "inviolable secret" from everyone except her mother, aware that "receiving money for toil" was sure to offend both her brother's masculinity and his genteel sensibilities—not to mention her own.[22] Women's employment outside the home was most often associated with downward social mobility and was undertaken out of dire necessity, not choice. Sarah recognized the social repercussions of her decision and worked closely with Frank to preserve her anonymity at all costs.[23]

Most importantly, Sarah's secrecy about her career meant that she was not obliged to expend her income maintaining the status quo at Hampton. Instead, she accumulated part of weekly paychecks in a bank account under the name of "Mr. Fowler," invested the other portion of her wage in stocks, and began to plan for the day when she and her mother would be able to set up a home of their own.[24] To achieve this goal, Sarah was compelled to revise her understanding of southern femininity: to revoke her complete submission to James by exercising her autonomy and withholding information about her career, and to see herself as an economic provider rather than an "unwanted dependent." Risking familial shame and social disgrace, Sarah embarked on a "new path" in an attempt to rebuild her elite identity and to attain her vision of the domestic ideal.

Like most elite southern women, Sarah Morgan found the transition to paid employment both physically and emotionally exhausting. Plagued by feelings of professional inadequacy, she regarded her newspaper work as a necessity that drained her already fragile state of health. And Frank, fearful that Sarah's "modest opinion of [her] own powers" may compel her to "march from the field of literature before the fight has fairly begun," spent much of his time encouraging his temperamental new writer. "You are, unhappily, in a condition in which it is necessary for you to exert to the utmost the talent which God has given you," he wrote. "I know too well how much it pains you to write anything for any eye to see, and I would not press you to continue, only that what you have already done proves that you can do everything, and more, that I predicted of you." Frank urged Sarah to consider her newspaper work as a grand expression of her moral influence as a woman: giving her a voice that allowed her to reach far beyond the confines of Hampton and into her community. "Your influence is no longer confined to your own household," he lectured her. "You have it in your power to preach to a larger congregation than Beecher and Spurgeon command, and with words as much loftier, and thoughts and aims as much purer, than theirs, as the nature of woman is higher than that of man."[25]

Although Sarah remained unconvinced of her ability to "do good to [her] people" through her work at the *News,* her personal circumstances compelled her to persevere. Throughout 1873, she penned over seventy editorials on topics ranging from French and Spanish politics to euthanasia, bores, race relations, and mothers-in-law. She also had the opportunity to write a series of articles on southern women. Unlike other elite ladies who confided their life experiences to a diary or a close friend, the very public genre of editorial writing granted Sarah a safe place to explore the injustices of her world—and to imagine alternatives—without the fear of familial or social reprisals.[26] Her editorials ranged over "The Use and Abuse of Widows," "Old Maids," "The Property of Married Women," "Work For Women," "Suffrage-Shrieking," "Age," "The Natural History of Woman," and other topics. In examining her writings, scholars have described Sarah as everything from a feminist to a "newly born woman and a budding . . . deconstructionist."[27] Many have failed to contextualize Sarah's writing, assessing her later, more radical views on motherhood and society alongside the editorials she wrote as a thirty-one-year-old single woman.[28]

Sarah's writing career spanned the 1870s, and her views changed over time. On one level, as E. Culpepper Clark has argued, her "essays were lectures to Frank on the dangers of marrying Sarah Morgan." The editorials she wrote were also autobiographical on another level. By examining her work from 1873–the year before she married Frank Warrington Dawson—Sarah's editorials highlight the set of challenges that confronted young, adult, single, elite, white women in the postbellum South. Sarah spoke candidly of the plight of Confederate belles who had sacrificed their traditional rite of passage during the Civil War only to find that southern defeat brought with it far more devastating consequences, such as loss of homes, possessions, finery, or men for courting. Like Sarah, many also faced the prospect of a single existence. Too many potential suitors had died for the Cause. Others returned home maimed in body or spirit. From this band of poor, dejected, sometimes dependent soldiers, young ladies often searched in vain for a suitable husband while subjected to pressure to marry from family and friends.[29]

While Confederate widows were regarded as true sacrificial patriots in the postwar South, the Confederate belle was not. Within years, her patriotic sacrifice was forgotten, and single women like Sarah were often branded as "old maid": a "withering epithet," which, she noted, "blasts a hardly matured women at twenty-five." Sarah felt the scorn of her new title, and devoted much of her editorial writing to the plight of the "old maid." "The most poignant as well as the most universal anguish is that produced by the terror of increasing years," she wrote in a piece titled "Age." "Certainly no other iron enters so deeply into the soul of woman. . . . To be pronounced *passeé* is more terrible to a woman than a good kicking is to a man. Insult can be avenged, but how may one resent the awful imputation of Age?"[30]

While Sarah acknowledged that even a "sweet sixteen shudders at the thought of being converted into a French participle Passeé," the widow, "that adder of men among women, is attractive, surrounded, irresistible at thirty, forty, fifty—yea, when past, by a quarter of a century, the age when the unmarried woman begins to read neglect and contempt in the manners of those around her." Sarah argued that widows perpetuated the poor condition of the "old maid" by "sinking the most indifferent men" with their natural magnetism and irresistible charms. "O for a law to abide by the vote of unmarried women on the question of enforcing the Hindoo [sic] Suttee, among the nations prolific of widows!" she declared. "And, if that be too flaming an advertisement of their perils and charms, O for a decree, like that of the Medes and Persians which altereth not, that no widow shall marry until the last girl has perished."[31]

In another editorial, Sarah Morgan addressed the "scarcely veiled . . . contempt" that marked the status of the "old maid." This stigma had existed in the antebellum South and persisted in the postwar period despite the physical and emotional legacies of war and defeat. In a world where elite femininity and the domestic ideal were epitomized by marriage and motherhood, single adult women without independent fortunes or households of their own were often viewed as "failures," or worse, as economic burdens who taxed the financial stores of the frugal postbellum household. As Sarah noted, the adult woman's single status eclipsed all else to define her identity and relegate her to the fringes of the community life. "It is doubtful whether civilization will ever advance so far that the name of the Old Maid will cease to bring a smile of contempt to human lips," she wrote. "While the idealized Mother is glorified by poets for tending her puny babies in her self-inflicted nursery, it is Old Maids like Miss Dix, Miss Nightingale and Miss Faithful who go about, bringing God's sunshine into darkened places, raising the fallen, loosing the prisoner's bands, and preaching Hope and Charity to men."[32]

Sarah constructed single womanhood as an honorable choice, far "superior" to the "infinite number of foolish virgins [who] prefer marrying men unworthy of a good woman's respect to facing the jibes and sneers of their mating and mated associates." "Put it to the vote a year, a month, a week after marriage and how many women would secretly black-ball their choice!" she added. "At least the Old Maid has no sickening conviction that only the name of a husband's love is hers. . . . She has no fear for the future; for, at the worst, her destiny is in her own hands, and she is not chained to a dead hope and a living despair. Shall we laugh at the multitude of Old Maids, or cry, Heaven help the Wives!"[33]

By depicting single life as a "noble choice" and not an unfortunate state imposed upon second-rate maidens, Sarah urged single women to recognize their agency. Using her position at the News and Courier, she wrote editorials on the importance of employment and self-support as an alternative way for financially dependent, single, adult women to nurture and honor the family unit. "The efforts making [sic] in the North to open a wider field of labor for women cannot be too highly praised," she argued in an editorial titled "Work for Women." "There are tens of thousands of delicately nurtured women, pining in want and in enforced idleness, to whom the possibility of earning a support for themselves, or for those dependent on them, would be an inconceivable blessing." "In the North," she noted, "numbers of women find employment in factories, shops, libraries and ticket offices." In the South, she asserted, women had only been "developed as rare exotics for the ornament of refined homes."[34]

With the coming of war and defeat, Sarah argued that these "helpless" southern belles had been "thrown as ruthlessly as broken flowers on the stones of an unsympathetic world." Convinced that even the most honorable gentleman would be "glad" to see his "most cherished" kin at work, Sarah called for an end to the "prejudice" that "shut [the woman] out from work she could do, perhaps better than the man to whom the preference is given."[35] Instead of languishing in "want and enforced idleness" within the households of their kin, Sarah urged "old maids" and women in similar circumstances to work outside the home, thereby enhancing their status as "worthy" and contributing members of their families and communities. By doing so they would become active participants in the quest for the domestic ideal instead of "sad-eyed, unwelcome dependents."[36]

Sarah's liberal comments on employment were made on the grounds of postwar necessity, not women's rights. Sarah argued that there was a sharp division between the Northern "chimera" of women's rights and woman suffrage, and the honorable cause of offering "means of self-support to that host of respectable mendicants who are ashamed to beg." Sarah reserved her contempt for "suffrage shriekers," who, through their "ravings," "injured" the call from "worthy women" to advance their sphere of "practical usefulness." "Woman suffrage is, of course, sheer nonsense," she proclaimed. "Shall maid and matron claim and exercise the privilege of electing the right woman to the wrong place? They will triumphantly prove themselves capable of blundering as systematically as the average male voter."[37]

Defeat may have thrown ladies into gainful employment, but for Sarah, it had not altered the proper state of relations between men and women. With fond recollections of her family life in Baton Rouge, Sarah believed that "woman's proper sphere was to be in perfect subjection to man," irrespective of her economic contribution. Women's employment was often necessary to ensure the attainment of the domestic ideal. Suffrage, she believed, offered no such advantages. In her editorial work, Sarah sought only to reposition the single, adult woman within her household and community: to grant her alternative ways to enhance her position, and to give her the tools to move from the margins of postwar life to the center. Equality with men was never part of this vision. Instead, Sarah Morgan offered readers an ideal: a vision in which women's work outside the home was accepted as a valued contribution to the domestic ideal, and one that rebuilt a single, adult woman's identity rather than destroying it. Sarah's vision, however, was far from the reality. Employment may have provided her with the opportunity to attain the domestic ideal, but its strong association with downward social mobility meant that it never became a central part of her postbellum identity. Like Mary Kelley's literary domestics, Sarah found herself unable to reconcile the inherent contradictions between her domestic life and her roles "as a public figure, economic provider, and creator of culture."[38]

Sarah Morgan's editorials created a sensation in Charleston, exciting widespread speculation on the identity of the author. "There is much anxiety here to know who is writing the social articles," Frank wrote excitedly in March; "they are doing *The News* good. Persons now read our editorials who never read them before."[39] Despite her resounding success, the demands of newspaper work, combined with the volatile environment at Hampton, soon wore down Sarah's already fragile state of health. In June, Dr Benjamin Watt Taylor diagnosed Sarah with gastritis (dyspepsia), an inflammation of the stomach lining. Alarmed by her deteriorating condition, Frank appointed her the *News and Courier's* official "undercover" correspondent for the season at Virginia's White Sulphur Springs, the preeminent summer retreat for the southern elite. While furnishing the paper with social articles on the guests, activities, and accommodations, Frank proposed that Sarah could also benefit from the healing properties of the springs, reputed to alleviate the effects of diseases ranging from dyspepsia to "chronic rheumatism, neuralgia, jaundice and scurvy."[40]

In mid-June, Sarah and her mother arrived at "the White": an "Eden" where the domestic ideal was downplayed and antebellum conceptions of gentility and social networking served to revive downtrodden elite identities. For the "homeless" Morgan women, who felt sure that Gabriella Morgan would never allow them to return to Hampton, the White Sulphur Springs provided them with the ideal environment in which to rebuild their identities as "aristocrats of Baton Rouge."[41] For decades, planters, professionals, politicians, and even presidents had flocked to the "breezy hills of Virginia" to escape the oppressive and unhealthy conditions that prevailed in the South between June and August. Gathering at the White Sulphur, elite southerners affirmed their gentility and status through unceasing rounds of balls, dances, visiting, and excursions to the springs. They promenaded through carefully manicured gardens, gazed at the majestic mountains, and marveled at the "four-story, four-hundred-foot-long-hotel" adorned with "arcades, columns, and porticos."[42] Even in the postwar period, when economic necessity had curtailed the "frills and furbelows" of many, young ladies could still be seen tripping gaily across the ballroom floor in a setting that evoked the old ways of life, not the hardship and struggle that characterized the new. "After a long and weary search for a terrestrial Paradise, I have, at last, discovered the original site of the garden of Eden," Sarah wrote with delight. Surrounded by genteel society, belles, balls, sumptuous dinners, and attentive and deferent black attendants, Sarah exhibited her gentility through her fashionable new wardrobe and by reestablishing social networks, which had always been regarded as an essential prerequisite for membership to the southern elite.[43]

As she resurrected her identity on her family name and antebellum status, Sarah's time at the White Sulphur exposed the precarious relationship between work and gentility: a theme she had barely touched on in her editorials on women's work. Employment furnished Sarah with her trip to the Springs and provided the requisite funds for fashionable attire. As she remarked in a letter to Frank, "no song, no supper!" "Mine earns breakfast and dinner in addition," she added. "I scarcely touch any of them, but it is reputable to have meals, you know, and my pen alone can earn them for me in future. Depend upon it, there is no service of the brain you can demand of me that I shall not be glad to give, even unto the whole of my kingdom."[44]

At the same time, Sarah faced the alarming prospect that her newly recovered status as a "proud Morgan" would be lost forever if her editorial work became publicly known. As Charlene Boyer Lewis has noted, antebellum families used their time at the Virginia Springs to "compete with members of their own group for a top place in the Springs hierarchy."[45] Sarah's letters indicate that the hardships of postbellum life had done little to dampen the social aspirations of many elite southerners, who looked to affirm their status by ostracizing "undesirable" or "unworthy" individuals from their select group. Sarah was painfully aware that her work as an "undercover correspondent" threatened to unleash a scandal that would terminate her interlude with fashionable society and leave her with nothing but the pity of her peers.[46] By the end of the season, she wrote to Frank in distress about the gossip and innuendo that pervaded her stay at the "White." "I cannot doubt that my 'official capacity' is freely whispered about," Sarah admitted. "I see people pointing me out at dinner. Day before yesterday four tables had me under inspection at once. . . . I grow sick to see men peeping at me over other people's shoulders, and hear them whisper something inaudible, but which I choose to interpret 'Correspondent.'" "Perhaps it had to be," she added, "but it makes me miserable." While she called for "old maids" to revoke their secondary status and rebuild their identities through "worthy" occupations, Sarah found herself unable to fulfill the ideal she had constructed for single southern women. She avoided the shame of her single status by referring to herself as a widow among new acquaintances.[47] Further, she became trapped in the contradiction between work and gentility. One may have facilitated the other, but for Sarah, the legitimacy of her elite identity was grounded on her acceptance as a member of Springs society and not as an employed correspondent. "I think I would be overwhelmed with shame if I was published," she admitted. While Frank declared her articles were "the best written, this season, from any watering place," Sarah founded her elite identity not on her professional achievements, but on her friendships with celebrated belles like Hetty Cary Pegram. Instead of embracing her new career and the professional status it afforded her, Sarah used her work to rebuild her postwar identity within an unstable antebellum framework of southern gentility.[48]

Sarah Morgan's resounding success at the White Sulphur Springs provided her with the income she required to bid Hampton farewell for good. After a short stay in Greenville, South Carolina, Sarah and her mother achieved their long-anticipated dream, moving into their own accommodations at the Gadsden House on Meeting Street in Charleston. With their "entire store for housekeeping" consisting of "silver forks and spoons, and five linen sheets," Sarah devised "a thousand means of employing every dollar I can earn" in order to attain a pleasing elite household. Still, the "bliss" of inhabiting their own home became a cause for "rejoicing." While she may have struggled to reconcile work with elitism, Sarah could not deny that employment had provided her with the requisite funds to establish a home of her own: a home in which she could finally marry her gentility with the postwar domestic ideal.[49]

Sarah Morgan's career as a writer largely ended with her nuptials to Frank Dawson in January 1874. Her new role as a wife, and later as a mother, did not rebuild Sarah's elite identity, but rather enhanced the identity that she herself had recovered through her work at the News and Courier. In the defeated South, economic necessity had compelled Sarah to step outside the traditional boundaries of elite femininity in order to resurrect a postwar self founded firmly on the antebellum tenets of home, family, status, and gentility.

Notes

1. Charles East, ed., Sarah Morgan: The Civil War Diary of a Southern Woman (New York, 1991), 47–8.

2. Ibid., 51.

3. Ibid., 85.

4. For an understanding of the household as the cultural foundation of southern society see Elizabeth Fox-Genovese, Within the Plantation Household: Black and White Women of the Old South (Chapel Hill, 1988); Catherine Clinton, The Planta-

tion Mistress: Woman's World in the Old South (New York, 1982); Steven M. Stowe, *Intimacy and Power in the Old South: Ritual in the Lives of the Planters* (Baltimore, 1987); Brenda E. Stevenson, *Life in Black and White: Family and Community in the Slave South* (New York, 1996); Marli F. Weiner, *Mistresses and Slaves: Plantation Women in South Carolina, 1830–1880* (Urbana, 1998), 54; Nancy Dunlap Bewcaw, "Politics of Household During the Transition from Slavery to Freedom in the Yazoo-Mississippi Delta, 1861–1876" (Ph.D. diss., University of Pennsylvania, 1996). On the household as a "haven from the outside world," see Leonore Davidoff, *Worlds Between: Historical Perspectives on Gender and Class* (Cambridge, 1995), 53; Lori Ginzberg, *Women and the Work of Benevolence: Morality, Politics and Class in the Nineteenth Century United States* (New Haven, 1990), 12.

5. On the pillaging of the Morgan home after the Federal invasion of Baton Rouge see East, *Diary of a Southern Woman*, 233, 247, 435, 153; see also 121.

6. For earlier interpretations that regard the Civil War as a watershed for southern women see Anne Firor Scott, *The Southern Lady from Pedestal to Politics, 1830–1930* (Chicago, 1970); Francis Butler Simkins and James Welch Patton, *The Women of the Confederacy* (Richmond, New York, 1936); Mary Elizabeth Massey, *Bonnet Brigades* (New York, 1966). For recent interpretations see George C. Rable, *Civil Wars: Women and the Crisis of Southern Nationalism* (Urbana, 1989); Drew Gilpin Faust, *Mothers of Invention: Women of the Slaveholding South in the American Civil War* (Chapel Hill, 1996); LeeAnn Whites, *The Civil War as a Crisis in Gender: Augusta, Georgia, 1860–1890* (Athens, Ga., 1995); Laura F. Edwards, *Scarlett Doesn't Live Here Anymore: Southern Women in the Civil War Era* (Urbana, 2000). For a more general examination of the survival of the planter class and the resurrection of their social values, see Michael Wayne, *The Reshaping of Plantation Society: The Natchez District, 1860–1880* (Baton Rouge, 1983); Jonathan M. Weiner, *Social Origins of the New South: Alabama, 1860–1885* (Baton Rouge, 1978); Laura F. Edwards, *Gendered Strife and Confusion: The Political Culture of Reconstruction* (Urbana, 1997).

7. Whites, *The Civil War as a Crisis in Gender,* 132–59; Edwards, *Gendered Strife and Confusion,* 107–44; Edwards, *Scarlett Doesn't Live Here Anymore,* 182–5.

8. East, *Diary of a Southern Woman,* 70.

9. For a biographical account of Sarah Morgan's early life see East, *Diary of a Southern Woman,* xv–xx.

10. Sarah's education was far less comprehensive than the education of most of her peers. See East, *Diary of a Southern Woman,* 136–7, 290. On women's education in the antebellum South, see Christie Anne Farnham, *The Education of the Southern Belle: Higher Education and Student Socialization in the Antebellum South* (New York, 1994); Anya Jabour, "'Grown Girls, Highly Cultivated': Female Education in an Antebellum Southern Family," *Journal of Southern History* 44 (February 1998): 23–64; Stowe, *Intimacy and Power in the Old South,* 142–53.

11. East, *Diary of a Southern Woman,* 80, 60–3. On reciprocity between men and

women see Joan Cashin, ed., *Our Common Affairs: Texts from Women in the Old South* (Baltimore, 1996), 10; Orville Vernon Burton, *In My Father's House Are Many Mansions: Family and Community in Edgefield, South Carolina* (Chapel Hill, 1985), 128; Faust, *Mothers of Invention*, 6.

12. East, *Diary of a Southern Woman*, 597. On the death of Sarah's father see 11–22; on loss of home see 247; on back injury see 333–7; on exodus to New Orleans see 473–88; on death of brothers see 597–602. On the Morgan family's observation of mourning rituals, see Nancy Schoonmaker, "Sarah Morgan: Death and Mourning as Religion and Ritual in the Nineteenth Century South" (M.A. thesis, University of North Carolina, 2001).

13. On the wartime experiences of young Confederate women, see Giselle Roberts, The Confederate Belle (Columbia, Mo. 2003).

14. For a full description of Hampton see James Morris Morgan, *Recollections of a Rebel Reefer* (London, 1918), 271.

15. For an examination of the postwar ideal of southern masculinity see Edwards, *Gendered Strife and Confusion*, 121–9. East, *Diary of a Southern Woman*, 282.

16. Sarah frequently mentioned the loneliness and depression she experienced at Hampton. See Dawson to Morgan, January 15, February 21, April 1, 10, 23, May 15, 18, 20, June 9, 1873, Francis Warrington Dawson Papers, William R. Perkins Library, Duke University, Durham, N.C. Unless otherwise cited, all correspondence between Morgan and Dawson is found in this collection.

17. East, *Diary of a Southern Woman*, 153.

18. See Dawson to Morgan, January 22, 27, 31, February 9, 1873. For biographical information on Frank Dawson see S. Frank Logan, "Francis W. Dawson, 1840–1889: South Carolina Editor" (M.A. thesis, Duke University, 1947); S. Frank Logan, "Francis Warrington Dawson: South Carolina Editor," *Proceedings of the South Carolina Historical Association* 2 (1952): 13–28; E. Culpepper Clark, *Francis Warrington Dawson and the Politics of Restoration: South Carolina, 1874–1889* (Columbia, 1980). On the relationship and subsequent marriage of Frank Dawson and Sarah Morgan see Dawson to Morgan, January 15, 19, 22, 31, February 9, 13, 15, March 16, April 17, 25, 26, May 18, June 10, 11, August 5, 18, September 6, 1873; Morgan to Dawson, August 4, 1873; Logan, "Francis W. Dawson," 85–106; E. Culpepper Clark, "Sarah Morgan and Francis Warrington Dawson: Raising the Woman Question in Reconstruction South Carolina," *South Carolina Historical Magazine* 81 (January 1980): 8–23.

19. Dawson to Morgan, January 22, 1873. On marriage proposals see Dawson to Morgan, February 9, March 5, April 24, 26, May 18, August 7, September 25, 1873.

20. Logan, "Francis W. Dawson," 99–100. Warrington Dawson (Frank and Sarah's son) related this story to Logan in a letter dated July 1, 1946.

21. Dawson to Morgan, March 4, 1873. On Sarah's first weeks as a writer see, for example, Dawson to Morgan, March 5, 7, 16, April 10, 1873. Sarah began her career as a writer for the *News*. In April, Riordan, Dawson, and Company bought the *Cou-*

rier and merged the two papers into one. The first edition of the *News and Courier* appeared on April 7, 1873.

22. Dawson to Morgan, March 16, 1873. See also March 5, April 14, 24, 25, May 20, June 22, July 9, 1873; Sarah Morgan, "Work for Women," *News and Courier,* April 15, 1873.

23. On the association between employment and downward social mobility see Rable, *Civil Wars,* 279, 282; Faust, *Mothers of Invention,* 81; Davidoff, *Worlds Between,* 78; M. J. Peterson, *Family, Love and Work in the Lives of Victorian Gentlewomen* (Bloomington, Ind., 1989), 120–1. On the incorporation of employment into the domestic ideal see Edwards, *Gendered Strife and Confusion,* 142.

24. Dawson to Morgan, March 18, April 1, 7, 14, 1873.

25. In her work on literary domestics, Mary Kelley argues that feelings of professional inadequacy were a result of the "female experience of intellectual restriction, frustration and belittlement" that "denied them a secure sense of their intellectual capacities, undermined their intellectual self-respect, and withheld intellectual self-confidence." See Mary Kelley, *Private Woman, Public Stage: Literary Domesticity in Nineteenth Century America* (New York, 1984), 104. Dawson to Morgan, March 7, 18, 16, May 15, 1873. The importance of Sarah's "moral influence" on the readers of the *News and Courier* became one of Frank's regular appeals to encourage Sarah to continue writing; see March 7, 16, April 10, 14, May 15, June 11, September 10, 1873.

26. Dawson to Morgan, March 16, 1873. In her study of American novelists, Anne Goodwyn Jones argues that writing fiction allowed women to cast their voices through a "mask" that allowed them to avoid "either literal alienation of physical departure or the psychological alienation of selflessness or madness." See *Tomorrow Is Another Day: The Woman Writer in the South, 1859–1936* (Baton Rouge, 1981), 24.

27. Scholars differ considerably in their interpretation of Sarah's diary and writings. Mary Katherine Davis argues that Sarah's work was "a reaction against chivalry, the code of honor, Southernism; not a positive assertion of female equality"; see "Sarah Morgan Dawson: A Renunciation of Southern Society" (M.A. thesis, University of North Carolina, 1970), 5. Charlotte Telford Breed contests this thesis and describes Sarah as a "new southern lady" who was motivated by the "diametrically opposed" forces of southernism and feminism; see "Sarah Morgan Dawson: From Confederate Girl to New Woman" (M.A. thesis, University of North Carolina, 1981). In her more recent study of Sarah Morgan, Clara Juncker contends that Sarah emerged from the Civil War "a newly born woman and a budding Louisiana deconstructionist"; see "Behind Confederate Lines: Sarah Morgan Dawson," *Southern Quarterly* 30 (fall 1991): 7. Charles East, who edited the most recent edition of Sarah's wartime diary, disputes all these viewpoints, arguing that Sarah never joined the "forces of the women's rights movement, but remained the independent she always was." He contends that her personal conflict between feminism and southernism was "never resolved." See East, *Diary of a Southern Woman,* xxxviii.

See also Katherine Cann, "A Most Awful and Insoluble Mystery: The Writing Career of Sarah Morgan Dawson," *Proceedings of the South Carolina Historical Association* (Columbia, 1990), 75–86. E. Culpepper Clark, biographer of Frank Dawson, examined Sarah's writing within the context of the couple's relationship; see "Sarah Morgan and Francis Dawson," 8–23. See also Logan, "Francis W. Dawson," 85–106.

28. Historians have frequently cited an undated essay titled "Comment on the Role of Women as Childbearers" as evidence of Sarah's feminist perspective. There is no evidence in the document or in the correspondence to suggest that this essay was written in 1873.

29. Clark, "Sarah Morgan and Francis Warrington Dawson," 14. Rable, *Civil Wars*, 270.

30. "The Use and Abuse of Widows," *News*, March 10, 1873; "Age," *News and Courier*, June 21, 1873.

31. Ibid.

32. "Old Maids," *News*, March 15, 1873.

33. Ibid.

34. Ibid.; "Work for Women," *News*, April 15, 1873. See also "Stitch! Stitch! Stitch!" *News and Courier*, April 10, 1873.

35. Ibid. Sarah's comments on work were not unusual for the time. Indeed, she may have been influenced by editorials and letters that appeared in the New Orleans *Daily Picayune* in the late 1860s. In a piece titled "A Woman's Plea," the paper urged men to leave clerking positions "for their less fortunate and more numerous sisterhood of spinsters, widows and girls" who otherwise remained "a burden to their friends, their families and themselves." Similar articles were published in the *Daily Picayune* throughout the early 1870s. See *Daily Picayune*, March 21, 1869, in Kathryn Reinhart Schuler, "Women in Public Affairs in Louisiana During Reconstruction," *Louisiana Historical Quarterly* 19 (July 1936): 696–701. Sarah was a resident of New Orleans in the late 1860s and it is likely that she read or heard about these letters and editorials. When she moved to South Carolina, she continued to receive a regular supply of newspapers from New Orleans.

36. "Work for Women," *News*, April 15, 1873.

37. Ibid. See also "Suffrage-Shrieking," *News and Courier*, May 20, 1873; "Two Hundred and Fifty Dollars for a Vote," *News*, April 4, 1873.

38. "Young Couples," *News*, March 29, 1873; Morgan to Dawson, July 29, 1873. See also "The Natural History of Woman," *News and Courier*, September 20, 1873. Kelley, *Private Woman, Public Stage*, 111.

39. Dawson to Morgan, March 16, 1873. See also March 12, April 24, 25, July 9, 1873.

40. Sarah's health had been fragile ever since she was thrown from a horse in 1863. See *East, Diary of a Southern Woman*, 333–7. For an account of Sarah's health in 1873 see Dawson to Morgan, January 31, February 11, March 16, April 10, 24, May 18, 20, June 10, 12, 13, 23, 25, July 18, 1873; Morgan to Dawson, September 8, 16, 24, 1873. Sarah also suffered from depression; see Dawson to Morgan, February

21, April 1, 10, 23, 25, 27, May 15, 18, 20, June 9, 13, 22, 25, July 21, 1873; Morgan to Dawson, September 10, 1873. On Sarah's impending trip to the White Sulphur Springs see Dawson to Morgan, May 18, 20, 26, 28, 29, June 9, 11, 12, 1873. For a comprehensive history of the White Sulphur Springs see Robert S. Conte, *The History of the Greenbrier: America's Resort* (Charleston, 2000). On the Virginia Springs see Charlene M. Boyer Lewis, *Ladies and Gentlemen on Display: Planter Society at the Virginia Springs, 1790–1860* (Charlottesville, 2001). On the healing properties of the Springs see Lewis, 62–3.

41. See Dawson to Morgan, July 4, 1873.

42. Dawson to Morgan, June 9, 1873. On the unhealthy conditions that prompted many southerners to visit the Springs, see Lewis, *Ladies and Gentlemen on Display,* 60.

43. "The Eden of the South: Summer at the White Sulphur Springs," *News and Courier,* June 26, 1873, 1. Sarah wrote nine pieces on the season at the Greenbrier. See "Beauty and the Beast: A Tale of the White Sulphur Springs," July 1, 1873; "A Summer Idyll: The Poetry and Prose of Life at the Springs," July 9, 1873; "A Season at the Springs: The White Sulphur in Full Blast—A Happy Company," July 16, 1873; "Style at the Springs: The Rush of Visitors to the Greenbrier White," July 23, 1873; "Scenes at the Springs: Stray Leaves from the Volume of Humanity," July 30, 1873; "Fashion at the Springs: The Belles of the White and their Ducks of Dresses," August 6, 1873; "Belles at the Springs: Apples of Discord in the Virginia Eden," August 13, 1873; "Scandal at the Springs: 'Tell Me, My Heart, Can This Be Love?'" August 21, 1873.

44. Morgan to Dawson, August 8, 1873. See also March 7, 16, 1873.

45. Lewis, *Ladies and Gentlemen on Display,* 152.

46. Ibid., 152. Charlene Lewis argues that the fierce competition among elite southerners dissipated after the Civil War; see 210. Sarah's letters and published articles indicate that this fierce competition was still alive and well in 1873.

47. Morgan to Dawson, August 17, 1873. See also August 1, 5, 12, 15, 1873; Dawson to Morgan, August 17, 20, 27, 1873.

48. Morgan to Dawson, August 1, 1873. For Frank's comments on Sarah's White Sulphur Springs work see June 25, 26, 29, July 23, 30, August 6, 13, 20, 1873. On Sarah's relationships with the elite White Sulphur society see Morgan to Dawson, August 5, 8, 12, 15, 1873.

49. On stay in Greenville see Morgan to Dawson, September 14, 15, 19, 1873. On preparations for Sarah's move to Charleston see Morgan to Dawson, September 15, 16, 19, 1873; Dawson to Morgan, 17, 19, 22, 1873.

3

"The Worst Results in Mississippi May Prove the Best for Us"

Blanche Butler Ames and Reconstruction

Warren Ellem

The experiences of Blanche Butler Ames were layered with many dimensions of identity: her individuality was significantly conditioned by region, informed by gender, constrained by race and class. The milieu in which Blanche came to womanhood and in which she lived the first six years of her marriage was political, and she participated in this milieu more actively than orthodox gendered ways prescribed.[1] The values that informed her multiple roles did not always dovetail with circumstances, and significant tensions arose between those values and identities. As the wife of a carpetbag U.S. senator from 1870 till 1873 and then governor of Mississippi till his resignation in 1876, and mother of three children during this six-year period, Blanche's experience as a Northern woman provides an insight into the ways in which the personal, familial, social, and political dimensions of her life interacted and intersected, and into the relationship of women to politics, political discourse, action, and power. Her life, while confirming in some respects the maleness of the political world in her time, indicates that some women entered actively and deeply into the political careers and decisions of their menfolk and thereby into the political life of the nation. Significantly, however, her engagement with politics did not grow out of any relationship to organized women's groups that have attracted the attention of historians to date, though she was aware of the campaigns those groups mounted. Rather her engagement grew out of familial relationships and was simultaneously propelled and constrained by them. Her relationship to political power and action may not have been "typical," but it does suggest that more attention needs to be given to women outside the organized reform movements if we are to comprehend the complexity and substance of women's involvement in the world of politics at state and national levels in the post–Civil War nation.[2]

Blanche, born in 1847, imbibed politics in her youth. Her father, Benjamin F. Butler, was intensely political. His public career in state and federal legislatures and in the Union army in the Civil War was long-lasting, varied, and dramatic. Sarah Hildreth Butler, Blanche's mother, involved herself deeply in her husband's career, counseling and advising him about courses of action he might best take, and defending him vigorously from criticism. Her mother's involvement in Ben Butler's military and political fortunes provided Blanche with a model of individuality in a companionate marriage. Unsurprisingly then, Blanche's conception of marriage envisaged intimate association between husband and wife within gendered roles that did not privilege one person over the other. Blanche had been courted by Adelbert Ames, who had won numerous brevets during the Civil War, been military governor of Mississippi, and was, as of early 1870, U.S. senator from Mississippi. The announcement of their wedding had been widely anticipated in Washington society circles early in 1870.[3]

Early on, Blanche established her independence. As preparations for their wedding advanced, she pointed out that the "style now [is] to leave out the word 'obey' from the marriage service," and informed him she had "not the least intention of making that promise." She further indicated, with a touch of humor, that she would add "when I feel like it" as the extent of her concession. She had previously played down patriarchal modes: "I wonder if you will ever succeed in inspiring me with that awe and reverence which some wives feel for the 'Lords of Creation.' I think not."[4] Plainly he need not anticipate that kind of subjection—and nor did he. For Adelbert, in whose life authority had been a significant presence, both in the power to command and to be commanded, the omission of the pledge bothered him not at all. "I only ask that you love me . . . obedience I do not believe in." Her only "requisite," also, was his love, in which her "happiness" was now located. She felt her love for him was redefining herself and undermining her accustomed "*self*- sufficiency and independence."[5]

Blanche loved life and people, and was frequently noted at Washington social events, where, according to the *Boston Morning Post*, she held "undisputed belleship." Their wedding, anticipated to be a stunning affair, took place in St Anne's Church at Lowell, Massachusetts, in the evening of July 21, 1870. It was reported widely, in major newspapers from Boston to New York to Washington. The 600 guests were worthy of the occasion, as "brilliant and fashionable [an] assembly" as had ever graced the church. In addition to the families on both sides, the governor of Massachusetts, William Claflin, was there, as were U.S. senators Charles Sumner, Zachariah Chandler, Henry Wilson, and Samuel Clarke Pomeroy; numerous ex-senators, congressmen, and generals; as well as public figures not formally connected to government such as the "prince of agitators" Wendell Phillips. The illness of Mrs. Grant was given as the reason for the absence of President Ulysses S Grant.[6]

The magnificence of the occasion and of the display embodied the triumphant glory of postwar republicanism. The two persons at the center of this occasion only confirmed that promise: Blanche, popular and intelligent, whose family had come immediately to the nation's aid when the crisis broke and had done much to make the Union cause a national and not specifically Republican cause; and Adelbert, whose life had revolved (and for four years dangerously so) around public service to the nation and who as U.S. senator was now committed to realizing the Republican ideal in Mississippi and elsewhere in the South. Their love embodied their personal fulfillment in each other, as they happily joined in lifelong commitment. It also affirmed for others the unlimited potential of free society in the restored nation.[7]

Blanche easily made the transition from the status of Washington belle to wife of a young and politically inexperienced senator from Mississippi. She enjoyed release from the constricting world of the belle. "There is one thing about this married life I appreciate above all others. It is the glorious sense of freedom." Determination, self-possession, and self-reliance seem to have taken "the place of 'doubt' and 'hesitation.'"[8] She had found "no forced affection or want of adaptability" and could not have asked for "happier" times.[9] Another element in the ease of her transition to her new role was her knowledge of the world of politics in which he as senator and she as a senator's wife moved. Having grown up in the political milieu of Massachusetts and in Washington, Blanche brought with her into her relationship with Adelbert a developed understanding of the modes and processes of politics, and of the demands of public life.[10]

She understood the needs of the political household and the social manners essential to its functioning. Courtesy was intrinsic to social exchange, to her relations to other people, and to her sense of self. The personal, social, class, and political aspects to her life fused with her gendered role of hostess as she entertained political friends of Adelbert and her father at dinners. The effort to return nearly 200 calls spoke eloquently of how fully, and perhaps exhaustively, Blanche identified with rituals of the so-cial-political community of Washington.[11] Blanche's conceptions were shaped also by her mother's insight into the importance of personal elements to political relationships. Sarah's involvement in Benjamin Butler's career may have been directed by the gender divide of the period into private communications, but it lost none of its pertinence. Blanche, who was very close to her mother, could hardly have been unaware of her mother's input into her father's career and conduct. Her subsequent assumption of such a role in her husband's political life and the fullness with which she carried it out suggests that for the Butler and Ames families, at least, the maleness of the public world of nineteenth-century America had been subverted by more female input than its formal prescriptions might suggest.[12]

Blanche's familiarity with the conventions of the social world of nineteenth-century state and national politics informed her relationship with the young senator from Mississippi. Ames lacked that experience and cultural familiarity with the workings of political relationships which she had absorbed as part of her growing up, and he found himself receiving not only family news and frequent expressions of happiness from his young bride, but also suggestions and comments that were not instructions but carried a meaning more insistent than a mere suggestion. They were involved together in their world. The closeness of their collaboration led her to refer to a policy Ames had put to the Military Committee as "*our* advise [*sic*]." In their marriage this sense of partnership deepened as she envisaged his work as "ours," and encouraged and supported him through her implicit understanding of the politician's craft.[13]

Blanche identified more positively with Ames's role as senator, then governor, than with the location of his political base, Mississippi. For the six years of their marriage until Ames's resignation from the governorship in 1876, Blanche was in Mississippi for seventeen months only. Anxiety over the dangers of the southern climate explained a large part of her decision to remain for much of the time in Lowell out of concern for their children's health.[14] Blanche loved her children deeply, finding great satisfaction in their feeding and nurture. These separations were felt keenly by both, but neither contested the values that dictated the separation.[15]

But it was not just the mysterious world of Mississippi that evoked concern in Blanche. Her disconnection with Mississippi, even when she lived within it, related to cultural, political, and social values, which functioned not only to inform her role and identity, but to alienate her from the society she now entered. To her, Mississippi was not hospitable country in any way. She understood the requirements of Ames's position and accepted, reluctantly, that they would have to make a household there. She remained skeptical that it was worth the effort to placate his southern white critics. "They are but a poor miserable set, who must be educated to what is just and proper. Nobody can conform to or be guided in the least by their crude uncivilized ideas." She lamented the "baleful climate, the lack of good will and refinement in the people," the absence of "amusements," libraries, and "social intercourse."[16]

As the governor's wife, from 1874 to 1876, Blanche had to negotiate between the necessary associations of her public world and her own personal values. She accomplished this to the satisfaction of the leading southern white ladies whose calls she returned. Ames's political friends, "all the carpetbaggers," she entertained over dinner at the Governor's Mansion. The reception held by Del and Blanche for state officers and the legislature indicated the limits of their social sphere. Their joint decision, to invite men only, was intended to avoid "trouble," that is, social intercourse between both genders of both races.[17] Blanche's conduct as the "First Republican Lady" later won praise from white Democratic leading ladies as a "gentlewoman . . . [who] permitted no social contact discreditable to the most exclusive of her class," but Blanche's relief that only one such reception was in prospect may have owed something to release from the conflict it precipitated within her value structure.[18]

Blanche had always enjoined Adelbert to keep her informed about affairs in Mississippi, and once criticized him for keeping "disagreeable or dangerous" information from her. She chided him for such omission, forgave him for the same provided he did not so offend again, at the same time demonstrating her knowledge of the situation in Mississippi and the strength of her identification with his success. In transmitting Butler's legal and political opinion on the effort by Ames's opponents to prevent the 1873 gubernatorial election in Mississippi, Blanche was doing more than relaying information.[19] She also helped prepare strategy in advance, revealing her knowledge of the system. Just as she wanted him to win once the decision was made to run for governor, so she wanted his administration to succeed. She "must always have the deepest [interest]" in his affairs for, as she saw it, "your life and thoughts must of necessity be those of your wife—who loves you."[20] The centrality of her role in his life, and in the political decisions of his career, was acknowledged as he negotiated the contending pressures placed on him to commit to run for the governorship in 1873 to prevent his Republican rivals from controlling the state. His and Blanche's expectation had been a continuing role for him in the U.S. Senate. As he alerted her to the developing strategy focussing on the governorship, he acknowledged, "I can make no definite plans till after consulting with you, my precious one."[21]

When she found that his request to President Grant in late July 1874 for troops to suppress white disorders in Vicksburg had been rebuffed, her initial reaction was his state of mind. She warned him against his nature, to "trouble and ponder over matters," with the risk of becoming "morbid, gloomy" and of taking sick. Reflecting her valuation of character, she was confident he would do his duty. The extent to which her perceptions were centered within her relationships was evident in her assurance that if affairs in Mississippi nonetheless went badly, he would have lost "nothing of any consequence" to him. The almost narcissistic security of her world—her class, race, region, family—underpinned her assurance to him as he contemplated the destruction of Republican government in Mississippi and the likely use of terror to effect it, that "We are, I think, superior to the good or evil fortune the state has power to bring to us. We should congratulate ourselves that we occupy such a favorable position."[22]

For Adelbert himself, the Vicksburg election of August 18, 1874—the terror, the refusal of the president to send troops, the white-liner victory—was a turning point. His letters evidence a redefinition of himself and his roles. He wanted an end to "our present peripatetic existence." Revealing how much his conceptions had taken shape in their discussions on his situation in Mississippi, and how large their relationship figured in his thinking, he compared "the advantages and disadvantages of my honors and duties with all their attendant good and evil" and found them nearly equal, and concluded that he was "now in a better frame of mind to nestle down with my family in some cosy corner than ever before." The reality to which he was responding was that "you constitute the best and greater part of my world."[23] Embracing Blanche's outlook on the state even as he indicated how much his service had been a joint undertaking with him as conduit, he affirmed that "We can say quits at any time, and she [Mississippi] will be my debtor." He had wearied of the "struggle, struggle all my life" and would now be "content to drift along with the current, without making a stroke—and this may be because there is nothing left but to drift." He was now doing his duty only, his heart no longer in it. His heart was elsewhere, with Blanche and their family.[24]

There remained, however, the matter of duty, and of pride—to Blanche, matters of no small moment. The very day that Adelbert announced he was in drift mode, she reacted to newspaper reports of the racial troubles in Austin in which six blacks were killed, and the lack of response from Governor Ames. He believed there was little he could do to protect blacks in situations like Austin in Tunica County, and that the president would not send troops if asked. Her response to these reports indicated how deeply she considered herself involved in the political strategy of his administration. "The thing I shall be most interested in as regards state affairs on my return to Mississippi will be the *reorganization* of the State Militia."[25] Just seven months into his first year as governor, in 1874, Blanche had foreseen difficulties ahead and offered advice to address the limitations she read into his conduct as governor. She impressed him from her vantage point in Massachusetts that he "must get control of the state and make *yourself* master of the situation. . . . [S]how that you can rule." In so doing, he would make Grant respect him and reinforce the obligations of the federal government to reconstruction. Thus he would thwart the efforts of "reorganized Ku-Klux" elements to control the state. She could not stand by and see the unholy combination of Grant's ambition for a third term and Ku Klux behavior triumph. "You see, sweetheart, I am ready for a fight." While welcoming newspaper reports that the federal government might intervene to "try to put a stop to the terrible outrages," she wanted "Mississippi in such a condition that she can take care of herself and control all disturbances, without aid, and this while my Love is Governor."[26] Her observation of the attorney general, Edwards Pierrepont, had already convinced her that, whatever is being said, "It is evident that you will have to 'paddle your light canoe' without assistance." To Blanche the crisis precipitated by the extralegal challenge of radical white-liners to Republican government in Mississippi was shaping as a personal and familial one as well as a political one, and she identified with his fortunes and honor powerfully.[27]

For her, this crisis, which by late 1875 had become a white revolution characterized by terror and violence, drew its principal importance from the centrality of her husband to its conduct. Drawing on the access of her father to the president and attorney general, Blanche sought to have put in place a process by which Adelbert could get access to federal troops immediately rather than through the current time-consuming and cumbersome process. That order to place federal troops at Ames's disposal, she and Butler believed, had been issued immediately, and so Ames's silence about its receipt puzzled her.[28] Though Adelbert had asked her to have Pierrepont alerted to the troop laws, she knew she had pushed her role beyond the limited brief he had given her. Concerned that she had been involved "more perhaps than you will think I am warranted in," she hoped he would not "resent a wife's meddling." The order was issued finally a week later, a delay in which the hand of Pierrepont can be seen, and coming just five days before the state election, it was too late to be of any use. Her fears of his displeasure proved unfounded.[29]

Blanche's role in his political career extended to the question of his res-ignation. Overwhelmed by the impending *"revolution"* of 1875 that the impotence of his party and the indifference of the U.S. government had underpinned, Adelbert announced to Blanche his decision "to resign after the election." He saw no reason to "fight on a hopeless battle for two years more." He had determined to leave the state as soon as his term was ended, and perhaps before. Several days later he raised with Blanche his inclina-tion "to resign the very first day I can do so honorably." Blanche, however, countered the proposal directly, opposing such action "while it would have the least appearance of your having been beaten and driven out of the state." She advised time and deliberation, a wait-and-see policy. He took her advice.[30]

Blanche's personal interest in Adelbert's career was complex. He was not only the conduit for their shared commitment to republicanism and to the Republican program of Reconstruction, but for their aspirations for political success with its rewards and status. More particularly, Blanche esteemed the position of U.S. senator very highly, and valued his reelection above the governorship. While she accepted the decision to run for gover-nor in 1873, her acceptance came after she understood that to be the most likely way to secure Adelbert's reelection to the Senate. While she would support him "in anything you think best to undertake," she remained unconvinced by the logic of the strategy.[31] Moreover her aspirations for his reelection to the Senate had evidently been a sustaining force for her during the trials of his governorship, as she reacted strongly against his statements to others in October 1875 that he "will not be a candidate again for any place," so "disgusted" was he at the indifference of the national government to the plight of black Republicans in Mississippi. Firmly she reminded him of her previous "good advice" about keeping one's counsel and one's options open, and not being pressured into unilateral declara-tions that preempted her wishes.[32] She saw his action as an unwelcome deviation from the consultation between them that had previously marked decisions of this nature. Emphasizing the collaborative nature of their relationship, she pointed out that such presumption represented a retrograde step, a step she described, with only a touch of jesting, as "a little exercise of your manly right to decide for yourself *and your family,* which I have not observed in you before." His action was unworthy of their relationship and she wanted the decision reversed. Nor was this merely a request. "Now I *demand it* as *my* right that you should take the Senator's position and then resign." Her preference for the senatorship reflected her own vantage point—her class, region, and race and her family and political associations—that web of values that interacted to underpin and inform (positively toward Washington and negatively toward Mississippi) her view of the world and of her place in it. She acknowledged she had a "great pride in this, Del" and considered it his duty to "gratify" her in this if at all possible." Though she knew his disillusion with politics, the prize of the Senate seat was too great to "throw away."[33]

In her awareness of the prescriptive limits assigned by the system to her formal participation in politics, she identified with his political role and career, rather than with the state he represented. When planning for their wedding, she observed that "'we' have gone into the Senate,"[34] but when Adelbert referred to the "days when we shall be working together for the interests of Mississippi," Blanche demurred. She saw herself delighting in him rather than in "working for Mississippi," pointing out it was difficult to get interested in a role from which one was excluded. Implicitly recognizing the gender dominance in their relationship and in the political structure, and his acceptance of it, she thought she might be more interested "If you will let me run at the next election. . . . But you won't—you will not dare." Her engagement with politics and with Mississippi, then, limited as it was by the gendering of political leadership and power, channeled itself through familial and personal contexts and was constrained by those contexts. The day before the 1875 election, she conceded that her own fulfillment in their relationship made her "so well content that I do not really think I am anxious enough about affairs in Mississippi—Except the desire that you should check-mate your enemies, and succeed in all you undertake."[35]

Her conception then of Mississippi politics was profoundly personal. Both her association with him and her love for him that wanted him to succeed, and the larger social and political cause—republicanism and the rights of blacks—were important in her political ideology. Yet so far as the struggle for republicanism in Mississippi went, it was secondary in her priorities and dependent on her perception of its connection to the fate of her husband. The relative silence in her letters about the freedmen and the meaning of Reconstruction to them is quite striking. More revealing perhaps of the extent to which she related to the freedmen through her culturally encoded racial ideology was her belief that they needed to struggle to realize their freedom. "[T]rouble and contest" were necessary for the "colored man" to develop "a spirit of self-reliance, [and] assertion." This struggle was inevitable, and she now assured him, contrary to his opinion, that "I do not think with you that it [the suffering of the black race] will be forever." From Massachusetts, where she found fulfillment in her family, her art, and the social life of Lowell, itself a world apart from that to which at that very time her husband was seeking in vain to restore order, Blanche did not think the situation as dire as he envisaged it. But even if it were, this was no occasion for him to despair. Rather, "As far as we are personally concerned, the worst results in Mississippi may prove the best for us."[36]

A striking example of her insight into political process was her role in Ames's resignation as governor. Blanche realized as soon as she returned to Mississippi in early December 1875 that Adelbert's impeachment by the incoming Democratic legislature was probable. She placed no confidence in the reports from her family via Democratic sources that impeachment would not proceed. She knew the Democrats had the numbers to impeach; they had a purpose to have "all the branches of the government" in their hands that his removal would deliver; and no morality to inhibit them from doing it. When the legislature voted twenty-one articles of impeachment (with two more to follow) on March 2, 1876, and after the removal of the black lieutenant governor A. K. Davis, Blanche knew conviction was a certainty. Her only regret about this was that Adelbert's name would be unfairly impugned. For herself, she told her mother, "you know I have never been contented with this country [Mississippi], and I hail with pleasure anything which will shorten our sojourn here." That anything did not include resigning while charges remained against him, a proposition Ames too rejected.[37]

While Ames's attorneys (recommended by Ben Butler) sought to construct a defense against impeachment, Blanche, aware of the futility of a legal defense, demonstrated her understanding of political process and of her husband in suggesting that an understanding could be reached. In essence, Ames indicated his willingness to resign, but stated that he "could not, and would not" leave his post with charges reflecting on his "honor or integrity" outstanding. The legislature then voted to dismiss the charges, and Ames resigned.[38]

Blanche's hand was evident in the conception and execution of the maneuver. She had suggested the "compromise with the Democrats" and she "induced" her husband to canvass the possibility with his attorneys. There is much about the compromise, including her husband's acceptance of it, which associates the settlement with her. Her "inducement" was probably essential for him to accept a course of action, which to an old soldier might well have seemed like abandoning the field in the face of the enemy. But she understood how much he had changed in himself from his unmarried days and how much their relationship had informed his new sense of identity, now deeply embedded in the familial context and increasingly removed from the warrior model of masculinity so prominent in his earlier life and career.[39] It was a transformation he willingly embraced. Those values that his relationship with Blanche brought forth—the reciprocation of love, sincerity, affection, understanding, and gentleness—sought resolution of conflict, in contrast to the heroic "male" values ascribed by cultural myth and that privileged aggression and triumph in "competitive battles."[40] Blanche knew her husband well in her construction of this compromise, which had sufficient aspect of armistice to it to allow him, and thereby her, an exit from impeachment and from Mississippi.

Blanche's father detested the compromise. Shaken that Ames and his attorneys, three men in whom he had "so much confidence," would participate in such a resolution of the crisis, he could "not conceal from you that the matter strikes the public ear unfavorably." When Blanche elaborated her role to her mother, admitting she felt "a little self-congratulatory," Butler said no more in criticism of the settlement. That letter would be the last she would write to her mother, who died of cancer one week after Adelbert's resignation, and the last from Mississippi, to which neither she nor he ever returned.[41]

Through her experience of Reconstruction and Mississippi, Blanche realized the limited importance to her of the social world of politics relative to her personal happiness. Yet her identification with her husband's political career and her response to the political crisis that confronted her husband had strained the boundaries of gendered roles. She exemplified in her fusing of political, familial, personal, racial, and sectional identities the profound interrelationships among private and public dimensions of politics, class, and race in post–Civil War America. The power she accessed was used for interests and issues connected with her husband's political career and the political ideology they shared, rather than for those championed by women's groups. She belonged with neither the politically active women visible in reform movements nor those women who accepted traditional definitions of their roles. Indeed the life of Blanche Butler Ames, in the period of her association with the South, questions in many ways the adequacy of traditional and current characterizations of women's relationship to politics, and to political action and power, in post–Civil War America.

Notes

I am indebted to Laura F. Edwards for her constructive commentary on an earlier draft of this paper presented at the Southern Historical Association Conference at Fort Worth in November 1999.

1. In the traditional conception of gender roles in the antebellum and immediate postbellum world, the realm of politics and of political action was a preserve of adult white males. Historians of the antebellum party systems have given us cause to rethink the adequacy of this conception in the light of women's participation at various levels in political activities; Rebecca Edwards, *Angels in the Machinery: Gender in American Party Politics from the Civil War to the Progressive Era* (New York, 1997), 13–29; Jean Baker, "Politics, Paradigms, and Public Culture," *Journal of American History* 84 (December 1997): 894–9. Participation in antislavery politics, not to mention the extraordinary contributions by women in many arenas during the Civil War to the saving of the nation, belied the continued exclusion of women from voting and holding office in the nation's "new birth of freedom" after the Civil War. Women continued in Reconstruction to engage in complex ways with political action and debate.

2. Laura F. Edwards, *Gendered Strife and Confusion: The Political Culture of Reconstruction* (Urbana, 1997), demonstrates the centrality of gender to the whole fabric of Reconstruction, and has broadened greatly our conceptions of the world of politics. On a different level, Virginia Jeans Laas, *Love and Power in the Nineteenth Century: The Marriage of Violet Blair* (Fayetteville, Ark., 1998), outlines in her subject, Violet Blair, a striking contrast with Blanche Butler Ames, who, like Blanche, was a member of the political elite. Blanche falls outside those women who were active in voluntary associations, addressed in Lori D. Ginzberg, *Women and the Work of Benevolence: Morality, Politics, Class in the Nineteenth-Century United States* (New Haven, 1990); and Israel Kugler, *From Ladies to Women: The Organized Struggle for Women's Rights in the Reconstruction Era* (Westport, Conn., 1987). Blanche believed in temperance, though, and questioned her husband when his letters indicated he had been having "drinks" with friends as he did his political rounds in Mississippi; Blanche to Del, October 22, 1871, Blanche Butler Ames, comp., *Chronicles from the Nineteenth Century: Family Letters of Blanche Butler Ames and Adelbert Ames. Married July 21st. 1870* (privately issued, 1957), 1:341.

3. Mrs. Sarah Butler to General Butler, August 25, 1861, in *Private and Official*

Correspondence of Gen. Benjamin F. Butler, during the Period of the Civil War (Norwood, Mass., 1917), 1:226–7. For a long and closely argued defense of Butler against criticisms of his generalship made in the New York *Evening Post* and *Herald*, see Sarah Butler to "Dear Sir," June 5, 1864; Benjamin F. Butler, Personal Correspondence, box 1, folder "1856–1865," Library of Congress. On one occasion, she suggested that an order of the Secretary of War "should be modified a little"; Mrs. Sarah Butler to General Butler, May 15, 1864, in *Private and Official Correspondence*, 4:219. She drew strategic matters to his consideration, less for him to reflect than to act on, combining in such recommendations the advantage for the Union with that for her husband; Sarah Butler to General Butler, May 8, 1864, in *Private and Official Correspondence*, 4:177. In military politics, she sustained him not only with her support but with shrewd advice on how to relate to Ulysses S. Grant; Sarah Butler to Benjamin F. Butler, June 17, 18, July 12, 1864; B. F. Butler Papers, Personal Correspondence, box 1, folder "1856–1865," Library of Congress. *Boston Morning Journal*, July 22, 1870.

4. Blanche to Del, June 26, 1870, *Chronicles* 1:178. Blanche to Del, June 9, 1870, *Chronicles*, 1:158. Blanche did not experience the "marriage trauma" that made some nineteenth-century women reluctant to commit to marriage; Nancy Cott, *The Bonds of Womanhood*, 80–1; Laas, *Love and Power*, 37.

5. Del to Blanche, June 28, 1870, *Chronicles*, 1:184. On the ideal of marriage for love in the mid-nineteenth century, Carl N. Degler, *At Odds: Women and the Family in America from the Revolution to the Present* (New York, 1980), 14, 18–9. Blanche to Del, May 22, July 9, 1870, *Chronicles*, 1:136, 186.

6. *Boston Morning Post*, July 22 1870; reprinted in *Vox Populi*, July 27, 1870; *Boston Morning Journal*, July 22, 1870, 2. Tallish, slim, with fair complexion, auburn hair tending to gold, and blue eyes, Blanche fitted perfectly with contemporary notions of beauty. *Boston Daily Evening Transcript*, July 21, 1871; *Boston Daily Advertiser*, July 22, 1870; *New York Sun*, July 22, 1870; *Boston Daily Advertiser*, July 22, 1870; *Vox Populi*, July 27, 1870; *Boston Morning Journal*, July 22, 1870. Admiral Farragut's absence was also attributed to illness.

7. *Boston Morning Journal*, Friday, July 22, 1870; *Boston Daily Advertiser*, July 22, 1870; *New York Herald*, July 22, 1870. On contemporary recognition of the importance of Benjamin Butler's contributions to the Union, especially in the first days of the Lincoln administration, see letters of Abraham P. Ely, January 31, 1865, and Edwin G Parker, January 26, 1865, Butler Papers, box 36, folder "January 21–31, 1865," Library of Congress; for similar acknowledgement from a much less sympathetic source, see Howard K. Beale, ed., *Diary of Gideon Welles* (New York, 1960), vol. 3, entry of January 14, 1865, 223.

8. Blanche Butler, Diary 1870–71, entry October 31, 1870, 12, Ames Family Papers, Sophia Smith Archives [hereafter AFP], box 3B, folder "Blanche's Diary (1870–71)"; reprinted in *Chronicles*, 1:207–23. Where Violet Blair found "empowerment" in being a "belle," and faced with some regret the prospect of giving up its attractions, Blanche found relief at having left the status of "belle"; Laas, *Love and Power*,

16–7, 37; also Karen Lystra, *Searching the Heart: Women, Men, and Romantic Love in Nineteenth-Century America* (New York, 1989), 233–5.

9. Blanche Butler Ames, diary entry of October 25, 1870, 1–2; AFP box 3B. The feeling of their being compatibly in love is a frequent source of mutual comment in their letters. During one period of separation, Blanche wondered, "Is it well to be so fond of a person that happiness depends entirely upon them?"; April 30, May 11, 1871, *Chronicles*, 1:269–70.

10. Blanche Butler Ames, diary entry of November 20, 1870, 26–7, AFP box 3B, for her knowledge of what Adelbert as a politician should expect when visiting Mississippi; on declining because of illness an invitation to lunch with Mrs. Grant and to receive in the afternoon, see Blanche to Mother, March 13, 1871, *Chronicles*, 1:234. Blanche to Del, May 22, 1870, *Chronicles*, 1:135.

11. Blanche to Mother, March 5, 1871, *Chronicles*, 1:230–1.

12. The bond between Blanche and her mother was typical of the strong mother-daughter bond observed by Nancy M. Theriot, *Mothers and Daughters in Nineteenth-Century America: The Biosocial Construction of Femininity* (Lexington, Ky., 1996), 76–7. On Blanche's close relationship with and love for her mother, Blanche to "Dear Mother," December 14, 1862; June 13, 1864; *Chronicles*, 1:87, 107–8. On the sharing of confidences, Mother to My dear Blanche, November 13, 1862, *Chronicles*, 1:85. On respect for her mother, Blanche, Diary, January 31, 1870 [1871], 36 AFP box 3B.

13. Blanche Butler Ames to Adelbert Ames, Lowell, May 5 1870, AFP box 24, folder 301; her emphasis. Blanche wrote two letters on May 5. The citation comes from the morning letter. Blanche to Del, October 18, 1871, *Chronicles*, 1:336. She foresaw the need for him to have a speech on hand when they made their first visit to Mississippi after their marriage, and suffered with him through his efforts at preparation and delivery. Blanche, Diary, November 20, 1870, 26–9; AFP box 3B.

14. For the first several years, when Adelbert was U.S. senator from Mississippi, months at a time were spent together in Washington, though the illness of their first child, Butler, sent Blanche and Butler back to Lowell. Between July 1870 when they married until his inauguration as governor in January 1874, she visited Mississippi twice for a period of about six weeks in total. When Ames became governor, Blanche lived in Jackson with him from winter to the end of spring/beginning of summer, usually January to early June, in 1874, 1875, and 1876, with the latter visit shortened to early April because of his resignation.

15. Blanche had none of the inhibitions of some mothers about breast-feeding, which concerned doctors; Sylvia D Hoffert, *Private Matters: American Attitudes toward Childbearing and Infant Nurture in the Urban North, 1800–1860* (Urbana, 1989), 146–8. Blanche was astonished to find people surprised that she breast-fed her babies and enjoyed observing the development of her children, even on occasion testing their capacities; *Chronicles*, 1:329, 335, 341, 372–3. Blanche to Del, May 26, 1872, *Chronicles*, 1:252–3; September 22, 27, 1875, ibid., 2:188–9, 191; Del to Blanche, June 3, 1871, ibid., 1:359.

16. Blanche Butler Ames, diary entry Saturday afternoon, 20–1; AFP box 3B. Blanche to [Adelbert], November 15, 1872; AFP box 24, folder 306. Blanche, Diary, November 20, 1870, 23–4; AFP box 3B. The charms of Natchez, though, won her over, as William Harris pointed out; William C Harris, *Day of the Carpetbagger: Republican Reconstruction in Mississippi* (Baton Rouge, 1979), 590.

17. Blanche to Mother, January 30, February 14, March 4, 1874, *Chronicles*, 1:644, 650, 657. Blanche could not see how to act on her mother's advice to remember "When there comes pressure either socially or politically, you belong to the colored people." Thursday morning, ibid., 1:654.

18. Undated handwritten note in Kate Power's handwriting, recollecting her mother's comment, Kate Markham Power collection, Mississippi Department of Archives and History. Kate was the daughter of the editor of the Democratic newspaper the *Jackson Daily Clarion* and became active in collecting and preserving historical recollections. Blanche to Mother, March 4, 1874, *Chronicles*, 2:656–7.

19. Blanche to Del, October 1, 1873, *Chronicles*, 1:584. Blanche to Del, August 1, 1873, *Chronicles*, 1:506.

20. Blanche to Del, October 1, 1873, *Chronicles*, 1:584. Blanche to Del, September 23, 1872, *Chronicles*, 1:378.

21. Del to Blanche, July 26, 1871, *Chronicles*, 1:308. Almost a year later, when a black Republican delegation expressed its support for his policies but suggested he should spend more time in Mississippi and buy some land, he understood that "I shall have to discuss the matter with you when I get to Lowell." June 3, 1872, ibid., 1:359.

22. Blanche to Del, August 1, 1874, *Chronicles*, 1:693–4. Blanche to Del, August 12, 1874, *Chronicles*, 1:706.

23. Del to Blanche, August 3, 1874, *Chronicles*, 1:696.

24. Del to Blanche, August 12, 1874, *Chronicles*, 1:707, 708; my emphasis. Another element in his disillusionment was the arrest of Thomas W. Cardozo on fraud charges relating to his tenure as circuit clerk of Warren County. Ames hoped Cardozo was innocent but the affair "gives me new cause to wish to be absolutely separated from it [Mississippi]." Del to Blanche, August 25, 1874, *Chronicles*, 2:14.

25. Blanche to Del, August 12, 1874, *Chronicles*, 1:709. Her emphasis.

26. Blanche to Del, August 15, 1874, *Chronicles*, 2:3–4. Blanche to Del, September 4, 1874, *Chronicles*, 2:22. She allowed that she may be seeking "something unattainable."

27. Blanche to Del, August 23, 1874, *Chronicles*, 2:12–3.

28. Footnote to letter of Blanche, October 25, 1875, *Chronicles*, 2:236–7. She had already, despite her reluctance to open their private letters to "the world," allowed her father to read portions of her letters from Del to Grant and Pierrepont, to galvanize them into some action against the "white-liners" in Mississippi; Blanche to Del, October 12, 1875, *Chronicles*, 2:215. On the white revolution of 1875, see Eric Foner, *Reconstruction: America's Unfinished Revolution, 1863–1877* (New York, 1988), 558–63.

29. "I have taken a good deal upon myself lately, Del." Blanche to Del, October 20, 1875, *Chronicles*, 2:229. Blanche to Del, October 20, 21, 22, 1875, *Chronicles*, 2:229–30, 232. Del to Blanche, October 28, 1875, *Chronicles*, 2:244. Pierrepont wrote to Ames, apparently as his response to Butler's lobbying, promising to send troops if the Democrats broke the peace, which was not what Butler had understood had been ordered. Del to Blanche, October 27, 1875, *Chronicles*, 2:241. The Democrats carried the 1875 state election decisively and won control of both House and Senate.

30. Del to Blanche, October 12, 1875, *Chronicles*, 2:217. Del to Blanche, October 18, 1875, *Chronicles*, 2:224. Del to Blanche, October 22, 1875, *Chronicles*, 2:232. Blanche to Del, October 28, 1875, *Chronicles*, 2:241.

31. Del to Blanche, September 21, 1872; Blanche to Del, October 21, 1872; *Chronicles*, 1:377, 399, respectively. She counseled him against believing political "friends," cautioning him that "people are [not] to be trusted in as a rule until they have proved the contrary." September 23, 1872, ibid., 1:378.

32. In her letter of September 3, 1875, Blanche had laid out a course of action by which he could attain the senatorship and then resign from a position of strength when he chose; *Chronicles*, 2:157–9. Her letter responded to his letter of August 30, 1875, where he told her he would not seek another office in the state; ibid., 2:151–2.

33. Blanche to Del, October 18, 1875; Blanche to Del, October 22, 1875; *Chronicles*, 2:224, 231–2.

34. Blanche to Del, May 24, 1870, *Chronicles*, 1:140.

35. Blanche to Del, Monday morning [June 13?], 1870, *Chronicles*, 1:162. Sylvia D. Hoffert, *When Hens Crow: The Woman's Rights Movement in Antebellum America* (Bloomington, Ind., 1995), 9, identifies the impact on women's "consciousness" of the adoption of universal white adult male franchise in the nineteenth century and cites particular instances in the lives of different women that led them to play prominent roles in the women's rights movement. Blanche, however, did not associate with the organized women's movement, though her father did, and did not share with Boston's elite women reformers their zeal for women's rights to public and political action; Debra Gold Hansen, *Strained Sisterhood: Gender and Class in the Boston Female Anti-Slavery Society* (Amherst, Mass., 1993), 11, 140–64; on Ben Butler, Kugler, *From Ladies to Women*, 35, 170. Blanche to Del, November 1, 1875, *Chronicles*, 2:247. She added, "In case the Democrats drive you out, Love, you will not come home to a family of mourners."

36. Blanche to Del, October 18, 1875; *Chronicles*, 2:223–4.

37. Blanche to Mother, December 8, 1875; February 6, March 1, 14, 1876; *Chronicles*, 2:256, 283, 310, 344–5. Harris, *Day of the Carpetbagger*, 696; Blanche to Mother, March 21, 26, 1876, *Chronicles*, 2:346–7, 351. Richard N. Current, *Those Terrible Carpetbaggers* (New York, 1988), 325.

38. Blanche to Mother, March 26, 1876, *Chronicles*, 2:351.

39. Blanche to Mother, April 2, 1876, *Chronicles*, 2:355; Harris, *Day of the Carpetbagger*, 697; Current, *Those Terrible Carpetbaggers*, 325.

40. Francesca M. Concian, *Love in America: Gender and Self-Development* (New York, 1987), 21–9. As early as August 4, 1873, Adelbert felt he "could without effort relinquish ambition for my family and home life"; Del to Blanche, *Chronicles,* 1:508.

41. Butler to Ames, April 1, 1876; B. F. Butler Papers, vol. 215, 312–4, Library of Congress; *Chronicles,* 2:354, says "public mind." Currently, *Those Terrible Carpet-baggers,* 325, notes that the Mississippi legislature published the charges against Ames anyway, which implied his guilt. Blanche to Mother, April 2, 1876, *Chronicles,* 2:355.

4

"College Girls"

The Female Academy and Female Identity in the Old South

Anya Jabour

In 1843, southern schoolgirl Margaret Graham wrote home to her mother from Georgia Female College (now Wesleyan College), repeatedly emphasizing that during her time away from home, she had adopted a new identity: that of the "college girl." At a wedding she had attended, Graham remarked, "Ophelia Longstreet & myself were the only college girls there, and I heard it said several times during the evening, though accidentally, that the college girls were the prettiest in the room. Mr Ellison gave the young gentlemen permission to pay us as much attention as they wished, & I assure you we had enough of it, for I believe some of them consider it quite an honor to walk with a college girl."[1]

Margaret Graham was not alone in her sense that leaving home for school allowed young southern women to explore a new identity. According to Elizabeth Fox-Genovese, a "deep sense of family" was "the primary influence upon a woman's identity" in the Old South. Well-to-do southern white women, she explains, moved directly from the family of origin to the new families that they formed with their husbands. Without alternatives to the roles of daughter, wife, and mother, southern women "relied upon family membership to define their identities"; they could look no farther than their immediate ties to parents, husbands, and children in their search to define themselves. Therefore, for slaveholding women, "the female self" was "predominantly a matter of family membership."[2]

As other scholars have demonstrated, however, young women in the antebellum South increasingly left their families behind for a period of months or years in order to attend school at a female academy, institute, or college either in their home region or in the North. In the female academy, southern women left their family ties behind to foster what Nancy F. Cott, in her classic study of women in the antebellum Northeast, called the

"bonds of womanhood." In the process, young southern women experi-
mented with a new form of identity, that of the "college girl" or "schoolgirl." While temporary, this new identity was, as Martha Vicinus has said
of English boarding school students, "simultaneously powerful and pe-
ripheral," and while southern daughters spent comparatively little time
away at school, the experience shaped the rest of their lives, introducing
them to a world in which identity rested not on family membership but on
participation in a female community.[3]

The academy experience is central to any investigation of well-to-do,
white, southern women's identities. Parents and educators alike viewed the
academy experience as important in training young southern women to
take their place in society as wives, mothers, and plantation mistresses and,
in the process, in confirming the family as the core of their identities. Indeed, in the most exhaustive study of southern women's education to date,
Christie Anne Farnham argues that southern women's schools prepared
young white women to fulfill the cultural ideal of the "southern belle."
Yet, as Steven Stowe has suggested, young women themselves often were
more impressed by "the immediate intimacy of shared womanhood" than
by the formal and the "informal curriculum" of the female academy.[4]

My research suggests that the female academy offered southern daughters a unique opportunity to establish a community of women and thus a
new context for female identity. While parents expected their daughters to
use their school years in order to prepare for a life devoted to family—
whether as daughters, wives, or mothers—young southern women often
emerged from the academy with a strong commitment, instead, to a female community of like-minded women and a group identity as "college
girls."[5]

When Penelope Skinner left home in 1832 to attend Miss Burk's School
for Young Ladies in Hillsborough, North Carolina, she wrote to her father,
"I remain forever your most Dutiful and affectionate daughter." This was
precisely what southern parents hoped for when they sent their daughters
away from home; as Farnham has suggested, wealthy southerners approved of higher education for women precisely because they hoped that
such training would be "preparation for pedestals" rather than a challenge
to accepted hierarchies of gender, class, and race. Parents expected their
daughters to return home as improved versions of themselves, not as
changed individuals, and they repeatedly reminded their daughters that
they should value their achievements in terms of pleasing their families
rather than for their own sake. Upon receiving a letter from his daughter

Susan, a student at Patapsco Institute in Endicott's Mill, Maryland, James McDowell rejoiced to see that her penmanship and grammar had improved, but he added: "I like still more that my dear little girl was a kind and dutiful child who did not forget her Father, but remembered him to love him and to do for him what made his heart thankful and happy."[6]

As young women left their families, however, they were exposed to new experiences that reshaped their ideas about themselves and thus their identities as southern women. In 1822, William Polk wrote a valedictory letter to his daughter Mary, who had recently left her home in Raleigh, North Carolina, to attend Mrs. Mallon's School in Philadelphia. "You are my dear Mary about commencing a new scene in life," he remarked. Mary Polk's father did not exaggerate when he described the female academy as "a new scene in life." For southern girls, leaving home for school was a defining moment, one that marked a shift from childhood to girlhood, from family to friends, and from parental approval to peer culture.[7]

Southern schoolgirls and their parents devoted significant attention to the major turning point of leaving home. The shift from home to school was fraught with anxiety for many girls. For some, the journey itself was a new experience, the first time they had ever left home without other family members. In the 1860s, Deborah Warren wrote to her daughter Julie, a student at St. Mary's School in Raleigh, North Carolina, to congratulate her on surviving what she called "the ordeal of leaving home." "Let me know how you got along journeying alone," she requested, "your first experience as an 'unprotected female.'"[8]

Upon arriving at the academy, many young women complained of homesickness. Julie Warren wrote from St. Mary's School to update her mother on her status and that of her sister, Fannie: "Of course we get home-sick sometimes," she admitted, "but we are determined to get along as well as we can, and to try to learn as much as we can."[9] For most girls, however, homesickness was soon replaced by a sense of belonging. Margaret Graham, attending Georgia Female College in Macon, wrote to her father in 1842: "I felt bad enough, I assure you, the first week I was here, being an entire stranger. I soon however became acquainted with the young ladies, and am now as happy and contented as one could wish." By the time she wrote to her mother the following week, Margaret described Macon as "a perfect paradise."[10]

Sallie Faison, who attended the Charlotte Female Institute in North Carolina, gave her mother a particularly detailed description of her journey to school, her initial homesickness, and her adjustment to school life. "We took an omnibus and came directly to the Institute, and as we approached the building who should we see but Mrs. Burwell, standing near the gate. [W]ell thought I how can I ever stay here I even dreaded to get out." Faison described the schoolmistress as a forbidding figure, "a very tall and stout lady dressed in purple calico." "I thought I would have to go home again in spite of every thing; but by the time we reached the steps I liked her a great deal better, and about dinner time I was completely carried away with her; and you ought to see me fly around her now." Sallie Faison's letter neatly summarized both the difficulties and the delights that young southern "school girls" experienced.[11]

In the female academy, southern schoolgirls found a community, one which embraced both faculty and students. Mary Kenan recognized the importance of this community when she wrote to her daughter, an Alabama student, in 1839: "Present my respects to all your teachers . . . [and] my love to the young ladys in your room."[12] Women teachers were the anchors of this community, charged with creating a home-like environment and giving motherly attention to their charges. Parents entrusted female schoolteachers and principals not only with their daughters' intellectual development, but with their physical well-being and moral purity. Writing to Peter Hagner to assure him of his daughter's good situation at the Virginia school he ran together with his wife, James Garnett praised "Mrs G's plan of deriving her influence over her Pupils rather from their personal regard, than their fears" and explained that she considered herself equivalent to a parent or guardian. As such, one of her primary missions was moral instruction: "Should she succeed in rendering a portion of them sensible, virtuous Women it will be her best reward on this side of the Grave."[13]

Southern parents admonished their daughters to pay close attention to their schoolteachers' lessons in behavior as well as their formal instruction. Writing to her daughter Ella, a student in Leesburg, Virginia, in the 1840s, Elizabeth Noland expressed much concern that her daughter would "gain the affection and good opinion of Mrs Edwards," her school principal. "Whilst under her protection, She must be your guide," she admonished. Similarly, A. M. Baker reminded his daughters to "undertake nothing where you feel yourselves at a loss without first consulting Mrs Granbery [?] and be sure you take her advice upon all occasions."[14]

Women were the dominant figures in the South's female academies. Even when men participated in the operations of the schools, schoolgirls reported the most contact with their female instructors. At the Charlotte

Female Institute, run by Mr. and Mrs. Burwell, Sallie Faison observed, "Mr Burwell has very little to do with the school." Thus, students' comments on their teachers highlighted their relationships with their female instructors. Emma Kimberly, a North Carolina student, echoed the sentiments of many schoolgirls when she confided to her father: "I love my teacher dearly, she is so good."[15]

Older women teachers played a key role in welcoming new students and in advancing their comfort. Although initially intimidated by Mrs. Burwell, Sallie Faison soon warmed to her. "She treats us just like a Mother would," she pronounced, noting that Mrs. Burwell took a personal interest in Sallie and her roommate, Mollie, by visiting with them in their room. Mary Virginia Early, a student at the Female Collegiate Institute in Buckingham County, Virginia, summed up older women's nurturing role in her description of a teacher named Mrs. Booth. "I am becoming more & more attached daily to my dear friend Mrs Booth," she wrote in 1839. "She is indeed a mother to us all."[16]

While older women were important maternal figures for their students, young women also found themselves attracted to younger, unmarried teachers. Admiration bordering on schoolgirl crushes was not uncommon. Lizzie Kimberly, a student at Raleigh, North Carolina's St. Mary's School in the 1850s, developed an intense attachment to her art teacher, Gertrude Bothamly. In the spring of 1859, she wrote rapturously: "It is warm here, and all the flowers are blooming, I have a good many given to me but I deny myself the pleasure of keeping them for I give them to one that I love better than myself, it is to one of the Teachers . . . I have always admired the name of 'Gertrude' I love it now because the one I love bears that name. I guess you think I am foolish, but I do love her more than ten thousand tongues can express. I never loved any body so before, love for her strengthens my whole soul, my mind, my body."[17]

While schoolmistresses of all ages were important role models, the students formed their most important attachments with other women of their own age. The importance of female friendships to nineteenth-century women has been well-documented. While women of all ages enjoyed close emotional ties to other women, school was a particularly important time for young women to form intense relationships with one another. As Stowe has written of students in southern female academies, a "dominant theme" in their letters home was "contentment and delight with sisterhood."[18]

The academy experience fostered close friendships. At boarding schools, dormitories were the focal point of female students' lives, as their lengthy letters naming and describing their roommates made clear. Lucy Warren's description of the "dormitory" at Raleigh's St. Mary's School was typical of girls' schools; the boarding house's quarters consisted of a long room with small alcoves "made up against the wall," where the girls slept.[19]

Living and studying in close proximity, southern schoolgirls often formed close friendships during their time in the female academy. Mary Louisa Read, a Virginia student, wrote to her cousin, Mary Carrington, about her friendship with "one of the finest girls you ever saw," Maryanna Mugee. "We are great cronies and are never satisfied unless we are together." When seated separately in the classroom, Read and Mugee communicated with each other by sign language. Friendship and kinship sometimes overlapped. A student at the Southern Female College in LaGrange, Georgia, in the 1850s confided to a friend: "Jennie you cannot imagine how much I love Cousin Mollie for she is the sweetest girl that ever lived I believe or she appears so in my eyes for you know love covers all defects."[20]

Female friendships in the academy often took on a romantic hue. As Farnham has noted in her study of antebellum female academies and colleges, "by at least the 1840s Southern women at boarding schools had developed the custom of patterning the relationships of best friends on heterosexual love as expressed in chivalrous courtship conventions," such as maintaining an exclusive relationship.[21] Southern schoolgirls recognized romantic friendships as special relationships marked by unique customs. Girls often exchanged gifts of candy and flowers to express their admiration for each other. Millie Birckhead's cousin Sallie, a student at Virginia's Piedmont Female Academy, explained, "I went in the woods after wild flowers we got a great many then we fixed up bouquet's and sent them to our loves." Sallie was delighted to have received four bouquets, including one from "Ida Fancouer . . . the sweetest little thing I ever knew." While flowers could be the mark of a special friendship, they also could be a sign of a girl's universal popularity. According to Sallie, "Ida Fancouer and the other pretty girls got a great many bouquets. . . . Miss Fannie Goss also gets a great many but I do not wonder at it for almost all the girls love her in school."[22]

Choosing deskmates was a ritual repeated at the beginning of each term that announced a special relationship. Writing to Olin Davis during the summer vacation in 1858, Nannie Nottingham could barely contain her eagerness to be reunited with her friend at Virginia's Wesleyan Female College. "Linnie I am almost crazy to see you dearest," she wrote. "I suppose you will not fail to choose our desk and remember we are partners for everything next session."[23]

Even more than sharing a desk, sharing a bed was a mark of a particularly close friendship. As Farnham has observed, students frequently shared beds with one another. While it is difficult (if not impossible) to know if girlish displays of affection such as hand-holding, hugging, and kissing extended to sexual intimacy, it is clear that students prized the night hours as a time to share confidences. Sharing a bed was a public statement of an important—often exclusive—relationship, as Greensboro, North Carolina, Female College student Jennie Johnson's cousin no doubt recognized when she demanded: "Who do you sleep with? . . . Have you a new darling, or do you still cling to Puss." Likewise, Louisiana Burge and her roommate, Mitt, "cried like two children" when illness forced Burge to withdraw from her classes at Wesleyan Female College. "She [Mitt] vowed that she had slept with me for three years and would have not [sic] other roommate," Burge wrote in her diary.[24]

The female community of classmates, roommates, and romantic friends was the primary reference point for academy students. A former student of Harrodsburg, Kentucky's Daughters' College known only as Daisy L. summed up the importance of belonging to the female community in a letter to her friend and schoolmate Belle Price at Christmas 1857:

> The Old Year is dying fast. . . . Pause, with your foot on the threshold and look back into the past. One year ago, to you I was a perfect stranger; I came here knowing no one; no kind hands were held out to welcome me; no eyes looked love into mine; no heart rose to welcome a sister-spirit . . . Now, I stand among you (shall I say it?) a beloved sister. Oh! God knows how I love you all, and thank you for it too![25]

The female academy was also a female community: a space inhabited and directed by women. In the female academy, what Gerda Lerner has termed "clusters of learned women" and "affinitive clusters" of female friendship overlapped; southern schoolgirls found both affection and intellectual challenges when they left home for school. This was an important precondition for an identity separate from the family circle. As scholars of women's colleges in the North and in England have pointed out, "formal institutions were alternatives to the nuclear family." In the context of such "woman-controlled spaces" as the female academy, young women forged loyalties to each other and to the values of the school that cut across—and sometimes superseded—their traditional loyalties to their families, kin, and neighborhoods. In the antebellum South as well, female academies offered a "social space . . . outside the family" where women-in-the-making could lead "women-focused lives" rather than lives oriented toward more traditional relationships with parents and other kinfolk, setting the stage for the creation of a southern women's culture.[26]

The "beloved sisters" of the female academy not only forged a female community, they also established a set of community standards. The standards that southern schoolgirls held for "college girls" indicated that while they continued to try to live up to their families' expectations in many respects, they filtered parental advice through their collective knowledge and only selectively followed the precepts of southern womanhood received from their elders.

Stowe has revealed that southern parents often felt ambivalence about sending their daughters away from home for the all-important academy experience, for girls on the brink of womanhood might adopt values and goals inconsistent with their parents' plans for them. Indeed, nineteenth-century parents and educators on both sides of the Atlantic were keenly aware of this danger. As Martha Vicinus observes of parents in Victorian England: "Many were certain that college would alienate well-to-do young women from their families and lead them to prefer the society of friends their own age." Yet, at the same time that parents urged their daughters to view school as only a brief prelude to domestic life and educators attempted to make academies as much like homes as possible, they also encouraged schoolgirls to focus their attention on the academy experience. Parents reminded their daughters repeatedly to make the most of their time at the female academy; school rules limited students' contacts with family members.[27]

Sally Lucas's letters from school in Alexandria, Virginia, to her father illustrated the tension between old responsibilities to family and new ones to school. "I fear you will think I have forgotten my duty as a daughter in not writing to you before," she began in 1850, assuring her father that she had "not entirely forgotten my duty but only delayed performing it . . . for my time is almost wholly preoccupied with my studies, and when not engaged with my duties in the school room there are many other things which claim my time and attention."[28] Sally Lucas was by no means the only southern daughter to find that "many other things" vied with her "duty" to her family during her stay at the female academy.

Parents of academy students attempted to maintain what another college-educated daughter, Jane Addams, would dub the "family claim." Occasionally joined by aunts and uncles, siblings, and grandparents, parents of academy-bound daughters filled letters with advice on what Richard Brumby, writing to Ann Eliza Brumby in 1858, called "all the essentials of a lady's education": everything from personal hygiene to study habits.[29] Family members generally agreed that girls should use their time at the female academy for self-improvement. Marcus Cicero Stephens advised, "the discipline of the Academy teaches you the use of the tools—points out the different routes of knowledge,—from that moment all depends on your own industry and discretion." Despite their consensus that daughters should use their time at the academy to improve themselves, parents' emphasis on different aspects of female education varied considerably. Some, like Brumby, insisted that "the great object of female education should be, the development of the girl into a lady"; others, like Elizabeth McPherson's brother, charged the girls to be "as studious as possible."[30]

Regardless of the specific goals they had for female education, southern parents urged their daughters to devote themselves wholeheartedly to the opportunities that the female academy afforded. Mississippi student Elizabeth Amis's mother urged her, "Study hard, and make good use of your time. . . . Always improve the present moment."[31] Southern daughters took this advice to heart. Penelope Skinner, hoping to convince her father both of her attachment to him and of her commitment to her studies, wrote from Miss Burk's School in Hillsborough, North Carolina: "I long to be at home once more I'm thinking about it all the time," but added "expect [sic] when I'm [in] school then my thoughts are about my lessons."[32]

One of the principal ways that schoolgirls demonstrated that they had improved their time was the regular grade reports sent home to parents. These reports, produced weekly, monthly, or quarterly, were an important part of the academy experience. Often students were required to write a letter home to their parents to accompany each grade report. Such letters usually contained apologies (or, sometimes, excuses) for low marks, self-congratulations for high marks, and promises to do better next time. Millie Birckhead, a student at Piedmont Female Academy in Virginia, sent her report to her father in 1861 with the notation, "The reports were Friday morning, and as providence happened I got perfect, and you cant imagin [sic] how happy I feel."[33] Emma Kimberly, writing to her father from St. Mary's School in North Carolina in 1857, took pains to explain the grading system to her father before commenting: "I think my report for this month is not so good as it ought to be, next month I am going to try to get a good one."[34]

Sending reports home to parents indicated, as Penelope Skinner wrote her father from Miss Burk's School in Hillsboro, North Carolina, that schoolgirls had "grown very industrious always having something to do." However, schoolgirls also used their reports as a way to measure their standing in the female community. Although reports often were sent directly to parents, schoolgirls kept close tabs on their marks. Often not only individuals, but the entire school knew each student's class standing; several schoolgirls commented on the practice of marks being "read out" in public.[35]

Although parents and students alike viewed good reports as evidence of daughters' dutifulness, southern schoolgirls also attached meaning to the reports as a measurement of their status in the group. Good reports were also a source of personal pride. Students regularly compared their marks to measure their standing amongst their peers. Virginia student Olin Davis boasted to her brother, "The past week I have 7 (the highest mark) on all of my studies and I hope that I will do the same through the seven weeks, or until the next reports go out." While her own report was "very good," Davis admitted that "it was not perfect" and compared her performance to "one of the girls" who "got 93 which I think was the highest number which any got."[36]

While reports home demonstrated their industriousness and attempts to meet their parents' expectations, schoolgirls themselves may have laid more emphasis on public performance. Students had ample opportunity to display their learning in public. Perhaps the most commonly noted performance was the end- of-term examination—an academy ritual to which students devoted significantly more attention than did their parents.[37] Not only were examinations public, but anybody in the audience—including men—could challenge the students. For some, this was a source of anxiety. Georgia student Margaret Graham worried in a letter to her father: "How I do dread the examination in July. I am constantly thinking of it. I expect if I learn anything before, I will be so embarrassed then, that I will forget every thing. But I will try not." Vicksburg, Mississippi, resident Emma

Shannon, who attended school in New Jersey in the 1850s, told her mother: "The idea of having to go up to the blackboard draw the figures and recite from books, kills me nearly."[38]

Despite such formulaic lamentations, many schoolgirls prized examinations as a time to display their knowledge. They dreamed of being "first" in their class, asked their parents and friends to attend the exams, and proudly reported their successes. Frances Moody, a student at Davenport Female College in Lenoir, North Carolina, begged her guardian and uncle to come to school to witness her examination. "I try to be first in my class and I have been first or with the first every time the marks have [been] read out," she noted with satisfaction, adding, "The examination will be the last of this month, you must come up if you can." Martha Turner, writing from North Carolina's Floral College in 1846, filled an entire letter with news of the impending examination. Closing, she remarked, "I have not wrote any thing yet but it is so near the examination that we cannot think of any thing except the examination." For Turner, the examination was clearly a much-anticipated event; she urged her father to attend the examination and asked her mother to make her a special dress for the occasion. Similarly, Mary Virginia Early, despite her protestations that she "expect[ed] to come up missing" at the examination, asked her mother to attend the event at the Female Collegiate Institute in Buckingham County, Virginia. Her cousin, Virginia Wilber, added a postscript in which she commented sagely: "She has appeared the most desponding creature, about her studies and composition you ever saw but I hope you comprehend her meaning. She is inviting you down to witness her examination, which she as well as I know, will result in bestowing honour [sic] upon her parents and credit to herself."[39]

Indeed, schoolgirls coveted the distinction to be gained by performing well both in lessons and at commencement ceremonies. At the end of the school term in 1832, Penelope Skinner gleefully reported receiving "twenty nine honours [sic]." Shortly before the Civil War, Louisiana Burge, a student at Wesleyan Female College in Macon, Georgia, competed fiercely for the "First Honor" of being named class valedictorian. When illness forced her to leave school before commencement, she proudly refused to accept the lesser honor of being named salutatorian, although another girl at the school, Kitty Cater, was happy enough to take her place.[40]

At some schools, the examination was part of a social event that included a concert and other celebrations. Martha Munroe, a student at

North Carolina's Salem Academy in 1843, gave her aunt and uncle an unusually complete description of the examination:

> The examination . . . took place on the 1st and 2nd days of June. We were examined in the Church, because the Chapel was not large enough for so many persons. On the sides of both galleries there were specimens of painting[,] drawing, needle-work, embroidery, & work on canvas exhibited. There were also a great many persons present at the examin[ation.] Sister Hatty had a recitation to say, & also a piece on the piano . . . besides having a part in the "Botany Dialogue." I had a part in the Astronomy, Chemistry, [and] Botany Dialogues, with about 20 or 30 more girls.

All of these displays, recitations, and dialogues were in addition to the public examinations in other school subjects, suggesting that southern schoolgirls—far from hastening through examinations—welcomed the chance to show off their learning.[41]

Students at female academies prized academic achievement. At a time when some educators worried that examinations, honors, and prizes might foster an unfeminine competitiveness in their female scholars, these daughters of the Old South embraced the opportunity to gain and to display their knowledge.[42] Moreover, while southern daughters clearly wished to please their parents and to demonstrate to their mothers' and fathers' satisfaction that they had used their time at the female academy well, their letters home also reveal the importance they attached to gaining the respect of their peers. Mary R. Kenan paid tacit homage to the importance that schoolgirls laid on their peers' opinion when she wrote to her daughter, a student in Marion, Alabama, in 1839, "I hope you will endeavor to improve in every way . . . as to merit and receive the commendation of all your friends."[43]

Southern schoolgirls' emphasis on public performance and their peers' approval tended to reinforce parental dictates to diligence and academic achievement. However, another aspect of schoolgirl culture—social life—coexisted more uneasily with parental expectations. As Stowe has pointed out, students in female academies placed more emphasis on their relationships with schoolmates than did their parents. The letters written by the young women in this study indicate that students' desire to participate in the social life of the boarding school could sometimes lead them to defy school rules and thus, indirectly, their parents.[44]

Student social life revolved around sociability, food, and frolic. To some extent, the physical layout of student dormitories encouraged sociability. However, school rules attempted to limit the scope of students' interaction by instituting rules that dictated study time, lights out, and so forth. At Sarah Wheeler's school in Wilmington, Delaware, "the rules of the school" specified that dormitory residents "must not speake to any pearson [*sic*] but to them that you sleep with." The rules at girls' schools, in fact, seemed endless. Each hour of the day was marked out for certain activities, and students' dress, grooming, and deportment were under constant scrutiny. Margaret Whitaker, a student at Chowan Female Institute in Murfrees-boro, North Carolina, did not exaggerate when she informed her father, "We are all watched very closely down here."[45]

Parents clearly expected their daughters to follow the rules. They in-spected their grade reports, which rated students' performance in "deport-ment as young ladies" as well as in academic subjects, closely, and urged their daughters to follow school rules. Most parents, like Susanna McDowell, expected their daughters "to cultivate a sociable and gentle manner" while away at school.[46] Schoolgirls' letters home to their parents generally emphasized their obedience and proper deportment. Sally Lucas, a Virginia student, proudly informed her father in 1850: "I have one thing to tell you dear Father which I know will give you . . . much pleasure and gratification. . . . It is that Mrs Wilner thinks I am a young lady of very good manners."[47]

Schoolgirls' eagerness to participate in the social life of the female acad-emy sometimes led them to break the all-encompassing rules typical of institutions of higher learning for women, however. In 1859, Julie Frances Lilly wrote to a friend from Greensboro College: "We were excused from recitations today and tomorrow but we have to keep the rules and study hours. You can imagine how many rules we keep and how much studying we do," she added with a touch of irony. Writing from Floral College in Harnett County, North Carolina, Julie Turner reported that she and her roommates, in defiance of rules mandating silence after hours, had "a heap of fun after studying [h]ours." Julie's sister Martha described boarding-school life: "We are studying hard and frolicking every time we get up stairs. [Y]ou may know how it is when sixty three of us girls get to-gether."[48]

In "frolicking," southern daughters defied their parents. In the context of "the rules of the school" at female academies and in light of the empha-sis that teachers, administrators, and parents placed on southern girls' good manners, such minor infractions of rules appear as an act of defiance against both adult authority and feminine ideals. Georgia student Louisiana Burge, whose "nature clamour[ed] for entire freedom," believed that her "independence, both of speech and action," cost her the valedictorian position. "Teachers don't like such independence," she noted sagely.[49] In following the injunctions to make the most of their time at school, some daughters acted in ways contrary to their parents' expectations of ladylike behavior.

Within the academy, students' adoption of a female community with its own standards, while often reinforcing parental dictates, also offered a subtle challenge to familial control. The ultimate goal of female education, according to J. McPherson, was "to make you the pride and honour of relations and friends."[50] But while parents warned their daughters to see school as a preparation for life, the very emphasis placed on using time wisely encouraged women to stress the academy experience as the most significant in their young lives. Although initiated and to some extent supervised by parents, the academy experience had the potential to introduce young women to experiences that made fulfilling their parents' expectations for their future—marriage and motherhood—less attractive.

Students emphasized the importance of the academy as a special time of life. Many young women agreed with a sentiment expressed in 1860 by a student at Virginia's Wesleyan Female College: "My school days are the happiest." In her 1897 alumnae address at Greensboro College (North Carolina), former student Sallie S. Cotton repeatedly recalled the days "when I was a schoolgirl," commenting that "'When I was a schoolgirl' is a refrain which sounds familiar to us all."[51]

"School days" were the "happiest" because the experience offered an opportunity to forge a new identity within the context of a community. During their time at school, daughters became "girls"—neither children, with loyalties to their parents, or women, with responsibility for marriage and motherhood. A letter written by Kentucky student Alice L. to her former schoolmate Belle Price illustrates this new identity. From home, Alice wrote: "I have had a very quiet time so far." Alice's home life was her own choice, she explained: "I shall not attend any parties this summer as I cannot do so and be consistent with my principles as a school-girl. I will not go to children's parties and if I go to young ladies' parties, of course I will be considered a young lady." Alice, who intended to return to school, saw her time as a "school-girl" as a special stage of life, a time when she was neither a child nor a lady. Her responsibilities at this time of her life were not primarily to either her parents or to her suitors, but to her schoolmates and her studies. Such comments suggest that southern schoolgirls, like Britain's "independent women," saw their years at school as "a glorious interlude, a special women's space in which duty to self and community took precedence over all outside obligations."[52]

The female academy was an important experience for southern women. As Elizabeth Fox-Genovese contends, the Old South was "a world that encouraged women to find their primary identities in the roles and relations of families."[53] However, the female academy offered southern daughters an alternative to an identity based on family connections: a sense of self anchored in female community. While their parents sent them to the academy to learn to be "southern ladies," these southern women-in-training emerged as examples of another prototype: the "college girl."

Notes

1. Margaret Graham to Mother, December 20, 1843, William P. Graham Papers, Southern Historical Collection, Wilson Library, University of North Carolina at Chapel Hill (hereafter SHC).

2. See especially Elizabeth Fox-Genovese, "Family and Female Identity in the Antebellum South: Sarah Gayle and Her Family," in *In Joy and in Sorrow: Women, Family, and Marriage in the Victorian South, 1830–1900*, ed. Carol Bleser (New York, 1991), 15–31, quotations from 16 and 19.

3. On southern women's education, see Catherine Clinton, *The Plantation Mistress: Woman's World in the Old South* (New York, 1982), chap. 7; Christie Anne Farnham, *The Education of the Southern Belle: Higher Education and Student Socialization in the Antebellum South* (New York, 1994); Anya Jabour, "'Grown Girls, Highly Cultivated': Female Education in an Antebellum Southern Family," *Journal of Southern History* 44 (February 1998): 23–64; Steven M. Stowe, "Growing Up Female in the Planter Class," *Helicon Nine* 17–18 (1987): 194–205; and Stowe, "The Not-So-Cloistered Academy: Elite Women's Education and Family Feeling in the Old South," in *The Web of Southern Social Relations: Women, Family, and Education*, ed. Walter J. Fraser, Jr., R. Frank Saunders, Jr., and Jon L. Wakelyn (Athens, Ga., 1985), 90–106. For quotations, see Nancy F. Cott, *The Bonds of Womanhood: "Woman's Sphere" in New England, 1785–1835* (New Haven, 1977); and Martha Vicinus, *Independent Women: Work and Community for Single Women, 1850–1920* (Chicago, 1985), 9.

4. See Stowe, "Not-So-Cloistered Academy," 92–7, quotations 92 and 93; and Stowe, "Growing Up Female," 201–3. The phrase "informal curriculum" is Christie Anne Farnham's; see *Education of the Southern Belle*, chap. 5.

5. This paper is part of a larger work-in-progress that explores the coming-of-age experiences of well-to-do white women in the nineteenth-century South. The women featured in this essay hailed from throughout the South, from Texas to Alabama and from Georgia to Maryland.

6. Penelope Skinner to Joseph Skinner, [October 3, 1832], Skinner Family Papers, SHC; James McDowell to Susan McDowell, January 28, 1843, McDowell Family Papers, Virginia Historical Society, Richmond, Virginia (hereafter VHS); Christie Farnham Pope, "Preparation for Pedestals: North Carolina Antebellum Female Seminaries" (Ph.D. diss., University of Chicago, 1977). See also Farnham, *Education of the Southern Belle*.

7. William Polk to Mary Polk, March 18, 1822, Polk, Badger, and McGehee Family Papers, SHC.

8. Deborah Warren to Julie Warren, Edward J. Warren Papers, SHC.

9. Julie Warren to Deborah Warren, February 15, 1866, ibid.

10. Margaret Graham to William Graham, October 29, 1842; Margaret Graham to Mother, November 5, 1842, William P. Graham Papers, SHC.

11. Sallie Faison to Martha Faison, October 2, 1869, Henry W. Faison Papers, SHC.

12. Mary R. Kenan to Mary Kenan, September 2, 1839, Kenan Family Papers, SHC.

13. James M. Garnett to Peter Hagner, February 1, 1823, Peter Hagner Papers, SHC.

14. Elizabeth Noland to Ella Noland, April n.d., 1844, and December 25, 1846, Ella Noland MacKenzie Papers, SHC; and A. M. Baker to Daughters, n.d., William Henry Wills Papers, SHC.

15. Sallie Faison to Martha Faison, October 2, 1869, Henry W. Faison Papers, SHC; Emma Kimberly to John Kimberly, April 7, 1857, John Kimberly Papers, SHC.

16. Sallie Faison to Martha Faison, October 2, 1869, Henry W. Faison Papers, SHC; and Mary Virginia Early to Elizabeth Early, October 26, 1839, Early Family Papers, VHS. See also Francis E. Moody to Marcus Moody, July 31, 1863, Sims Family Papers, SHC.

17. Lizzie Kimberly to John Kimberly, March 5, 1859, John Kimberly Papers, SHC.

18. In addition to Carroll Smith-Rosenberg's classic essay, "The Female World of Love and Ritual: Relations Between Women in Nineteenth-Century America," in her *Disorderly Conduct: Visions of Gender in Victorian America* (New York, 1985), 53–76, see Carol Lasser, "'Let Us Be Sisters Forever': The Sororal Model of Nineteenth-Century Female Friendship," *Signs* 14 (August 1988): 158–81; and Steven M. Stowe, "'The Thing, Not Its Vision': A Woman's Courtship and Her Sphere in the Southern Planter Class," *Feminist Studies* 9 (spring 1983), 113–30. On female friendship in southern schools, see Farnham, *Education of the Southern Belle*, chap. 7; and Stowe, "Not-So-Cloistered Academy," quotation 96.

19. For examples of schoolgirls' letters home, see Frances Moody to Marcus Moody, July 31 and August 10, 1863, Sims Family Papers, SHC; for quotation, see Lucy Warren to Deborah Warren, October 14, 1865, Edward J. Warren Papers, SHC.

20. Mary Louisa Read to Mary V. Carrington, May 28, 1829, Carrington Family Papers, VHS; and Til to Jennie, March 25, 1857, Harris Family Papers, Special Collections Department, Robert W. Woodruff Library, Emory University (hereafter Emory).

21. Farnham, *Education of the Southern Belle*, 155–6, 165.

22. Sallie to Millie Birckhead, April 23, 1864, Edward F. Birckhead Papers, Special Collections, Perkins Library, Duke University, Durham, North Carolina (hereafter Duke).

23. Nannie Nottingham to Olin Davis, August 13, 1858, Beale-Davis Family Papers, SHC.

24. Farnham, *Education of the Southern Belle*, 163; M. Love to Jennie Johnson, February 14, 1859, Duke; and Richard Harwell, ed., "Louisiana Burge: The Diary of a Confederate College Girl," *Georgia Historical Quarterly* 36 (June 1952): 143–64, quotations 151–2.

25. Daisy L. to Belle Price, December 25, 1857, Charles B. Simrall Papers, SHC.

26. Gerda Lerner, *The Creation of Feminist Consciousness: From the Middle Ages to Eighteen-seventy* (New York, 1993), 224 ("women-focused lives"), 226–7 ("clusters of learned women" and "affinitive clusters"), 233 ("social space . . ."). Lerner explains: "Since the locus of women's gender indoctrination has so often been the family, the social space necessary for liberating women has had to be a space outside the family" (233). See also Vicinus, *Independent Women*, 7 ("woman-controlled space" and "Formal institutions . . ."); and Patricia Palmieri, *In Adamless Eden: The Community of Women Faculty at Wellesley* (New Haven, 1995).

27. Stowe, "Not-So-Cloistered Academy"; and Vicinus, *Independent Women*, 128 (quotation), 171.

28. Sally Lucas to William Lucas, Lucas Family Papers, VHS.

29. Richard Trapier Brumby to Ann Eliza Brumby, April 3, 1858, Ann Eliza Brumby Papers, SHC.

30. Marcus Cicero Stephens Letters, SHC; Richard Trapier Brumby to Ann Eliza Brumby, April 3, 1858, Ann Eliza Brumby Papers, SHC; and J. McPherson to Elizabeth McPherson, [April 1837], Ferebee, Gregory, and McPherson Family Papers, SHC.

31. Mother to Elizabeth Amis, [August 3, 1851] and [1851?], Elizabeth Blanchard Papers, SHC.

32. Penelope Skinner to Joseph Skinner, postscript to Tristrim Skinner to Joseph Skinner, August 21, 1832; see also Penelope Skinner to Tristrim Skinner, July 18, 1833, Skinner Family Papers, SHC.

33. See for example the monthly reports for Lizzie and Emma Kimberly from St. Mary's School, January 1860, John Kimberly Papers; Margaret Graham's report from Georgia Female College for the quarter ending April 1, 1843, William P. Gra-

ham Papers; Mary Faison's report from the Charlotte Female Institute for the month ending December 15, 1869, Henry William Faison Papers, all in SHC. For quotation, see Millie Birckhead to Edward Birckhead, April 7, 1861, Edward F. Birckhead Papers, Duke. On grade reports, see Farnham, *Education of the Southern Belle*, 88–9.

34. Emma Kimberly to John Kimberly, March 7, 1857; see also March 7, 1856, and March 14 and April 7, 1857, John Kimberly Papers, SHC.

35. For quotation, see Penelope Skinner to Joseph Skinner, [January 9, 1832], Skinner Family Papers, SHC; on the custom of being "read out," see Francis Moody to Marcus Moody, August 10, 1863, Sims Family Papers, SHC.

36. Olin Davis to Brother, January 16, [1858; misdated 1857], Beale-Davis Family Papers, SHC. See also Emma Crutcher to Levina Crutcher, June 5, 1858, Crutcher Shannon Family Papers, Center for American History, University of Texas at Austin (hereafter UT).

37. For examples of schoolgirls' comments on examinations, see for example Penelope Skinner to Joseph Skinner, [October 3, 1832] and [December 22, 1832], Skinner Family Papers; Martha Turner to Carolina Turner, April 24, 1846, Harnett County (North Carolina) Papers; Margaret Whitaker to Cary Whitaker, May 26, 1853, William Henry Wills Papers; Olin Davis to Brother, January 16, [1858; misdated 1857], Beale-Davis Family Papers, all in SHC. For less common parental notice of examinations, see for example W. McPherson to Elizabeth McPherson, May 30, 1835, Ferebee, Gregory, and McPherson Family Papers; and Cary Whitaker to Anna Whitaker, May 24, 1829, William Henry Wills Papers, SHC. See also Farnham, *Education of the Southern Belle*, 89–90.

38. Margaret Graham to William Graham, October 29, 1842, William P. Graham Papers, SHC; and Emma Shannon to Levina Shannon, March 16, 1858, Crutcher-Shannon Family Papers, UT.

39. Francis Moody to Marcus Moody, August 10, 1863, Sims Family Papers, SHC; Martha Turner to Caroline Turner, November 6, 1846, Harnett County Papers, SHC; and Mary Virginia Early to Elizabeth Early, August 11, 1840, Early Family Papers, VHS. See also Til to Jennie, March 25, 1857, Harris Family Papers, Emory; and Francis Moody to Marcus Moody, August 10, 1863, Sims Family Papers, SHC.

40. Penelope Skinner to Tristrim Skinner, [December 22, 1832], Skinner Family Papers, SHC; Harwell, "Louisiana Burge," 152, 154, and 157. "Cater" spelled as in printed version.

41. Martha Rowena Munroe to Mr. and Mrs. Hendly Varner, June 22, 1843, Varner Family Papers, Duke.

42. Nancy Green, "Female Education and School Competition: 1820–1850," in *Woman's Being, Woman's Place: Female Identity and Vocation in American History*, ed. Mary Kelley (Boston, 1979), 127–41.

43. Mary R. Kenan to Mary Kenan, September 2, 1839, Kenan Family Papers, SHC.

44. Stowe, "Not-So-Cloistered Academy," 93–6.

45. For quotations, see Sarah Wheeler to Mother, April 21, 1833, Southall and

Bowen Family Papers, SHC; and Margaret Whitaker to Cary Whitaker, May 26, 1853, William Henry Wills Papers, SHC. For other examples of school rules, see Lucy Warren to Deborah Warren, October 14, 1865, Edward J. Warren Papers, SHC; and Til to Jennie, March 25, 1857, Harris Family Papers, Emory. See also Thomas Woody, *A History of Women's Education in the United States,* 2 vols. (New York and Lancaster, Pa., 1929), 1:434–41; and Farnham, *Education of the Southern Belle,* 130–9.

46. For quotations, see Susanna McDowell to Susan McDowell, January 2, [1842], VHS; and monthly reports for Lizzie and Emma Kimberly from St. Mary's School, January 1860, John Kimberly Papers, SHC.

47. Sally Lucas to William Lucas, May 22, 1850, Lucas Family Papers, VHS.

48. Julia Frances Lilly to Minerva Ewing, December 20, 1859, Preston H. Turner Papers, SHC; Julie Turner to Caroline Turner, [ca. 1846], and Martha Turner to Henry Turner, February 3, 1847, Harnett County Papers, SHC.

49. Harwell, "Louisiana Burge," 146, 154.

50. J. McPherson to Elizabeth McPherson, [April 1837], Ferebee, Gregory, and McPherson Family Papers, SHC.

51. For first quotation, see Hollie to Olin Davis, June 15, 1860, Beale-Davis Family Papers, SHC. See also Mattie F. to Josephine Southall, October 5, 1871, Bowen and Southall Family Papers, SHC. For second quotation, see Mrs. Sallie S. Cotton, Alumnae Address, May 25, 1897, Edward F. Birckhead Papers, Duke.

52. Alice L. to Belle Price, Charles B. Simrall Papers, SHC; Vicinus, *Independent Women,* 124.

53. Fox-Genovese, "Family and Female Identity," 31.

II

The Civil War Era

5

"'Tis True That Our Southern Ladies Have Done and Are Still Acting a Conspicuous Part in This War"

Women on the Confederate Home Front in Edgefield County, South Carolina

ORVILLE VERNON BURTON

Nearly thirty years ago historian Mary Elizabeth Massey mourned the dearth of historical research investigating the Confederate home front. While acknowledging that the war's military engagements and political developments merit close and persistent attention, she maintained that the everyday experience of men and women on the home front, when understood in their proper social and economic context, can illuminate the war's outcome and cast new light on the ways in which warfare transforms the lives of noncombatants.[1] This chapter, looking closely at the role of women on the Confederate home front in Edgefield County, South Carolina, focuses primarily on the changes in daily life and consciousness of southern white women during the war era. The war necessarily modified southerners' relationships among themselves, their families, and their communities.[2]

Just as the Civil War resulted in emancipation for African American enslaved peoples, so, too, southern white women felt new freedom and opportunity, as well as more responsibility. They had to work for themselves and for their families in order to survive the very war that was to "protect" them. In rural Edgefield the role of women was understandable only in terms of a highly complex network of kin and neighborhood relationships within a fairly restrictive, patriarchal hierarchy. Independence was an independence of white male family heads from one another, and in no way included autonomy for women, slaves, or free blacks. During the war an Edgefield officer explained to his wife, "For while men can manage to work for themselves, and can fight the battles of their country if necessary, Females are very dependent." This concept of female dependence necessarily changed during the Civil War.[3]

The Civil War was not one unified experience. The forty-eight months of war meant very different things to different people, even within the same class and within the same geographical region. The stories of the Civil War for women in Edgefield are diverse. Each story is unique, yet patterns emerge.

The story of Leila Griffin, for example, is similar to many of her class. Although slaves performed daily chores in well-to-do households, women from elite families still had formidable domestic responsibilities. One Edgefield soldier, from a less well-off household, remembered that his mother had one slave to help her in the house, yet he recorded, "In a family of 8, it took my mother's whole time to cook, sew, and keep the house." A woman like Leila, the mistress of a plantation, oversaw all household production. Food, clothing, linens—anything intended for domestic consumption—was grown or made under her eye. She directed slave gardeners in raising vegetables and fruits, and kitchen slaves in canning and drying the surplus for winter. Preserves, relishes, and delicacies the mistress put up herself, and Leila Griffin did this skillfully enough to win prizes for her brandied peaches and melon preserves at the district agricultural fair. The plantation mistress raised the poultry that put eggs and meat on her table, ensured that the cows were milked and butter churned, and every fall oversaw the processing of several dozen hogs into hams, bacon, sausage, and lard. Entrusting none of this produce to the slaves who cooked and served food, the mistress carried keys to the smokehouse, pantry, and storerooms, doling out supplies daily when she ordered meals.[4]

An enormous amount of time went into the production of clothing—spinning, weaving, and sewing. Because of the proximity of Horse Creek Valley and the other antebellum textile mills, Edgefieldians could buy cloth more easily than many in the South. A former soldier mentioned that his mother did not have to spin and weave; "as there was a large cotton factory nearby, we could buy our cotton goods at the factory cheaper than we could make it at home."[5] On a plantation the size of the Griffins,' most of the cloth for slave clothes would have been purchased rather than spun and woven, but a set of cotton garments for summer and woolen for winter still had to be cut and sewn for sixty-one slaves. In addition to accomplishing part of this endless task, Leila had to make the everyday clothing for herself and her family, including her eight children and one on the way, and keep it in repair. Very few southern women had sewing machines at that time, and even if Leila Griffin had one, she probably never sat down without sewing, mending, or knitting in her hands.

War changed the easy availability of cloth; Edgefield mills had to produce for the army before selling to the public. During the war Leila set some of the slave women to spinning and weaving cotton and wool, from which she made clothing for the children and for her husband at the Virginia front. In 1861–62 shortages were not as severe as they would later become, when dyes had to be made from bark and berries and buttons improvised from seeds, pieces of gourd, or anything that could be covered with cloth and attached. By winter 1864, the manager of Eloise and Johnson Hagood's plantation in Edgefield could not obtain any wool and was forced to have the cattle sheared and the hair carded and spun with cotton in order to make slave clothes.[6]

War multiplied Leila's administrative responsibilities and decreased the available resources for coping with them. Still the plantation's chief nurse, she would have found it harder to procure medicines. Meals had to be prepared without items such as sugar, salt, spices, coffee, and tea, which gradually disappeared as the Federal blockade of the southern coast squeezed off imports. Coffee made from parched grain and tea from blackberry leaves or sassafras were tasteless but patriotic; sugar and salt, however, were harder to forego. They could be given up at the table, but were essential ingredients in preserving fruit and curing meat. Because of the Union blockade and the neutrality of Kentucky, salt became scarce and rose drastically in price. In May 1861, a sack weighing 210 pounds cost 65 cents; by October, the same sack cost between seven and eight dollars. Leila had to hoard her supply of salt as if it were gold dust.[7]

Other essential articles underwent similar radical increases in price—wheat, flour, cornmeal, meats, bacon, fabric, iron, tin, copper, and utensils. Because prices rose more quickly than the currency depreciated, some scholars argue that scarcity was a more important factor than monetary policy in causing inflation. As early as spring 1862, food prices were four to six times greater than they had been in 1860. Between October 1861 and March 1864, the commodities index rose by an average of 10 percent a month. The price index for commodities that equaled 100 in 1861 reached 763 by 1863. Real wages, on the other hand, fell 65 percent during the war. In spite of attempts at tax reform to alleviate it, inflation persisted and became even more acute after the Union victories at Gettysburg and Vicksburg in the summer of 1863. In 1864, forty-six dollars purchased what one dollar did in 1861. Paper money was increasingly regarded as useless.[8]

Reacting to the ravages of inflation, Edgefieldians on the home front preferred to make exchanges in kind. As the war dragged on, more and more advertisements appeared in the *Edgefield Advertiser* for bartering. On October 5, 1864, the Granite Manufacturing Company ran one offering to barter drills and skirting for commodities at the following prices: corn, 50 cents per bushel; fodder, 50 cents per hundredweight; flour, $7.00 per barrel; and bacon, 12 1/2 cents per pound. An October 20, 1864, advertisement offered to barter salt for pork, sugar for bacon, homespun for flour, bacon, or wheat, and salt for corn, wheat, or flour. A July 6, 1864, advertisement offered yarn for flour and sugar for bacon, and a July 20, 1864, advertisement wanted to exchange salt for corn, wheat, flour, or bacon. Few of these mentioned prices. During the last two years of the war, the primary object of many of those on the home front was staying financially afloat. The formerly enslaved Annette Milledge, an Edgefieldian whose mother regularly did the owner's family marketing, remembered that in the final days of the war a roast cost $70 in Confederate money. In mid-January 1865, an Edgefield woman recorded prices after shopping in Augusta: "$30 yd muslin, coffee $30 lb tea $150 Other things in proportion."[9]

Leila and other women had to deal with this situation. Leila tried to keep some seventy people on the plantation fed. The responsibilities of food and clothing could have occupied 100 percent of her time, but she also became her husband's agent in directing the overseer and monitoring the crops. J. B. Griffin seems never to have written separately to B. F. Spradley, the overseer, who was literate; instead his letters are full of instructions for Leila—where, when, and how much cotton and grain to plant, to be economical with the corn, to have the wheat sunned, and dozens of other agricultural matters. The unaccustomed hours outside gave her an embarrassingly unladylike suntan, which, her husband assured her, made him only more proud of her for "this is not time for *fair faces* and *tender hands*."[10]

A fair face and tender hands were the mark of elite womanhood on both sides of the Mason-Dixon line, but they had special significance in the South's caste society. Pale skin and soft palms implicitly distinguished the gentry from the dark faces and callused hands of the African Americans who toiled for them, and from the sunburned wives and daughters of yeomen and poor who worked in the fields by necessity. Ladies like Leila Griffin could regain their fair complexions; how easily they would relinquish the independence acquired during the war and slip back into antebellum gender roles was a matter for conjecture. Despite his praise for Leila's managerial abilities, J. B. Griffin clearly did not anticipate that their relationship would be permanently changed. He expected to return to his role as patriarch and protector, allowing her to "retire" to domestic concerns.

Leila's reaction to the unaccustomed responsibilities thrust upon her by the war we cannot know, for her letters to Griffin have not survived. Some planters' wives stepped hesitantly into the absent husbands' shoes and were at times almost overwhelmed by the frustrations of coping with recalcitrant slaves and unfamiliar routines. Others developed competence and confidence as they succeeded at new tasks and learned to make decisions. The tone of Griffin's letters suggests that Leila was among the latter. He seems to have relied on her judgment and ability, frequently responding to queries by advising her to "do as you think best," or "do the best you can." In none of his letters did he voice any doubt about her ability to cope, even with a crisis. Griffin never took issue with Leila's ability to look after the plantation; he praised her development into "a *first rate* manager" and teased that she would make a "right-managing Widow."[11]

She was up before daylight to get everything done, and she still prepared special boxes of food and handmade clothing to send to her husband and wrote the letters that he expected to receive regularly, even as he acknowledged her extra workload. Although Griffin lamented his absences from his family and inability to care for them, it seems clear that, despite homespun and high prices, Leila and the children were not in want. Indeed, when he was later stationed along the Carolina coast in the winter of 1862–63, he casually requested her to send him provisions and large sums of money.

Not until the last months of the war, when Sherman's troops were marching through Georgia, was his presence really essential at home. The plantation house burned to the ground, and, having no home, Leila and the younger children went to live off the plantation. She left the more than fifty slaves on the plantation under the supervision of her fifteen-year-old stepson Willie.[12]

By the end of the war, when Leila and the children were in pressing need, the military situation was also desperate, and Griffin was denied permission to go to his family. True emergency stripped away chivalrous rhetoric. "My Darling you are now thrown upon your own resources and you must do the best you can," he wrote matter-of-factly. At the end, when defeat closed in around South Carolina, Griffin would no longer be able to claim the role of patriarchal defender of women and children: "I will try to [take] care of myself, and you take care of yourself and the Children."[13]

The Griffins survived the war, but, devoted Confederates that they were, they lost everything financially. Another member of the Edgefield planter class had a story with a different ending. Doctor Dewitt Clinton Tompkins, a farmer with twenty-eight slaves, did not remain long at the front. Yet, while he was in service, his resourceful and unscrupulous spouse, Hannah Virginia Smyly Tompkins, had not only successfully managed the family's two-thousand-acre plantation, but had hoarded more than thirty bales of cotton each year that were subsequently sold for 30 cents a pound in gold. Thus the Tompkins family, thanks to Virginia Tompkins, entered the postwar period with 20,000 dollars in hard cash, a move up in the relative wealth of their community.[14]

It is well to remember when we concentrate on women during the Civil War that many antebellum elite women were not exactly "sheltered" before the war. They often bore responsibility and deprivation, especially when living in a "new country" as settlers, or when tending plantations while husbands were away in the legislature or on militia reviews. A significant difference is that at these times antebellum elite women had more white males close by, especially relatives on whom to rely.[15]

Within the less wealthy groups in Edgefield were many yeoman families. They might have owned some farmland, or have been tenants. A topic that needs investigation in the South is what Philip Paludan described in the North as "invisible farmers"—mothers, wives, and daughters who, year in and year out, hoed, gardened, ploughed, tended animals and crops, gathered hay, picked corn. Probably this kind of farming activity was so common by all people in the South, male and female, black and white, that it was rarely commented upon. Nevertheless, during the Civil War, with husbands and sons on the front, yeoman women took a more active role in the running of farms. As a result of this experience, and of the decimation of male landowners and overseers caused by the conflict, one might expect that more women would be operating farms in 1870 than before the war in 1860. Instead, the opposite occurred. Both the percentage and actual number of women operating farms in 1870 decreased. While women took on more active roles in some areas of community life, farm operation remained primarily in the male domain. In fact, as tenantry replaced slavery after the war, a woman was less likely to manage the farm without the help of an overseer.[16]

Church records often contain parts of the stories of these yeoman families, and the records of two churches in Edgefield have information on two such, the Timmerman family and the Ouzts family. These families seem to have borne maximum casualties during the war; nine of sixteen Ouzts family members and six of eleven Timmermans all served in Company K and all lost their lives at the front. The widows had no income to fall back on. Each spouse of each of the married Ouzts and Timmerman soldiers who died in Tompkins Company K moved to the Graniteville textile mills for employment.[17]

Before the Civil War six districts contained textile mills; the most successful and largest was in Edgefield District, Graniteville, where 169 males and 230 females worked. In the antebellum years, wives did not work in William Gregg's Edgefield cotton mills; neither did many of the male heads of families, but their children often did. During the war, however, not only fathers but also adult women began to work in the mills. The women who went to work in the mills during the Civil War gained an experience that they were either reluctant to forego after the war or, alternatively, eager to escape. In any event, the experience altered white southern women's view of themselves and their world.[18]

As expected, women did take a larger role in industry during the war. Opportunities for women became available in cities like Augusta, just across the Savannah River from Edgefield, where fifteen hundred seamstresses worked for the Confederacy. Indeed, the Confederate government became an important employer of women. Just on the border of Southwest Edgefield District in Aiken, Henry William Ravenel noted in his diary of August 10, 1864, "govt. work has been the means of giving a living to many person who have lost their all during the war. Widows of Officers & soldiers, refugees without a home, & other destitute persons thus have been enabled to live." He commented that "The necessities of war have given rise to many kinds of business & employment before unknown." In December 1864, seven men in Greenwood, about seven miles to the northeast from Edgefield District, incorporated "The Ladies Card Factory."[19]

The absence of husbands and sons rendered greatest hardship on those least wealthy. By 1862, one sixth of the number of white families enumerated in the 1860 census were petitioning for relief. In early March 1862, the *Edgefield Advertiser*, in an editorial entitled "The poor ye have always with you," noted that "The duties of war have called away from home the sole supports of many, many families, who must suffer . . . unless the

States, and individuals blessed with abundance, shall come forward with open hands to the relief of the destitute."[20]

Initial attempts at relief in Edgefield were local efforts to aid the families of soldiers. By December 1861 the local paper admitted that the district fund to aid soldier families was exhausted. Six months later the women of Edgefield formed a voluntary association, The Southern Sisters' Aid Society, which assisted destitute military kinfolk. By the end of 1862 similar organizations appeared in many crossroads communities throughout the district. A typical event organized and run by The Southern Sisters' Aid Society was the November 1862 Wednesday evening "Fair and Tableaux" in the Masonic Hall, where "Fancy articles and refreshments, including *real store-bought Coffee*, will be sold." All proceeds went to destitute families.[21]

Money to help the destitute was enthusiastically pledged, but harder to come by. Appealing to fellow pledgers to remember their covenant, the faithful recounted that "Many of the privates in the Company left their families destitute." Reminding their neighbors that their guarantee to the soldiers' families was "a just and noble cause, and it is your cause as well as ours," the faithful pleaded that others attend the next meeting of the association on Saturday.[22]

However, Edgefield's voluntaristic, hierarchical, and paternalistic local society was overwhelmed, and the reciprocity from the wealthy in turn for the yeomen and less wealthy fighting the war failed. As the war wore on, government officials at various levels ostensibly took over the task of caring for destitute military dependents. With the involvement of the government, men supervised the programs and relegated women to subsidiary roles. The state took on the paternalistic role to help the families of soldiers but provided no guidelines. Funds were distributed at the caprice of the local Boards of Relief, all of whom were male, and thus reinforced the notion of male paternalism, as the representatives of the state with the power to bestow largesse at their whim.

In November and December 1862, 444 families were on the relief roles; a year later 727 families were receiving more than $30,000. Linking the extant lists of the relief boards to the manuscript census records in an Edgefield database shows the obvious. Most families on relief had no real estate listed in the 1860 census (40 percent of households in 1860 had no real property), and the heads of those families on relief in 1860 had been mostly farmers, millers, or factory workers. Still, those who had property and were on the relief rolls sometimes received more money from the local relief board than did those who were propertyless. No members of the planter class ever appeared on the relief roles.

In looking at the need for relief, the state did not see women as individuals; rather they were viewed as the spouses and family members of soldiers. The paternalism of the antebellum South was shifted so that the responsibility was that of the state while the soldier, as household head and patriarch, was away at war. Thus, in his governor's message of 1862, Edgefieldian Francis Pickens called for aid not for women and children, but for the families of soldiers. Relief was not a form of welfare, but an obligation to soldiers.[23]

Edgefield's Governor Milledge Bonham argued that it was the state's duty to insure that no soldier's family was needy. Bonham called on the South Carolina legislature to raise taxes if necessary to increase relief for the families of soldiers. If the state had been willing and capable of providing substantial relief to the families of soldiers, then the military might have had a less severe problem with desertion. Alexander Baron Holmes, whose family were refugees in Edgefield, noted that four poor deserters who had gone home were court-martialed and sentenced to be shot. "Thank God I was not in the shooting squad. Those men were 'regulars' who had not been home in three years, their families were starving, and they could not get furloughs, but went anyway and were convicted of desertion, and were murdered."[24]

According to former governor and senator James Henry Hammond, the material hardships and the need for survival even motivated poor white. women to cross that forbidden white female–black male interracial barrier. As early as September 1863, James Henry Hammond, in a petition requesting a magistrate for the southwestern section of Edgefield, wrote, "The country around there is without exaggeration in a desperate condition. Negroes are uppermost, openly keeping white, & some very pretty, girls, & getting children by them. They do not conceal that they steal corn, meat & everything they can to support the fathers & mothers of their Sweet heart. There is not a Magistrate any [where] in reach." This startling postscript sounds like the ravings of a paranoid man, but many whites were worried about being so outnumbered by the slaves, and interracial unions of free black men and white women did occur.[25]

While financial hardship fell disproportionately on poorer women, women of all classes suffered the pain of lost loved ones. Many diaries and letters describe the grief. When Dr. Charles Richard Mosley from near Ninety-Six died in spring 1864, his sister-in-law recorded in her diary, "It seems our best men are all being killed. Emma and I went to see Kittie last week—she is overwhelmed with grief and his poor children do feel it sadly! Oh, when will this cruel war end!" A friend wrote the widow, "his loss is irreplaceable to the State, District, and to his family oh! Who can ever fill his place."[26]

Within the cacophony of multitude stories of women in the Confederacy, a pattern of increased influence emerges. Waging a war necessarily changed the role of women in the community, and the record for Edgefield women shows that the Civil War had a significant impact. Some of Edgefield's white women, barely surviving, took it upon themselves to write lengthy petitions to the government asking for relief and fair treatment. Some daughters from the planter and middle classes succeeded in the professions of teaching, nursing, and clerking. These and other women found that the exigencies of the Civil War enabled them to make a more substantial and active contribution to community life; these women envisioned a broader, more active position for themselves in the social and political life of the South.

Thus, there was no one story.

You will find that years later these stories became unified, a story—a memorial even—of loyalty and devotion to the Cause after it was long lost.[27]

Notes

The quotation in the chapter title is from James B. Griffin to Leila Griffin, February 26, 1862, the Papers of James B. Griffin. The letters of James B. Griffin are a privately held family collection, now in the possession of Jack Gunter, Sr., of Dallas, Texas. Photocopies have been placed in the South Caroliniana Library, Columbia, South Carolina, and in the Center of American History, University of Texas at Austin. The letters have been transcribed and annotated and placed at the center of a book; see Judith N. McArthur and Orville Vernon Burton, *A Gentleman and an Officer: A Military and Social History of James B. Griffin's Civil War* (New York, 1996).

1. Mary Elizabeth Massey, "The Confederate States of America: The Homefront," in *Writing Southern History: Essays in Historiography in Honor of Fletcher M. Green*, ed. Arthur S. Link and Rembert W. Patrick (Baton Rouge, 1965), 24–72. The major study of the Confederate home front is still Charles W. Ramsdell, *Behind the Lines in the Southern Confederacy* (Baton Rouge, 1944). Mans A. Vinovskis took social historians and especially the authors of community studies to task for virtually ignoring the impact of the Civil War on people and society, in "Have Social

Historians Lost the Civil War? Some Preliminary Demographic Speculations," *Journal of American History* 76, no. 1 (June 1989): 34–58.

2. For description of Edgefield District see Orville Vernon Burton, *In My Father's House Are Many Mansions: Family and Community in Edgefield, South Carolina* (Chapel Hill, 1985).

3. James B. Griffin to Leila Griffin, February 26, 1862, Griffin Papers. On independence and republicanism in the South, see J. Mills Thornton III, *Politics and Power in a Slave Society: Alabama, 1800–1860* (Baton Rouge, 1978); Stephen Hahn, *The Transformation of the Georgia Upcountry: 1850–1880* (New York, 1983). J. William Harris, *Plain Folk and Gentry in a Slave Society: White Liberty and Black Slavery in Augusta's Hinterlands* (Middletown, Conn., 1986); Lacy K. Ford, Jr., *Origins of Southern Radicalism: The South Carolina Upcountry, 1800–1860* (New York, 1988).

4. This section on Leila Griffin draws from McArthur and Burton, *A Gentleman and an Officer.* Thomas Jefferson Howard, Civil War Veterans Questionnaires (1915), 6 and (1922), 6. *Edgefield Advertiser,* October 24, 1860. On the plantation mistress see Anne Firor Scott, *The Southern Lady from Pedestal to Politics, 1830–1930* (Chicago, 1970), 22–44; Catherine Clinton, *The Plantation Mistress: Woman's World in the Old South* (New York, 1982), 100–45, for descriptions of the responsibilities of planters' wives. Elizabeth Fox-Genovese (*Within the Plantation Household: Black and White Women of the Old South* [Chapel Hill, 1988]) departs significantly from Scott and Clinton in contending that, with the exception of sewing, white women have been credited with much work that was actually performed by female slaves under their supervision. An especially useful collection on southern marriage and women is Carol Bleser, ed., *In Joy and Sorrow: Women, Family, and Marriage in the Victorian South, 1830–1900* (New York, 1991). Although not about the planter class, for insights on antebellum southern womanhood also see Suzanne Lebsock, *The Free Women of Petersburg: Status and Culture in a Southern Town, 1784–1860* (New York, 1984); and Jean E. Friedman, *The Enclosed Garden: Women and Community in the Evangelical South, 1830–1900* (Chapel Hill, 1985).

5. Thomas Jefferson Howard, Civil War Veterans Questionnaires (1915), 6 and (1922), 6.

6. Mrs. Thomas Taylor et al., eds., *South Carolina Women in the Confederacy,* 2 vols. (Columbia, 1903), 2:51. Hagood was from Barnwell, but his wife was the daughter of Senator A. P. Butler, and he had a plantation in Edgefield.

7. See for example *Charleston News and Courier, "Our Women in the War": The Lives They Lived, the Deaths They Died* (Charleston, 1885), 10–7, 60–5, 399–443, 426–49, for examples of how women did without. A superb description and analysis of white women in the Confederacy is George C. Rable, *Civil Wars: Women and the Crisis of Southern Nationalism* (Urbana, 1989).

8. Civil War historian James McPherson, however, links the problem of inflation in the Confederacy to the paper money issued to cover government debt; issues of

notes rose from 119 million in 1861 to 400 million in 1862. The commodity index increased by twenty-eight times between January 1861 and January 1864. The money supply increased elevenfold; Eugene M. Lerner, "Inflation in the Confederacy, 1861–1865," in *Studies in the Quantity Theory of Money*, ed. Milton Friedman (Chicago, 1956), 173; James McPherson, *Ordeal by Fire: The Civil War and Reconstruction* (New York, 1982), 199–200; Ramsdell, *Behind the Lines in the Confederacy*, 20–1, 75; Lerner, "Inflation in the Confederacy," 163–78; Richard Cecil Todd, *Confederate Finance* (Athens, Ga., 1954), esp. 110, 117.

9. George Rawick, *The American Slave*, vol. 4, Georgia Supplement Series I (Westport, Conn., 1977), 433–7; Ella Watson Diary, January 25, 1865, 5, Ella Watson Papers, South Caroliniana Library.

10. James B. Griffin to Leila Griffin, April 25, 1862, Griffin Papers; examples of letters concerning instructions to Spradley are March 17, 23, 26, and 30.

11. Rable, *Civil Wars*, chap. 6; Scott, *The Southern Lady*, chap. 4. Not all absent husbands were as supportive and confident as Griffin. See for example the Laurens County couple described in Joan Cashin, "'Since the War Broke Out': The Marriage of Kate and William McClure," in *Divided Houses: Gender and the Civil War*, ed. Catherine Clinton and Nina Silber (New York, 1992), 200–12. James B. Griffin to Leila Griffin, January 10, 1862, Griffin Papers.

12. Quite likely some of these slaves had taken care of Willie as a younger boy, hunting and fishing with him, and they might have wondered who was supervising whom.

13. James B. Griffin to Leila Griffin, February 14, 1865, Griffin Papers. Drew Gilpin Faust ("Altars of Sacrifice: Confederate Women and the Narratives of War," *Journal of American History* 76, no. 4 [March 1990]: 1200–28) analyzes the reaction of planters' wives to the failure of their husbands to live up to the patriarchal ideal during the Civil War.

14. Arthur S. Tompkins, undated memorandum, the Papers of Daniel Augustus Tompkins, SHC. Howard Bunyan Clay, "Daniel Augustus Tompkins: An American Bourbon" (Ph.D. diss., University of North Carolina, 1951), 2, 4–5. According to their son Arthur, Virginia Tompkins made better crops during the war with the aid of the overseer than her husband had before the war. Virginia's father was a first cousin of John C. Calhoun.

15. For the experience of women who moved to new and frontier areas in the South, see Cashin, "Since the War Broke Out."

16. Phillip Shaw Paludan, *"The People's Contest": The Union and the Civil War, 1861–1865* (New York, 1988), 157. Farms operated by women determined from manuscript censuses in Edgefield Data Base. See discussion of this phenomenon and the cultural discussion of patriarchy in terms of farming arrangements in Burton, *In My Father's House Are Many Mansions*, chap. 7.

17. *Edgefield Advertiser*, July 6, 1864; Hortense Woodson, *Peter Ouzts I and His Descendants* (Edgefield, S.C., 1949); Elijah Timmerman Papers and McKendree

Methodist Church Records (both in South Caroliniana Library). Free School Reports, Edgefield, in South Carolina Department of Archives and History, Columbia, S.C.

18. Harry Hammond to Emily C. Hammond, July 22, 1864, Hammond Bryan Cummings Papers, South Caroliniana Library; J. H. Taylor, "Manufactures in South Carolina," *DeBow's Review,* n.s., 2 (January 1850): 24–29; Edgefield, S.C., Database.

19. Arney Robinson Childs, ed., *The Private Journal of Henry William Revenel, 1859–1887* (Columbia, 1947), 199. *Charleston News and Courier,* February 16, 1864; Mrs. James Conner et al., *South Carolina Women in the Confederacy,* vol. 2 (Columbia, 1907), 57. There is no record of whether this incorporated factory ever actually produced materials.

20. *Edgefield Advertiser,* March 2, 1862. See also, for example, July 31, 1861, August 7, 1861, January 11, 1865. J. W. Patton, "The Work of Soldiers' Aide Societies in South Carolina during the Civil War," *Proceedings of the South Carolina Historical Association,* 1937, 3–12. Mrs. A. T. Smyth et al., *South Carolina Women in the Confederacy* (Columbia, 1903), 111, 146; Francis Butler Simkins and James Welch Patton, *The Women of the Confederacy* (Richmond, 1930), 18–34.

21. For relief societies see *Edgefield Advertiser,* June 26, July 10, October 16, 30, November 6, 13, 1861, passim July–October 1861, November 26, 1862, March–April 1863, January 1865.

22. *Edgefield Advertiser,* December 4, 1861.

23. *Journal of the House of Representatives of the State of South Carolina, 1862* (Columbia, 1862), 11.

24. *South Carolina Senate Journal, 1863* (Columbia, 1863), 10, and *Journal of the House of Representatives of the State of South Carolina, 1863* (Columbia, 1863), 74. Scrapbook of A. Baron Holmes, in the possession of the family, original with Mr. A. Baron Holmes III, Charleston, S.C. I am also grateful to David Parker's sharing of his copies of the notebook with me. See also David Parker, "The Edgefield Saga of Charleston's Noted Holmes Family," *Edgefield Advertiser,* February 1, 1989, 3, 4. On a less sympathetic report of a deserter's execution, see *Edgefield Advertiser,* March 18, 1863.

25. H. Howard et al., to M. L. Bonham, September 1863, Materials 1863–64, Milledge Luke Bonham Papers, in South Carolina Department of Archives and History. See Burton, *In My Father's House Are Many Mansions,* especially chap. 4.

26. Ella Watson, Diary, n.d.; N. G. Aiken to Lou Watson Mosley, March 1, 1864, Ella Watson Papers.

27. Much credit for the creation of the unified memory of one white Confederate story goes to the United Daughters of the Confederacy. For South Carolina see Mrs. Taylor Thomas et al., eds., *South Carolina Women in the Confederacy,* 2 vols. (Columbia, 1907). Beginning in 1990 with volume one of *Recollections and Reminiscences, 1861–1865 through World War I,* the South Carolina Division of the United Daughters of the Confederacy (UDC) is publishing materials collected around the

turn of the century and has now reached volume five (1994). As far as I know, no one has drawn the connection between the agrarian protests and interracial politics of the Populists in the 1890s and the creation of the UDC in 1894. In South Carolina, noncombatant Pitchfork Ben Tillman was consolidating his power, instituting a new state constitution, and replacing the Civil War heroes Wade Hampton and Matthew Calbraith Butler in the U.S. Senate. The introduction to the recent publication of memories from the South Carolina UDC has a poignant discussion of the Confederate flag flying over the state capitol.

6

Ministries in Black and White

The Catholic Nuns of St. Augustine, 1859–1869

Barbara E. Mattick

Although since the 1980s there has been a growing interest in evaluating the impact of the Catholic Church on American history, relatively little has been written on the Catholic Church in the South, and women's history has been dominated by analyses of Protestant women from the Northeast. This northeastern view emphasizes the development of networks and bonds between women in urban settings through voluntary associations, mothers' clubs, and charitable works. Activities in such groups as the Woman's Christian Temperance Union ultimately led to political involvement of women and to social change. As Elizabeth Fox-Genovese points out, however, the South was overwhelmingly rural, and there was little opportunity for the development of such networks. She says, "Most rural southern women lived their lives within and interpreted their identities through the prism of specific households." Another historian, Jean Friedman, says that southern women were also slow to embrace change because of the constraints on them imposed by a strongly evangelical Protestantism as opposed to the generally more liberal Protestantism of the Northeast.[1]

This chapter discusses the contributions Roman Catholic nuns made to the education of young women in St. Augustine through their establishment of St. Mary's Academy, a school for white girls, and through their work with blacks during the first few years after the Civil War. It also examines how their vocations as women religious (another name for nuns or sisters) enhanced their ability to carry out their mission in the predominantly Catholic community of St. Augustine, Florida, in the mid-nineteenth-century South just before and after the Civil War. One of the main purposes is to evaluate their role in imparting traditional values to the students.

Since the twelfth century, the Roman Catholic Church has provided an avenue for women to have ministries devoted to prayer, education, and service to the needy. Women who felt the call to such a life in the Catholic Church generally had to be between the ages of fifteen and thirty-six, of reasonable intelligence, and of high character to be accepted into a religious order. They also had to leave their families and embrace three primary vows: poverty, chastity, and obedience. With such qualifications, it is incongruous that the lives of nuns were shaped by the medieval perceptions of a woman as an "immature, inferior, and evil being, incapable of directing her own life and requiring constant surveillance lest she fall." European convents often adopted rules of silence except during prescribed times and demanded that women separate themselves from the world, including their families.[2]

The first nuns came to the United States in the 1790s. The country as a whole then was "avowedly Protestant" and did not trust Catholics, considering them to be superstitious idolaters. With the great influx of immigrants from Ireland and Germany between 1829 and 1859, the number of Catholics increased rapidly. Sisters were recruited by the American Catholic Church to operate schools, hospitals, orphanages, and other agencies to assist the needy; indeed, thirty-nine foundations—communities of sisters—were established in the antebellum period. Most of the Catholic immigrants who came to the United States in the 1830s and 1840s went to northern cities, where American workers often saw them as threats to jobs. Soon anti-Catholic sentiments raged in the North, and nuns and priests, often foreign-born, were subjected to physical and verbal attacks and accused of lurid sexual immorality, murder, and infanticide. Such attacks were justified in the eyes of their perpetrators because they considered the decision of nuns to live single lives of celibacy to be unnatural, and their sworn obedience to their superiors, including the pope, to be anti-American. They even accused Catholics of plotting to take over the country for the pontiff. Unlike the North, however, the South was primarily rural, with comparatively few immigrants and even fewer Catholics. Thus the anti-Catholic rage of the North was not prevalent in the prosperous antebellum South.[3]

For nuns in particular, however, their lives challenged the accepted concept of true womanhood or domesticity that was embodied by motherhood and submission to a husband. According to Alexis de Tocqueville in his 1840 commentary on American life, "[I]n the United States the inexorable opinion of the public carefully circumscribes woman within the narrow circle of domestic interests and duties and forbids her to step beyond it."[4]

The ideology of domesticity arose from middle-class Protestants in the Northeast. It emphasized the essential role of the family in imparting cultural values and in maintaining social order. Women were the primary agents in the process: "Woman as wife and mother represented a beacon of stability, a preserver of tradition, in a society undergoing unprecedented industrial development, urban growth, and geographical expansion." Women, indeed, owed it to society to fulfill the prescribed roles of wife and mother. In "The Cult of True Womanhood, 1820–1860," Barbara Welter has described what was expected of women in antebellum America. The four primary virtues were piety or religious devotion, sexual purity, submissiveness, and domesticity. Religion was the province of women, for men were supposedly too occupied with the day-to-day life of business to be concerned with piety. Women, though, could pursue piety without neglecting their responsibilities of caring for the home. Sexual purity was not necessarily expected for men, but for women its "absence was unnatural and unfeminine." Without purity, a female could not be a true woman.[5]

Although social norms allowed for "single blessedness," considering a single life to be better than a "loveless or unhappy marriage," most women fulfilled these ideals of womanhood in the state of marriage and from a home. In their homes, women were expected to exercise piety, not only teaching their children, but also bringing men "back to God." They were to make their homes places of comfort and cheer by nursing the sick, maintaining a well-ordered household, and gracing their surroundings with beauty. Girls, therefore, had to learn to be proficient in various kinds of needlework and in drawing-room skills such as singing and playing an instrument. Academic education for women was fine as long as it did not interfere with the primary goal of becoming a good homemaker. The seminaries and academies for girls emphasized that their programs would not hinder the development of the skills of domesticity, but would "enlarge and deepen" a girl's ability to fulfill her God-given role of wife and mother.[6] Protestants feared that nuns encouraged young girls they taught in parochial schools to follow their example in entering convents, thus eroding the stabilizing influence of wives and mothers. The establishment of Protestant schools for girls became a focus of concern for the Protestant community, for through education they believed they could combat the growth of convents and the entrenchment of Catholicism in America.[7]

Catholics, however, defended their convent schools by claiming that the nuns supported and fostered the very ideals of motherhood and domesticity espoused by the Protestants. Furthermore, nuns fully realized that most young women were destined to be wives and mothers and insisted that they made no effort to coerce those who did not have a vocation for the religious life. They encouraged all women to live for God. In fact, the four qualities identifying the antebellum true woman basically dovetailed with the virtues of the ideal nun as defined in the rules and constitutions of various religious sisterhoods. The convent institutionalized the true woman's attributes of piety, purity, and submissiveness in a nun's religious calling and her vows of chastity and obedience. Rather than encouraging the girls in the academies to enter the convent, the main goal of the teaching nuns was to prepare their students to be proper wives in middle- and upper-class homes. Curricula were similar to those offered at northern Protestant seminaries for girls. Nuns, therefore, supported rather than thwarted the enculturation of young girls with the ideals of domesticity. The ideal of domesticity was common throughout the country, but was especially strong in the South. An examination of the work of Catholic nuns in St. Augustine, Florida, provides a vehicle for evaluating the validity of these paradigms in regard to a southern Catholic community in the middle of the nineteenth century.[8]

In the last months of 1859, Bishop Augustin Verot, the Roman Catholic vicar apostolic for Florida, brought to St. Augustine some Sisters of Mercy to establish an academy for girls, along with three Christian Brothers from Canada to establish a day school for boys. Jean-Pierre Augustin Verot was consecrated vicar apostolic of Florida and titular bishop of Danaba in Baltimore, Maryland, on April 25, 1858, and arrived in St. Augustine on June 1, 1858. Although Florida had been a flourishing center of Catholicism as a Spanish colony, by the time Verot assumed his new post it was a struggling mission field with only three or four priests. Between 1821, the end of the Second Spanish Period when Florida became part of the United States, and 1857, few bishops had visited Florida.[9] Verot's attentions to St. Augustine were, therefore, greatly appreciated by the Catholics there. The affection with which he was regarded by the people of St. Augustine was expressed in the announcement of his return from a recruitment trip that appeared in the local newspaper, the *St. Augustine Examiner:* "We need not say how great is the joy of his spiritual children, who so well appreciate the winning qualities of this worthy Prelate. It is with unfeigned pleasure we welcome and record his safe return to the 'Ancient City' and the great success he has attained in his tour in Europe."[10]

The cheerful announcement of Verot's return was a reflection of St. Augustine's close relationship with the Catholic Church in spite of the recent years of neglect. The Ancient City, settled by Catholic Spaniards nearly three hundred years before, remained a Catholic town. In 1860, St. Johns County, for which St. Augustine was the seat of government, had 2,000 Catholics in six churches, more than twice as many as the Methodists who were the next most numerous denomination. The largest concentration of Catholics was in St. Augustine, with an estimated population of 952 white and 376 black Catholics.[11] The city was actually a Catholic enclave in Florida, for like most of the rest of the South in 1860, the state was rural, and most of its inhabitants were Protestant. There had been an influx of Protestants when Florida was transferred from Spain to the United States in 1821. Yet, in spite of the alarm of the Catholic bishop who wrote in June 1823 that St. Augustine was "overrun with Methodists and Presbyterians," the Ancient City remained a Catholic town and Protestants remained in the minority. Furthermore, the Protestants who came into Florida were not overtly antagonistic to Catholics.[12]

The Catholics of St. Augustine, therefore, were overjoyed when the bishop returned with six priests and "two Religious Ladies and several other persons to aid him in the Florida Mission." He also had five students at the Theological Seminary of Baltimore preparing for the work in Florida. Before the end of the year, Verot also recruited five Sisters of Mercy from Providence, Rhode Island. The Sisters of Mercy were led by a young Mother Superior, Mary Ligouri from Virginia, who was only twenty-five years old. By 1860, there were nine other sisters at the newly established St. Mary's Convent in St. Augustine. Sisters in the order all had religious names beginning with "Mary" and were sometimes referred to using only the second name. Sister Mary Ragina, from Florida, probably joined the convent after it was established.[13]

In December 1859, shortly after the arrival of the Sisters, the "Ladies of the Roman Catholic Church" held a fair. The newspaper reported that the proceeds from the event were to be "devoted to the education projects now in movement in this City. A very worthy object which should be cheerfully and faithfully sustained by our people, both Catholic and Protestant." The Sisters started St. Mary's Academy, a boarding school/day school for white girls, after the first of the year. According to the census, there were eight boarding students who ranged in age from twelve to sixteen years old and were all from Florida. This was the first Catholic convent school in the state.[14]

The education of their youth continued to be one of the major concerns of the citizens of St. Augustine. In reviewing recent internal improvements of the city, the editors, in the January 7, 1860, edition of the *Examiner*, rejoiced over the awakening of an interest in education and proclaimed, "San Augustine is in a fair way to be celebrated for the plenteousness and excellence of her school privileges, not on a sickly and fluctuating basis, but we hope and believe possessing the very best elements of permanency." A month later, however, the editors gave a totally unexpected strong warning against the establishment of church-related schools:

> We are however in one danger which indeed should be *no* danger to lofty and liberal minds. The moment our schools erect fortifications of *sect* and *ism* around them, that moment, we honestly believe, they strike the first blow at their own ruin. The school room is not the place to teach religious dogmas; these legitimately belong to the Sunday-schools and the consecrated teachers of religion; the development of the intellect, the training and storing the mind with knowledge, accompanied and hallowed by those mild influences and examples which inculcate practical piety, are the department of the presiding spirits in the school-room. The *worth of a school for youth*, does not hinge upon the question [illegible] Methodist or Episcopal or Roman Catholic. It hinges upon *this* rather—Is it a source of *light?* is the young mind wisely and successfully trained there? Are those principles formed in it which it will do to guide our life by in after years? Are children taught to revere the majority of broad moral right? Are they fitted for true noble manhood and womanhood? We are opposed in every sense and on every ground to sectarian schools.

Bishop Verot was discouraged by this public reaction, but pressed forward with the establishment of the schools.[15]

In spite of the *Examiner*'s strong warnings against church-related schools, a little more than a year later, the same editor had almost euphoric praise for the schools that had been established in St. Augustine by the Catholic Church, St. Mary's Academy for white girls, the day school for white boys, and two free schools, presumably for poor whites:

We have great cause for gratulation [*sic*] when we consider the great progress in the educational system in our city; too much gratitude cannot be felt by the citizens of St. Augustine, to the Catholic Bishop and Priests, under whose auspices the schools connected with that Church have been established, and to the Sisters and Brothers who are engaged in instructing our youth . . . The girls are under the care of the sisters, 'tho always remarkable for their good manners, and gentle bearing—have now the added charm of intellectual improvement; one cannot too much admire the gentle courtesy and modesty of their demeanor—much of this is natural to them, but one can also see the effects of careful training; it could scarcely fail to be otherwise under the supervision of Ladies so eminent for their piety, and themselves of cultivated minds and manners.[16]

No explanation is given for this radical change in attitude concerning parochial schools, other than, perhaps, extreme pleasure in the results of the Sisters' teaching methods under the guidance of Mother Mary Ligouri. All looked well for the school, but in the same month as the editorial's publication, the country erupted into the Civil War.

The intensity of tensions between the North and South had been building steadily since the Compromise of 1850. Because of the strong anti-Catholicism that was prevalent across the country at mid-century, most Catholic leaders had refrained from political discussions that did not have a direct bearing on the Catholic Church. On January 4, 1861, however, Bishop Verot delivered a sermon at the church in St. Augustine that launched him into the political arena. The occasion was the Day of Public Humiliation, Fasting, and Prayer proclaimed by President Buchanan in a spiritual effort to avert the disintegration of the Union. Verot's message, "Slavery & Abolitionism," strongly condemned the North for the widespread practice of refusing to assist in the capture and return of runaway slaves, a rebelliousness that flagrantly violated the Fugitive Slave Act of 1850 and justified the South's consideration of secession. The sermon also denounced abolitionists for blasphemously trying to use the Bible to condemn slavery as a "moral evil, and a crime against God, religion, humanity, and society." Verot countered that slavery had "received the sanction of God, of the Church, and of Society at all times, and in all governments," and cited biblical and historical examples to support his argument. Verot's defense of slavery and states' rights was published and widely quoted throughout the South, and gained him the reputation of being a "rebel bishop."[17]

Verot defined slavery as a "state of dependency of one man upon another 'so as to be obliged to work all his life for that master with the privilege in the latter, to transfer that right to another person by sale.'" The master, however, did not own the slave, but only had a right to the slave's labor and that of the slave's children. According to Verot, masters also had responsibilities toward their slaves. Some treated their slaves like animals, but the bishop said,

> A man, by being a slave, does not cease to be a man, retaining all the properties, qualities, attributes, duties, rights and responsibilities attached to human nature, or to a being endowed with reason and understanding, and made to the image and likeness of God. A master has not over a slave the same rights which he has over an animal, and whoever would view his slaves merely as beasts, would have virtually abjured human nature, and would deserve to be expelled from human society.[18]

His sermon also delineated six conditions under which slavery could be considered "legitimate, lawful, approved by all laws, and consistent with practical religion and true holiness of life in masters who fulfil [sic] those conditions:" (1) repudiate the slave trade, for slaves brought into the country from Africa had not really been captured in war, but were caught and sold as trade items; (2) respect the rights of free colored persons; slavery was not based on color, but on property rights, and it was unjust to re-enslave a free person; (3) do not take advantage of colored females, who were frequently subjected to immorality; (4) honor, respect, and encourage slave marriage and keep families together; (5) provide adequate food, clothing, and shelter; and (6) provide a means for slaves to know and practice religion. To seal these reforms, Verot proposed that the Confederacy adopt a servile code to outline the rights and duties of slaves.[19]

Verot frankly addressed the immorality some masters forced upon their female slaves: "It is but right that means should be taken to check libertinism and licentiousness, and that the female slave be surrounded with sufficient protection to save her from dishonor and crime. The southern Confederacy, if it should exist, must rely on morality and justice, and it could never be entitled to a special protection from above unless it professes to surround Slavery with the guarantees that will secure its morality and virtue." Such concern for female slaves and the open admission that the sexual abuse they often suffered was criminal was startling, especially coming from a southern bishop. It should be noted, however, that Verot also held racist ideas. His emphasis on the need to keep slave families together to avoid sexual immorality was based on the belief that "the strength and violence of animal propensities is in the inverse ratio of intellectual and moral faculties, which are decidedly weaker in the African race, as all persons of experience will testify."[20]

On January 10, 1861, six days after Verot delivered his sermon, Florida seceded from the Union; little more than three months later, the Civil War began with the Confederacy's April 14 firing on Fort Sumter. Union troops took possession of St. Augustine on March 10, 1862. So many people fled the city that the Sisters of Mercy closed St. Mary's Academy in May, and on August 17, Bishop Verot personally conducted most of them to join other Sisters of Mercy in Columbus, Georgia, for the duration of the conflict. The few who remained lived in great poverty, and the work that had been going very well before the war suffered a major setback. During the Civil War Sister Mary Ann, one of the St. Augustine Sisters of Mercy from Ireland, provided nursing care after the Battle of Olustee, at the Savannah Hospital and at the prison camp at Andersonville.[21]

The Sisters of Mercy returned at the end of the war in 1865 to reopen St. Mary's Academy. There were other schools in St. Augustine shortly after the war ended. The Freedmen's Bureau had opened a school for black children during the war, funded by taxes on black citizens in the Union-held city, and in 1866 Governor David Selby Walker had established a state system of schools for blacks. Bishop Verot welcomed the peace and turned his attention toward ministering to the needs of the freedmen in the areas under his charge.[22]

It was impossible for the Sisters of Mercy to maintain schools and religious classes for both whites and blacks. In 1865, therefore, Verot went to LePuy, France, his hometown, to recruit some Sisters of St. Joseph to come to St. Augustine to teach blacks and convert them to Catholicism. Of the sixty French sisters who volunteered, eight were chosen. Verot made it clear that they were to teach newly freed slaves in Florida and Georgia, saying, "I have five or six hundred thousand [sic] Negroes without any education or religion . . . for whom I wish to do something." He was compelled not only by genuine concern for the Negroes, but also by the Florida legislature's recent action to provide schools for blacks and by the efforts already in place by Protestant teachers from the North. In explaining the urgent need for teachers, he told his French audience, "[W]e must make a beginning by establishing schools—a necessity. The [northern] Protestants have anticipated us here: they have opened free schools which the Negroes attend in great numbers. . . . We must, therefore, prepare for the contest . . . in procuring religious instruction for this simple and docile race."[23]

In September 1866, the eight French sisters arrived in St. Augustine, staying at first with the Sisters of Mercy. In November, with six new postulants from Savannah (which was also under Verot's jurisdiction), the Sisters of St. Joseph opened a school for black children. According to the biography of Mother Marie Sidonia Rascie, who was in charge of the school, the black children were "proud of being taught by French sisters, whom the people [of St. Augustine] despised on that account." In February 1867, Mother Sidonia sent five sisters to establish a similar school in Savannah, teaching out of a "rickety frame building on the grounds of St. Johns Cathedral."[24]

The citizenry of Savannah was unhappy at having a school for blacks and did not welcome the Sisters, some referring to them as "nigger sisters." Bishop Verot's announcement of the school's opening was met with "whispering of disapproval" throughout the congregation. Even so, the school opened with fifty students and went on to provide night classes for adults. In October, four more sisters arrived, and the Mother Superior went back to St. Augustine with three new sisters. Back in the Ancient City, they also established a school for white boys.[25]

As alluded to by Bishop Verot in his appeal for French support, the Protestant American Missionary Association (AMA) had sent both men and women to the South to teach the freedmen. Based on the Georgia record of this organization, most of the teachers were single, white women in their twenties, with a missionary zeal to Christianize the freed blacks. In these respects they were not very different from the French Sisters of St. Joseph. Most of the AMA teachers, however, were from New England, primarily Massachusetts; few were foreign. The most critical difference between them, though, was that most AMA teachers were evangelical Protestants and adamantly anti-Catholic. The AMA was driven by a fear that moral society, as defined by members of the mainstream northern middle class, was crumbling, and identified "Romanism, rum, and ignorance" as major agents of the decline. They considered Roman Catholics to be their chief rivals in seeking the souls of the freedmen. Indeed, that was true in St. Augustine, where in 1867 three-fourths of the population was Catholic, including the majority of freedmen. Catholics tended to be just as strongly anti-Protestant. Added to that, the AMA teachers were Yankees. Catholicism was so strong in St. Augustine that the AMA did little work there compared to their efforts in other parts of Florida. In the long run, however, neither the AMA nor the Catholic Church was successful in developing a strong membership among the freedmen, for the black community was more drawn to the rising African American denominations such as the African Methodist Episcopal Church.[26]

Although there was some initial opposition to the work of the Sisters of St. Joseph with the blacks, St. Augustine soon embraced the nuns. Acceptance was made easier because they were everything the AMA teachers were not: they were Catholic, not Protestant and were from France, not New England. Furthermore, they were sponsored by the beloved Bishop Verot, who had been such a champion of the Confederacy. By August 1867, a citizen identified only as "Observer" wrote the editor of the *St. Augustine Examiner* commenting on the Sisters' work among the freedmen:

> We hear . . . that the Sisters of St. Joseph have met with success in training the coloured children of St. Augustine. The Catholic children belonging to the coloured population are now far above the level of their comrades of African origin belonging to other churches or no church at all; and we cannot give too much praise to these devoted Sisters of St. Joseph, for having left their happy country and all the comforts of *"la Belle France"* to assist in the great work of the moral regeneration of the African race. What they have done hitherto is a sure pledge of greater success for the future. Their conquests on ignorance, barbarism, vice and brutal habits entitle them to far greater praise than that which is given to conquerors who mark their passage by fire, devastation, and torrents of blood,

presumably referring to the recent Union aggressors.[27]

Over the next several years, the Sisters of St. Joseph established other schools for freedmen in St. Augustine and nearby communities. In 1868, Mother Julia and a novice established a mission in Mandarin, near Jacksonville, Florida. There they taught white and black children separately; the more than forty white students were instructed in the church, while twenty-seven black pupils were taught in the sacristy, a 12–foot by 16–foot room with one window. In St. Augustine, the Sisters had sixty black pupils. In 1869, they ran two schools in the town, one for colored boys and girls and one for white boys, and in 1870 also established a school for colored children in Jacksonville.[28]

As the Sisters of St. Joseph were establishing their schools for blacks and the poorer whites in St. Augustine and nearby communities, St. Mary's Academy under the Sisters of Mercy had resumed its place as the favored institution dedicated to the education of the Ancient City's white girls to make them refined young women. What constituted "noble womanhood" and "noble manhood" as mentioned by the editors of the *Examiner* in their February 11, 1860, comments about education in St. Augustine? From the same editorial, it is clear that behavior was a critical factor, and some idea of what was expected is revealed by the glowing report that "The school girls, bless their little hearts, are growing gentler and more gracefully lady-like, under the influence of gentle and lady-like teachers. The school-boys, while the roughness which belongs to mischievous boyhood is not yet wholly eradicated, are yet becoming more deferential and gentlemanly in their manner." The editors also praised the academic advances made and the increased powers to think and reason, all of which would prepare the students for adulthood.

According to their advertisements in the *Examiner* in 1866, the Sisters of Mercy offered a full course of instruction for young ladies that would meet these expectations, which included reading; writing; grammar; orthography (spelling); arithmetic; geography; history; rhetoric; natural philosophy; algebra; geometry; chemistry; astronomy; French, German, and Spanish languages; music, vocal and instrumental; drawing; and plain or ornamental needlework. Tuition for boarders was four hundred dollars a year, with extra charges for instruction in the foreign languages, art, and music. Needlework was offered free of charge to the boarders.[29]

As a parochial school, the curriculum was steeped in strong Catholic teaching. The basic goal of Catholic schools was to "fortify the soul with Christian education" by "training the intellect and memory in truth, teaching the heart and will—which are the springs of moral action—to obey the dictates of conscience and thus acquire virtue, and enlightening and controlling the conscience by the sanction of religion, so as to make it an effective guide to conduct." In addition to academic training, therefore, there would have been daily prayers and religious instruction.[30]

The excellent reputation of the academy was reflected in a report that appeared in the *Examiner* in the fall of 1868. Bishop Verot had gone to the North and returned with three new Sisters of Mercy to join the faculty at St. Mary's. According to the paper, the Sisters, "yielding to motives of zeal and feeling the impulse of the missionary spirit, cheerfully renounced the comforts, blandishments and advantages of home and changed them with

the sacrifice, privations and comparative poverty of a country lately deso-
lated by evil disaster and war." Speaking of their work at the academy, the
paper continued,

> They have already commenced to teach the young daughters of the
> 'Ancient City' in St. Mary's Academy, which has now been in exist-
> ence for ten years [actually only eight] and earned a just reputation
> throughout Florida for the solid and accomplished education which it
> gives to young ladies. With the addition of these three new members,
> the school cannot fail to become more prosperous; doubtless it will
> sustain its reputation of a first class school for young ladies, and we
> hope it will draw large numbers of young ladies from the county and
> neighboring cities

that they would "receive more fully all the benefits of the Institution," and
pointing out what a bargain it was at only two hundred dollars a year, half
of the prewar rates.[31]

The academy had to compete with other schools that advertised in the
Examiner: Mrs. M. M. Reid's Boarding and Day School for Young Ladies in
Palatka, Florida, and the Bay Side Seminary, A Home School for Young
Ladies, in Oyster Bay, Long Island, New York. A citizen identified only as
"Observer" wrote the editor of the *Examiner* in 1867, extolling the work
of the Sisters of Mercy: "[W]e willingly take this opportunity of congratu-
lating with our fellow citizens of St. Augustine and the country around for
the good opportunity they enjoy of giving a thorough, classical scientific
and above all genteel and moral education to their daughters." "Observer"
thought that "it was a very superfluous and rather dangerous experiment
to send those young plants of the South to northern latitudes in the hostile
soil, with so good and substantial opportunities of a good education at
home."[32] Such accolades regarding St. Mary's Academy were common in
the *Examiner.*

Another laudatory remark regarding St. Mary's Academy commented
that the Sisters had succeeded in making the girls not only graceful but
also intellectual. A review of other comments about the academy, however,
demonstrates that special appreciation was accorded the training the girls
received in the finer arts and skills, such as needlework and other handiwork. The prevailing attitudes toward what were suitable activities for
young ladies were represented in the *Examiner* in an article entitled,
"Woman's Scepter, the Needle," in which the writer asserted,

There is something extremely pleasant; and even touching . . . if very sweet, soft and winning effect—in this peculiarity of needle work, distinguishing woman form [sic] man. Our own sex is incapable of any such by play, aside from the business of life; but women . . . have always some handiwork ready to fill the tiny gap of every vacant moment . . . a needle is familiar to the finger of them all . . . and they have greatly the advantage of us in this respect. The slender thread of silk or cotton keeps them united with the small, familiar, gentle interests of life . . . Methinks it is a token of healthy and gentle characteristic when women of high thought and accomplishments love to sew.

It was with great enthusiasm, therefore, that the *Examiner* reported two years later that the French Sisters of St. Joseph not only taught French as their native tongue, but also taught "fancywork" to the boarders at St. Mary's. In such ways, the Sisters of Mercy and St. Joseph fostered the domestic skills and behaviors considered essential for true ladies.[33]

In 1869, a public school was finally established in St. Augustine. The 1868 state constitution had provided for the creation of a public school system, but action was slow in coming. A local Board of Public Instruction was organized in St. Augustine in May 1869 when an agent for the Peabody Education Fund, a nonsectarian body, helped organize a free school committee made up of leaders from St. Augustine's major churches. The town government also contributed toward the support of the Peabody School, and the first classes were held in City Hall. After the Freedmen's Bureau school was closed, a second Peabody School was established for blacks. According to a short article in the *Examiner*, a loan of $800 was obtained to repair the schoolhouse, and the board resolved to apply for state funds to open that school and others in St. Johns County immediately. The Peabody School would be for whites, but the colored school would be continued.[34]

In August 1869, the Sisters of Mercy returned to their convent in Rhode Island and turned St. Mary's Academy over to the Sisters of St. Joseph, who continued their work with white and black students for decades to come. Bishop Verot served St. Augustine until his death in 1876. Two years before his death, at the laying of the cornerstone for a new motherhouse for the Sisters of St. Joseph in St. Augustine, he summarized the spirit of their work by saying, "Wherever these sisters are established they aim above everything else to procure the glory of God by doing good to their neighbor. This building will be a convent, a novitiate for candidates to the sisterhood, and normal school for the training of teachers who will devote their lives to the Christian education of youth." The new building brought about the permanency longed for by the people of St. Augustine, for the Sisters of St. Joseph remain in the Ancient City and continue to teach the community's youth.[35]

Both the Sisters of Mercy and the Sisters of St. Joseph made significant contributions to the cultural development of St. Augustine. As nuns, they assumed a life that was counter to the prevailing ideas concerning a woman's domestic responsibilities to marry and raise her own children, duties that were considered essential to maintain stability in society. It was their commitment to the rules of their orders, their disciplined lives, and their devotion to a life of service, however, that empowered them to become beloved and respected members of the Catholic community in St. Augustine as they became mentors for rising generations of southern ladies and black youth.

The story of the nuns in St. Augustine shows that the strong anti-Catholicism associated with the North in the 1850s had little hold in the South. It also demonstrates the irony that these women, whose lives were restricted by their religious vows and rules of their respective orders, were at the same time, because of those restrictions, free to go to strange lands in ways that were out-of-bounds for other women. Their teachings for white girls, however, were consistent with the prevailing values and prescribed behaviors for American women. In that regard, these supposedly rebellious and dangerous women were actually part of the establishment, fulfilling the expectations of a white, male-dominated society.

Notes

1. Elizabeth Fox-Genovese, *Within the Plantation Household: Black and White Women of the Old South* (Chapel Hill, 1988), 78, 81; Jean E. Friedman, *The Enclosed Garden: Women and Community in the Evangelical South, 1830–1900* (Chapel Hill, 1985).

2. Thomas P. McCarthy, *Guide to the Catholic Sisterhoods in the United States* (Washington, D.C., 1952), passim; Mary Ewens, *The Role of the Nun in Nineteenth Century America* (New York, 1978), 35, 38–9, 87, 326.

3. Randall M. Miller, "A Church in Cultural Captivity: Some Speculations on Catholic Identity in the Old South," in *Catholics in the Old South: Essays on Church and Culture*, ed. Randall M. Miller and Jon L. Wakelyn (Macon, Ga., 1983), 11–2; John Higham, *Strangers in the Land: Patterns in American Nativism, 1860–1925* (Westport, Conn., 1981), 113.

4. Alexis de Tocqueville, quoted in Joseph G. Mannard, "Maternity . . . of the

Spirit: Nuns and Domesticity in Antebellum America," in *The American Catholic Religious Life: Selected Historical Essays*, ed. Joseph M. White (New York, 1988), 129.

5. Mannard, *American Catholic Religious Life*, 131–4; Barbara Welter, "The Cult of True Womanhood, 1820–1860," *American Quarterly* 18 (summer 1966): 152–4.

6. Welter, "Cult of True Womanhood," 162–70.

7. Mannard, *American Catholic Religious Life*, 135.

8. Ibid., 142. See also Fox-Genovese, *Within the Plantation Household*, 203.

9. Michael V. Gannon, *Rebel Bishop: The Life and Era of Augustin Verot* (Milwaukee, 1964), 23.

10. *St. Augustine Examiner*, October 29, 1859. Hereafter cited as *Examiner*.

11. U.S. Census, Miscellaneous Statistics, 1860. St. Johns County then included what is now Flagler County. Gannon, *Rebel Bishop*, 25.

12. Michael V. Gannon, *The Cross in the Sand* (Gainesville, 1965), 152. In 1860, Florida had a population of 140,424. There were only a few cities and towns: the largest included Pensacola (pop. 2,876), Key West (pop. 2,832), Jacksonville (pop. 2,118), Tallahassee (pop. 1,932), and St. Augustine (pop. 1,914); Joseph C. G. Kennedy, *Population of the United States in 1860* (Washington, D.C., 1864), 54; George E. Buker, "The Americanization of St. Augustine, 1821–1865," in *The Oldest City: St. Augustine, Saga of Survival*, ed. Jean Parker Waterbury (St. Augustine, 1983), 158.

13. *Examiner*, October 29, 1859; Gannon, *Cross in the Sand*, 168. Typescript from the Archives of the Sisters of Mercy, Providence, Rhode Island, on file at the Archives of the Sisters of St. Joseph, St. Augustine, 301.2, hereafter cited as Archives; U.S. Census, Population Schedules, St. Johns County, 1860. The census taker misspelled Mother Ligouri's name, entering it as Legoria.

14. *Examiner*, December 31, 1859; Karen Harvey, *St. Augustine and St. Johns County: A Pictorial History* (Virginia Beach, 1980), 117.

15. *Examiner*, February 11, 1860; Gannon, *Rebel Bishop*, 29.

16. *Examiner*, April 6, 1861.

17. Verot, A., *A Tract for the Times. Slavery & Abolitionism Being the Substance of a Sermon. Preached in the Church of St. Augustine. Florida, on the 4th Day of January 1861. Day of Public Humiliation, Fasting and Prayer* (New Orleans, 1861), 5; Gannon, *Rebel Bishop*, 31.

18. Verot, *Tract*, 15; Gannon, *Rebel Bishop*, 31.

19. Verot, *Tract*, 5; Gannon, *Rebel Bishop*, 45–52.

20. Verot, *Tract*, 18–9.

21. Gannon, *Rebel Bishop*, 66 n. 46; Jane Quinn, *The Story of a Nun: Jeanie Gordon Brown* (St. Augustine, 1978), 73, Archives, 301.2; Edward F. Keuchel, "Sister Mary Ann: 'Jacksonville's Angel of Mercy,'" in *Florida's Heritage of Diversity: Essays in Honor of Samuel Proctor*, ed. Mark T. Greenberg, William Rogers, and Canter Brown Jr. (Tallahassee, 1997), 100.

22. Thomas Graham, "The Flagler Era," in Waterbury, *The Oldest City,* 185; Gannon, *Rebel Bishop,* 129–30.

23. Gannon, *Cross in the Sand,* 183–4; Gannon, *Rebel Bishop,* 117.

24. Sister Thomas Joseph McGoldrick, "A Study of the Contributions of the Sisters of St. Joseph of St. Augustine to Education, 1866–1960" (Master's thesis, University of Florida, 1961), 24; Mary Alberta, "A Study of the Schools Conducted by the Sisters of St. Joseph of the Diocese of St. Augustine, Florida, 1866–1940" (Master's thesis, University of Florida, 1940), 3.

25. Mary Alberta, "Study of the Schools."

26. Joe M. Richardson, "We are truly doing missionary work: Letters from American Missionary Association Teachers in Florida, 1864–1874," *Florida Historical Quarterly* 54 (October 1975): 184; Jacqueline Jones, *Soldiers of Light and Love: Northern Teachers and Georgia Blacks, 1865–1873* (Chapel Hill, 1980), 19, 25, 155. Joe M. Richardson, *The Negro in the Reconstruction of Florida, 1865–1877,* Florida State University Studies no. 46 (Tallahassee, 1965), 86; Gannon, *Cross in the Sand,* 184.

27. *Examiner,* August 17, 1867.

28. Gannon, *Cross in the Sand,* 184. Mary Alberta, "Study of the Schools," 8.

29. *Examiner,* November 10, 1866.

30. Mary Alberta, "Study of the Schools," 49.

31. *Examiner,* October 17, 1868.

32. *Examiner,* August 17, 1867.

33. *Examiner,* November 3, 1866, July 6, 1867, May 30, 1868, March 20, 1869.

34. From 1868 to 1897, George Peabody, an American philanthropist then living in England, donated $3.5 million to encourage education for all races in the South. Between 1868 and September 1897, Florida received $67,375 from the fund. J.L.M. Curry, *Brief Sketch of George Peabody, and History of the Peabody Education Fund Through Thirty Years* (New York, 1969), 147; Graham, "The Flagler Era," 185; *Examiner,* May 8, 1869.

35. Quinn, *Story of a Nun,* 79.

7

The Rise of the United Daughters
of the Confederacy, 1894–1914

KAREN L. COX

When President-General Lizzie George Henderson attributed the United Daughters of the Confederacy's (UDC) rapid growth to God's influence in 1907, she was able to point to membership rolls for proof of what she regarded as Divine assistance. The UDC filled a void in the lives of thousands of southern women eager to join a voluntary organization whose goals were, by definition, conservative. Attracted by the organization's mission, they responded by joining in large numbers. One year after the UDC was formed in 1894, twenty chapters were chartered representing women in Tennessee, Georgia, North Carolina, South Carolina, Virginia, Maryland, Texas, Kentucky, and Washington, D.C. Within two years, there were 89 chapters, and by the third year 138 chapters were actively pursuing the organization's goals. The UDC's growth was so phenomenal that within a few years railroad companies offered the Daughters discounted travel to their conventions. The small group of women who met in Nashville in 1894 had grown to nearly 30,000 women, a remarkable rise, in just ten years. The Texas Division alone reported nearly 5,000 members in 1902, and by the end of World War I, the organization claimed a membership of nearly 100,000 women.[1]

Southern women joined other organizations as well, but joined the Daughters in greater numbers. In 1902, when the UDC had close to 30,000 members, the total membership in the southern state federations of the General Federation of Women's Clubs (GFWC) was less than half that number. Southern state memberships in the Woman's Christian Temperance Union (WCTU) in 1900, the last time the organization kept such records, were less than 6,500.[2] At their peak, southern suffragists numbered just over 13,000. The UDC offered southern women something unique. Like other organizations, it offered a social and cultural outlet and the opportunity to engage in progressive reform. UDC membership, however, meant that women could use that opportunity to vindicate the Confederate generation and simultaneously uphold the values of their race and class. Ironically, it also gave them respectability within the traditionally male sphere of politics—a cachet they often used to their advantage.[3]

The UDC was active at the local, state, and national levels. It was primarily an urban voluntary organization; chapters were organized in small towns and cities and were required to have a minimum of seven members. When three chapters formed within a state, a state division was created whereby officers were elected at annual conventions.[4] While most of the membership of the UDC was drawn from the South, chapters were organized wherever seven white female descendants of Confederate ancestors banded together. During the early twentieth century, the Daughters were represented in several states outside of the region—in California, New York, and Illinois, to name a few. Thus, the UDC's claim that it was a national organization was legitimate.

Southern women were attracted to the UDC for many reasons. Prestige and elite social status accompanied membership in the organization. Women were able to command considerable influence through the UDC, as they perpetuated a conservative ideology and agenda consistent with the politics of white supremacy. Southern women who lived outside the region, in places like Ohio, Montana, and Pennsylvania, joined the organization despite living in what they described as a "hostile atmosphere." According to the UDC, the organization had such a stronghold in San Francisco that "women of Northern birth" were in a desperate search for a relative "whose services to the Confederate cause might render them eligible" for membership.[5] The UDC's initial success was certainly helped by the natural constituency provided by the Ladies Memorial Associations (LMA). Cofounder Anna Davenport Raines insisted that members of memorial associations join the UDC. Katie Cabell Currie of Texas, an early officer and later president-general of the national organization, sent a message to the 1898 Alabama state convention urging memorial associations "to merge into the Daughters of the Confederacy." Two years later, Mississippi's president, Josie Frazee Cappleman, noted that members of memorial associations, as well as their daughters and granddaughters, were "gradually falling into the new order of [UDC]." At the 1903 meeting of the Georgia UDC, state historian Mildred Lewis Rutherford reiterated the plea of her fellow Georgian, Anna Davenport Raines, that "the members of one general body should be the members of the other."[6]

Kate Mason Rowland, who served as the general organization's corresponding secretary in 1896 and 1897, encouraged women to join the UDC, expressing great confidence in the Daughters' mission. A frequent contributor to the *Confederate Veteran*, she contacted numerous individuals, often women of prominence in their local communities, to organize a UDC chapter. "We are the latest of the hereditary societies," Rowland wrote one woman, "but we do not wish to be the smallest." In a letter to the head of a United Confederate Veterans (UCV) camp imploring him to encourage members of its auxiliary to join the UDC, she bragged, "[I]f it is considered an honor now to have descent to a Revolutionary Patriot, we esteem it equally glorious to belong to the families of those who fought in a cause so holy and as just in 1861–65."[7]

Most of the women who joined the UDC within the first decade of its founding belonged to the second generation of women active in the Lost Cause. Their mothers had belonged to memorial associations, and now they wished to assume their place within the new order. Others were new to the work of the Lost Cause, particularly northern women who had married southern men and were accepted into the organization based on the biblical principle that "the twain shall be one flesh." As the organization grew, however, the leadership became increasingly concerned that not all southern women were worthy of becoming Daughters. Aware of the drawing power of an organization perceived as elite, UDC leaders were intent upon preserving the UDC's exclusive reputation. They wanted the organization to grow, but also wanted a membership that exemplified upper-class or patrician values. Cofounder Anna Raines argued that voluntary associations were not "compelled to receive as a member one who is morally or otherwise objectionable."[8]

The extraordinary growth experienced by the UDC during its first two decades actually alarmed leaders, who subsequently recommended restrictions on membership. In her report to the General Convention of 1911, President-General Virginia McSherry of West Virginia proposed that chapters were "not obliged to accept as a member one who is not personally acceptable to the chapter." In 1912, her successor, Rassie Hoskins White of Tennessee, recommended precautionary measures to further limit eligibility. "As the organization grows in strength, popularity and prominence," she asserted, "membership in it becomes more desirable, and therefore should be hedged about and protected by more stringent rules." White knew something about status, as she had married a banker in her hometown of Paris, Tennessee, and was regarded as one of its prominent residents.[9]

Though women were attracted to the UDC because of its social status, clearly the organization's success rested on an active membership with the desire and ability to accomplish broad objectives intended to the vindicate Confederate men and preserve Confederate culture for future generations. Many women joined the organization out of a real sense of duty and responsibility to honor the Confederate generation and to instill the values of those men and women among future generations of white southerners. Mississippian Virginia Redditt Price referred to the work of the Daughters as fulfilling a "sacred obligation." Indeed, vindication of the Confederate generation was "the promise you virtually make when you become a UDC." Price prized her membership in the organization and proclaimed that because she had been born and reared in the South, she valued her membership in the UDC above her membership in other women's organizations. Caroline Meriwether Goodlett, cofounder of the organization, concurred. After repeated requests to join the Daughters of the American Revolution (DAR) in the early 1890s, Goodlett proclaimed, "I am prouder to be known as a Daughter of the Confederacy."[10]

Membership in the UDC also seemed to touch an emotional chord with southern women. Addressing the 1913 UDC convention in New Orleans, President-General Rassie White reflected upon the importance of the UDC to its members. "Long ago I discovered it was not a hobby with any of us, but is and has been from the very beginning, a serious work," she told those in attendance. White felt that defending the Confederate past gripped "the very hearts of Southern women." Indeed, the Daughters were personally motivated to defend the actions of their mothers and fathers, and their membership in the UDC had become central to their lives. As White's daughter remarked accusingly, "[I]f you are not talking 'Daughters' you are thinking 'Daughters.'"[11]

The UDC swiftly became a powerful and influential women's organization in the early twentieth century, not only in terms of its numbers, but also in its ability to accomplish goals on behalf of Confederate causes. It was an organization that allowed southern women to assert their influence as public figures and to maintain their image as traditional women. As President-General Rassie Hoskins White put it, "I love the United Daughters of the Confederacy because they have demonstrated that Southern women may organize themselves into a nationwide body without losing womanly dignity, sweetness, or graciousness."[12]

As the UDC grew in numbers and influence, behaving like "southern ladies" gave the organization respectability while also serving as the source of its power. "We are not a body of discontented suffragists thirst-ing for oratorical honors," Anna Raines reminded members in 1897, even though some members participated in the suffrage movement. Instead, they considered themselves a "sisterhood of earnest, womanly women." Ten years later when the UDC held its convention in Norfolk, within a short distance of the Jamestown Exposition, President-General Lizzie Henderson reminded delegates that people from around the world who had come for the exposition were interested in how southern women "con-duct their conventions." She advised delegates to keep the scrutiny of "hy-percritical eyes" in mind and urged each delegate to uphold the reputation of southern women as "high-toned, courteous, gentle-mannered ladies."[13]

Women who joined the UDC between 1894 and 1919 were, in many respects, a diverse group. Daughters also belonged to a variety of women's organizations, including hereditary societies such as the DAR, Colonial Dames, the Daughters of 1812, and, in the West, the Daughters of the Re-public of Texas. UDC members also belonged to the WCTU, the Young Women's Christian Association (YWCA), and the King's Daughters, a Christian organization of single women whose work often benefited com-munity hospitals. Some Daughters were suffragists, while others were virulent antisuffragists. The UDC was active in cities as dissimilar as Sa-vannah, Georgia, and Tacoma, Washington. Its membership included Epis-copalians, Presbyterians, Methodists, Baptists, Jews, and Catholics. The di-versity within the UDC, however, was balanced by those factors that made these women similar: gender, race, class, and a common Confederate heri-tage.[14]

Comparisons between the UDC and other women's organizations prove difficult when there was such a cross-pollination of membership. The goals of one were often the goals of another; education and reform were central to the agenda of many women's organizations. Many women's groups also had a similar organizational structure in which the real work was being done at the state level. What made the UDC different was its emphasis on Confederate culture with its goal of preserving the values of their race as well as class.

The oldest members of the UDC, those born between 1820 and 1850, had experienced the Civil War as adults. In many cases, at least one male relative had died in battle. When the war was over, these women became members of their local LMA. In fact, they had engaged in considerable Confederate memorial activity by the time the UDC was founded; becom-ing a member of the Daughters was just another stage in their evolution as

Lost Cause women. Finally, their activity as public women extended beyond the celebration of the Lost Cause, as they joined numerous women's organizations, many of which were reform-oriented.

UDC cofounder Caroline Goodlett was representative of this older generation. Born in 1833 in Todd County, Kentucky, she was in her late twenties when the war broke out. Her brother was killed during the first year of the conflict, and throughout the war she helped sew uniforms, roll bandages, and care for wounded soldiers. She became active in memorial work immediately after the war. In 1866, she joined a benevolent society that raised money for artificial limbs for Confederate veterans. Goodlett also belonged to the Monument Association in Nashville and headed the Ladies' Auxiliary to the Tennessee Soldiers' Home. In many respects, Goodlett's role in the creation of the UDC was the culmination of her experience as an active participant in the Confederate tradition.

After her term as the first UDC president, Goodlett turned her attention to reform in her own state. She served on the Board of Managers of the Protestant Orphan Asylum and Mission Home, was vice president of the Humane Society of Nashville, and was a member of the Ladies' Auxiliary to the Masonic Widows' and Orphans' Home. Goodlett explained to a later president of the UDC that she did not seek notoriety from her Confederate work. "I am known in my own State," she wrote, "as a woman who is interested in all measures proposed for the good of the people of the State." In fact, she lobbied her legislators to pass a bill raising the age of consent from sixteen to eighteen years. She proposed a bill to build a home for "feeble-minded children" and urged the state legislature to "abolish whipping women in the Penitentiary." Goodlett obviously saw her work in behalf of Confederate veterans as one of her many reform interests.[15]

Cornelia Branch Stone, a contemporary of Goodlett, offers an instructive example of women whose experiences in other voluntary organizations prepared them for UDC's top office. A resident of Galveston, Texas, Stone was born in 1840 and became president-general of the UDC in 1908. She also belonged to the Confederated Southern Memorial Associations (CSMA), the Daughters of the Republic of Texas, Colonial Dames, and DAR. Serving as president-general of a state division was regarded as critical experience before ascending to the UDC presidency, and Stone's case was no exception. Her leadership in other organizations, moreover, was typical of women who served as president-general of the UDC in the first two decades of the organization. By the time Stone came to head the UDC, she had served as president of the Texas Woman's Press Association, as first vice president of the Texas Federation of Women's Clubs (TXFWC), and corresponding secretary for the Colonial Dames.[16]

A position of leadership in the UDC was regarded by many as a significant public achievement. Election to the organization's highest office, president-general, meant election to one of the most powerful political positions a southern woman could hold in the late nineteenth and early twentieth centuries. The president-general of the UDC wielded considerable power, as she summoned the support of literally thousands of southern women when it suited her cause. Moreover, as the UDC grew in size and influence, the president-general was invited to represent the organization at veterans' reunions, at monument unveilings, and at the meetings of other women's organizations. Presidents Theodore Roosevelt, William Howard Taft, and Woodrow Wilson all hosted a UDC president-general at the White House.[17]

Many UDC members, like Goodlett and Stone, engaged in some aspect of progressive reform. Virginia Clay Clopton, a member from Alabama once married to U.S. Senator Clement C. Clay, Jr., and later to a judge, lobbied for woman suffrage through the Equal Suffrage Association for more than twenty years. Rebecca Latimer Felton of Georgia, the wealthy widow of former U.S. Congressman Dr. W. H. Felton, supported woman suffrage and worked to reform education for the uplift of rural white women. While with the TXFWC, Cornelia Stone, described by a contemporary as "one of the bright and brainy women of the Southland," chaired a committee that lobbied for an amendment to better enforce her state's poll tax law to increase funds to public schools. Historian Judith N. McArthur argues that southern women increasingly participated in reform even though they faced criticism for their public activity. UDC members, however, were able to avoid much of this criticism because of their dedication to rehabilitating the image of Confederate men.[18]

Most of the women who joined the UDC between 1894 and 1919 were born after 1850. Of the fifteen women elected president-general of the UDC between 1894 and 1919, more than half were born after mid-century. They were literally daughters of the Confederacy, and often they were daughters of Confederate officers. Some of them were children during the Civil War and had memories of its devastating impact on their families. Those women born during or soon after the war experienced Reconstruction as children or teenagers, and had participated in Memorial Day exercises as young girls. Their opinions about the war were largely shaped by Confederate men and women whose loss was transformed into bitterness, particularly during Reconstruction. For nearly all whites in the region, Reconstruction was the South's "tragic era," an insult added to injury. Carpetbaggers, scalawags, and "ignorant" freedmen, they believed, had forced change on an unwilling South. Not surprisingly, they regarded the Ku Klux Klan (KKK) of Reconstruction as the South's redeemer.[19]

UDC members born after 1850, therefore, developed their perceptions about the Old South based on their parents' memories. Nevertheless, this generation of southern women was moved to defend the patrician culture of the Old South and to seek vindication for their parents. Images of plantations and faithful slaves held more appeal than the "dark days" of Reconstruction in which they had grown to maturity. The agrarian past, moreover, provided a stark contrast to the problems of industrialization they associated with plans for a "New South"—a term that was an expletive in their vocabulary. By the time this younger generation of women reached adulthood, the Old South had been idealized through the narrative of the Lost Cause. So too had the women of the Old South, who were portrayed as models of femininity to be both celebrated and emulated. For this generation, myth had replaced reality.[20]

UDC members had much invested in preserving the social structure and culture of the Old South. Clearly, they shared the privileges that accompanied membership in their race and class. And while information on the rank and file of the UDC has not been preserved, an examination of the presidents-general in the period between 1894 and 1919 suggests an organization led by social elites who were related by blood or marriage to men of power and influence in the region.

Ellen Foule Lee (president-general, 1897–99) was married to Robert E. Lee's nephew Fitzhugh Lee, governor of Virginia in the late 1880s. Lizzie George Henderson (president-general, 1905–7) attended Fair Lawn Institute in Jackson, Mississippi, described as "a young ladies' school of the Old South." She was the daughter of U.S. Senator James Z. George, author of the "Mississippi Plan" that included the infamous disfranchisement clause adopted by southern state governments to sidestep the Fifteenth Amendment. Daisy McLaurin Stevens (president-general, 1913–5), another Mississippian, was the daughter of Anselm J. McLaurin, who served as that state's governor and later as U.S. senator. She was educated locally at the Brandon Female Seminary and was married to a state judge. Virginia Faulkner McSherry (president-general, 1909–11) of West Virginia was the daughter of Charles J. Faulkner, a U.S. congressman and later minister to France before becoming a member of General Thomas "Stonewall"

Jackson's staff. Cordelia Powell Odenheimer (president-general 1915–17) of Maryland was the daughter of a Confederate captain. Mary Poppenheim (president-general 1917–18) was the daughter of a Confederate officer and graduated from Vassar in 1888, where she was vice president of the student body.[21]

These presidents-general were not atypical of the membership. They initially joined the UDC as members of the rank and file and made their way to the organization's senior position by first holding local and state offices. Of the fifteen women who served as president-general between 1894 and 1919, seven (46 percent) of them were under the age of fifty when they were elected. Among the eight remaining presidents-general, one half of them were less than sixty years old. The oldest woman to assume the post of president-general, Cornelia Branch Stone, was sixty-seven when elected. The youngest woman, Hallie Alexander Rounsaville of Georgia, was just thirty-seven when she assumed the UDC's highest office in 1901; eleven years earlier, at the age of 26, she was a charter member of the national DAR. On the whole, the Daughters were women who had the youthful energy required to meet the organization's objectives. They were not, as has been assumed, the "gray-haired friends" of the UCV.[22] And though these younger representatives may not have experienced the war firsthand, their quest to vindicate Confederate men and women was extremely personal. Indeed, the men and women they wished to honor were their parents and grandparents.

Mildred Lewis Rutherford, probably the best-known member of the UDC, is representative of the generation of Daughters who had grown up in a defeated region. Born in Athens, Georgia, in 1851, Rutherford need to look no further than her own backyard for evidence of war's destruction. She was educated locally at the Lucy Cobb Institute and later became its president. In 1888, at the age of thirty-seven, she was elected president of the Athens Ladies' Memorial Association—a post she held the rest of her life. Between 1901 and 1903 she served as president of the Georgia Division of the UDC and in 1905 was appointed "Historian-General for Life" in her state. She eventually became historian-general for the general organization, a post she held for five years during which time she became a celebrity within Lost Cause circles.[23]

Rutherford crusaded for "truthful" histories of the Civil War, often appearing in 1860s costume, her hair in Spaniel curls. All Daughters considered "true history" to be a primary means of achieving vindication. Rutherford used her position of leadership to promote a prosouthern view of events, and she defended traditional roles for men and women as well as the preservation of white supremacy. She believed that women of the Old South, plantation mistresses to be exact, represented a feminine ideal worthy of preservation. For Rutherford, true men were chivalrous and true women were genteel and deferential to their men. African Americans, moreover, should remain faithful to their former masters if the New South were to resemble the Old South she longed for.[24]

Rutherford's stance on the question of woman suffrage reveals the influence tradition and the Lost Cause had on her life. A member of the Georgia Association Opposed to Woman Suffrage, Rutherford vociferously condemned the drive to win the vote, believing that many of the South's traditions were under attack. Not only were states' rights in jeopardy, but so were traditional gender roles. In expressing her "violent" opposition to suffrage for women, she personally addressed the Georgia House of Representatives committee that dealt with the question of woman suffrage. The irony of this overtly political action, given that she was opposed to women's involvement in politics generally, was apparently lost on her.[25]

Rutherford opposed the amendment by summoning images of the Old South. "[Go] back to your ideals of manhood," she scolded committee members, and "remember chivalry of old, yours by inheritance." Rutherford believed that women should also look to the past, "back to the home and those God-given rights." Like other Lost Cause women, she celebrated female role models of the Old South and admonished her female peers to "turn backward in loving emulation to the ideals set by the mothers and grandmothers of yesterday."[26]

Though a celebrity among UDC women, Rutherford was typical of the Daughters in many respects. For while she worked to preserve tradition and the values associated with Confederate culture, she did so by taking advantage of the public forum created in part by Lost Cause women, but also by social change. Advancements in education, progressive reform, and women's increased participation in voluntary organizations opened new doors for southern women, creating a dilemma for women like Rutherford who sought to remake the New South in the image of the Old. At the same time, the politics of Jim Crow supported her expression of conservative values and racist beliefs.[27]

In many ways Rutherford and members of the UDC stood at the crossroads of the Old and New South. They were very much a product of the past and romanticized the Old South, yet they were visibly caught up in the changes occurring in the New South, particularly those affecting women. As historian Marjorie Spruill Wheeler argues, southern suffragists understood that their activities as "New Women" were often tempered by the fact that these same southern women were also "hostage" to the Lost Cause and its traditional definitions of womanhood.[28]

The Daughters, continuing in the footsteps of the LMA, intended to resurrect southern men from the doldrums of defeat by reassuring them that the cause they fought for was just and that women were willing, if only rhetorically, to reassume a primarily domestic role. And even though the Daughters had become influential public women, they continued to present their work as that of a helpmeet.

More than any other single UDC member, Elizabeth Lumpkin, a favorite speaker at veterans' reunions, eloquently expressed these sentiments. Born in Georgia in 1880 to former planter elite, Lumpkin was educated and grew up listening to stories of the Confederacy from her father. Like many young women of her generation, she came to admire white womanhood in the Old South as characterized by the "southern lady." Referring to that feminine ideal, she told a group of Georgia veterans in 1904, "I would rather be a woman than a man. . . . What woman would not, if she could be a Southern woman and be loved by Southern men?"[29]

Lumpkin's speeches were purposefully crafted for the moral uplift of aging Confederate men. When she addressed throngs of veterans, she regaled them with stories of their youth when, according to the Lost Cause fiction in which they all believed, southern men were real men. Then she returned to the present, proclaiming how much the women of her day envied Confederate women. "We can work with tireless fingers, we can run with tireless feet for these men; but they [Confederate women] could love and marry Confederate soldiers!"[30]

The local press hailed Elizabeth Lumpkin's gifts as an orator wherever she spoke. The *Confederate Veteran* remarked that her speaking ability was not exaggerated, and that her oration at the Louisville reunion was "thrilling and penetrating." Dr. F. L. Powell, another speaker at the reunion, described her sway over the audience by proclaiming, "[Y]ou could put a flag in her hands and conquer the world."[31] Lumpkin was the Confederate woman reincarnated, devoted to the purposes of the Lost Cause. According to legend, southern women were the last to give up the fight. Similarly, Lumpkin had a "never say die" attitude regarding the agrarian past; in fact, it became a central theme in her speeches. "If we say that the glory of the Old South is dead," she dramatically told veterans, "skeleton hands will rise again and fold the old flag in loving embrace, socketless

eyes will blaze again with the glory of that dear past, and skeleton teeth
will chatter again the old Rebel yell." It is no wonder that Lumpkin's
speeches were often interrupted by "thunderous applause."[32]

The image of womanhood Lumpkin projected was based in tradition,
yet it was tradition personified by the public activity of women and a New
South. Lumpkin was an enormously popular public figure in the Lost
Cause because she represented traditional womanhood—cultivation, refinement, and gentility. Yet, in significant ways, she was a "New Woman."
She was well educated and skilled in oration—able to step outside the
bounds of domesticity, stand atop the speakers' platform at a veterans' reunion, and still be admired for typifying tradition. This blending of Old
and New South identities worked well for Lumpkin and was the formula
for success for thousands of women who participated in the Lost Cause in
the early twentieth century.

One of the most striking aspects of this extraordinary group of southern women in the UDC was that they had, to a degree, been emboldened
and empowered by the women they admired: the women of the 1860s.
Confederate women, according to the Lost Cause narrative, had one foot
planted in the domestic sphere and one in the public sphere. On the one
hand, women of the "old regime" were described as "the finest types of
true womanhood; refined, cultivated, gentle; devoted wives, good mothers,
kind mistresses, and splendid homemakers." Yet they were also lauded for
being more patriotic than southern men, for being "Spartan women" or
women who demonstrated "Spartan endurance." Indeed, Lost Cause literature often portrayed Confederate women as individuals who maintained the virtues of domesticity even as they rose to face the public challenges of war. To the extent that their Confederate mothers had been
"liberated" by the gender upheaval caused by the experience of war,
women of the Lost Cause had been liberated, but only to that extent.[33]

The same terms used by Lost Cause devotees to characterize Confederate women were often invoked to describe the Daughters. UDC members
were often portrayed as powerful yet genteel women. Kate Litton Hick-
man, a founding member of the UDC, was described by a friend as "a
Josephine in diplomatic power and a Marie Antoinette in graciousness and
in the power of winning hearts." Such characterizations indicate how the
Daughters managed to maintain their image as traditional yet public-
minded women.[34]

While the Daughters existed to honor tradition, much of their activity,
collectively and individually, also placed them in the category historians
describe as "New Women." Indeed, the Daughters carved a niche for them-

selves in the political culture of the New South as preservers of tradition. The source of their power, in fact, lay in their ability to employ the "indirect influence" of the southern lady in order to gain access to politicians, as well as to maintain control over the public celebration of the Lost Cause. They also drew power from the example set by women of the 1860s. Just as women had played a critical public role in the Confederate cause, the Daughters had a critical public role to play in the vindication of the Confederate generation. It was the Daughters' charge, Florence Barlow asserted as editor of *The Lost Cause*, to come to the "defense of Southern integrity."[35]

Tradition was important to the Lost Cause because it defined not only the role that women were to play, but men as well. Within the Confederate tradition, both women and men accepted a particular set of traits as "typical" of southern womanhood and southern manhood. Such ideas were largely derived from the Lost Cause narrative, a class-based fiction in which such ideals were represented by the Old South elite. The Lost Cause narrative generally ignored poor whites, and former slaves were little more than racist caricatures of devoted "uncles" and "mammies." Moreover, the term *faithful slaves* grouped males and females together, disregarding their individuality.[36]

The men and women who constituted the generation of the sixties, therefore, were the men and women whom the Daughters chose as role models for their own generation. Mildred Rutherford argued as much as late as 1912, when she said, "[T]he men of today and the women of today are adjusting themselves to the Old South remade." While the Daughters sought to emulate southern womanhood of the 1860s, however, their male contemporaries were often criticized for their lagging interest in the ways of the Old South. UDC members, in fact, often prodded or made excuses for the South's "New Men" who were disinterested in emulating their Confederate fathers, and for good reason.[37]

The South's New Men were markedly different from their Confederate fathers. In the Old South, men had earned their living in a plantation economy, while New Men, according to the emerging myth, were self-made businessmen who helped build the towns and cities of the New South. These younger men were less interested in preserving their Confederate heritage than in creating a foundation for their own power based on their business interests.[38]

The South's New Men also operated in a world that had changed considerably since the Civil War. Many of these young men had fought in the U.S. army, rather than against it, during the Spanish-American War. According to historian Nina Silber, northerners accepted the South's military service as proof of southern "manliness" as well as patriotism. Southern men held views consistent with men who lived outside the region. They employed the language of empire, a language in accord with racial theory in the 1890s. Anglo-Saxonism and the belief in the superiority of "white civilization" were, to be sure, consistent with the goals of southern politicians. In the late nineteenth and early twentieth centuries white supremacy, politically sanctioned in the South, had become integral to the new emphasis on American nationalism.[39]

The world and the self-image of New Men, therefore, stood in stark contrast to the provincial world of their fathers. While Old South men lived in a region that relied solely on agriculture, New South men lived in a region that offered them economic diversity. In the New South, business was more diversified. In addition to agriculture, men engaged in mining, textiles manufacturing, and railroad building. A region consumed with business interests, however, spurred discussion that pitted the values of this New South with the agrarian values of the Old. The Daughters blamed New Men for the trend to abandon the agrarian past, and Confederate veterans joined in the criticism. New Men, according to UDC and UCV members, were more concerned with making money than with honoring their ancestors.

To be sure, New Men were much less likely than their female contemporaries to see their Confederate fathers, the defeated, as role models. They regarded themselves as more powerful and successful, eager to shed the burden of defeat. As historian Glenda Gilmore explains in *Gender and Jim Crow*, the South's New Men "had ample evidence that the older generation of men had mistreated white women by failing to provide for them after the Civil War." They believed that they had proven themselves better able to provide for southern women. They certainly made a point of proclaiming their allegiance to the patrician ideals of the Old South. And they regarded disfranchisement and their success in reestablishing white supremacy as evidence of their chivalry and ability to protect white women. Yet they were clearly focused on the region's future, and their interests were linked to the new business ventures of the era.[40]

New Men may have been reluctant to take an active role in the Confederate celebration, but they were willing as businessmen and as elected public officials to assist the Daughters. Indeed, as UDC petitions for monument funds came before local and state governments, men often granted the Daughters the financial support they sought. Though appreciative of receiving financial assistance, the Daughters nevertheless believed that these same men should join them in the campaign to honor the generation of the sixties.

Members of the UDC and UCV lamented the lack of enthusiasm displayed by the new generation of leading southern men. "Our younger men," wrote a member of the UDC in 1911, "are sordidly forgetting the past in the getting of a dollar." Speaking to a meeting of the UDC in Nashville, Judge J. M. Dickinson complained that "at times Southern men seem lethargic if not indifferent" to the commemoration of their heritage. An article in the *Confederate Veteran* went further, claiming that the Sons of Confederate Veterans (SCV) "had in many respects become a hindrance rather than a blessing to the cause for which it was created." New Men, in other words, appeared to eschew a role in the Confederate celebration, choosing instead to devote their attention to business and industry.[41] By the beginning of the twentieth century, southern men had deferred to southern women as "the sole protectors of the honor of ancestors." Still, women continued to criticize them for their conspicuous absence from the Confederate celebration.[42]

The founding of the SCV in 1896 did not do much to change women's minds about what they generally viewed as men's apathy. "It is good for women to do their part," a South Carolina Daughter wrote in 1897, but "we cannot make healthy manhood by standing in its place and assuming its obligations." She was not alone in her belief that young men, both in and out of the SCV, had an obligatory role to play in continuing the celebration, nor was she alone in her awareness that responsibility for the Lost Cause celebration had been shifted almost entirely to women.[43] One veteran complained of the complacency of the SCV membership, noting that the majority of its members had left the duty of preserving Confederate culture "to the willing Daughters." He plead with the SCV not to allow "commercialism" to affect their duty to this important work, arguing that "there is no excuse for man allowing money to dwarf exalting memories."[44]

UDC members were clearly frustrated by this lack of interest in behalf of the Lost Cause. In their view, young men ignored the fact that they were morally and politically indebted to their Confederate ancestors. Yet according to historian Donald Doyle, many of these men, though sons of Confederate veterans, were not descended from planter families and, therefore, were not personally motivated to preserve agrarian traditions. Thus, the Daughters' continued reverence for their forbears, many of whom were of the planter class, set them apart from New Men whose fathers had been common soldiers. Still, women's dedication in the face of men's indifference served as a powerful bargaining chip for the UDC. New Men may have been unwilling to join women in the Confederate celebration, but these same men resolved to support UDC objectives financially, through allocations from local and state budgets and private donations. Indeed, the UDC demanded that male descendants of Confederate veterans participate in the effort to preserve Confederate culture, even if they only provided financial support.[45]

By the end of the first decade of the twentieth century, the Daughters had toned down their criticism of New Men, and began to make excuses for what they had once regarded as apathy. They agreed instead to accept men's considerable financial participation in the Lost Cause. President-General Lizzie Henderson offered her own explanation about why the responsibility for preserving southern heritage was not shared equally by the SCV. After all, they too were lineal descendants of Confederate veterans. The SCV, she told the Daughters, "are the busy men of today . . . They do not have time for these things." A few years later, in 1913, President-General Rassie White also excused SCV members by stating that they were "active business men with little time to give to this work." If the SCV did not have the time, the UDC was still committed to honoring the generation of the sixties. Indeed, the Daughters accepted the task as their very own, maintaining their dedication to honor the Confederate dead and to serve those still living.[46]

From its beginning in 1894, the UDC saw its role as defender and preserver of Confederate culture as similar to the role played by southern women of the Confederacy. Tapping into the wellspring of sentiment for the Confederate generation, and following the example of the women of the sixties in active support of a cause, the UDC steadily grew in numbers and influence. "As the women of the South in the past were steadfast, true, and loyal," Elizabeth Lumpkin reminded Georgia veterans, "so the women of the South in the future will be loyal and true forever." The Daughters abided by this model of loyalty and made a conscious attempt to conform to the image of the "Southern lady." That southern men often referred to UDC members as the finest examples of womanhood is a testament to their success in living up to the ideal.[47]

The Daughters played a prominent role in the public life of the South from the 1890s through World War I. They reaffirmed the region's conservative traditions, even as they expanded woman's sphere. The extent of their influence provides ample evidence that traditional methods of feminine power were effective, particularly when used in support of conservative goals. Yet this era was also a time when increasing numbers of southern women went to college, engaged in occupations outside the home, and attacked the evils of society as organized reformers. UDC members were part of this new tradition too. They achieved enormous success because they were able to draw upon both traditions. The most visible of their accomplishments, of course, are the hundreds of monuments that mark the southern landscape. Yet even these stone testimonials barely hint at what the Daughters accomplished in their campaign to vindicate Confederate veterans.

The results were mixed at best. By their own account, UDC members achieved great success in their campaign to resurrect Confederate culture. For southern blacks, however, that success came with negative repercussions. By promoting a vision of the New South based on the Old, the Daughters helped to preserve white supremacy for at least one more generation—the generation of massive resistance to racial integration.

Notes

1. "United Daughters of the South," *Confederate Veteran* (hereafter cited as *CV*), December 1895, 374–7; "Daughters of the Confederacy," *CV,* January 1897, 34; and "United Daughters Reunion," *CV,* October 1897, 498–503. Actual figures on the total number of members in the UDC are unavailable for the first few years, but the published minutes of the annual conventions sometimes provide approximate estimates of total membership. I have estimated 30,000 members by 1904 based on a report in 1902 that claimed 25,000, of which close to 5,000 were from Texas; "Daughters of the Confederacy," *CV,* January 1902, 9. At the 1913 convention, President-General Rassie White claimed in her report to the convention that the UDC had a "membership of over 90,000," *Minutes of the Twentieth Annual Convention,* 13, Virginia Historical Society. The figure of 100,000 was reported in the *Minutes of the Twenty-Fifth Annual Convention,* 324. The Tennessee UDC, for example, grew by 1,000 members between 1906 and 1907; see "The Tennessee Division, UDC," *CV,* June 1907, 301.

2. The total is derived from WCTU membership records for the states of Alabama, Arkansas, Georgia, Louisiana, Mississippi, North Carolina, South Carolina, Tennessee, Texas, and Virginia as published in the *Women's Christian Temperance Union, Convention Minutes for 1900* (Chicago, 1900), facing page 112.

3. Membership numbers from *General Federation of Women's Clubs, Membership Records (Directories)*, 1890–1910, GFWC Archives, Washington, D.C. Source of membership numbers for southern suffragists comes from Elna C. Green, *Southern Strategies: Southern Women and the Woman Suffrage Question* (Chapel Hill, 1997).

4. The organization's annual meetings were, and still are, known as "general conventions" and will hereafter be referred to as such.

5. Historical Report, *Minutes of the Tenth Annual Convention*, 119.

6. "Convention Alabama Division UDC," *CV,* April 1898, 155; UDC, *Minutes of the Seventh Annual Convention*, 98–9; Mildred Rutherford, "Confederate Monuments and Cemeteries," *CV,* January 1903, 17.

7. Kate Mason Rowland to Mrs. R. Halm, and Kate Mason Rowland to Colonel Oswald Tilghman, in Kate Mason Rowland Letterbook, 1896–97, UDC Collection, Eleanor S. Brockenbrough Library, Museum of the Confederacy, Richmond, Va. (hereafter cited as MC).

8. A. M. Raines to Mrs. Parsley, February 10, 1896, Parsley Family Papers, Southern Historical Collection (SHC).

9. Quotation from Virginia McSherry, President-General's Report, UDC *Minutes of the Eighteenth Annual Convention*, 98–9; quotation from White, President-General's Report, UDC, *Minutes of the Nineteenth Annual Convention*, 95.

10. "Why I Am a UDC?" Virginia Redditt Price, *Our Heritage*, September 1913, 2; Caroline Goodlett to Mrs. L. H. Raines, April 24, 1894, T. S. Rutherford Scrapbook, vol. 11, MC. Historian Anastatia Sims found that the UDC was the most popular of the women's voluntary organizations in North Carolina, often affecting the membership rolls in other organizations; see Sims, *The Power of Femininity in the New South: Women's Organizations and Politics in North Carolina, 1880–1930* (Columbia, 1997).

11. Address of Mrs. Alexander White, *Minutes of the Twentieth Convention*, 12–3.

12. Ibid., 13.

13. Raines, quoted from "Daughters of the Confederacy," *CV,* January 1897, 34. Woman suffrage provoked a hostile reaction from white southerners because it threatened "Southern Civilization," in which traditional "southern ladies" played an important role in maintaining the status quo. Historian Marjorie Spruill Wheeler argues that southern suffragists were held "hostage" by the limited thinking imposed upon them by the Lost Cause; see Wheeler, *New Women of the New South: The Leaders of the Woman Suffrage Movement in the Southern States* (New York, 1993), 33–37. Henderson quoted from "United Daughters of the Confederacy," *CV,* October 1907, 440.

14. Hallie Alexander Rounsaville of Georgia, who served as state president and then president-general (1901–03), was a charter member of the national DAR.

15. "The President of the NCDC," *CV,* October 1894, 307; "The Daughter of the Confederacy," *CV,* February 1901, 36; "Founder of the UDC," *CV,* November 1914, 496; Mrs. C. M. Goodlett to Mrs. Edwin G. Weed, ca. 1900, UDC Collection, MC. Additional information on Goodlett can be found on the Internet at <http://www.hqudc.org/Founder.htm>.

16. *CV,* July 1909, 310; *CV,* December 1909, 590; Mrs. James Britton Gantt, "Mrs. Cornelia Branch Stone," *CV,* May 1911, 210. Stone's predecessor, Lizzie George Henderson, was president of the Women's Missionary Union as well as the Greenwood Woman's Club.

17. William Howard Taft hosted a White House reception for the entire UDC delegation when the organization held its annual convention in Washington, D.C., in 1912.

18. On Virginia Clay Clopton, see her memoir *A Belle of the Fifties: Memoirs of Mrs. Clay of Alabama, Covering Social and Political Life in Washington and the South, 1853–1866* (Tuscaloosa, Ala., 1999); on Rebecca Felton, see LeeAnn Whites, "Rebecca Felton," in *Visible Women: New Essays on American Activism,* ed. Nancy Hewitt and Susan Lebsock (Urbana, 1993); "Mrs. Cornelia Branch Stone," *CV,* May 1911, 210. See also Judith N. McArthur, *Creating the New Woman: The Rise of Southern Women's Progressive Culture in Texas, 1893–1918* (Urbana, 1998), 3–5.

19. Most UDCs revered the first Ku Klux Klan (KKK) and included it in their Lost Cause publications. Laura Martin Rose wrote a primer for children on the KKK. The Daughters tended to distance themselves from the second Klan of the early twentieth century, primarily because of class differences.

20. Grace Elizabeth Hale writes about the idealized Old South within the Lost Cause narrative in *Making Whiteness: The Culture of Segregation in the South, 1890–1940* (New York, 1999), 43–75; see also, Jacquelyn Dowd Hall, "'You Must Remember This': Autobiography as Social Critique," *Journal of American History* 85, no. 2 (September 1998): 43–65. On emulating antebellum women, see McArthur, *Creating the New Woman,* 3.

21. Information on presidents-general gathered from the following sources: on Lizzie Henderson, "Elizabeth George Henderson," Subject File, Mississippi Division of Archives and History (MDAH), Jackson, Miss., and "Mrs. Lizzie George Henderson," *CV,* December 1905; on Virginia Faulkner McSherry, see *CV,* April 1916, 152; on Daisy McLaurin Stevens, "Daisy McLaurin Stevens," Subject File, MDAH, and "New President General UDC," *Our Heritage,* November 1913, 4; additional information on UDC presidents can be found in Mrs. Bryan Wells Collier, *Representative Women of the South* (published by author, 1925); additional biographical information by Tommie LaCavera can be found in "Ex-Presidents General," *UDC Magazine,* April 1994–March 1995.

22. Thomas Connelly and Barbara L. Bellows mistakenly identify the early UDC as "grayhaired" in *God and General Longstreet: The Lost Cause and the Southern Mind* (Baton Rouge, 1982), 2.

23. Fred Bailey, "Mildred Lewis Rutherford and the Patrician Cult of the Old South," *Georgia Historical Quarterly* 77, no. 3 (fall 1994): 509–35; Collier, *Representative Women of the South,* 147–8; Genealogy and Biography, Mildred Lewis Rutherford Collection, Hargrett Rare Book and Manuscript Library, University of Georgia, Athens (UGA). Rutherford was also crowned "Patron Saint of the UDC"; additional biographical information from Tommie LaCavera, "Mildred Lewis Rutherford," *UDC Magazine,* February 1992, 14.

24. See Hale, *Making Whiteness,* 61–2; Rutherford's addresses and speeches are collected in the Mildred L. Rutherford Collection, UGA.

25. Circular, n.d., "Observations and Comment," by James Callaway, in Mildred

Lewis Rutherford Scrapbooks, Hargrett Library, UGA. Callaway states that Rutherford "gave an address before a committee of the House of Representatives."

26. Rutherford, "Address to the Georgia House of Representatives," handwritten, Mildred Lewis Rutherford Scrapbooks, UGA.

27. *Address delivered by Miss Mildred Lewis Rutherford, Historian General United Daughters of the Confederacy*, New Willard Hotel, Washington, D.C. (Athens, Ga., 1912), 19.

28. Wheeler, *New Women of the New South*, 3–37.

29. "Miss Lumpkin to Georgia Veterans," *CV*, February 1904, 69–70; Jacquelyn Dowd Hall analyzes Elizabeth Lumpkin's role in the Lost Cause celebration in her article "'You Must Remember This,'" 452–7; Gaines Foster, *Ghosts of the Confederacy: Defeat, the Lost Cause and the Emergence of the New South, 1865–1913* (New York, 1987), passim.

30. See also *CV* (February 1904), 69–70.

31. "Address by Miss Elizabeth Lumpkin," *CV*, July 1905, 298–9.

32. Ibid.

33. *Minutes of the Fifteenth Annual Convention*, vol. 2, page 11; "The Women of the Confederacy," *The Lost Cause*, October 1902, 37. This same article described the women as "fearless, yet shrinking; bold, yet timid, unyielding, yet gentle."

34. Quotation from "United Daughters Reunion," *CV*, October 1897, 502.

35. Florence Barlow, "Daughters of the Confederacy, Their Mission," *The Lost Cause*, December 1900, 72.

36. References to the men and women who grew up in the Old South and went on to defend the Confederacy are central to Lost Cause ideology. On the development of the "faithful slave" fiction, see Leon Litwack, *Been in the Storm So Long: The Aftermath of Slavery* (New York, 1979).

37. Men who were eligible to join the Sons of Confederate Veterans were not as apt to join the organization as women of the same generation were to join the UDC. And, as Gaines Foster has noted, the SCV membership "never became an important group," Foster, *Ghosts of the Confederacy*, 197. Those who sustained the Lost Cause, in effect, were the UCV and the UDC. For discussions of the ideal woman of the antebellum South, see Anne Firor Scott, *The Southern Lady from Pedestal to Politics, 1830–1930* (Chicago, 1970); Elizabeth Fox-Genovese, *Within the Plantation Household: Black and White Women of the Old South* (Chapel Hill, 1988); George C. Rable, *Civil Wars: Women and the Crisis of Southern Nationalism* (Urbana, 1989); Wheeler, *New Women of the New South*, 5–7; and Drew Gilpin Faust, *Mothers of Invention: Women of the Slaveholding South in the American Civil War* (Chapel Hill, 1996).

38. For the purpose of this study, "New Men" are those men who were the sons of Confederate veterans who may or may not have been members of the SCV. They were men of the same generation as many of the women who joined the UDC. The UDC often referred to these men as descendants of Confederate veterans who had turned their back on their heritage in their quest to make money. I refer to them as

"New" because the UDC often remarked on the differences between these men and the generation of their fathers, the men of the Old South. Other definitions of who "New Men" were can be found in Dwight Billings' study of the rank and file membership in the 1890s North Carolina state legislature: *Planters in the Making of a "New South": Class, Politics, and Development in North Carolina* (Chapel Hill, 1979); Vann Woodward, *Origins of the New South, 1877–1913* (Baton Rouge, 1951); Glenda Gilmore refers to these men as "New White Men" in *Gender and Jim Crow: Women and the Politics of White Supremacy in North Carolina* (Chapel Hill, 1996). In *New Men, New Cities, New South: Atlanta, Nashville, Charleston, Mobile, 1860–1910* (Chapel Hill, 1990), 87–96, Don H. Doyle argues that "New Men" in the South's urban centers were not "new" in the sense that they were younger than members of the old planter class, but "new" in that they were self-made men who had earned their wealth since the war through business, and not through agrarian, investments.

39. On nationalism, Anglo-Saxonism, and empire see the following: Charles Reagan Wilson, *Baptized in Blood: The Religion of the Lost Cause, 1865–1920* (Athens, Georgia, 1983), 163; Gilmore, *Gender and Jim Crow*, 62–3; and Nina Silber, *The Romance of Reunion: Northerners and the South, 1865–1900* (Chapel Hill, 1997) 174–8. On "manliness" see Gail Bedennan, *'Manliness' and Civilization: A Cultural History of Gender and Race in the United States* (Chicago, 1995), 6–7. Historian David Blight further suggests that African Americans became "sacrificial offerings on the altar of reunion," in *Race and Reunion: The Civil War in American Memory* (New York, 2001), 139.

40. Gilmore, *Gender and Jim Crow*, 64–7.

41. "A Model Appeal—What a Daughter Says," *CV*, September 1911, 416; Judge J. M. Dickinson, "Women and Men of the South," *CV*, November 1909, 537; "What May Be Expected of Our Young Men," *CV*, February 1912, 56.

42. "What May Be Expected of Our Young Men, " *CV*, February 1912, 56.

43. Mrs. Thomas Taylor, "South Carolina Daughters," *CV*, January 1897, 14.

44. Herbert Mitchell, "A Plea to the Sons of Veterans," *CV*, October 1909, 484–5; "General Evans to Sons and Grandsons," *CV*, January 1910, 3.

45. For further discussion of Confederate men's failure as seen by New White Men, see Gilmore, *Gender and Jim Crow*, 65–7.

46. Henderson, "United Daughters of the Confederacy," *CV*, June 1906, 245–6; see also Mrs. Alexander White, "Greeting and Counsel with the Daughters," *CV*, March 1913, 250.

47. "Miss Lumpkin to Georgia Veterans," *CV*, February 1904, 69–70; Lost Cause periodicals often showered women of the UDC with compliments for following in their mothers' footsteps.

III

The Segregation Era

8

Keepers of the Hearth

Women, the Klan, and Traditional Family Values

GLENN FELDMAN

Much has been written in recent years about race, racism, race relations, and civil rights. Some of it has been about the Ku Klux Klan. Some, also, about women. But little has been written about women and the Klan.[1] This is so largely because the KKK was a white, Anglo-Saxon, Protestant, male organization. Members *had* to be males—by the very definition of the organization itself. So most historians have concentrated on the male. Only in the last decade have scholars probed the relationship of women to the KKK.[2]

As a result of such scholarship, many informed people know that women, far from being invisible, actually played an important role regarding the Klan. Women played several conspicuous and important roles in the order. As wives, girlfriends, mothers, sisters, and daughters of the 115,000 male members of the Alabama Ku Klux Klan, for example, and as forceful members of their communities, women during the 1920s shaped the order, its ideology, its goals, and the implementation of its program (sometimes at the end of a whip).[3] Some women joined the Klan movement—if not the KKK itself—along with their children, in auxiliary groups. And many who did not join, even semiformally, played a crucial— if less visibly obtrusive—part in shaping and carrying out the Klan's program, principally in women's "spheres": family, child-rearing, religion, morality, and education.

Although the activities of Klanswomen and fellow female travelers usually focused on the moral, civic, and educational thrusts of the Klan, there was considerable overlap among race, class, ethnicity, gender, and religion. Klan activity had much to do with the preservation of societal order against a host of changes, perceived and real. This meant the protection and preservation of a "southern way of life" that included white supremacy, patriarchy, ethnic purity, and social and political conservatism—all of which relied on bonds of a moral and religious orthodoxy.[4]

Also, women—black and white—played a vital role as conspicuous targets and victims of the KKK. The sheeted order is often thought of as a militant and terrorist wing of white supremacy, which it was. But it was much more during the first half of the twentieth century. Along with black victims, the KKK targeted virtually anyone who represented an aberration, and thus a threat, to Alabama's majority and exceptionally homogenous society. An "outsider"—racially, religiously, ethnically, culturally, morally, and with respect to traditional gender roles—risked becoming a target of repression and even violence in Alabama. Female victims of the Klan, often targeted by other women, supplied visible, corporeal, and even visceral examples of women who had "gotten out of their proper place," thus posing a threat to the community.[5]

In Alabama's intensely religious environment, a Calvinist concern for personal morality reigned paramount, largely because of a curious reading of St. Paul's admonition to the early Christians to treat the body of faith as a whole community. Actually, St. Paul can be read as a call for the toleration and acceptance of diversity in society—even in the religious community. Yet the relevant passages more commonly employed in the white evangelical South were a license, indeed a heavenly mandate, for intolerance and the rooting out of nonconformity. Translated into southern evangelical society, this admonition rapidly gained momentum as a license for ordinary folk to police the personal morality and, indeed, the customs, habits, and idiosyncrasies of their neighbors in the name of purity, decency, and wholeness. Women were vitally important, both as the policers and the policed. Men, more often than not, wielded the blunt instruments that drove the morality lessons home. But it was women—often in vital concert with men—who decided what the curriculum should be.[6]

Thus, women functioned both as the coauthors and the victims of a kind of misogynistic terror that kept them tethered to narrow and traditional roles outlined by southern patriarchal society.[7] Klan repression of women concerned the maintenance of "proper" relations between the races, including preserving of women's "proper place" in society and maintenance of widespread notions of "acceptable" ethical behavior. As historians have shown, the line between racial order and sexual order was mutually supportive and symbiotic. Along with class hierarchy, caste and gender order were variants of a comprehensive social world that was comfortable to the vast majority of southern whites.[8]

To this triangular formulation may be added a fourth angle: a traditional family-values morality that buttressed established relations. This morality, overarching southern community, long served as a foundation for southern society in the same ways that white supremacy, material privilege, and male domination did. This religious-based system of conservative mores often served as the bridge between white supremacy, class hierarchy, and paternalism, interlocking caste, class, and gender into a mutually supportive foundation. For most white southerners, this moral link made race, class, and gender assumptions seem God-ordained, and an almost impregnable way against fundamental change.[9]

Emotion and intolerance were important by-products of the reliance on religious orthodoxy to provide the social cement. "Threats" to social orthodoxy were sometimes discerned in the most innocuous of events. Where there were minimal threats—the mildest of liberal reform impulses, for example—a "slippery slope" approach or extreme version of "guilt by association" was used to discredit that threat. Social Gospel advocates and labor organizers were immediately branded with the foolproof epithet of "Communist agitator." W. J. Cash wrote that "Southerners didn't think; they felt," and for that he has been roundly castigated by some distinguished minds. But Cash was onto something. Emotion and its cousin irrational intolerance were powerful by-products of the reliance on "old-time religion" and religious conformity. Assaults on the status quo were not just efforts at reform, they were rejections of God's word itself. The momentousness of preserving the Good Society made the defensive effort a highly emotional one.[10]

During the 1920s, Alabama experienced an orgy of Klan violence. While most of it was racial in nature, much was also tied to the forcible maintenance of gender roles and morality. During the frenzy of violence in Alabama, Kluxers routinely targeted females—mostly for violating narrow social conventions and notions of traditional morality, but sometimes for being too racially tolerant. Aside from its obvious contradiction of its own tenets about chivalrous behavior, the Klan's targeting of female victims spoke volumes about the people in the secret order. Women had only just received the franchise in 1920. The perception of the "flapper"—despite her rarity in actuality—terrified men and women comfortable with the old "separate spheres." The automobile and new contraception methods foreshadowed female independence and sexual freedom. Divorce rates were up and growing numbers of women entered the workforce. Gender relations, like racial and ethnic purity, came under assault during the 1920s. Men and women tied to the Klan worked to return to a simpler, "purer" time when women "knew their place," "darkies" were obedient and content, immigrants were from northern Europe, and Yankee agitators stayed at home.[11]

The "protection" of white womanhood was the circumscription of women. Divorce, contraception, female suffrage, automobiles, post–World War I labor unrest, Freudian psychology, the "New Immigration," modernist values, and the debate over alcohol all contributed to an atmosphere of extreme uncertainty. The Klan may have been the most extreme expression of a native white Protestant backlash, but it was no aberration from the white Protestant majority. The Klan's representative and majority nature was the main reason, not only for its popularity and geographical diffuseness in the 1920s, but also for the lack of much criminal, legal, or moral opposition. Opposition was expedient, pragmatic, and self-serving.[12]

To repel assaults, the KKK enforced local conventions. Although men usually wielded the whips and blunt instruments, women functioned as the Klan's essential "eyes and ears." In this role, women helped set the agenda of enforcement of community orthodoxy—much of which perpetuated traditional male-female relations. Offenses varied in severity and in whether they were actual infractions of the law or only personal vices. Kluxers might visit a man who had been accused of adultery, spousal abuse, or not providing for his family, or a woman accused of adultery or running a prostitution ring. Other offenses were not nearly so serious or public. The Klan visited people for transgressions such as drinking, dancing, gambling, "parking," or being too courteous to African Americans, or for not reconciling with a previous spouse, dating after divorce, or remarrying.[13]

It was also not uncommon for the self-appointed custodians of morality to become addicted to their roles as morality commissars and to feeling superior to their wayward neighbors. Exclusive membership in a "moral elite" was a powerful incentive to join the KKK and its morality police. In one south Alabama county where the Klan was particularly strong, a small-town mayor identified five of the most active Kluxers as two blacksmiths, a barber, a bricklayer, and a shoe repairman. The sixth was the village drunk—before 1924. "Ever since he's sworn off," the mayor explained, "he's been all hell in favor of virtue."[14]

During the Klan's heyday in Alabama, violent incidents of morality policing exploded in number and severity. The state had experienced vigilantism before, but nothing had been seen on this scale since Reconstruction. Various estimates of 1920s floggings—not to mention cross-burnings, kidnappings, threats, and disappearances and killings—numbered between 600 and 800.[15] Although black males were the largest group of Klan targets, white women also comprised a significant number of victims. In 1927 Florence nightriders dragged Bertha Slay from her bed to her front yard, tied her husband and sisters to chairs in order to watch, bent her over a barrel, and whipped her with such gusto that they exhausted themselves and had to take a break. Trading their switches for an automobile fan belt, the hooded group resumed the beating and demanded a "confession" for Slay's part in a neighborhood scandal. Despite their best efforts, they did not get one.[16] In St. Clair County, masked Knights lashed a sickly teenage girl and her mother for allowing a black man to teach them how to drive. Chilton County Klansmen repeatedly terrorized an old woman known as "Aunt Becky," the widow of a Confederate veteran, because she insisted on continuing to run a restaurant after her husband died. Her pleas to police and local politicians fell on deaf ears. In a case that combined sadism and sexuality with controlling women not under the direct eye of a male, the Crenshaw County Klan visited Fannie Clement Daniels twice. A seventeen-year-old divorcee who had moved back home to take care of her mother upon her father's death, Fannie Daniels apparently violated local sensibilities by dating a young farmer. The Klan warned her to stop seeing the young man. At a second visit, this time at midnight, masked Knights broke down her front door, snatched a shotgun from her mother, bruised the old woman, and ordered Fannie to dress suitably to go in search of her boyfriend. As she changed from nightclothes, several of the hooded men refused to leave her bedroom, preferring instead to stay and leer. Growing impatient, the men threw the young woman across the bed, hiked up her dress, and whipped her. Then they took her to the living room for more questioning. When Fannie showed signs of being unbowed, one of the Klansmen struck her across the face with the back of his hand. "Give her some more," another Kluxer called from the back of the room, "she ain't had enough."[17]

Elsewhere, Klansmen in the state dealt just as roughly with divorced women who attempted to date again or remarry. Such anomalies to the ideal of lifelong monogamous marriage threatened greater social order because marriage was viewed by the majority as divinely inspired. An episode from south Alabama illustrates just how grotesquely community mores could become twisted once they were subject to a pathological obsession with the morals of others. A Baptist preacher officiated at the wedding of a couple who had both been married before and, apparently, officiated at their flogging as well. L. A. Nalls, witnesses testified, performed the wedding ceremony and later presided over a brutal flogging of the newly-weds in their front yard. After a savage beating—administered in front of the couple's several small children—the Klan reverend took up a collection for the bleeding woman, offered her $3.50, a jar of ointment for her wounds, and some pastoral words. "Sister, you were not punished in anger this evening," the preacher said, "you were punished in a spirit of kindness and correction to set your feet aright and to show your children how a good mother should go."[18]

Many white Alabama women supported and participated, as informers, in this sort of morality policing. Klansmen from across the state corrobo-rated how their wives and other women identified "immoral" persons in the community.[19] Mildred Ruth Heaton and Lowis Cowan, two Alabama women, recalled years later that during the 1920s everyone in their social circle knew who was, and was not, a member of the "secret" order. Both argued that the Klan was a good thing; that it punished people for drinking alcohol, adultery, and nonsupport. Others related that many times the lo-cals were happy these types of ethical problems had been dealt with by the Klan.[20] Indeed, such expressions of support for the Klan—even at its most violent—reflected a larger consensus. Birmingham's police commissioner publicly applauded violent Klan raids on teenage dances that sometimes featured alcohol and petting. W. B. Cloe's defense of the Klan was an al-most perfect articulation of the connection between racism, nativism, and intolerance—and the drive to preserve societal order. In a statement in which he disparaged blacks, Jews, and Asians, Cloe defended vigilantism. "Klansmen are a good bunch of men," otherwise "they wouldn't be knocked so much. . . . I say 'God bless them.' It may be your sons or daugh-ters who are going to hell."[21] R. F. Elmore, judge of Alabama's Seventeenth Circuit Court, instructed a grand jury investigating a string of Klan as-saults that the order was worth supporting, even to the point of jury nul-lification, because it bolstered social order and hierarchy. The KKK, Judge Elmore charged the jurors, "stand[s] for just what you and I stand for: . . . the constitution . . . white supremacy . . . the public school and education . . . [and the] chastity of women."[22] An Etowah County court allowed Kluxers to deliver a popular broadsheet to jurors while they were actually in session. "Remember," the Klan circular instructed the jurors, "every criminal, every gambler, every thug, every libertine, every girl ruined, ev-ery [home] wrecker, every wife beater, every dope peddler, every moon-shiner . . . every pagan papal priest . . . every white slaver, every brothel madam, every Rome-controlled newspaper is fighting the Ku Klux Klan. Think it over. Which side are you on?"[23]

Many Alabamians agreed that vigilantism and perhaps hypocrisy were preferable to immorality. Some women naively compared vicious Klan assaults to childhood whippings. Others felt that local communities had a right, indeed a civic responsibility, to regulate personal conduct. Some evangelicals felt it was their moral duty to note and correct the ethical shortcomings of their neighbors and to preserve social order—by force if necessary. One Klanswoman remembered that the policing of community morality "gave people a feeling that they were doing the right thing . . . like they were doing the[ir] Christian duty."[24] This ethos was reinforced in a society in which well-received hooded Klan groups called upon Protestant congregations and their ministers, often in the midst of Sunday morning services, and presented grateful pastors with envelopes stuffed with cash. Klan lecturers such as Methodist minister Earl Hotalen crisscrossed the state to defend white supremacy as essential to the preservation of an unpolluted heritage and praised the Klan at religious and civic gatherings as an organization dedicated to morality, chivalry, Bible study, and public schools. Klansmen wore robes, Hotalen explained, not to conceal their identities, but to bolster the social order and symbolize the purity of Jesus Christ. The Klan would unmask only when "our Lord, the Prince of Peace, shall come again . . . when Satan . . . shall have been bound in chains, and when bootleggers . . . rapists . . . [and] gamblers . . . no longer encumbered the earth."[25]

Behavior that threatened the family—especially undiluted whiteness— received special attention. In January 1925 Klan chapters around the state launched a campaign to close houses of ill repute. Within a week, masked Kluxers burned crosses in front of ten Birmingham homes thought to be brothels. A raid on one bordello yielded a special prize when Knights discovered a former policeman enjoying the sexual favors of black prostitutes. In other episodes, Talladega Knights charged an elderly farmer with housing prostitutes, making moonshine, and hosting dances. A flogging followed. In Birmingham, armed Klansmen organized a caravan consisting of a truck and several curtained cars and issued a general invitation to the press to accompany the mob on its anti-prostitution crusade.[26]

As the "eyes and ears," women were often the driving force behind the Klan's regulation of extramarital sex in the community. Shortly after New Year's Day 1926 a dozen armed Klansmen, accompanied by an off-duty deputy sheriff, invaded three Chinese restaurants in downtown Birmingham to search for alcohol, and raided couples consisting of only one married person in small private dining rooms said to be havens for adulterous couples. Gun-wielding Klansmen bullied, searched, and finally "arrested" three women and three men and took them to the county jail. Once there, though, the raid came to an end as Jefferson County's chief deputy tore up the "warrants," released the "prisoners," and declared the whole thing to be a huge mistake.[27] During the 1920s, Klan mobs across Alabama also lashed men and women suspected of adultery; forced several "shotgun weddings" to take place; beat husbands accused of nonsupport and spousal abuse, and a man who refused to allow his wife to visit her sick mother; assaulted a man who refused to remarry his former wife; kidnapped a man for legally separating from his wife; caned teen couples for "parking" on lovers lanes; lashed a separated mother of four for having "improper" sexual relations with men she was dating; brutalized a janitor for spying on school-age girls in the bathroom; tried to hang a farmhand for cursing in front of a woman; and used brass knuckles on a doctor whom they charged with having sexual relations with a female patient.[28] All of their victims were white.

Incidents that crossed lines of color, ethnicity, or religion raised special passions. Race was not just an emotional issue. White supremacy had a definite rational logic to its maintenance. Economic rewards accompanied white supremacy and institutionalized racism: better parks, playgrounds, libraries, schools, public amenities, health care, housing; safer neighborhoods; access to credit; a continued source of cheap labor for employers; and a leg up on job competition for common whites. Such economic benefits were as important and powerful as the social and psychological benefits whites felt from this legal and institutionalized caste system.[29]

Ethnic purity raised similar passions. Knights terrorized a Greek man for marrying a native white woman, a Jew for trying to marry a Protestant, a Romanian confectionery store owner and a German tailor for trying to date native women, and a Catholic druggist who said he could date married Protestant women.[30]

Such things did not go on completely uncriticized. Virginia Foster Durr, noted Montgomery liberal and sister-in-law to later Supreme Court justice Hugo Black, disdained the Invisible Empire. More commonly, criticism of the Klan emanated from the most conservative sources in the state—the Big Mule/Black Belt coalition of powerful and wealthy industrialists and planters. Jealous of the Klan's political strength and the resonance of its moral program with many plain Alabamians—and especially worried that unsubtle Klan enforcement of the racial status quo might eventually risk the involvement of the federal government and real racial change—these conservatives mounted an eloquent critique of the order's violent enforcement of morality and ethics. Predictably, their opposition to the order's violence was itself rooted in preference for time-tested notions of what constituted proper relations between the sexes and the races. A Covington County editor denounced the beating of women—for any excuse—as uncivilized, and demanded that southern gentlemen take up arms to protect white womanhood from the depredations of hooded mobs. "Where are they now . . . [the] men . . . the pride of the Southland?" he lamented. "Do they sleep? . . . Is the spirit of the Old South waning?"[31] Prominent Black Belt Democrat John Bainbridge damned the 1920s Klan while praising the Reconstruction order and its racial conservatism—not an unusual combination among Alabama elites. He took special issue with the group's targeting of white women through its moral police squads of "brave tom tits." Bainbridge described these Klansmen as indulging their Freudian fantasies to "spank some neighborhood [Mary] Magdalene" and recommended a liberal use of buckshot as suitable remedy.[32] The state's leading patrician mouthpiece, Grover Hall of the *Montgomery Advertiser*, lambasted the Klan's morality enforcement as "appalling . . . Every blow of the lash . . . on the body of a defenseless . . . woman is a blow at . . . [the] State and [the] law. So long as masked men may go into an Alabama home to . . . satisfy . . . their lust for cruelty . . . so long will Alabama harbor anarchy and barbarism."[33]

On several occasions, women took up arms against attacking Klansmen, with mixed results. A Decatur madam repulsed one Klan mob by wielding a shotgun and calling out the names of regular customers she recognized in the mob. The daughter of an elderly striking railroad worker came to his defense only to be flogged herself by his attackers. A wife who interspersed herself between Kluxers and her husband wound up with her clothes being ripped off. A young woman eagerly learned how to operate a firearm after her husband was brutalized, while an elderly woman unsuccessfully attempted to foil the flogging of her daughter by brandishing a shotgun. Two spinster sisters, though, drove off a Crenshaw County Klan mob with a pair of shotguns only to have their furniture shot full of holes later.[34]

More telling was the reaction of Alabama law enforcement and juries, made up of the friends and neighbors of Klan members. Rarely did local law enforcement arrest Knights, no matter how violent they were. In those few instances in which they did, acquittals usually occurred. Virtually all convictions were overturned by higher courts. At a fundamental level, the goals of the hooded order were seen as noble and worthy of societal endorsement and protection. Of all the travesties of justice in 1920s Alabama, perhaps none was more egregious than the flogging and killing of Annie Mae Simmons, an elderly black woman. The sensational 1927 case, brought by an ambitious state attorney general, included incriminating testimony of three (black) eyewitnesses and the confession of the flogging squad's ringleader. Still, a Crenshaw County jury returned a verdict of not guilty in a case that featured squabbling between state police officer witnesses and apparent complicity between law enforcement and the defense team. But mostly, as one defense attorney boldly stated in open court, the killers would not be convicted because Annie Mae Simmons occupied the lowest rung on society's ladder and her death was of no consequence. A black accomodationist who profited handsomely from his close relationship to the white power structure, Oscar Adams repeatedly refused to speak out against the Klan. "While the means of correction are unlawful," he wrote about the earlier double lynching of an interracial couple, "the spirit behind the act must be considered righteous and altogether pleasing."[35]

Women in Alabama—as auxiliaries of the Klan, members of the Women of the KKK (WKKK), Kamelias, and individuals connected to the order in less formal ways—played a major role in the 1920s Klan program aimed at encouraging patriotism, "100 percent Americanism," and public education. Alabama women spearheaded KKK and WKKK drives to ensure that all children were properly schooled in the prevailing white, Anglo-Saxon, Protestant variant of American patriotism. Again, the goal was to short-circuit threats to the status quo in a rapidly changing world. A manifestation of this concern was the Klan drive to ensure that all Alabama children of classroom age had American flags flying in their schoolrooms. In Talladega County and other places where this was not already the case, local women affiliated with the KKK bought flags and bestowed them upon schools with great flourish and ceremony.[36]

Initiations of new Klan members gave the order ideal opportunities to overwhelm communities. Women played conspicuous roles. In 1922, Anniston's KKK held festivities on a large sandbar in Oxford Lake, featuring a barbecue beneath a huge electric cross, fireworks, and several parades as four hundred area men formally joined the outfit. Over a thousand robed Klansmen and women attended the event, carried to Anniston on special trains from around the state. Similar extravaganzas took place across Alabama during the Klan's heyday in the 1920s. In 1925 and 1926, "Klan Day" at the Lee County Fair drew 10,000 spectators, including 2,000 costumed Klansmen, as 200 "aliens" received initiation into the hooded order. Hundreds of WKKK women, dressed in full Klan regalia, took active part in all of the festivities, accompanied by men and children, also in full Klan dress.[37]

Male Klan leaders went to great lengths to recruit women. During the early 1920s rival efforts at recruiting women reached a fever pitch in Alabama as part of the greater internecine struggle for control of the Knights of the KKK, Inc., between two Alabamians who both claimed to be head of the national order. The Knights' originator, Methodist clergyman Joseph Simmons, organized a group of Birmingham women into a group called the Kamelias after the famous male white supremacist organization of the Reconstruction era, the Knights of the White Camellia. Alabama dentist Hiram W. Evans, who was soon to displace Simmons as the nation's leading Klansman, responded by organizing his own group of Alabama women into a state branch of the Women of the Ku Klux Klan. The WKKK group grew to absorb the Ladies of the Invisible Empire, Queens of the Golden Mask, the Grand League of Protestant Women, the Order of American Women, Puritan Daughters of America, and other like-minded women's groups.[38]

For some families, the Klan was an essential part of family life, and women were fundamentally involved in the order's activities. Around the state, Klan chapters, often with the active involvement of women, donated money to hospitals, visited sick children, bought food and clothing for widows and toys for the needy at Christmas time. The Clay County chapter paid for funerals, the Tuscaloosa den raised money to pay for a new Boy Scouts campground, and a Huntsville klavern bought a memorial room at the city hospital.[39]

Klansmen and women were motivated by more than doing good or a love of learning. Many supported public education because they feared parochial education and the "un-American" and "un-democratic" indoctrination and ethnic, working-class challenges they associated with Catholicism. While civic and educational efforts appealed to some Klan types whose motives were beyond reproach, these activities also struck a common chord among nativists, religious bigots, and members of the middle class.[40] Supporting public education was a way of fighting Catholic schools, just as efforts at the inculcation of "American" values were often imbued with a dread of immigration, alcohol, political machines, and religious faiths other than Protestantism. Many Alabamians harbored a profound fear of a church they saw as evil, foreign, and menacing, and Klan literature and ideology betrayed an obsession with so-called "aliens," while a host of Alabamians interpreted "Americanism" to include only white Anglo-Protestant culture.[41]

It is impossible to divorce Klan support of public education in Alabama from an environment in which the Klan also abused Catholics, Jews, Greeks, Italians, and others whose religion or ethnicity varied from the Anglo-Protestant norm. Hooded speakers regaled receptive audiences with tales of how Catholics buried a rifle under their churches every time a male child was born for use in an eventual papal takeover of America and how Catholics dominated the World Court to "Romanize" the United States and force "papal aliens" into the country. When they "learned" that the 1917 U.S. dollar bill was "really" covered with secret Catholic symbols, dutiful Klansmen ripped off the corner of bills where they believed the pope's picture was hidden. A favorite theme concerned the "unnatural" male domination of women in convents. Klaverns in Alabama hosted itinerant "escaped nuns," female Klan lecturers who posed as former Catholic nuns, to titillate audiences with tales about the carnal lust of priests and the evils of parochial education. These "nuns" displayed leather bags, which, they told their wide-eyed audiences, were used to cremate the infant products of priest-nun sexual unions in the basement furnaces of Catholic churches. Such stories emphasized the plight of helpless young girls locked in dungeon-like convents with high walls, iron windows, and bolted doors—and elicited actual tears of rage from emotionally overwrought Protestant audiences.[42]

Klan groups in Alabama responded by burning a Catholic church and school at Pratt City, organizing boycotts of stores owned by Catholics, pressuring businesses to fire Catholic employees, blocking construction of Catholic churches, burning crosses in front of Catholic churches and schools, and, on one occasion, raiding a Mobile playground where frightened kindergarten children mistook the sheeted men for ghosts. Birmingham's boisterous city elections of 1917 turned on anti-Catholic prejudice, and Thomas E. Kilby won the governorship in 1919 partially by exploiting the issue. Two years later, Sylacauga Klansmen beat a Catholic druggist senseless because he bragged about dating Protestant women. The anti-Catholic fervor, like white supremacy, was intimately bound up in "protecting" white, American, Protestant women from infection by unclean and un-American "outsiders." The mania reached a low point in 1921 when an itinerant preacher, named "The Marrying Parson," shot and killed a Catholic priest in broad daylight in downtown Birmingham because he had officiated at the wedding of the parson's daughter to a white Puerto Rican Catholic. Himself a member of the Klan, the Baptist preacher admitted the deed, but still benefited from a Klan defense fund to secure the talents of an ambitious young attorney named Hugo Black. The jury, anchored by a foreman who was also a Knight, returned a verdict of not guilty largely because Black had the courtroom's lights turned down and insinuated that the groom was part African American.[43]

Because most American Catholics were of Irish, Italian, or eastern European descent, immigration and liquor were indelibly imprinted on the anti-Catholic fervor. Along with concern about papal domination came the worry that people only one generation removed from the old country would not embody the same loyalties. These anxieties reflected the powerful insecurities of an earlier generation of immigrants whose memories of their parents' and their own odysseys to America were remarkably short-lived. And the Klan damned the hierarchy of the Catholic Church and allegiance to "a foreign prince" while demanding loyalty above all to a hierarchical Invisible Empire. Likewise, the order spewed republican ideology while notoriously failing to practice it within its ranks.[44] Sensational events such as the Red Scare of 1919–20 and the Sacco and Vanzetti trial fueled popular nervousness. In 1928, immigration, Catholicism, white supremacy, and alcohol found virulent expression in opposition to the presidential candidacy of New York governor Alfred E. Smith. A "wet," Catholic, Irish product of New York's Tammany Hall, and a relative liberal on the race issue, Smith's nomination as the national Democratic standard bearer precipitated the deepest crack in the "Solid Democratic South" since Reconstruction. In places like Alabama, it meant virtual war between those who insisted that Smith had to be accepted to ensure traditional Democratic protection of white supremacy and those, like the Klan, who viewed his candidacy as intolerable.

In Alabama, Klan forces united with prohibitionists, women temperance advocates, and evangelical Protestants to wage a ferocious campaign against Smith's candidacy and, but for some familiar Black Belt electoral shenanigans, would have carried the state for Republican Herbert Hoover.[45] Far from being demure observers of the millennial conflict in Alabama, women took part as major players in the unfolding drama. As male Klan leaders damned "Popish plots . . . the papal menace . . . and the papal monster," and warned Alabamians that the Catholics would use mind control, Jesuit assassins, and hoarded gold reserves to win the day, female allies in the powerful Anti-Saloon League and the Women's Christian Temperance Union locked arms with the KKK.[46] Horace C. Wilkinson and Hugh A. Locke, leading racial and religious bigots and Klan leaders, organized the "Anti-Smith Democrats," with the conspicuous assistance of women from the Anti-Saloon League and the WCTU. The rump group negotiated a bizarre compact with former Populist O. D. Street and the Alabama Republican Party to list twelve prominent Democrats as Alabama electors for Herbert Hoover. Reflecting their growing political power and intimate involvement in the 1928 "bolt," two women made the critical elector slate: Mary T. Jeffries, president of the Alabama WCTU, and Zue Musgrove Long, sister of L. B. Musgrove, a multimillionaire coal operator, Klansman, failed senatorial candidate, and prohibitionist extraordinaire.[47]

The 1928 campaign brought out the worst in Alabama as both sides stooped to the lowest forms of a "politics of emotion." The term includes the manipulation and/or exploitation of ingrained feelings on emotional issues such as race, but also abortion, prayer in schools, patriotism, the "character" or personal morality of political candidates, gun control, or the flying of the Confederate flag. Throughout southern history, elite white southerners have persuaded many plain whites to ally themselves with their class "betters" by appealing to these emotional, rather than substantive, issues. Race and racism are part of the "politics of emotion" and a contrasting "politics of reason." While race was perhaps the most powerful emotional issue for white people, it was also a substantive issue. Concrete economic rewards accompanied white supremacy—both for plain whites and patricians. As the primary economic competitors with blacks, poor whites stood to gain much by the preservation of white supremacy. As members of a select caste, whites, no matter how humble, enjoyed more freedom and better schools, parks, libraries, neighborhoods, public amenities, and access to credit. The South's planters and industrialists profited from the preservation of white supremacy as well, both in emotional terms and in concrete economic terms such as the perpetual supply of cheap labor and a strong wedge dividing potential biracial action along class lines.[48]

Both sides in the 1928 bolt used the emotional appeals. Bourbon Democrats, including Marie Bankhead Owen—whose father and two brothers served in the U.S. Senate and House of Representatives—resorted to religious-baiting and racial demagoguery to attack Hoover. The Klan/ Hoovercrat alliance, though, proved the equal to its Bourbon adversaries. Bob Jones, a noted Montgomery evangelist and Klan fellow traveler, bragged that Birmingham was the most typical Anglo-Saxon city in America and criticized large Northern cities as being made up mostly of unwashed "foreigners." "If Catholic Al Smith is elected," the religious leader warned, "the gates to immigration will be thrown open. I had rather see a saloon on every corner . . . than to see the foreigners elect their candidate." Jones urged rejection of Smith by informing Alabamians that "God Almighty" had called on southerners to be His chosen people for the sacred mission of saving America from wickedness.[49] A. J. Barton, a zealous Baptist, stumped against Smith by reassuring mixed Klan and women temperance audiences that "They say we are intolerant, but I have never been so happy in all my life as I am in supporting Herbert Hoover. He is not a negro lover."[50] Senator and Klan darling J. Thomas Heflin did yeoman service by damning the "insidious papal monster . . . [and] the invisible government of Rome" at every opportunity, warning that Smith's election meant the systematic genocide of all American Protestants by the Knights of Columbus. On several occasions, Heflin predicted his own assassination at Jesuit hands. A firm believer in white supremacy who had once enforced his understanding of Jim Crow by gunning down a black man on a Washington, D.C., streetcar, Heflin appealed to Alabama women by resorting to familiar themes. He had earlier raised his profile by defending the lynching of "fiendish brutes in human form" in classic terms: because "Southern womanhood is the priceless jewel of the southern household [and] we will safeguard it and protect it with the last drop of our blood." Women had a duty to oppose Smith because Rome was "aim[ing] her brutal, arrogant and unholy propaganda at the sacred circle of the American . . . Protestant home . . . [and] real Americans."[51] State Republican and Masonic leader O. D. Street's variant of opposition to Al Smith and traditional Democracy bordered on outright misogyny. Street's anti-Catholic bigotry was so raw, in fact, that he distributed an imprint from the Spanish Inquisition that depicted Catholic priests amputating a Protestant woman's breasts with the caption: "She nursed a heretic child."[52]

The 1928 presidential campaign was so divisive and emotional in Alabama that certain episodes in it rival any in American political history for their bizarre nature. Long accustomed to feeding on the emotional issue of race in its politics, Alabamians of both sexes again hewed to a "politics of emotion"—and, in effect, rehearsed their roles for what would be common political practice in the state for years to come. Because of the long-standing race issue and related issues, including the Reconstruction legend, emotion was deeply engraved in Alabama's political culture and a large part of the political socialization of plain Alabamians. In August 1928, a pathological low point of sorts was reached when the powerful Nathan Bedford Forrest Klan Den in Wahouma held a political rally for the whole family. As two hundred men, women, and children cheered, one local Klan leader after another stood to denounce Smith for his Catholicism, his moral depravity in opposing Prohibition, and the impurity of his heritage. After the speakers had whipped the crowd into a frenzy, a Klan leader held up a Smith mannequin before the crowd and asked them what they wanted to do with it. "Lynch him! Lynch him," they chorused in a macabre though unconscious imitation of Christ's passion at the hands of Pontius Pilate. The presiding Klansman took out a long knife and slit the dummy's throat, red mercurochrome spurting forth to simulate blood. Assisting Knights rushed the stage to tie a noose around the mannequin's neck and drag it around the hall. Men, women, and children kicked and shot the Smith doll as a Klan emcee assured his audience that, come November, Smith would be lynched "with good Christian votes."[53]

At less debased gatherings, race, gender, and ethnic issues combined with moral and religious dynamite. Women temperance activists joined Klan leaders and leading evangelicals to denounce Smith's candidacy. One prominent Methodist minister warned that if Smith were elected, the Democratic Party would become the "party of Rome and rum for the next hundred years." A Birmingham woman and member of the WCTU charged that every woman who planned to vote for Al Smith was an "emissar[y] of the Devil." "It is useless," she sobbed, "to pray that the wicked will change their votes."[54]

The planter-industrialist oligarchy that formed the nucleus of conservative democracy in Alabama, as in other southern states, was well practiced in the craft of race-baiting. Although patrician and Klan-connected women found themselves on opposite sides of the Smith-Hoover question, actually women on both sides hewed to, and pursued the maintenance of, narrow and traditional versions of race and gender relations. In doing so, planter and industrialist types invoked the emotional specter of Reconstruction drummed into every southern schoolboy and schoolgirl by the age of ten. The caricature was replete with corruption, "ignorant" black rule, Yankee and federal oppression, and dire threats to white womanhood.[55]

The imagery was powerful, pervasive, and of long-standing effectiveness in the South. "We have a white man's government in Alabama, and we are going to keep it unless federal bayonets again tear our heritage from us," a leading Bourbon declared. Future Alabama governor Frank M. Dixon warned that Hoover's election would reconstitute the Reconstruction era's "Negro rule" in the South and again bring "down the heels of the ex-slaves on the throats of Southern men and women."[56]

Women were part and parcel of this type of conservative Democracy, just as they were intimately bound up with the Klan-evangelical attempt to derail Smith's candidacy. Mabel Jones West, president of the Alabama Women's League for White Supremacy, was a major player in contesting the bolt. West's repudiation of the Klan and her endorsement of the Democratic candidate spoke volumes because she had, herself, been a leading member of the Women of the KKK. Noting her disappointment that the WKKK had allowed itself to be "prostituted" into supporting a Republican, West reduced the election to the critical issue of race. As paradoxical as it may now appear, for West and thousands of others who remained loyal to Alabama's Democratic Party in 1928, the preservation of white supremacy meant rejection of the Invisible Empire. "When the time comes when we must choose between the Ku Klux Klan and . . . white supremacy," she announced, "let the Ku Klux Klan go to the devil." Knowing her stand against the Klan would be controversial, West forewarned against any retribution from the sheeted order. "I am not afraid of the Ku Klux Klan," she announced, "And that includes [grand dragon] Jim Esdale and [politico] Horace Wilkinson."[57] Other Alabama women who put white supremacy above all things, ironically, repudiated the KKK-prohibitionist heresy of backing a Republican candidate. One female native of Alabama was especially upset at the prospect of having to use the same bathroom as African Americans. "Think of a Secretary of Commerce having to stoop to niggers . . . [and] nigger politicians . . . to win," she complained. She and other southern white women at the Commerce Department called the black employees "'Hoover's Chocolates,'" and "[we] all wish we could make him eat them."[58]

Other Alabama women found the wellspring of their support for the 1920s Klan and its doctrines in their notions of religion and in the nostalgia and affection they felt for the Klan of their fathers during Reconstruction. A self-described "Old Lady of the South" from Prattville backed the 1920s Klan, she explained, because her father had been in the original order that "cleansed our public offices of Negroes, carpetbaggers, and scalawags." "I can very well remember the Reconstruction Days," the old woman recalled, "when the White people of the South were oppressed and mistreated by this ungodly corruptible group. I can remember my father saying the Ku Klux Klan will never die. 'It was here yesterday, today, and forever.' And I firmly believe that God has a working hand through this organization. . . . [I]f it wasn't for the Ku Klux Klan in the Reconstruction Days, America would have been a mongrelized nation."[59] This feeling of a traditional society in moral crisis was part of the Klan ethos during the 1920s. Male Klan members were hopeful that the organization of women into the order would shore up society's ethical foundation because it "has long been conceded that the Protestant women of America have wielded the greatest influence in this country for greater morality, political purity . . . better citizenship and the maintenance of the high standards of the home."[60]

During the 1930s, a smaller KKK shifted gears to focus on Jews, Communists, labor unionists, and other threats to the class-based status quo. Class had been a part of the 1920s KKK appeal and raison d'être. Members of the Invisible Empire often disparaged Roman Catholics as members of a dirty working class, attacked unionists in the labor unrest following World War I, and painted Jews as the radical "brains" of an international conspiracy to use blacks as the dupes of global revolution.[61] Still, at its root, the "change" in Klan targets was only ostensible. As in previous incarnations, Alabama's Klan activity still revolved around a xenophobia broadly understood: people who personified "foreign" threats to cultural homogeneity, especially white supremacy. Ethnicity and religious regularity factored into the equation as well. Jews, "Godless Communists," and labor organizers, especially the new biracial Congress of Industrial Organizations (CIO), were all dangerously suspect in the South because they were closely associated with class insurgency. But their most egregious sin was in threatening racial purity and stability by promoting biracial activity for reform.

The "Scottsboro Boys" tragedy encompassed all of these threats: black males accused of raping white women, Jewish defense attorneys from New York, Communist involvement in raising money for the boys' defense. Accordingly, the KKK involved itself intimately in the proceedings, at times surrounding the various courthouses in Scottsboro and, later, in Decatur, threatening to lynch the defendants and their attorneys, and physically clashing with black and white Communists marching in Birmingham for the boys' release.[62]

The explosive combination of race, radicalism, and sex led to increased tensions in a number of places during the Depression. In the summer of 1931, Birmingham erupted into full-blown hysteria when a deranged black Communist kidnapped four young white women from Mountain Brook, easily the wealthiest neighborhood in the state. He held the women hostage in nearby woods for four hours while occasionally spouting radical propaganda, and eventually shot three of them, killing one. Simmering tensions boiled over, giving way to a summer reign of terror in which Klansmen, police officers, and corporation security guards wreaked havoc on the city's black population. Before the outbreak ended, white mobs with Klan involvement burned and bombed black businesses, shot several African Americans at random, and assaulted numerous others.[63]

Many white men and women in Alabama were sure that Jewish labor organizers and Communist activists wanted to break down—forcibly if necessary—the wall between black men and white women. As the "hardest hit Depression town in America," according to the federal government, and as the new home of the southern branch of the Communist Party, however small, Birmingham became an emotion-filled battleground during the Depression.[64] The vaunted atheism connected to Communism lent a millennial quality to the fight against radicalism and for the preservation of white supremacy. To defend the southern white home and "protect" women, the KKK rode again. Native Alabamian and imperial wizard Hiram Evans warned blacks in Birmingham to stop "breathing [the] hot communistic airs of racial equality or there would be trouble."[65] In the central part of the state, an Autauga County woman explained her support for, and belief in, the KKK in terms of a religious and patriotic duty because America had become "a nation of contemptible filth." The sheeted order rode because they were on a mission from God. "Instead of the carpetbaggers and scalawags of years past," she complained, today we have to contend with "Communism . . . the NAACP and other Jewish controlled organizations as peddlers to create hate and brainwash the minds of the American people [and] destroy our Christian faith . . . and the American Way of Life."[66]

As Klan and police forces clashed with Alabama's few thousand black Communists during the Great Depression, women gave and received right along with the men. In the streets of Birmingham, anti-radical vigilantes beat female Communists into unconsciousness with blunt objects and rubber hoses. Black women excitedly asked Communist organizers when the next rally was going to be held so they could "whup them a cop." Joint Klan and police groups went on nocturnal searches for black radicals and sometimes satisfied themselves with assaulting whatever women and "dirty black bitch[es]" they found at home. As sharecropper clashed with landlord and Klan ally in the Black Belt, women became casualties right along with the men. A Klan attorney in Clarke County, although "not an advocate of lynch law," told Black Belt whites that he still had "red blood in my veins and I believe it is no more contemptible to string up a Negro in the face of high heaven than it is to pounce upon an unprotected white woman and defile her. . . . The proper thing to do is to crack their necks with the least possible delay."[67]

Yet the same protections did not extend to black women. After a group of Klan-like vigilantes, with the apparent involvement of law enforcement officers, riddled the body of a black Sharecroppers Union leader with bullets, the mob returned to his Lowndes County home that night. They hung his wife from a tree several times before cutting her down and, for good measure, lashed a female friend who had come to stay with the grieving woman. Near Dadeville, a black preacher informed the Klan that a black female Communist was hoarding dynamite. That evening they raided her home and beat her so ferociously that they broke her spine.[68]

Although the "second Klan" faded as a political entity after the 1928 election, it continued to exist as a force to be reckoned with well into the 1930s and beyond. World War II marked a relative hiatus in Klan activities in Alabama. Thirty or so klaverns and a thousand hard-core members remained through the war years, but the organization increasingly attempted to dissociate itself from unflattering comparisons with Adolf Hitler and Nazism. In 1945, though, pent-up racial tensions exploded and gave rise to another period of intense Klan activity in Alabama. Although this period has not been as closely studied as other eras, the KKK, at least in Alabama, was very active—and in ways quite reminiscent of the 1920s order.[69]

The post–World War II Klan demonstrated profound concern for the growing racial independence of returning black soldiers and the attempts of African Americans to secure voting rights. Like the 1920s order, though, the 1940s KKK exhibited intense interest in preserving traditional morality and familiar gender roles—roles that had changed when women entered the workforce in numbers to produce war materials. When race was involved, the mixture became explosive. Markedly lower class and more working class than in its heyday, the post–World War II Klan garnered strong support from fringe evangelical sects rather than from the mainline Protestant denominations that had been its lifeblood. In a real sense, the 1940s KKK served as the militant arm of popular white supremacy in Alabama. The growing racial crisis brought ordinary white Klansmen together with Big Mule industrialists and planters in a broad white alliance to combat federal movements toward expanded civil rights. Overlap existed between the KKK and the "Dixiecrat" movement of the States' Rights Party, in which plain-white segregationists locked elbows with privileged planters and industrialists. The Klan's revisited obsession with moral authoritarianism was decidedly plebeian, and it appealed strongly to the emotions and sensibilities of plain whites. But, like other pan-white movements in Alabama's past, the coalition most benefited the state's more powerful interests.

From its outset, the 1940s Klan organizers—themselves alumni of the 1920s order—reassured an increasingly nervous middle class that their goals were purely racial, sexual, and moral: only the "protection of white womanhood and white supremacy," in the words of Alabama grand dragon Will Morris. Only "honky-tonk operators, common brier-patch prostitutes, and people of that type . . . [and] the colored man [who did not know] his place" need be concerned, Morris reassured the public.[70] In a sensational act of Klan terrorism in June 1948, the KKK, upset over two white female instructors' sleeping in close proximity to a group of black Girl Scouts, united in a huge midnight mob of robed and gowned Klansmen who descended on a Bessemer Girl Scout camp, ransacked the tents of the two white instructors, accused them of practicing Communism, and ordered them to vacate the campgrounds within twenty-four hours. Badly shaken, the instructors immediately cancelled the remainder of their two-week course and fled. Meanwhile, the county sheriff and his chief deputy informed the press that they considered the Klan raid to have been "a good thing," failed to make any arrests, and instead reported that their informal survey of nearly a hundred local residents favored the Klan's action because "folks around here don't like Negroes and whites living together." A local Klan leader and physician carefully denied the group's involvement "as an organization," but defended the raid. "If I saw a mad dog or a snake I would shoot it," he explained, "And some people act like mad dogs and snakes."[71]

A year to the day of the raid, morality and gender concerns again took center stage in a sensational manner. One hundred armed and costumed Klansmen struck at the Jefferson County home of Edna McDanal, a white woman. As she tried to load a shotgun and pulled the masks off several of her assailants, Kluxers slugged her over the head with a blackjack and dragged her outside to witness a giant cross burning in her yard. They read her a list of charges that included selling alcohol and pornography, prostitution, statutory rape, and dancing in the nude on her front porch, and, in turn, threatened her with beating, hanging, and burning at the stake. Residents later testified that a Baptist preacher and two other ministers were in the Klan mob and that Graysville's police chief gave the Klan procession an escort replete with lights and siren wailing. A male neighbor who had watched the entire midnight spectacle enthusiastically endorsed the action because Edna McDanal was an immoral woman.[72]

In separate incidents, the postwar Klan regulated caste, sex, and ethics. Kluxers brutally flogged two white men and a white woman because she had given birth to three children out of wedlock. An Assembly of God preacher removed his hood to pray over the victims before they were beaten. Walker County Klansmen savaged an elderly coal miner who failed to provide for his family because he had broken his back at work. He suffered a nervous breakdown. In nearby Dora, Klansmen kidnapped and terrorized three young couples—including simulating their hangings—because they did not approve of their dating. The Tuscaloosa Klan, meeting as the "Tuscaloosa Social Club" in a county building, made plans to punish black dishwashers and white waitresses for talking together in local restaurants.[73] Accused of being a member of a Klan flogging squad, one Holiness Pentecostal preacher got up, walked across a courtroom to the witness box, and struck his female accuser in the face. The presiding judge excused him when he asked to be forgiven.[74] In 1949, Kluxers abducted navy veteran Billy Guyton Stovall from his home and covered his back with welts because he had violated local sensibilities by allowing his wife to take a part-time job. Incensed by his beating, Stovall's young wife vowed to defend her home with firearms. "I'd do it," she pledged, "I'd not mind at all seeing them drop one at a time."[75]

Although some Alabama women actively opposed the KKK of the 1940s, female opinion was by no means universal on this point. Birmingham's elite League of Professional and Business Women and the Council of Church Women publicly criticized Klan violence—if not its actual goals and beliefs.[76] A woman of standing proposed that Birmingham adopt an antimask ordinance, but was rebuffed by Mayor Cooper Green—himself a 1920s member of the order. Although he personally approved of such a law, the mayor claimed, his two fellow city commissioners, Jimmy Morgan and Eugene "Bull" Connor, were unmoved.[77]

More ordinary Alabama women spoke out as well. Jennie Bartran Gentleman asked the governor to do something about the KKK. "We are ... [ultimately] responsible for the Klan!" she admonished Governor "Big

Jim" Folsom. "Please . . . use your position to fight this thing of prejudice, ignorance, and hate . . . [and] give our children the heritage their fathers fought for." "I am not a Jew, Catholic, or Negro, just an American," she explained, and "I am sick to death of the Ku Klux Klan!"[78] Another Alabama woman put the issue as well as anyone: "The people themselves in Alabama are responsible for the Ku Klux Klan. It will also be the people who ultimately must change their way of thinking."[79]

Still, on balance, many Alabama women were sympathetic to the Klan's principles and ideology, if not its actual methods. One, who described herself as a virulent opponent of the KKK, revealed that her brand of opposition actually had more to do with southern touchiness over its honor and reputation than the white supremacist tenets of the organization. "[T]he harm . . . [that] the . . . Klan has done to Dixie is beyond the scope of mention," she declared; "it has disgraced us" in the eyes of the nation. The stupidity of the Klansman was "not a God-given ignorance as the savages of the 'Dark Continent' possess," she explained, "Their's [is] a man made ignorance, an ignorance bathed in prejudice, hatred, and deceit . . . a form of ignorance that is truly dangerous."[80]

However, a large number of women were outright supporters of the Klan in the 1940s. "Every Southern white woman who has suffered a fate worse than death in the clutches of THE BLACK BEAST," one woman said in relying on the old "rape excuse" for the basis of her support, "was outraged by an ANTI-KLANSMAN." A Gardendale woman favorably compared the Klan's spate of morality violence to a positive type of parental discipline and publicly thanked the Kluxers for performing a valuable community service. Another applauded the particularly vicious attack on Edna McDanal. "How would you like it for some woman to get out in front of your little girls and dance naked?" she asked. "When [the Klan] . . . take[s] one out and whip[s] them it is for some disgraceful act by god-fearing men and god-loving men."[81]

The relationship between women and the Ku Klux Klan as an organization was multilayered and varied. Some women served the organization in vaguely positive, or at least neutral, forms. Some helped drive the organization's effectiveness as a blunt instrument of racial, religious, nativist, gender, and moral repression. Others were victimized by the group—both in literal and figurative ways. Still others participated in the KKK as the perpetrators of victimization as individuals, only to, paradoxically, contribute to their own continued victimization as the members of a repressed group.

The women who actively engaged in the Klan's more insidious program of moral authoritarianism did so as more than just victims who came to identify with their male oppressors and thus embrace their values. Many actively collaborated with Klansmen and consciously felt that they benefited. Some willingly acted to uphold the interrelated racial, class, and gender hierarchy of southern society. Others, in a curious kind of way, sought a different advantage. Through their adherence to local moral orthodoxy—enforced, if the need arose, by violence—these women sought conformity status and comfort of conformity. By toeing the local line on family values and race and gender roles, many women won for themselves enhanced status as upstanding, reliable, and solid members of their communities. By doing so, they found themselves welcomed by their sisters and brothers into the warm and nurturing sunlight of local acceptance. They did not have to worry about the social discomfort that is often the price of minority dissent, or concern themselves with the price such dissent might mean for their husbands,' fathers,' and brothers' careers or their children's and their own social lives. Men and women alike found the allure of this warm acceptance to be too appealing and too powerful to resist with what was almost certain to be futile dissent. But, in becoming reliable parts of the dominant white southern community and its enforcement mechanisms, such women were active perpetuators and beneficiaries of the southern status quo.

Notes

1. Some of the classic works on the Ku Klux Klan are David M. Chalmers, *Hooded Americanism: The History of the Ku Klux Klan* (1965; reprint, Durham, 1987); Wyn Craig Wade, *The Fiery Cross: The Ku Klux Klan in America* (New York, 1987); Patsy Sims, *The Klan* (New York, 1978); Kenneth T. Jackson, *The Ku Klux Klan in the City, 1915–1930* (New York, 1967); and Arnold S. Rice, *The Ku Klux Klan in American Politics* (Washington, DC, 1962). The "populist-civic school" of Klan historiography is best represented by Shawn Lay, ed., *The Invisible Empire in the West: Toward a New Historical Appraisal of the Ku Klux Klan of the 1920s* (Urbana, 1992); and Leonard J. Moore, *Citizen Klansman: The Ku Klux Klan in Indiana* (Chapel Hill, 1991).

2. This topic is fortunate to have been the focus of Nancy MacLean's excellent study *Behind the Mask of Chivalry: The Making of the Second Ku Klux Klan* (Oxford, UK, 1994). Kathleen M. Blee first addressed the issue in fascinating detail in *Women of the Klan: Racism and Gender in the 1920s* (Berkeley, 1991).

3. This figure is taken from Glenn Feldman, *Politics, Society, and the Klan in*

Alabama, 1915–1949 (Tuscaloosa, Ala., 1999), 16, 20. Alabama grand dragon James Esdale claimed 150,000 members during the 1920s but this figure is probably inflated. The figure of 115,000 is reasonable, although Wayne Flynt put it at around 95,000 in Leah Rawls Atkins, William Warren Rogers, Robert David Ward, and Wayne Flynt, *Alabama: The History of a Deep South State* (Tuscaloosa, Ala., 1994), 431–2. See also William Robert Snell, "The Ku Klux Klan in Jefferson County" (M. A. thesis, Samford University, 1967), 55–6, 77.

4. MacLean, *Behind the Mask of Chivalry,* 91–2.

5. In the 1920 census, Alabama was home to 2.35 million people, about 62 percent white and 38 percent nonwhite. That is where the state's heterogeneity ended. Almost 99 percent of the state's white population was native born; 78 percent lived in rural settings; and 96 percent identified themselves as Protestant Christians. Over 84 percent of these Protestants were either Baptist or Methodist. The clear majority of Alabama's half-million urban residents could be found in only three cities: Birmingham, Mobile, and Montgomery. Catholics made up only 3.4 percent of the overall population; Jews comprised less than 1 percent. U.S. Department of Commerce, Bureau of the Census, *Fourteenth Census of the United States: Population, 1920,* vol. 3, *Population, 1920; Composition and Characteristics of the Population by States* (Washington, D.C., 1922), table 1, 54, tables 10 and 11, 66–8; *Religious Bodies: 1916,* part 1, *Summary and General Tables* (Washington, D.C., 1919), 238–9, and *Religious Bodies: 1926,* vol. 1, *Summary and Detailed Tables* (Washington, D.C., 1930), 142–5. The dean of southern religious history, Samuel S. Hill, Jr., wrote that it is "legitimate to speak of a transdenominational 'Southern church' embracing what may be called 'popular Southern Protestantism,'" in *Southern Churches in Crisis* (New York, 1967), 73.

6. I Corinthians 10:6–33 may be read as a basis for intolerance of diversity in moral matters, while I Corinthians 12:4–28 may fruitfully be read as a prescription for tolerance of diversity. For an intriguing look at a similar climate of community monitoring and intolerance, set in Catholic Paris of the sixteenth century, see Barbara B. Diefendorf, *Beneath the Cross: Catholics and Huguenots in Sixteenth-Century Paris* (Oxford, UK, 1991), especially 28–36, 37, 48, 53, and, for incredible brutality performed in the name of religious orthodoxy, see 100–3.

7. This point is in contradistinction to Kathleen M. Blee's interpretation of women's involvement in the Klan as having been a liberating experience that qualified as part of feminism. See Blee, *Women in the Klan,* 35, 51–2, and 178. This liberation may have been the case in the regions that Blee concentrated on in her study, the Midwest and West, but it was not the case in Alabama nor, do I think, generally in the South.

8. Jacquelyn Dowd Hall, *Revolt Against Chivalry: Jesse Daniel Ames and the Women's Campaign Against Lynching* (New York, 1979); and "'The Mind That Burns in Each Body': Women, Rape, and Racial Violence," in *Powers of Desire: The Politics of Sexuality,* ed. Elizabeth Ann Snitow, Christine Stansell, and Sharon Thompson (New York, 1983), 328–46; Joel R. Williamson, *The Crucible of Race: Black-*

White Relations in the American South Since Emancipation (New York, 1984); Glenda Gilmore, *Gender and Jim Crow: Women and the Politics of White Supremacy in North Carolina* (Chapel Hill, 1996). And various essays in Jane Dailey, Glenda Elizabeth Gilmore, and Bryant Simon, *Jumpin' Jim Crow: Southern Politics from Civil War to Civil Rights* (Princeton, 2000).

9. Both Nancy MacLean's *Behind the Mask of Chivalry* and Kathleen M. Blee's *Women and the Klan* do an excellent job of tying together race, class, and gender issues in their analyses of the 1920s KKK.

10. On fundamentalist and literalist intolerance of religious liberalism and the Social Gospel, see MacLean, *Behind the Mask of Chivalry*, 93–4, 120. On Cash, see C. Vann Woodward, "The Elusive Mind of the South," in *American Counterpoint: Slavery and Racism in the Black-White Dialogue* (Boston, 1971), 265–83. Bruce Clayton provides a more appreciative reading of this Cash insight in "W. J. Cash: A Native Son Confronts the Past," in *Reading Southern History: Essays on Interpreters and Interpretations*, ed. Glenn Feldman (Tuscaloosa, Ala., 2001), 18. Similar terms sometimes used to discuss the forced conformity of the South are "siege mentality," the "savage ideal," and the "closed society." See also Bruce Clayton, *The Savage Ideal: Intolerance and Intellectual Leadership in the South, 1890–1914* (Baltimore, 1972).

11. A dated, but still excellent, source for the contextual background of the dizzying changes that occurred during the 1920s is Frederick Lewis Allen's journalistic account *Only Yesterday: An Informal History of the 1920s* (New York, 1931). See also Leslie Woodcock Tentler, *Wage-Earning Women: Industrial Work and Family Life in the United States, 1900–1930* (New York, 1979), and MacLean, *Behind the Mask of Chivalry*, 31–3, 118–9.

12. See the concept of "pragmatic opposition" versus "principled opposition," in Feldman, *Politics, Society, and the Klan in Alabama*, 8–9, 326–7.

13. Mildred Ruth Heaton and Lois Cowan interview with Linda Jean Thorpe, February 1, 1974, Oral History Collection (henceforth OHC), Mervyn Sterne Library, University of Alabama at Birmingham Archives, p. 4; Vern M. Scott Reminiscences, 1988, p. 15, Talladega County Historical Association, Talladega, Alabama; Snell, "Ku Klux Klan in Jefferson County," 144–5, 153; *Montgomery Advertiser*, July 23, 1927.

14. William G. Shepherd, "The Whip Wins," *Collier's Magazine* 81 (January 14, 1928), 31–2 (quoted).

15. Ku Klux Klan file, Tuskegee Institute News Clipping Files, reel 28, 1927, Tuskegee University Archives (henceforth TUA), Tuskegee, Alabama. *New York Times*, July 12, 1927, December 2, 1927, 22; *Montgomery Advertiser*, July 10, 12, 1927; William G. Shepherd, "The Whip Hand," *Collier's Magazine* 81 (January 7, 1928), 8, and "The Whip Wins," 32; Editors, "The South Aroused to Midnight Floggers," *Literary Digest* 94 (July 30, 1927), 8–9.

16. Ku Klux Klan file, reel 28, 1927, TUA; *New York Times*, July 11, 14, 18, 1927; *Montgomery Advertiser*, July 10, 14, 20, 1927; *Atlanta Constitution*, July 22, 1927.

17. *Montgomery Advertiser*, October 2, 20, November 26, 1927; *Montgomery Examiner*, July 7, 1949; Michael Newton and Judy Ann Newton, *The Ku Klux Klan: An Encyclopedia* (New York, 1991), 142, 391; Shepherd, "The Whip Wins," 32.

18. *Montgomery Examiner*, July 7, 1949; Newton and Newton, *The Ku Klux Klan*, 391, 412.

19. Vern M. Scott Reminiscences, 1988, 15, Talladega County Historical Association (henceforth TCHA), Talladega, Alabama; Snell, "Ku Klux Klan in Jefferson County," 144–5, 153; *Montgomery Advertiser*, July 23, 1927. This practice was, apparently, the same in Georgia and elsewhere. MacLean, *Behind the Mask of Chivalry*, 121.

20. Heaton and Cowan interview, 4, OHC; Vern M. Scott Reminiscences, 1988, TCHA.

21. *Birmingham News*, April 21, 1925.

22. *Montgomery Advertiser*, November 1, 1927.

23. *Pittsburgh Courier*, November 6, 1926.

24. Blee, *Women in the Klan*, 80.

25. Alabama Ku Klux Klan newsletter 5 (March 1927): 1 (quoted), in box G192, folder "Ku Klux Klan, 1927," Alabama Governors Papers, Bibb Graves Papers, Alabama Department of Archives and History (ADAH), Montgomery, Alabama.

26. *Birmingham News*, January 17, 21, 1925; Irving Beirman, "Birmingham: Steel Giant with a Glass Jaw," in *Our Fair City*, ed. Robert S. Allen (New York, 1947). E. C. Sharp interview by Ralph H. Compton, ca. 1974, OHC; Bibb County KKK file, Shelby County KKK file, and Talladega County KKK file, in KKK Research Files, Department of Special Collections, Harwell Goodwin Davis Library, Samford University (SUDSC), Birmingham, Alabama.

27. Ku Klux Klan file, reel 25, 1926, TUA; *New York Times*, January 5, 1926; *Atlanta Constitution*, January 5, 1926; *Birmingham Age-Herald*, January 4–14, 1926. The action of the chief deputy, also a member of the Klan, precipitated a cause célèbre within and without Birmingham's Klan ranks.

28. Lee County KKK file, KKK Research Files, SUDSC; KKK file, reel 20, 1924, and reel 23, 1925, TUA; *New York Telegraph*, July 19, 1927; *New York Graphic*, July 18, 1927; *Birmingham News*, February 26, March 1, 21, 27, 1925; *Atlanta Constitution*, October 9, December 6–7, 1921; Snell, "The Ku Klux Klan in Jefferson County," 79–83, 116, 120.

29. *Atlanta Georgian*, March 30, 1922; *Montgomery Advertiser*, April 12, May 21, September 4–8, 1922, October 2–8, 1923; *Birmingham Age-Herald*, March 13, 1927; William R. Snell, "Masked Men in the Magic City: The Activities of the Revised Klan in Birmingham, Alabama, 1915–1940," *Alabama Historical Quarterly* 34 (fall and winter 1972): 221.

30. Alabama Ku Klux Klan newsletter 4 (June 1926): 7, in box 16, folder 11, Associations Records, ADAH; Ku Klux Klan scrapbooks, vol. 1, and the Charles A. Fell Memoirs, vol. 2, part 1, 101–28, both in the Birmingham Public Library Archives (BPLA), Birmingham, Alabama; Papers of the NAACP, part 1, reel 13, Library of

Congress (LC), Washington, D.C., and Microforms and Documents Department (AU-MADD), Ralph Brown Draughon Library, Auburn University, Auburn, Alabama; Virginia Van der Veer Hamilton, *Hugo Black: The Alabama Years* (Baton Rouge, 1972), 84; Glenn Feldman, *From Demagogue to Dixiecrat: Horace Wilkinson and the Politics of Race* (Lanham, Md., 1995), 67. For some, Alabama was such a homogenous place that encounters with persons of diverse backgrounds were almost exotic. A Jewish man who lived over forty years in Montgomery, yet still was known, albeit affectionately, as "the foreigner," told of a 1920s sidewalk encounter with a woman who stopped him and asked: "Are you a Jew?" When he responded in the affirmative, she stepped back, looked at him again, and said, "My, you're a real live Jew, aren't you?" See "Reminiscences," p. 9, folder 1, Eugene Feldman Papers, ADAH.

31. Virginia Foster Durr interview, 7–8, Oral History Office, Columbia University, New York. *Covington County (AL) News*, reprinted in the *Montgomery Advertiser*, July 17, 1927.

32. John Bainbridge to Editor, *Montgomery Advertiser*, September 13, 1927.

33. *Montgomery Advertiser*, July 11–2, 1927.

34. *Decatur Daily*, August 10, 1975; Ku Klux Klan Collection, Blount County Historical Society, Blountsville, Alabama. Feldman, *Politics, Society, and the Klan in Alabama*, 47–9, 61, 72, 100, 147, 301, 395 n. 28.

35. *New York Times*, November 21, 1927; *Montgomery Advertiser*, October 2, November 25, 1927.

36. Talladega County KKK file, KKK Research Files, SUDSC; *Sylacauga (Ala.) Advance*, February 4, 24, May 10–3, 22, June 21, July 26–9, October 18, 27–30, 1925, and October 20, 27, 1926.

37. Alabama Ku Klux Klan newsletter 4 (June 1926): 7, in box 16, folder 11: "Ku Klux Klan, Associations Records," and newsletter 5 (March 1927): 2–4, in box G192, folder "Ku Klux Klan, 1927," Alabama Governors Papers, Bibb Graves Papers, both in the ADAH; E. C. Sharp interview by Ralph H. Compton, ca. 1974, 1–4, OHC.

38. *Atlanta (Ga.) Imperial Knighthawk*, June 13, October 3, 1923, May 14, July 16, 23, and 30, October 29, 1924; *Memphis (Tenn.) Commercial Appeal*, August 22, 1924; *Montgomery Advertiser*, September 27–8, 1921, January 20, March 28, June 21, August 22–4, and December 17, 1923; Snell, "The Ku Klux Klan in Jefferson County," 55–6, 77. Women lobbied to be active in the Klan movement. They wanted to "stand alongside our men and help" rather than be "patted on the head and told not to worry," one woman wrote in a Klan publication. An "unhappy wife" agreed by asking why native-born, white, Protestant women should be excluded from the KKK along with such unseemly groups as the "Knights of Columbus, Jews, or negroes?" Blee, *Women of the Klan*, 24–9. By 1923, thirty-six states had WKKK groups operating in them. The WKKK banner included other related women's groups such as the Ladies of the Invisible Eye, Ladies of the Cu Clux Clan, Ladies of the Golden Den, Hooded Ladies of the Mystic Den, Ladies of the Golden Mask, the White American Protestants, and the Dixie Protestant Women's Political League.

39. Chalmers, *Hooded Americanism*, 79; Jackson, *The Ku Klux Klan in the City*, 82–3. Not every Protestant minister in Alabama during the 1920s was a fan of the secret order, but the majority were members or at least sympathizers. Still, there were a few solitary individuals who did voice genuine outrage at the Klan's methods and uneasiness with its goals. See Feldman, *Politics, Society, and the Klan in Alabama*, 104.

40. Blee, *Women of the Klan*, 93; MacLean, *Behind the Mask of Chivalry*, 93, 96–7, 99.

41. MacLean, *Behind the Mask of Chivalry*, 118–20.

42. Ibid. See also Blee, *Women of the Klan*, 86–93, 90.

43. Dozier to Coyle, 1917, box 7, folder 25, Alabama Pamphlets Collection, and Emmetts to Kilby, August 1, 1921, folder "Law Enforcement, 1920–23," Alabama Governors Papers, William W. Brandon, both in the ADAH. See also Charles A. Fell Memoirs, vol. 2, part 1, 1–28, BPLA; *New York Telegraph*, October 20, 1921; *New York World*, October 17, 1921; *Memphis Commercial Appeal*, April 13, 1922; Marvin Y. Whiting, "'True Americans,' Pro and Con: Campaign Literature from the 1917 Race for the Presidency of the Birmingham City Commission," *Journal of the Birmingham Historical Society* 6 (July 1980): 11; and Michael A. Breedlove, "Progressivism and Nativism: The Race for the Presidency of the City Commission of Birmingham, Alabama, in 1917," *Journal of the Birmingham Historical Society* 6 (July 1980): 3–4; Paul M. Pruitt, Jr., "The Killing of Fr. Coyle: Private Tragedy, Public Shame," *Alabama Heritage* 30 (fall 1993): 24–37.

44. MacLean, *Behind the Mask of Chivalry*, 92–3, 95–7; and Blee, *Women and the Klan*, 92–3.

45. J. Mills Thornton III, "Alabama Politics, J. Thomas Heflin, and the Expulsion Movement of 1929," *Alabama Review* 21 (April 1968): 83–112; and J. Wayne Flynt, "Organized Labor, Reform, and Alabama Politics," *Alabama Review* 23 (July 1970): 163–80.

46. Alabama Ku Klux Klan newsletter 6 (April 1928): 2, (June 1928): 1 (quoted), (July 1928): 1, 7, (January 1929): 4, Oliver Day Street Papers, ADAH.

47. "Call for Conference of Anti-Smith Democrats" and "A Resolution Adopted by Conference of Anti-Smith Democrats," August 13, 1928, J. F. Hines Papers, SUDSC. See also box 26, whole folder "Intolerance," and the Alabama Ku Klux Klan newsletter 7 (January 1929): 3, both in Oliver Day Street Papers, ADAH.

48. The concepts of a "politics of emotion" and "God and Country Issues" are explained in Glenn Feldman, "Introduction: The Pursuit of Southern History" in *Reading Southern History*, 6, and the term "politics of emotion" itself appears in the book's index.

49. Marie Bankhead Owen, "Hoover's Religion" statement, October 23, 1928, box 5, folder 14, William Brockman Bankhead Papers, ADAH; *Birmingham Age-Herald* and *Birmingham News*, August 14, 1928 (all quotations).

50. Ibid. See also box 19, folder 4, State Democratic Executive Committee Records, ADAH; "A Resolution Adopted by Conference of Anti-Smith Democrats,"

August 13, 1928, J. F. Hines Papers, SUDSC; and the Alabama KKK newsletter, April, September, October, and November issues, Oliver Day Street Papers, ADAH.

51. J.A.J., "Roman Treason Against Our Homes," *Kourier Magazine* 3 (April 1927): 21 (first and third quotations); Senator J. Thomas Heflin in the *Congressional Record*, Senate, extract, February 18, 1927, and 63rd Cong., 2d sess., LI, p. 2893 (second quotation), J. Thomas Heflin Scrapbooks, MF-652, SUDSC.

52. "Governor Smith's Membership in the Roman Catholic Church and Its Proper Place as an Issue in This Campaign," box 26, folder "Intolerance," Oliver Day Street Papers, ADAH.

53. *New York Times*, July 8, 1928, 2; *Birmingham Age-Herald* and the *Birmingham News*, July 8, 1928.

54. Alabama Women's League for White Supremacy, clipping (woman quoted), box 210, folder "Birmingham City Commission," Alabama Governors Papers, Benjamin Meek Miller Papers, ADAH; Rogers et al., *Alabama*, 440 (other quotations).

55. For a good explication of the "Dunning School" of Reconstruction historiography, see Fred Arthur Bailey, "E. Merton Coulter and the Political Culture of Southern Historiography," and "Charles Sydnor's Quest for a Suitable Past," both in Feldman, *Reading Southern History*, 32–48, 88–111.

56. Huddleston to Hammill, October 4, 1928, box 210, folder "Birmingham City Commission," Benjamin Meek Miller Papers, ADAH; *Birmingham News*, November 5, 1928; Hugh D. Reagen, "Race as a Factor in the Presidential Election of 1928 in Alabama," *Alabama Review* 30 (fall 1993): 6–7, 12–7.

57. *Birmingham News*, November 4, 6, 1928; *Birmingham Age-Herald*, November 16, 1928.

58. "Anonymous" (Commerce Department Employee) to Cole Blease (quoted), ca. 1928, box 5, folder 14, William Brockman Bankhead Papers, ADAH.

59. Declaration (quoted), folder "KKK-Prattville," Boone Aiken Papers, Auburn, Alabama, in possession of the author. A decidedly minority counterpoint was expressed by liberal pariah Virginia Durr. Durr vehemently opposed the 1920s Klan, although her maternal grandfather had ridden with Nathan Bedford Forrest and, after the war, founded a local klavern. She also remembered clearly her Klan uncle reminiscing about beating blacks with baseball bats during Reconstruction because they attempted to vote. Virginia Foster Durr interview, 7 (quoted), Oral History Office, Columbia University, New York.

60. Klan publication quoted in Blee, *Women of the Klan*, 32. "Klan recruiters portrayed themselves as a movement of righteous Protestants beleaguered by forces of immorality" (Blee, quoted on 80). Klan propaganda stressed the order's effectiveness at arresting the 1920s "drift toward immorality." MacLean, *Behind the Mask of Chivalry*, 99.

61. Blee addressed the connection between Catholicism and the working class in *Women of the Klan*, 93. MacLean described Klan dislike of Socialism and Communism for their usurpation of male proprietary rights over women and children in *Behind the Mask of Chivalry*, 118–9.

62. Angelo Herndon (circular), "The Scottsboro Boys: Four Freed! Five to Go!" ca. 1931, p. 9 (quoted), box 5, folder 30, Alabama Pamphlets Collection, ADAH.

63. *Birmingham Reporter*, August 15, 1931; *Southern Worker*, August 15, 29, and September 12, 1931; Robin D. G. Kelley, *Hammer and Hoe: Alabama Communists During the Great Depression* (Chapel Hill, 1990), 84.

64. Feldman, *From Demagogue to Dixiecrat*, 104. As part of its heritage as a battleground for class and racial issues, Birmingham was once home to black radicals Hosea Hudson, Angelo Herndon, and, later, Angela Davis.

65. *Pittsburgh Courier*, December 21, 1940; "Communism and the Negro," *Kourier Magazine* 8 (September 1932): supplement, 5, 23; "Communists Stirring Southern Negroes," *Kourier Magazine* 9 (October 1933): 19–20.

66. Declaration (quoted), folder "KKK-Prattville," Boone Aiken Papers, Auburn, Alabama, in possession of the author.

67. Helen Long affidavit, December 30, 1936, part 3, 967–9, Joseph Gelders testimony, part 3, 775; Jane Speed, Kenneth Bridenthal, and Harriet Flood affidavits, January 12, 1937, part 3, 961, 970–3; Belle W. Barton affidavit, December 7, 1936, part 3, 973–6, all in the United States, Senate, Committee on Education and Labor, 75th Cong., 2d sess., *Violation of Free Speech and Rights of Labor, Hearings Before Subcommittee* (1937–38); *Birmingham Afro-American*, February 17, 1934; KKK File, reel 46, 1934, TUA.

68. Kenneth T. Jackson, "On the Alabama Front," *The Nation* 141 (September 18, 1935): 329–30; *Southern Worker*, July 25, August 1, 29, 1931; Kelley, *Hammer and Hoe*, 40–3.

69. Glenn Feldman, "Soft Opposition: Elite Acquiescence and Klan-Sponsored Terrorism in Alabama, 1946–1950," *Historical Journal* 40, no. 3 (1997): 753–77.

70. *New York Times*, July 22, 1946 (quoted); *Louisville Courier-Journal*, June 23, 1949 (quoted).

71. Testimony of Herbert M. Levy, p. 129, in the United States, Congress, House, Committee of the Judiciary, Subcommittee no. 3, *Beatings and Cross-burnings in Alabama Towns*, 81st Cong., 2d sess. (1949). Hereafter cited as *1949 House Hearings on the KKK*. See also Thompson to Selden, August 13, 1948, folder 2: "Ku Klux Klan, 1948–1950," Alabama Governors Papers, James E. Folsom, Sr., ADAH; *Columbus Recorder*, June 24, 1948; Morris to To Whom it May Concern, June 22, 1948, box 8, folder 21, Birmingham Mayoral Papers, Cooper Green Papers, BPLA.

72. "It Sure Was Pretty," *Time* 54 (November 7, 1949): 24. See also Edna McDanal interview, June 24, 1949; Hugh McDanal and J. E. Woods interviews, June 12, 1949; Dester Lott and Jerry Ensor interviews, June 13, 1949; Mr. and Mrs. Virgil Cook and Mr. and Mrs. Grady Ensor, Cal Nations, and W. E. Mitchell interviews, June 14, 1949; and George Bensko to Torrence (statement), June 23, 1949, all in box SG 12644, folder "KKK, 1949, no. 5," Alabama Governors Papers, James E. Folsom, Sr., Papers, ADAH (henceforth, Folsom Papers)

73. KKK File, reel 108, 1949, TUA; part 5, reels 19 and 20, Papers of the NAACP, LC and AU-MADD; William Hamilton, William Rochester, Flossie Rochester,

Emmett Atkins, and Martha Gladys Rochester interviews, June 23, 1949, box SG 12644, folder "KKK, 1949, no. 5," Folsom Papers; "Anti-Negro Groups" file, reel 108, 1949, and reel 112, 1950, Tuskegee Institute News Clipping Files, TUA; *Tuscaloosa News*, May 28–31, 1949.

74. *Louisville Courier-Journal*, October 28, 1949; New York *Daily Worker*, November 6, 1949; *Birmingham News*, October 26–9, 1949.

75. Testimony of [Mr.] Lake, 184–94, in *1949 House Hearings on the KKK*; *Montgomery Advertiser*, June 16, 1949; *Birmingham News*, June 17, 1949.

76. "Program Convention, 1949," association box 8, Alabama Associations Records, American Legion Records, ADAH; Warner to Folsom, June 21, 1949, folder 3: "Ku Klux Klan, 1949," Folsom Papers; "Sheeted Jerks," *The Nation*, 169 (July 2, 1949): 2.

77. Green to Parker, June 28, 1949, box 8, folder 21, Birmingham Mayoral Papers, Cooper Green Papers, BPLA.

78. Jennie Bartran Gentleman to Folsom, June 13, 1949 (quoted), box SG 12644, folder "KKK, 1949, no. 4," Alabama Governors Papers, Folsom Papers.

79. Citizen to Folsom, July 3, 1949 (quoted), box SG 12644, folder "KKK, 1949, no. 8," Alabama Governors Papers, Folsom Papers.

80. Whitfield to Folsom, July 15, 1949 (quoted), box SG 12644, folder "KKK, 1949, no. 6," Folsom Papers.

81. Anonymous to Folsom, June 18, 1949 (first quotation), box SG 12644, folder "KKK, 1949, no. 6," and Pitts to Folsom, June 27, 1949 (second quotation), box SG 13479, folder "KKK, 1949," both in Folsom Papers.

9

A Warm, Personal Friend,
or Worse Than Hitler?

How Southern Women Viewed Eleanor Roosevelt,
1933–1945

PAMELA TYLER

An essay that undertakes to reveal what southern women thought about Eleanor Roosevelt must first acknowledge the protean nature of southern women. They were not monolithic in their backgrounds, educations, or experiences, and they certainly were not unanimous in their views of the complex and controversial Mrs. Roosevelt. Southern womanhood in the 1930s and 1940s included spinners in cotton mills, clubwomen, domestic servants, college girls, wives and mothers struggling against the demands of the cruel Depression economy, Democratic precinct workers, matrons of Charlotte and Atlanta reading their urban dailies, widows in rural hamlets reading only the Bible and the *Grit* newspaper. They were African American women reading secondhand copies of the *Chicago Defender* sent back home by brothers and sons, women whose men were far away in military service, weathered women who picked cotton and strung tobacco, privileged women who spent their time entertaining and being entertaining, female professionals competing in a man's world, activist women working to repeal the burdensome poll tax, sheltered women completely oblivious to the poll tax, women fighting to end lynching, and women who felt safer precisely because the deadly practice of lynching flourished. In such a welter of identities, how could there be a single view of anything?

Two quotes from southern women will illustrate just how far from unanimity they were on the first lady. "I have admired you for many years," confided an Alabama woman. "I and countless others here feel that you are our warm, personal friend." A Mississippi woman, however, compared ER to the blackest villain of the age. "I am sure that if a poll were taken to find out the most hated person in our state, you would run Hitler a close race."[1] So one must begin by admitting that it is fatuous to claim and an impossibility to know what *the* southern woman" felt about Eleanor Roosevelt. It is, however, possible to identify patterns of support for her, and of opposition to her, among women in the South. Evidence for these patterns rests, as far as possible, upon the women's own words to and about Mrs. Roosevelt.

What exactly were Eleanor Roosevelt's connections with the American South while her husband was president? The peripatetic first lady was a frequent visitor to the South during FDR's presidency, speaking on college campuses, inspecting New Deal facilities, addressing gatherings of women. Forces of enlightenment stirring in the South found a sympathetic supporter in Eleanor Roosevelt, whose keen sense of social justice responded to many southern-based ills. She was an opponent of the poll tax, an advocate for organized labor in southern industry, and a champion of racial justice. She praised the Southern Tenant Farmers Union, supported the New Deal's most progressive programs (many of which had a profound impact on the South), and functioned as an important part of a network of progressive southerners that included Lucy Randolph Mason, Aubrey Williams, Will Alexander, Clark Foreman, Mary McLeod Bethune, Virginia Foster Durr, and Frank Porter Graham. Southern women's views of this first lady were inextricably bound up with their opinions about the aspects of southern life in which Mrs. Roosevelt interested herself.

Eleanor Roosevelt's own views of the American South evolved as she became better acquainted with a wide range of southerners. Her husband had a famously close relationship with the region, anchored at his beloved Warm Springs, Georgia, home. To this modest cottage he retreated as often as circumstances would allow. Georgians, and by extension other southerners, relished the fact that the president sojourned among them and delighted to claim FDR as one of their own. Not so with his missus, however. "We didn't like her a bit," asserted a Warm Spring matron.[2] Rexford Tugwell vouched for the accuracy of that statement and alleged that ER "considered all these people down there rednecks." He went on, "I never heard anybody around the Warm Springs place say a good word for her. She didn't like it, and they didn't like her, and that's the way it was." Though she made occasional duty trips to join Franklin at Warm Springs, she habitually arrived late and departed before he did.[3]

What accounts for Mrs. Roosevelt's distant coolness toward her husband's retreat and its people? Warm Springs was Franklin Roosevelt's place to relax, devoid of the duties and obligations associated with his cherished Hyde Park home. The Georgia sanctuary's leisurely pace, liberally spiced with cocktails, jokes, and gossip, all of which FDR adored, perhaps explains what the ever-earnest Eleanor disliked about the atmosphere at the spa/rehabilitation center. However, her negativism extended beyond one Georgia village. Before her husband became the thirty-first president of the United States, she had avoided contact as much as possible with the entire southern region. She disliked the southern climate, the mosquitoes, the characteristic Spanish moss, and the sound of the southern drawl, which allegedly grated on her ears. Beyond doubt, the harsh segregation and grinding poverty of the region depressed her. Jonathan Daniels put it plainly when he wrote that Eleanor Roosevelt "did not care for the South."[4]

Nevertheless, the rigors of her upbringing, nourished by the wellsprings of her own genuine kindness, had instilled in Eleanor Roosevelt a virtually infallible graciousness of manner. In the South, the nation's most traditional region, good manners, courtesy, and form mattered greatly. Eleanor Roosevelt unfailingly displayed these traits wherever she went. Thus many southern women, themselves bred to be custodians and transmitters of etiquette and grace, came away from an encounter with the poised and gracious first lady with warm feelings toward her. One example will suffice to demonstrate the point.

When the first lady spent a hectic but by no means atypical sixteen hours in North Carolina in the summer of 1937, she followed a schedule that would have foundered a Marine. Greeted at dawn at the Raleigh railroad station by a flock of Democratic women leaders, she immediately entrained for her destination, an agricultural experiment station "down East" near Wallace, some forty miles from coastal Wilmington, where her schedule would begin with a hearty breakfast on the lawn. ER and her secretary worked steadily on answering correspondence. "We hadn't been on a minute—even before the train started to pull out—when Mrs. R and Malvina turned two seats so they faced each other," recalled May Thompson Evans, a North Carolina woman then serving as assistant director of the Women's Division of the Democratic National Committee. "Malvina whipped out her little portable typewriter."[5] Only when the train slowed for the stop at Wallace did the disciplined ER stand and settle her hat upon her head, ready to face the cheering thousands. A hot drive in an open car over red clay roads swirling with dust took her to breakfast, where she accepted a basket of strawberries and the honor of having a new hybrid named the "Eleanor Roosevelt." Next, she "dashed about" a nearby re-settlement project, examining homes, furniture factory, and school, asking questions all the while. She sat through an outdoor pageant, "From Settle-ment to Resettlement," which the homesteaders had written for her visit, jumped from her perch on a wooden bench onto the improvised platform to square dance when invited up, addressed the crowd, and still made it back to Wallace in time for a one o'clock luncheon in her honor. Stealing one hour of solitude upstairs at her hostess's home, she dictated "My Day" and dispatched it to the Western Union office. She then headed for the town center to open the Strawberry Festival with appropriate remarks, re-ceived the obligatory serenade from the Fort Bragg military band, and heard oratory from state and local dignitaries, after which her presence was required at an interview with the press, a reception for several hun-dred clubwomen, and finally a buffet supper for one hundred local citizens. Shortly before nine o'clock that evening, she boarded her train for Wash-ington.[6]

Mrs. Roosevelt displayed an exquisite courtesy throughout that hectic day. Scheduled to drive in an open car over dirt roads, she offered no com-plaint about either the heat or the dust, both of which had the locals apolo-gizing profusely. Presented with a basket of strawberries, she praised them as "the largest [she had] ever seen" and sampled them. Touring, she voiced eager and intelligent interest in all facets of the resettlement project's op-eration. At the amateur pageant, she smiled and applauded at intervals and, when invited to join the performers in square dancing under the noonday sun, she did not plead fatigue or the heat but joined right in. When she was overcome with coughing as she spoke to her audience, she poured water for herself and laughed, "You know, I think I must have swallowed some dust this morning." Given three books by amateur North Carolina histori-ans, she paused to leaf through each one in turn and tactfully expressed appreciation. There was nothing perfunctory or formulaic about her public appearances; she participated at every turn with gusto. One state official noted her energy and marveled, "Why, she outwalked women down there who are accustomed to walking."

She went beyond the packed schedule to take on an extra chore, crossing the street in Wallace at a child's pleading to go to her friend's sickroom and chat with the young convalescent. ER's report of the incident reveals more of her unassuming courtesy. "It occurred to me that the mother might have some objection to having her child visited without permission," she wrote delicately, "so I waited at the door until the father and mother appeared from the street and took us upstairs."[7]

Remembering the busy day decades later, May Thompson Evans asserted that "everybody who was there was impressed." Demonstrating an unfaltering ability to consider the feelings and meet the expectations of others required that Eleanor Roosevelt ignore her own discomfort or boredom, but successfully masking pieces of herself in this way was a long-standing practice of hers. A woman who participated in the busy day's activities reported approvingly, "[n]ot one thing that was done for her pleasure, comfort or entertainment escaped her appreciation."[8] Traditionally, southern ladies knew that southern hospitality involved making others feel appreciated and special. On this day in 1937, Eleanor Roosevelt was herself the very personification of the southern lady.

A few days after the North Carolina visit, a local woman reflected that "everyone loves Mrs. Roosevelt more than ever now and we marvel in her ability and her strength to do so much." In this woman's view, the first lady's visit had intensified the warm regard with which many local women viewed her. "We are even more consumed with admiration for you now that we have had this personal contact with you," she assured ER.[9]

Yet, only five years later, a group of white women of North Carolina denied Eleanor Roosevelt even a modicum of hospitality. This time the scene was Salisbury, a small city located in the Piedmont region of the state. Mrs. Roosevelt again undertook a strenuous schedule, touring the nearby Cannon textile mill, visiting the YWCA, reviewing a parade, leading a discussion forum. However, African Americans were the real focal points of her stop: She addressed the annual convention of women of the African Methodist Episcopal (AME) Zion church and was guest of honor at a luncheon with AME Zion officials at the home of an African American college president. The local arrangements committee had hoped to secure the cooperation of a prominent white woman in whose home the first lady could rest and refresh herself at some point during the day. But, in the words of a newswoman who had interviewed ER in a Salisbury hotel room, "no 'nice' home would receive her." To a woman, Salisbury's white matrons spurned the chance to extend hospitality to the president's wife, forcing the embarrassed committee to book an impersonal hotel room for ER's use. The admiration and love so evident in 1937 had seemingly evaporated by 1942.[10]

These opposite episodes feature different places, different women, and different circumstances. Yet it is safe to say that Eleanor Roosevelt's failure to accept and defend the racial status quo underlay the enmity of Salisbury's white women. Her decision to socialize in easy, familiar terms with a contingent of African Americans constituted a significant breach of the southern racial code. By sitting down to have iced tea and baked chicken with her black hosts, she jolted Salisbury middle-class white women and left them talking about her for weeks afterward. The indignant southern white view of this event held that "[r]ather than embarrass [her] colored friends [she] insulted the whole state." In the southern hierarchy of racial etiquette, dining with blacks was exceeded only by romantic and sexual attachment to Negroes as the most offensive kind of interracial intimacy. Such democratic displays of friendly courtesy led to venomous southern gossip about the first lady, with widespread rumors centering on her alleged sexual promiscuity with African Americans. Learning that her visit to Salisbury would include so much time spent with Negroes, the town's white women offered a united front of ostracism, only slightly broken when a YWCA executive managed to recruit a few white ministers' wives to meet her train. Their efforts at outreach ended at the railroad station, however; the imperative of racial etiquette trumped all other considerations, and Salisbury's frigid welcome was intended to underscore that fact.[11]

Out of the Salisbury visit grew a rumor that ER had imperiously demanded accommodations for several black women at the local hotel, an "urban myth" that proved so potent that southern editors contacted the White House for confirmation or denial. Eleanor herself commented that, while this rumor was inaccurate, she felt it did no good to deny it. Whenever asked about "social equality," she rejected the concept, reminding listeners that "in a democracy we can choose our friends according to our own individual desires." But, she maintained, the blatant unfairnesses governing the daily lives of minorities in this country impeded the U.S. war effort and should be addressed, the sooner the better.[12]

The Warm Springs matron who snarled, "We didn't like her a bit," had added, by way of explanation, "She ruined every maid we ever had." By the summer of 1942, when ER stopped in Salisbury, North Carolina, potent rumors of "Eleanor Clubs" were swirling through a Southland already shaken by the changes brought by war and feeling quite vulnerable. Despite a monochromatic advertising campaign, not every Rosie the Riveter was white; when the lure of defense jobs beckoned African American women, many had responded with alacrity. Hourly wages in the defense industry that equaled the going rate of pay for a full day of housework exercised a powerful pull.[13]

In the American South, even white women of slender means frequently enjoyed the part-time services of a maid-of-all-work. Wives of more comfortable status usually employed full-time help, while wealthy women hired two, and sometimes three, servants to free them from all the demands of cooking, cleaning, and childcare. The cruel limits of employment possibilities meant that black women who wanted work had found it chiefly in white men's fields or white women's homes, constituting a plentiful labor pool in which white women fished with very little silver on their hooks. For example, a physician's wife in Chapel Hill, North Carolina, recalled that, during the 1930s, she paid three dollars a week to her maid.[14] The war's voracious demand for labor created opportunities for black women undreamed of even a year or two before. One woman, who found work in an aircraft plant, summed up the effect: "Hitler was the one got us out of the white folks' kitchen."[15]

When the long-standing southern tradition of cheap household help began to erode, white women felt the change keenly. "I'm sure my cook has joined the Eleanor Club," Virginia Durr recalled hearing rich southern women say. "Every one of them has. You can't walk downtown any more because they will come up and just push you in the gutter."[16] Unable, after a systematic inquiry, to discover any Eleanor Clubs in reality, Howard Odum theorized in 1943 that malicious southerners had simply created them out of whole cloth in order to disparage Mrs. Roosevelt, whom they blamed for inspiring their previously subservient cooks to become more assertive. He singled out southern *women* in particular for keeping anti-Eleanor sentiment boiling, reporting that women's groups "in the highest brackets of southern society" took evident pleasure in repeating sordid rumors regarding Mrs. Roosevelt and the Negro and in telling each other about the initiation rites allegedly required of pledges to the "club." During the war, Arthur Schlesinger, Jr. discovered, even "a charming southern gentlewoman" was capable of a hysterical tirade on race, which culminated in her pointed denunciation of the first lady, whom she identified as the chief northern agitator causing unrest among a previously contented population of southern Negroes. "Everyone in the South," she informed her shocked listener, "hates Mrs. Roosevelt."[17]

Having the services of a housemaid was a badge, a visible indicator of a certain status for white women in the South; for some of them, being unable to find or keep one represented a threat to that status, while for all it constituted an unaccustomed burden. Eleanor Roosevelt was not the only figure criticized for her stand on economic justice for domestic servants. Jessie Daniel Ames, highly controversial in her role as leader of the Association of Southern Women to Prevent Lynching, drew less resistance from conservative southern women for her anti-lynching stand than for her advocacy of better wages for maids. "I was not popular. The women could take all of this other but the matter of what they paid their cooks was their own business. And I was just interfering, giving them ideas."[18] But there was no talk of a "Jessie Club." Eleanor Roosevelt's very public role as the embodiment of New Dealism made her an irresistible target for southern housewives' frustrations. Southern women's grumbling over the labor situation focused on the first lady and her maddeningly egalitarian ways. From her resignation from the Daughters of the American Revolution to protest their segregationist policy, to her frequent consorting with the very dark-skinned Mary McLeod Bethune, to her appearance at an interracial dance at a Washington USO (United Service Organization) during the war, Eleanor Roosevelt behaved in ways that deeply offended some southern women.[19]

While some southern women vilified Eleanor Roosevelt, others recognized her genuine kindness and sincere humanitarianism. All across the South, there were women who responded to her care and concern with an outpouring of admiration and affection. The best evidence for this assertion lies in box after box of correspondence at the FDR Library, where the response of southern women to the first lady's gentle invitation, "I want you to write to me freely. I want you to tell me about particular problems which puzzle and sadden you,"[20] can be measured in thousands of pages. Genteel or crude, educated or unschooled, these correspondents displayed a genuine warmth for Mrs. Roosevelt, however they expressed it.

Their response came like a tsunami. "It is one o'clock in the morning. I could not sleep for thinking of writing you and explaining how we are treated," said a mill worker's wife. "[T]hough you are the President's wife, I believe you could come into my cabin home & we could very comfortably have tea together," wrote Vera Dossey. "You have a talent for making everyone feel at ease." An Atlanta matron confided, "When you are proud it makes me happy and when you are rudely criticized it hurts me." "[S]ence I been sick have greatly injoyed reading of your kindness . . . you are a mother to us all and I read about how much you done for the intrest of the needy," wrote another. "I no the Lord will give you a crown."[21]

Many struggling southern women sent poems to Eleanor, trustingly requesting her to have them set to music, assuring her that they would be listening to hear their work on the radio. The FDR Library contains three full boxes of nothing but such verses to ER, giving proof of the central role of both the radio and the first lady by the 1930s. An Alabama sharecropper's wife enclosed a note of explanation with her verses. "[Y]ou being the first Lady of our Land people will do things for you they wont do for me." Relying on the economic pattern she knew best, she offered to work the cultural fields on halves. "[I]f you can find someone that will write the music and sell the song for half they get I sure will thank you a thousand times." A North Carolina woman's poem gives insight into aspects of Mrs. Roosevelt's behavior that inspired admiration and affection among women. Called "Mrs. Roosevelt Did," it catalogued her kind actions and asked if the reader would have done the same "if good fortune placed you as First Lady of the Land": "Would you visit many workrooms,/ Smiling kindly, scorning none,/ There to manifest your interest/ In the work that is being done?. . . Would your interest in the lowly/ Take you to the slums one day,/ Just to raise their plane of living,/ New ideas put into play?" Other stanzas asked if the reader as first lady would "stoop to help the underprivileged," "rush to catch a train each day, speaking, planning, helping others," "talk to throngs of young folks," "give a party to little children," and "keep a special diary for the public." For every question the refrain was the same: "Mrs. Roosevelt did." The poet captured the maternal qualities that Eleanor Roosevelt often displayed, ministering especially to the young, the old, the weak, and the powerless. These traits resonated particularly for women trained for generations to do the same.[22]

Many Americans came to view Eleanor Roosevelt, with some justification, as a virtual fairy godmother who could grant their deepest yearnings. Women wrote to ask for her old clothes, to urge her to buy their handicrafts, to describe in agonizing detail their latest health crisis, and to beg for assistance when financial disaster loomed. However, sometimes they asked enough to choke a horse, or so it seems. When a Virginia woman's husband secured a government job through ER's intervention with the appropriate agency, the fortunate wife promptly took up her pen again. "I have a sister also who needs work and my mother is a widow and she needs help," she informed Eleanor.[23]

The 1939 visit of the British royal couple generated a glare of media attention. Southern women followed the stories and newsreels along with the rest of an excited populace, reading of evening gowns and afternoon dresses, of entertainments planned and menus offered, marveling that the democratic Roosevelts had served hot dogs and beer (as well as much more elaborate fare) to the king and queen of England when they hosted a picnic at their Hyde Park estate. United in their verdict that ER had conducted herself splendidly as hostess for their majesties, delighted southerners wrote their approval. One woman, "overflowing with pride," praised the first lady for her "dignity and *natural* poise." A Georgia matron linked Mrs. Roosevelt's ease with royalty to her much-reported skills with the masses: "Any person like you, who can sympathize & walk with the lowly and underprivileged, can have no fear of walking with a King & Queen. Anyone with such a heart and background as you & our beloved president have, need never fear of doing the proper thing." Mrs. Blanche Hall probably voiced the sentiments of many when she wrote simply, "It would be nice to see a king and queen, but to me I had rather see you in person."[24]

The example of Eleanor Roosevelt was richly inspiring to women and girls in the South, where a thoroughly patriarchal society routinely relegated females to a secondary position. Tenant farmer husbands exercised tyrannical control over financial resources, never allowing wives to "tote the pocketbook" or have input in spending decisions. In the region's cotton mills, women outnumbered men in the labor force, but placing women in supervisory positions over men remained a rigid taboo. Poll taxes kept millions of poor women voteless as struggling husbands simply refused to pay them for their wives, thereby maintaining politics as a masculine endeavor, the Nineteenth Amendment notwithstanding. Whether we consider the memoirs of the well-bred Virginia Durr, in which she fumed over "the role that southern girls had to play . . . always fooling the men and being pleasant and putting up with anything" to get a husband, or the evidence of a southern woman who half-joked that she never tasted salt fish until she was grown (because by the time she had picked all the bones out of the breakfast fish for her brothers, it was time for her to go to school), or the accounts of southern holiday feasts at which women sometimes served the men, waited in the kitchen while they dined, and then fed themselves on what remained, the evidence indicating women's inferior position in southern society in the 1930s and 1940s is overwhelming.[25]

During Franklin Roosevelt's twelve years as president, southern women could contemplate the example of a new kind of first lady. Eleanor Roosevelt routinely traveled unescorted by husband, son, or any other male, and addressed large audiences of men and women with authority and confidence. In daily newspaper columns, magazine essays, and question-

and-answer formats, she stated her opinions forthrightly. Her powerful example of liberated womanhood found both admirers and detractors. The liberation that she had achieved, painfully, after personal crises in the 1920s, shocked traditionalists who preferred conventional, deferential, "ladylike" behavior. As an admirer put it, by "refus[ing] to step into her little mould in the biscuit tin of President's wives that was ready and waiting for her," Eleanor Roosevelt became, in her view, "one of the greatest things that has ever happened to [the women of America]."[26]

Whenever Mrs. Roosevelt visited the South, women flocked to hear her speak. In Raleigh, North Carolina, in 1934, the local press estimated that approximately 90 percent of her listeners were female, constituting "the largest gathering of their sex for an indoor event in the history of Raleigh." On that occasion, with thousands turned away for lack of seating, she emphasized fair wages, organized labor, better pay for school teachers, the importance of women registering and voting, and the need for women to subject government officials to close scrutiny to prevent dereliction of duty. Though she eschewed the label "feminist," her ideas about women were, in many ways, untraditional.[27]

Admiration for the pathbreaking ER was particularly keen among *young* women, both on southern college campuses and in the region's mill towns. Shortly before FDR's first election, lecturing at the Women's College of the University of North Carolina, Eleanor encouraged political awareness and brought the welcome message that candidates would soon be nominated and elected on their qualifications alone, "without regard to sex." Students might joke about the frantic spiffing up of campus that an ER visit prompted, as well as their increased attention to personal neatness, but they clearly loved her for the ideals she cherished and the work she promoted. In turn, Eleanor drew energy from exposure to audiences of idealistic young women, whether collegiate or industrial. When Josephus Daniels addressed the graduates at his state's Women's College a few years later, he called the first lady "the real sister of every woman who thinks and labors to make this a better world." Mrs. Roosevelt had recently extended gracious hospitality to a female delegation of seven Alabama cotton mill workers, welcoming them as her houseguests in the White House when they came to Washington for a labor conference, taking her breakfast with them each morning. The awestruck young working women, he told his privileged audience, "found as cordial a welcome as the wives of royalty" and detected in their hostess "an understanding of the conditions under which woman workers live and a desire to improve them." Mailing an excerpt of these remarks to ER, Daniels reported that his audience of college women gave their greatest applause to these lines in his commencement address. An eighteen-year-old female factory worker from Tennessee summed up ER's influence as a powerful role model: "Say, she's swell," she told a reporter in 1935. "Why, I'm not ashamed of being a girl any more."[28]

Perhaps because of the stifling limitations of education, income, gender roles, and workload, few African American women in the South seem to have accepted Eleanor Roosevelt's sincere invitation to write to her of their lives and needs. There are letters from black women living outside the South, taking her to task for her use of the term *darky* in her autobiography, thanking her for her steady decency toward their race, and, toward the end of World War II, deploring the extent of racism embedded in the United States. The well-known correspondence between the first lady and the brash and articulate young Pauli Murray—black, female, and southern—forms the great exception to the absence of epistles from southern black women. Murray pressed ER steadily to do more to make the concept of "liberty and justice" meaningful for Negroes, while ER patiently pointed out significant political obstacles to rapid change but never dampened Murray's ardor for reform by any ill-considered negativism. Occasionally in her frank exchanges with Murray, ER cautioned, "This letter is confidential and not for publication," a caveat that the younger woman respected. Ultimately, Murray recognized ER's capacity for growth. "Mrs. Roosevelt went to the very perimeters of whatever her limitations were. She went to the very boundaries of those limitations. And that is what makes her great in my eyes . . . you can see this painful growth, step by step by step." In addition to the first lady's contributions to improved conditions for black Americans, Murray attributed the revival of the women's movement to ER's example.[29]

Female Democratic Party activists down South also held Eleanor in high regard. The story of the first lady's efforts to promote women within the party and her solid understanding of party politics, gained in the 1920s in her work with the Women's Division of the New York State Democratic Party, is by now well known. As first lady, she used her influence skillfully to encourage women in state Democratic organizations, networking widely, sending words of support, occasionally intervening at the federal level to help achieve some desired effect. Southern women activists, living in a society in which male resistance to female autonomy was endemic, developed a special regard for her; they could see exactly what she was doing to advance the cause of women and of reform. The dean of the Women's College in North Carolina, an enthusiastic Democratic activist, thanked ER for the "inestimable contribution" she was making and predicted that her "spiritual and intellectual life [would] influence the trend toward a more decent civilization for many years to come."[30]

The Roosevelt administration depended greatly upon women for organization and votes. Southern women took prominent roles in the Women's Division of the Democratic Party, where they worked with Mollie Dewson and Eleanor Roosevelt to promote a liberal political agenda and to liberalize the party in their region. For activist southern women who hewed to a liberal agenda, pushed for reforms, or promoted progressive solutions to community problems, Eleanor Roosevelt was a particular inspiration. North Carolinian May Thompson Evans (serving first as state president of the Young Democrats and later as assistant director of the Women's Division of the Democratic Party) recalled of ER, "She influenced women to organize to secure the legislation that they believed in. She hammered away at that all the time," and added, "Her impact was terrific."[31]

Correspondence in the papers of the Women's Division of the Democratic National Committee shows that southern women worked diligently at the grassroots political tasks of raising money, broadcasting radio programs, and boosting subscriptions to the *Democratic Digest*. The letters also reveal that the leaders who motivated local workers to "hammer away" at these tasks drew their energy from contact with Eleanor Roosevelt herself. Mrs. Roosevelt combined deep and special interest in the political action of women with her good memory for names to establish a feeling of relationship through what one southern woman called "moment-contacts." Southern women activists battled gender prejudice and a deep, almost genetic conservatism as they worked for a better society along New Deal lines. That they had a sympathetic ally in the White House sustained them through some hard times. The southern woman who headed the Democratic Women's Division wrote gratefully to ER after the 1944 campaign, "You have been wonderful to us when we have turned to you for help, and I cannot tell you how much it has meant to feel that we could come to you when we confronted difficulties and that you would understand our problems." She closed her letter by reminding Mrs. Roosevelt of the "loyalty and affectionate admiration of women" for ER, which she had observed at countless political meetings where, she wrote, "they always speak out from full hearts of your courage and leadership." Eleanor Roosevelt's effect upon the sometimes lonely liberal contingent of southern women was dramatic. "All of a sudden you felt that you were not by yourself," recalled Virginia Foster Durr. "We knew that Eleanor just had to pick up the telephone and call Franklin. We had the feeling of having the power of the government on our side."[32]

Eleanor Roosevelt's well-known role as pipeline to her husband thrilled southern women activists; their concerns stood a fair chance of being related to the president himself by his wife. One southern woman who particularly relied on the ER-to-FDR apparatus was Lucy Randolph Mason. Bluest of bluebloods, the Virginian Mason organized for the CIO in Dixie, a daunting task in a region notoriously hostile to unionization. Eleanor's sympathy for industrial workers, her concern over their exploitation, and her belief in the right of labor to organize and bargain collectively were widely known. When "Miss Lucy" reported the particularly oppressive tactics being used against labor down South, ugly efforts at intimidation, even kidnappings and beatings, ER's concern was genuine. Many of Mason's letters to ER are marked in hand "The President has read," clear evidence that ER passed them on to FDR with a request that he take an interest.[33]

In late 1938, Mason's distress mounted over a situation involving textile workers at the Merrimac Mills in north Alabama. There, union-busting officials had evicted seventy-three families from company housing, targeting only the union members. With winter fast approaching, Mason, haunted by the thought of exhausted women struggling to shelter their little children, drove herself to find tents and blankets for them, to no avail. There exists a handwritten note from Mason to ER, scrawled while both were attending the Southern Conference for Human Welfare (SCHW) meeting in Birmingham. In it Mason asked ER to meet her and three "desperate people who are evicted from their homes" for five minutes, "in the rear wing on the Negro side." Mason, hoping that FDR could be moved to order CCC (Civilian Conservation Corps) tents for the homeless southerners, wanted ER to hear personally from them. That is exactly what happened. After the encounter, ER carried her message to FDR and, subsequently, the federal government provided tents for evicted workers. With this clear indication that Washington supported workers' efforts to unionize, the situation was resolved when pragmatic mill management ceased evictions and signed a contract with the textile workers of Merrimac. "You had a very significant part in the final solution," Mason told Eleanor, "and all of us are deeply grateful."[34]

Mason continued to feel grateful to ER. Working in a region whose elites were hostile to the principles of economic and racial justice that Mason held sacred, she frequently poured out her concerns to the first lady. Whenever Mason was in Washington or New York, she wrote asking if ER could see her. Quite often, Eleanor made time and they had lunch or at least some face-to-face time. From this connection, Mason drew the courage and strength to go on with very difficult CIO work in the South, while ER gained information on southern economic, racial, and political realities. She clearly valued Mason, requested that she keep her up-to-date on the South via letters in between visits, and looked to her for suggestions on how she might use her position to foster economic justice in the South. Just before ER met with the Georgia Rural-Urban Women's Conference in Atlanta in 1938, for example, Mason wrote, in a typical exchange, to say that ER could help the cause of labor unions in the South "tremendously" by saying "something about your belief in labor unions and your long associations with the Women's Trade Union League." ER obliged.[35]

Mason's admiration for Mrs. Roosevelt knew no bounds. She joined the chorus of southern liberals who implored a reluctant ER to attend the second conference of the controversial SCHW, urging "we need you because you are the most beloved, trusted, respected, and admired woman in America." On another occasion, she confided to ER, "You always renew my faith in life and humanity," and yet again, she proclaimed, "[T]hank God Mr. Roosevelt is President and you *are you.*"[36]

If Eleanor Roosevelt was the soul of the New Deal, in her emphasis upon the needs of helpless or disadvantaged individuals, it stands to reason that she was distressed by much of what she found in the impoverished, racist, class-ridden South. Her distress made her eager to help the region. The bottom line is really this: Any southerner who accepted the status quo with equanimity found ER a menace, because she worked tirelessly for change. Harvard Sitkoff concluded of her, "Certainly no individual did more to alter the relationship between the New Deal and the cause of civil rights."[37] Southern politicians traditionally had promised little and delivered less, keeping taxes low and government services few. To pacify the masses, they commonly promoted tension and clashes between working-class whites and blacks, fomenting race hatred as a leitmotif to deflect criticism from their own shortcomings. To the extent that the New Deal empowered people who had never enjoyed the safety of the middle-class mainstream, which it did by creating opportunities for those southerners, black and white, who had lived on the margins of life, it challenged the privileges of the southern elite and the southern middle class.

Newly empowered southerners became wage earners, bank depositors, homeowners, and voters. They voted their interests, which meant voting for Franklin Roosevelt and his New Deal. A southerner who deplored these developments would have groused about FDR, but FDR was hard to hate. He palpably radiated bonhomie and special fondness for the South; his easy charm helped to soothe many who, as the years went by, felt increasingly uneasy about the New Deal. His praise for southern hospitality, inclusion of southerners in his Cabinet and White House staff, and general responsiveness to the South led many flattered southerner traditionalists to feel that, as one put it, the nation was "taking [the South] back into the Union."[38] It was far easier for an anti–New Deal southerner to dislike Mr. Roosevelt's *wife*, a wordy woman who opposed the poll tax, advocated higher wages for domestic servants, spoke positively of the rights of labor, quite obviously rejected the principle of "woman's place," and treated everyone, whether tenant farmer, mill worker, washwoman, or the queen of England, with respect. Unlike her husband, she had not been elected to any office, had no mandate to exercise power, and could not pour out blessings from the alphabetic cornucopia of New Deal programs onto a suffering land. But to many southerners, the contrast between Franklin and Eleanor was simple: she was all stick and no carrot. Interpreting her challenges to the constants of race, gender, and class arrangements in the South as a reproach to the South and its way of life as well as an unwarranted interference by an unelected busybody, many southerners resented her bitterly. A woman who had frequented social gatherings at Warm Springs remembered Eleanor Roosevelt coolly: "She always made us feel like we were under inspection." Of FDR, she recalled, "He was fun, but *she* . . ." And here, she allowed her voice to trail off.[39]

It is a difficult task to privilege a mere handful of voices out of all the thousands and thousands of pages of correspondence that southern women directed to Eleanor Roosevelt. Some sent venom, others the elixir of friendship. While one vowed across the miles, "you are the sweetest person I have ever known," another snarled, "That race riot in Detroit is a terrible and horrible thing . . . due largely . . . to your unwise talks and actions. Why don't you stay home and quit talking and writing on everything under the sun?"[40] For every southern woman who praised Mrs. Roosevelt, there were others who denounced her because she threatened the way of living that they preferred. The southern economic and racial status quo found energetic defenders in southern women. Said the sister of the owner of a giant southern textile enterprise, "Burlington didn't need [unions] . . . If you got a union in a mill . . . they stir up trouble." Commented another, "The Negroes were better off under slavery. Southerners are the only people who understand how to treat the Negro."[41]

Writing in spring 1945, when Eleanor Roosevelt was a widow of one month, one correspondent, taking notice of an aspect of the first lady's personality that others had remarked on over the years, expressed sentiments that many southern women might have seconded. In the midst of the emotional and logistical upheaval of moving out of the White House, ER had nevertheless written in "My Day" of her hope that a particular robin would return to her feeder in this, the last spring of the war. "Your not being too busy to tell us about the robin tells me again, that you have time to be interested in the little things of life," the Tennessee woman wrote appreciatively, "and *that is why you are so useful to humanity.*"[42] Some southern women would have liked ER much better had she confined her interests to matters like robins and bird feeders, but this unusual first lady's restless spirit drove her to take an interest in so much more, in sharecroppers' rights, cooks' wages, and the plight of "millbillies" and "lintheads." This fact, coupled with southern fealty to gender conventions, accounts for the extremes of feeling that Eleanor Roosevelt aroused in the American South while her husband was president.

Resting on the twin pillars of white supremacy and patriarchy, the South in the 1930s and 1940s discovered that the president's wife threatened both. For some, the discovery was stimulating and encouraging, for others, a highly unwelcome realization. In this duality lies much of the explanation for southern responses, both positive and negative, toward Eleanor Roosevelt. To employ the phrase used by the woman quoted above, what really constituted being "useful to humanity"? Southern women answered the question in various ways, and judged Mrs. Roosevelt accordingly.

Notes

1. Louise O. Charlton to ER, October 2, 1936; Katherine Hazard to ER, June 28, 1943, both in Eleanor Roosevelt Papers, Franklin D. Roosevelt Library, Hyde Park, N.Y. Hereafter cited as ER Papers.

2. Quoted in Theo Lippman, *The Squire of Warm Springs: FDR in Georgia, 1924–1945* (Chicago, 1977), 91.

3. Rexford Tugwell interview with Emily Williams, March 30, 1979, 41–2, transcript in FDR Library.

4. Doris Kearns Goodwin, *No Ordinary Time* (New York, 1992), 315, 333; Ruth

Stevens, "*Hi-Ya Neighbor*" (n.p., 1947), 38–9; Harold Ickes, *The Secret Diary of Harold Ickes: The First Thousand Days 1933–1936* (New York, 1953), 240–1; Joseph Lash, *Eleanor and Franklin* (New York, 1971), 296–7; Blanche Wiesen Cook, *Eleanor Roosevelt 1933–1938*, vol. 2 (New York, 1999), 154–5; Jonathan Daniels, *Washington Quadrille: The Dance Behind the Documents* (New York, 1968), 207. Frank Friedel, *FDR and the South* (Baton Rouge, 1965) remains the best account of Roosevelt's attachment to Warm Springs.

5. May Thompson Evans interview with Thomas Soapes, January 30, 1973, 24, transcript in FDR Library.

6. Account of day drawn from "First Lady Brings Message of Cooperation to Wallace," *Raleigh News and Observer,* June 12, 1937; Eleanor Roosevelt, "My Day in Wallace," *Raleigh News and Observer,* June 13, 1937; May Thompson Evans interview.

7. ER, "My Day in Wallace," *Raleigh News and Observer,* June 13, 1937.

8. Mrs. J. A. Yarbrough, "A Close-up of the First Lady," *Charlotte Observer,* June 20, 1937, clipping in box 659, ER Papers.

9. Lewellyn (Mrs. John) Robinson to May Thompson Evans, June 18, 1937, in May Thompson Evans Papers, Department of Archives and History, Raleigh, N.C.; and Robinson to ER, July 10, 1937, in ER Papers.

10. Among Salisbury's citizens in 1942 were the Hanfords and their five-year-old daughter Liddy, who would grow up to become Elizabeth Hanford Dole. Valerie Nicholson, "No 'Nice' Home Would Receive Her," *The Pilot* (Southern Pines, N.C.), November 15, 1962, in North Carolina Collection clipping file, Davis Library, University of North Carolina-Chapel Hill.

11. J. S. McRae, Greensboro, N.C., to ER, June 22, 1943, in ER Papers.

12. Ibid. ER quote from undated *News and Observer* clipping (Carroll Kilpatrick, "Malicious Rumor") in Josephus Daniels to ER, December 22, 1942, ER Papers; Jonathan Daniels, *White House Witness: 1942–45* (New York, 1975), 100. See also ER correspondence to Pauli Murray, in which she commented at length about "social equality." In her public statements about race, ER was circumspect and far from radical. While urging justice and fair treatment, she avoided endorsing militant action and, on occasion, counseled black Americans to proceed slowly in their march toward racial equality.

13. Lippmann, *The Squire of Warm Springs,* 91.

14. Norma Berryhill, interviewed by Mary Friday, March 9, 1978, 27, transcript in Southern Oral History Collection, Wilson Library, University of North Carolina-Chapel Hill (hereafter cited as SOHC).

15. Fannie Christina Hill, "Rosie the Riveter," in *Modern American Women: A Documentary History,* ed. Susan Ware (Belmont, Calif., 1989), 246.

16. Hollinger F. Barnard, ed., *Outside the Magic Circle: The Autobiography of Virginia Foster Durr* (Tuscaloosa, Ala., 1985), 114.

17. Howard Odum, *Race and Rumors of Race* (Chapel Hill, 1943), 25, 79–87;

Arthur Schlesinger, Jr., *A Life in the Twentieth Century: Innocent Beginnings, 1917–1950* (Boston, 2000), 272–4.

18. Jessie Daniel Ames, interviewed by Pat Watters, 35, transcript in SOHC, 35.

19. For the controversy over ER's resignation from the DAR see Allida Black, "Championing a Champion: Eleanor Roosevelt and the Marian Anderson 'Freedom Concert,'" *Presidential Studies Quarterly* 20 (fall 1990): 719–37. On ER's friendship with Bethune, see Cook, *Eleanor Roosevelt,* vol. 2, 159–61. ER's visit to a non–Jim Crow canteen in the nation's capital in 1944 prompted impassioned disapproval from southerners who deplored her presence at an occasion where young white women mingled with black servicemen. See for example Hendrix Rowell, Pine Bluff, Ark., to Congressman Charles McKenzie, March 15, 1944, in ER Papers.

20. Eleanor Roosevelt, "I Want You to Write to Me," *Woman's Home Companion* 60 (August 1933): 4.

21. Mrs. J. W. Hallman to ER, January 29, 1934, quoted in Jacquelyn Dowd Hall et al., *Like a Family: The Making of a Southern Cotton Mill World* (Chapel Hill, 1984), 293; Vera Dossey, Fountain Run, Ky., to ER, January 22, 1945; Mrs. W.T.S. Dickey, Atlanta, Ga., to ER, March 2, 1939; Sarah Jane Lee, Crab Orchard, Ky., to ER, n.d. [December 1937]; second, third, and fourth quotes in ER Papers.

22. Mrs. H. A. Harris, Havana, Ala., to ER, July 10, 1940; Mrs. Will Carter, "Mrs. Roosevelt Did," *Raleigh News and Observer,* n.d. [1936], all in ER Papers.

23. Mrs. Everett Marks, Richmond, Va., to ER, March 12, 1937, in ER Papers.

24. Ruth Campbell, Richmond, Va., to ER, June 13, 1939; Betty Lou (Mrs. E. G.) Duke, Palmetto, Ga., to ER, June 10, 1939; Mrs. Blanche Hall, Fort Bellvoir, Va., to ER, May 10, 1939, in ER Papers.

25. Margaret Jarman Hagood, *Mothers of the South: Portraiture of the White Tenant Farm Woman* (Chapel Hill, 1939), 160; Hall et al., *Like a Family,* 72; Sarah Wilkerson Freeman, "The 'Second Battle' for Woman Suffrage: Southern White Women, the Poll Tax, and V. O. Key's Master Narrative of Southern Politics," forthcoming in *Journal of Southern History*; Barnard, *Outside the Magic Circle,* 103; Norma Berryhill, interviewed by Mary Friday, March 9, 1978, 2–3, SOHC; Jimmy Carter, *Christmas in Plains* (New York, 2001), passim.

26. Fannie Hurst, "A First First Lady," *The Democratic Digest,* March 1935, 7.

27. "Mrs. Roosevelt Expresses Confidence in the Future," *Raleigh News and Observer,* June 12, 1934.

28. On opinion among southern college women, correspondence from Anne Firor Scott to the author, September 18, 1997; Eleanor Roosevelt quoted in Sarah Wilkerson-Freeman, "Women and the Transformation of American Politics: North Carolina, 1898–1940" (Ph.D. diss., University of North Carolina, 1995), passim; Josephus Daniels to ER, June 8, 1937, in ER Papers. Mill worker and labor organizer Eula McGill discussed the stay at the White House in her interview with Jacquelyn Dowd Hall, SOHC. See also "This Is On You," in student newspaper of Woman's College of University of North Carolina, March 23, 1945, clipping in Eleanor

Roosevelt file, North Carolina Collection, University of North Carolina-Chapel Hill. University of North Carolina president Frank Porter Graham told ER that, in his state, "[m]any of your staunchest supporters are Alumnae of the Woman's College"; FPG to ER, May 14, 1940, in ER Papers. Susan Ware, *Still Missing: Amelia Earhart and the Search for Modern Feminism* (New York, 1993), 143.

29. On "darky," see Mrs. Esther Carey to ER, April 13, 1937; on racism during the war, see ER to Pauli Murray, October 3, 1944, and Katie Robinson to ER, March 1, 1944, in ER Papers. See Pauli Murray's memoirs, *Proud Shoes: The Story of an American Family* (New York, 1956) and *Song in a Weary Throat: An American Pilgrimage* (New York, 1987). Pauli Murray interview with Thomas Soapes, February 3, 1978, transcript in ER Oral History Project, FDR Library.

30. Blanche Wiesen Cook particularly stresses Eleanor the canny politician in her excellent biography, *Eleanor Roosevelt*, vols. 1 and 2 (New York, 1992 and 1999). Dean Harriet Elliott to ER, October 16, 1943, ER Papers.

31. May Thompson Evans interview, 9.

32. Evans interview, 57–65 in transcript; Gladys Avery Tillett to ER, November 27, 1944, in ER Papers; Barnard, *Outside the Magic Circle*, 127.

33. For examples of letters so marked, see various correspondence from Lucy Randolph Mason to ER in series 70, boxes 321 and 322 of ER Papers. See also John Salmond's excellent biography of Mason, *Miss Lucy of the CIO: The Life and Times of Lucy Randolph Mason 1882–1959* (Athens, Ga., 1988).

34. Lucy R. Mason to ER, undated [November 1938]; Mason to ER, November 28, 1938; Mason to ER, December 9, 1938, all in ER Papers.

35. Lucy Randolph Mason to ER, February 11, 1938, in ER Papers.

36. Lucy Randolph Mason to ER, February 10, 1940; January 8, 1942; February 1, 1938, all in ER Papers.

37. Harvard Sitkoff, *A New Deal for Blacks* (New York, 1978), 65.

38. Stevens, *Hi-Ya Neighbor*, 50.

39. Quoted in Lippmann, *Squire of Warm Springs*, 221–2.

40. Alice Winston Spruill, Rocky Mount, N.C., to ER, June 20, 1939; anonymous, Memphis, to ER, June 23, 1943, both in ER Papers.

41. First quote, Cornelia Spencer Love interview with Lee Kessler, January 26, 1975, 47, transcript in Southern Oral History Program, UNC; second quote from Schlesinger, *A Life in the Twentieth Century*, 272.

42. Sarah Hunter, Johnson City, Tenn., to ER, May 12, 1945, in ER Papers; italics mine.

IV

The Era of Social Change

10

Esther Cooper Jackson

A Life in the Whirlwind

SARAH HART BROWN

When Esther Cooper, executive director of the Southern Negro Youth Congress (SNYC), introduced W.E.B. Du Bois to the 850 delegates crowded into the chapel of Columbia's Benedict College for SNYC's 1946 Youth Legislature, she had already shown her willingness to make "the great sacrifice" Du Bois would soon call for. An admirer of Du Bois since childhood, Cooper embodied the hope, energy, and militancy of the message he proclaimed that day in what has become known as his "Behold the Land" speech. He asked young people to stay in the South and work for justice because "the oil and sulfur; the coal and iron; the cotton and corn; the lumber and cattle belong to you the workers, Black and white, and not to the thieves who hold them to enslave you," underscoring both her deep commitment and her views about the cynical racism of southern planters and their capitalist allies.[1]

As the wife of a recently returned World War II veteran and mother of a young daughter, her experience paralleled most of her contemporaries' lives. Yet Cooper displayed progressive intellectualism and personal independence rare among American women of her day. Du Bois had described the importance of training "exceptional men" in his famous 1903 "Talented Tenth" essay, but surely the diminutive, feminine Esther Cooper fit into that fraction singled out for leadership. Her colleagues called her "high principled, serious, and fearless," a leader who "brought new fervor and imagination to the struggle for freedom." A natural and self-assured feminism also resulted from Cooper's dedication to equality. When, after nearly fifteen years of marriage, she adopted the practice of using her husband's surname, the change resulted not from a turn toward tradition but because he faced prosecution as a Communist under the Smith Act, and she wanted to show public support and solidarity. "I guess," she said sixty years later, "we were just advanced" in the 1940s.[2]

The Cooper family's history provides some clues about its "advanced" daughter. Her father, George Posia Cooper, served with Theodore Roosevelt in Cuba and then in the army of occupation in the Philippines at the end of the Spanish American War. In 1917, about two months after the birth of his second daughter, Esther, he received lieutenant's bars at "the first Officers' Training Camp for Negroes" in Iowa. His unit served in France with distinction, and in 2002 Esther still kept "some plates and the silk apron he brought back to me from Paris." George Cooper remained in the army for thirty years, until 1928, when he took a job at the Bureau of Printing and Engraving in Washington. Although his own father, Anderson Cooper, had been "the first colored teacher in Rutherford County, Tennessee," the George Cooper family always lived in Arlington, near his first posting at Ft. Meyer, Virginia. Even after his retirement, Esther Cooper Jackson said, he loved to ride horseback at Ft. Meyer.[3]

Lieutenant Cooper's pride in his three active, talented daughters—Kathryn, Esther, and Paulina—never flagged. "He was the kind of father who would clap louder—embarrass us, even in grade school," Esther said. She regretted that he died just before her college graduation in 1938: "I knew if he came to Oberlin he'd be the proudest [parent there]—and the last clap—he was looking very much forward to it." Cooper treasured education, music, and books. Esther remembered that "even before we had electricity—we were still using lamps—[my parents] had plenty of books." The girls took piano lessons and the family used a Victrola to play the records her father selected: Marian Anderson, Roland Hayes, Enrico Caruso, and many others. The Coopers had sets of encyclopedias, read the Harvard Classics, and never missed an issue of *The Crisis*, the monthly magazine of the National Association for the Advancement of Colored People (NAACP), edited by Du Bois until 1934. "Around the dinner table we discussed Jim Crow, and the history of African Americans, and we read Du Bois's column [in *The Crisis*]."[4]

Books, music, and politics played a large part in their lives, but the Cooper parents also planned recreational outings in ways that, as much as possible, shielded their young children from the sting of segregation—family picnics, trips to "the circus in Washington (because it was segregated in so many other places) . . . and to the black theaters on 'U' Street where we saw movies; and we did a lot of things at home together." In the summers, too, the sisters felt a respite from Jim Crow. The family vacationed in Sea Isle

City, New Jersey, or in Cleveland and other parts of Ohio with their mother's family. "It was wonderful," Esther remembered, "because when we went to [Sea Isle City or] Cleveland we could go to the beach."[5]

Esther's mother became the social activist in the family and perhaps the paradigm for her namesake daughter. And Esther Irving Cooper followed in the footsteps of her own female ancestors, including a stalwart abolitionist great-grandmother who brought her free black family across the Appalachians from North Carolina to Ohio by ox-cart in the 1850s, and her aunt, a conductor on the Underground Railroad. In 1913 Esther Irving won a civil service job with the U.S. Forest Service by taking the exam in Cleveland. Her race turned out to be a surprise at the agency, and although the offer held, "there was some discrimination." Soon thereafter she married George Cooper, and although she took a leave of absence before the birth of her first daughter and stayed at home during the children's earliest years, she continued in government service after they entered school. Later she taught business subjects at the National Training School for Women and Girls in Washington, founded by her good friend, the black educator and civil rights advocate Nannie Helen Burroughs.[6]

But Esther Irving Cooper's heart belonged to her community volunteer work—she served as a leader of her church, a founding member of the ecumenical group Church Women United, local president and state officer of the Parent Teacher Association (PTA), and an officer of the American Legion Auxiliary. She founded local and state committees to support progress in education and to establish recreational facilities for her community's children. "I used to get my braids pulled in schools sometimes when a student would say 'you think you're so cute 'cause your mother's in the school every day.' And my mother *was* always there," her daughter claimed, "she was president of the PTA; and she was always taking delegations down to Richmond to the capitol." With others from the NAACP and the Southern Conference for Human Welfare, Esther Irving Cooper organized pickets to protest the 1939 premier of *Gone with the Wind* because it "distorted our history and the role that blacks played in their own liberation." She lost a race for National Democratic Committeewoman by a slim margin, and fought long and hard to increase the local black vote. Most of all, she worked with and for the NAACP, first in the Washington branch, then as a founder and long-time president of the Arlington branch of the organization.[7]

Esther Cooper Jackson recalled her mother's public accomplishments, but remembered even more her private admonitions "to be kind to others—she wouldn't let us say anything about any other racial group" or make any kind of racial slurs.

> There was a Jewish storekeeper in the neighborhood, Finklestein, and black kids would make all kinds of remarks, but not us. . . . Then, I remember some of the blacks in the neighborhood would say a verse in front of the Chinese laundry: "Chinese, Chinese, eat dead rats, chew them up like ginger snaps." And my mother said . . . you shouldn't say things like that about other people. . . . And the "n" word was never heard in our house. . . My mother would say "colored," she'd say African-American—I don't think she used the word black either, or my dad—they used colored a lot—but the "n" word, that was absolutely a no-no, even in reporting a story—we just did not use it.[8]

Because the segregated black schools in Arlington did not meet their standards, the Coopers sent their children to schools in the District of Columbia after the fifth grade. Esther attended Lovejoy Junior High School and then Dunbar High School, a very prestigious African American institution. Students at Dunbar, where Esther joined the National Honor Society, often outperformed white students in Washington on standardized tests, and 90 percent of them went on to college.[9]

During the years of school in Washington, one or two of the Cooper girls usually resided during the week with their "Uncle" George, their mother's cousin, George Richardson, and his wife, Ida. Dr. Richardson, a lawyer as well as a physician and the first black on the Washington city council, possessed "a tremendous library." "When I was quite young," Esther said, "I used to sit at his feet, and he would read the Washington papers and interpret world history." In the early 1930s he cautioned her "not to believe everything you are reading in the paper about what's going on in Russia, about the first and second five year plans. . . . There's a big experiment going on in that country," he said, "and you have to read between the lines." George Richardson remained an important influence in young Esther's life: "He was a scientist, and a very wonderful, loving, well-read man. . . . Frederick Douglass, Harriet Tubman, Abraham Lincoln, my Uncle George, my parents, these people were our heros."[10]

Regardless of the advantages of an essentially upper-middle-class upbringing, at least in its cultural elements, Esther and her sisters grew up in the Jim Crow South. Virginia maintained separate, substandard schools for African Americans; most libraries and recreational facilities were off-limits; they could not drink cokes at soda fountains or dine in local restaurants; and other indignities, large and small, confronted the growing girls despite their parents' protective care. "We knew from early childhood," she said, about "Jim Crow on all the transportation in Arlington; and sometimes we would just get so fed up with it that my sisters and I would get up and walk all the way across the bridge to Washington." As the nation's capital, Washington had integrated its public transportation, unlike its schools, "though one could not try on hats and shoes in places like Woodward and Lothrop." Their father, rather than receiving a deserved promotion, remained a junior officer until his retirement in the late 1920s, though often, his youngest daughter Paulina wrote, "the lights would burn late into the night at the family home in Ft. Meyer as he instructed a White candidate toward a higher rank."[11] These shameless but legally supported inequities added to their parents' sacrifices and expectations and, catalyzed by the depth of their education in black history and American history, not only at schools like Dunbar but in family settings, pushed Esther and her sisters toward excellence and toward challenging the segregated system that limited their reach. In the six years following her graduation from high school in 1934, Esther Cooper gained broader understanding of her people's grievances and of the national response to economic distress. As a college and graduate student in the years of the Great Depression, she studied American social problems and worried about the state of democratic capitalism in the United States—about race and class and oppression of the poor.

College meant Oberlin, in Ohio, which Jackson says was "supposed to be one of the 'liberal' institutions" in the 1930s but had fewer than ten black students during her four-year tenure, and Fisk, the black college in Nashville where W.E.B. Du Bois first felt the sting of southern segregation. She found Oberlin "very challenging" and, like other black students in her generation, "felt the weight of doing well because it was for the whole race." She applied herself vigorously to the academic work at hand, made both white and black friends among progressive students, had good relationships with several professors, and graduated with awards from the sociology department. Despite obvious racism among some in Oberlin's administration, the institution's intellectual freedom encouraged Esther Cooper's native interests and curiosity. "There were all kinds of radical activities taking place" on campus; "it was an open kind of situation where one could discuss a different point of view in the classroom and in organizations to which one belonged." During this time she began to consider herself a socialist and participated in the progressive student movement as a member of the leftist American Student Union and the pacifist Fellowship of Reconciliation. Members of the Young Communist League invited her to meetings, but as part of Oberlin's "large peace movement" she went mostly to argue, opposing the Communists' militant call for American involvement in the war beginning in Europe.[12]

The budding sociologist accepted a scholarship to Fisk University for graduate school, both because she wished to work with the eminent scholar Charles S. Johnson, then chair of Fisk's Social Science Department, and in order "to study at a black college and one that had its roots in struggle." As part of her scholarship she lived in a Methodist settlement house near the campus for her entire tenure at Fisk (1938–40) and worked with neighborhood families. This experience led her "off the main roads in Nashville," where she "saw for the first time the southern poverty of blacks . . . living in very horrible conditions." She came to know the hopelessness of these families and began thinking about the need for systemic change in American economic and social life. "Seeing these conditions, I felt that no small amount of change would do. . . . It helped steer me to radical politics." Her work experiences in Nashville probably also affected her thesis topic, "Negro Women Domestic Workers in Relation to Trade Unionism." As a part of this research she not only interviewed southern women but traveled to northern cities where "there had been some attempt to unionize domestic workers." There she witnessed the same appalling conditions that had inspired Ella Baker and Marvel Cooke's *Crisis* article "The Bronx Slave Market" just a few years before. Her thesis compared the plight of American domestic workers with the more favorable position of those in the Scandinavian countries that had unionized domestic workers. Addison T. Cutler, an economist and former Columbia University professor, directed it.[13]

Esther Cooper found "a number of white professors who were excellent" at Fisk, like Dr. Cutler and Dave and Naomi Robison, a faculty couple with whom she developed a close relationship. She also became friendly with several black members of the faculty, including the well-known muralist Aaron Douglas and William Allen, a musician who later became a prominent newspaper reporter in California. These members of Fisk's faculty were part of

> a group of radical professors there, at Fisk and [Tennessee] A&T [College], and they would introduce students they thought might be interested to Marxist literature. That's how I first started reading some

of this literature, from some of my professors. They would see students in their classes who had expressed opinions or ideas and they'd invite them over. One professor [Dr. Cutler] had what I called a little "Anne Frank" room—he kept all kinds of literature and would invite those students he was impressed with to read the literature.[14]

As the Spanish Civil War escalated in the late 1930s, the ranks of pacifists among American socialists declined. Influenced by her own reading and by her radical friends, Esther "began to shift and understood that there are wars and wars . . . that one had to support certainly the Civil War and the Revolutionary War . . . and I wasn't such a hard pacifist after that." She began reading the *Daily Worker* regularly; stories about labor organizers, workers, and the ongoing "Scottsboro Boys" case and other southern tragedies enlivened its columns. She became a Communist while at Fisk, because "the Communist Party . . . was, really, the one organization that was out in the streets and organizing" not only against capitalist inequity but against institutionalized racism. Like many others on the American left, her openness to the party came as a response to the collapse of capitalism in the 1930s and to what John Diggins calls "Russia's highly propagandized economic success" in that decade; but Esther found most inspiration for her choice in the American party's longtime dedication to equality for African Americans. She joined the party during the Popular Front period, years when the party doubled in size to about 82,000 members, became "almost respectable" (according to party chairman Earl Browder), and, as Ellen Schrecker has written, "served as the unofficial left-wing of the New Deal, its cadres and rank and file supplying manpower and leadership for a wide array of social reform movements and progressive political groups." In 1939 Esther attended the second annual conference of the Southern Conference for Social Welfare in Chattanooga, widening her contacts among southern liberal and leftist activists. "The two years in Nashville . . ." she recalled, "were very interesting and happy years."[15]

Not long after her party affiliation, Professor Charles Johnson asked Esther Cooper to give visiting activist and fellow Virginian James E. Jackson a tour of the Fisk campus. A recent pharmacy master's degree graduate of Howard University, Jackson made Fisk his headquarters while he worked with Howard professor Ralph Bunche as an investigator, gathering material for Gunnar Myrdal's ground-breaking *American Dilemma: The Negro in a White Nation*. Jackson had joined the Communist Party when he was sixteen, in 1931, the same year he and his father faced the indignities of a ceremony in which the Richmond Boy Scouts reluctantly awarded him a medal as the first black Eagle Scout in the state. Virginia's governor hung the award around each white Eagle Scout's neck, then simply threw James Jackson's metal toward the black Scout seated separately on the far end of the stage. Jackson's politics might also have been rooted in the anger he felt as a boy observing the lives of hardworking, indebted workers from Richmond's "sweatshops of tobacco"; early on he determined to "some day . . . strike a blow at this bloody system." The year before he joined the Myrdal study he had done just that: the twenty-one-year-old was thrown in jail as the leader of a successful strike of black women tobacco stemmers organized by the new Southern Negro Youth Congress. Insults like the Boy Scout ceremony, one of many which compounded the general offense of life in the Jim Crow South, his keen sensitivity to the working-class poverty around him, and a progressive upbringing in a family not unlike Esther Cooper's led Jackson to believe deeply in the necessity for radical transformation of America's political economy. Active in the left-oriented student movement while a student at Virginia Union University and Howard, and now deeply involved in SNYC, James Jackson's attraction to the brilliant, serious Esther Cooper—and hers to him—seems natural.[16]

Some of Cooper's radical friends in Nashville already knew "Jack," and they invited her to a dinner in his honor at a faculty home. "What impressed me most about him at the time," she wrote fifteen years later, "was his sincere and passionate desire to change the Jim Crow South and to unite Negro and white in bringing about that change." Though an exhausted Jack (then traveling across the lower South for the Myrdal study) slept through the movie on their first date, he wrote her soon afterwards that the best part of his Fisk visit had been meeting her: "a native unselfishness, a will to serve and to sacrifice, an ardent devotion to our cause, symbolized in the youthful beauty of a charming lady—and that's Esther to me."[17]

The Southern Negro Youth Congress had been formed as an outgrowth of the 1936 National Negro Congress conference in Chicago, at which young people voiced the need for a southern-based movement to fight poverty and racism. Because the leader of the youth movement, Edward Strong, left the country temporarily to attend the World Youth Congress in Geneva, James Jackson and Chris Alston, a black auto worker, shouldered the responsibility for planning the first SNYC conference. They attracted about five hundred delegates to Richmond in February 1937. At this first meeting several young Communists were elected as SNYC officers, and one of the speakers on the first day was Angelo Herndon, a young

party member whose appeal of his Georgia conviction for inciting insur-
rection awaited a U.S. Supreme Court decision. But Dr. Mordecai W.
Johnson, widely respected president of Howard University, delivered the
keynote address challenging youth "to go into the South and make
changes," and throughout its life SNYC would operate as a Popular Front
group—that is, while many of its leaders were Communists, the party
never controlled the organization, and liberal church, university, and civic
leaders always supported its work, sending speakers and youth delegations
to annual conventions. In 1937 SNYC's "advisory committee consisted of
distinguished individuals in the field of politics and education," such as
Mary McLeod Bethune; Charlotte Hawkins Brown; Abon Hosley of
Tuskegee, president of the National Negro Business League; Atlanta University president Rufus Clement; and Fisk sociologist Charles Johnson.[18]

Dr. Johnson might have encouraged his student Esther Cooper to ob-
serve SNYC's second "All-Southern Negro Youth Conference" in Chattanooga, but she did not attend—or meet James Jackson and Edward
Strong—until the third conference, which brought about 650 young
southerners to Birmingham in April 1939, the spring before Jackson's visit
to Fisk. "I went and met a lot of really activist young people there," she
said, "It was a real eye-opener for me, and a very important period in my
life." After she completed her master's degree in May 1940, Cooper received a telegram from Jackson and Strong inviting her to become a volunteer in SNYC's summer voting rights campaign, a project just initiated at
the organization's fourth annual conference in New Orleans. SNYC had
moved its headquarters from Richmond to Birmingham, with Strong, a
Texas native, party member, and former head of the youth division of the
National Negro Congress, as executive director. A recent Rosenwald scholarship offer for Ph.D. study with sociologist Robert Park at the University
of Chicago, a plum for any sociologist, must have complicated Cooper's
decision. But her will to serve—and her heart—pulled her toward Birmingham: "I discussed it with my mother, and she said, go ahead, try it.
And then I stayed there—what was it?—seven years."[19]

Goals of SNYC's "right to vote" campaign launched at the New Orleans
meeting included the elimination of the poll tax, an end to literacy requirements for voting, and protection from physical and economic intimidation
for black registrants and voters. In June the Birmingham NAACP, the CIO,
and local educators cooperated in a community kickoff event at the Sixth
Avenue Baptist Church. Members of the League of Young Southerners
(LYS), an idealistic, predominantly white group of young people closely

connected to the Southern Conference for Human Welfare and also recently based in Birmingham, actively assisted SNYC's organizing and field work. Despite the Byzantine difficulties of managing an interracial alliance in Jim Crow Alabama, SNYC and LYS worked together to publicize the Geyer anti–poll tax bill then introduced in Congress, and set up classes to teach prospective registrants about the problems and pitfalls of Alabama's voter registration process. Foreshadowing the sixties generation of civil rights activists, volunteers taught black Alabamians "precisely what their rights were with respect to the poll tax, property qualifications, and voter registration for veterans," and SNYC volunteers called the "Caravan Puppeteers" began putting on puppet shows in rural and urban venues with topics such as how to vote, how to register, how to fight the plantation owner, and so forth. Mill managers and planters seldom suspected that such subversive messages might be imbedded in seemingly harmless theater. In addition to voting rights activities, members of SNYC poured their energy into union organizing efforts in mills and mines, worked with students; wrote articles, plays, and broadsides against injustices such as police brutality or the causes of rural poverty; or joined in the national anti–poll tax or anti-lynching campaigns of the Southern Conference for Human Welfare.[20]

That first summer Esther and Jack were arrested handing out anti–poll tax literature at one of the Tennessee Coal and Iron Company's sites, the Hamilton Slope mine. During a shift change, the couple became separated from their LYS colleagues and were

> picked up at gunpoint by the superintendent of the plant. . . . They took us to this little shack in the middle of the place [to await arrival of the police]. But Henry Mayfield was in the next shift that was to go down into the mine, and he was president of the UMW local. He and the men refused to go down into the shift and surrounded the shack where we were being held, and forced them to release us. This was our hero, Henry Mayfield.[21]

They remained close to Mayfield, a native of rural Alabama, union activist, and vice chairman of SNYC, who was a long-time stalwart of the Alabama Communist Party. They also knew and loved Hosea Hudson, the former sharecropper turned steelworker and union organizer whose story was told in his autobiography and in Nell Irvin Painter's magnificent *Narrative of Hosea Hudson: His Life as a Negro Communist in the South*.[22]

In his book *When the Old Left Was Young*, Robert Cohen comments on

SNYC's "idealism regarding the working class" as a motivating force for community organizing "beyond the campus." Most of SNYC's leaders had become activists through the campus-based student movement, but they tried hard to enlist workers, black and white, in the cause of building a more democratic South. Members of LYS and SNYC, Robin D. G. Kelley writes, "shared a common democratic socialist vision, espoused a militant interracialism, and pledged full support for the CIO organizing campaign and a civil rights agenda." "We very deliberately tried to involve white young people," Esther Cooper Jackson said, "and most of them were out of the colleges, but there were some young trade unionists. And . . . in the coal mines it was the black miners who really initiated all the organization, but we got some young white coal miners in . . . I remember delegations of young white people who actually participated in all of our conferences." SNYC's leaders embarked upon their ten-year mission in Birmingham "fueled by both Marxist ideology and the new dynamism of the labor movement," says Cohen, and keenly aware that no other "militant" organizations existed specifically to fight Jim Crow and disfranchisement.[23]

On a personal level, the experience of being a part of SNYC in the years just before World War II must have been both exciting and difficult. Just finding a place to live presented difficulties, especially in the beginning. Ed Strong and his wife, Augusta Jackson, had secured an apartment in a low-income housing project ("the best housing for blacks in Birmingham"), and during part of the summer of 1940 almost the whole Birmingham staff lived at least part of the time in their apartment, among them James Jackson, Esther Cooper, New Yorkers Louis and Dorothy Burnham, the poet Warren Cuny, and another young activist from Harlem who put on puppet shows. When the crowd got too large for the cots in the Strong's apartment, some of them moved to the nearby home of Sallye and Frank Davis (who were probably not, like most of these young people, members of the Communist party, though their daughter Angela would be the most famous American Communist of the next generation). But these were serious young militants on a mission, not members of a house party, Esther reported: "We were sitting up all night writing fliers—we had one of those old mimeograph machines. And something was happening [that we had to address] almost every weekend—some policeman, some shooting. We were too exhausted, even if we wanted to, to be involved in hanky panky."[24]

About a year later—in May 1941—Esther Cooper married James E. Jackson in Bessemer, Alabama. "Yep, we just decided to get married and went . . . we had a witness, but no money for rings. And about two days later he went into Louisiana to do organizing work with rural workers for about five or six weeks—some honeymoon!" Despite his frequent absences, from the beginning the couple was surrounded by a warm circle of friends; members of SNYC's staff established close friendships that lasted a lifetime. Three very active couples became especially close: Esther Cooper Jackson served as administrative secretary of the organization from 1940 until 1943, while her husband was educational director (really a traveling organizer); Augusta Jackson, Executive Director Ed Strong's wife, edited SNYC's monthly newspaper, *Cavalcade: The March of Southern Negro Youth*; and Louis Burnham, a close friend of James Jackson's from student days, first coedited the newsletter, then became organizational secretary of SNYC in 1942, bringing in his new wife and coworker, Dorothy. They all worked in the field, and the men encouraged and appreciated the women's contributions as leaders, an unusual circumstance in the 1940s South. Esther Jackson noted that "it certainly wasn't widespread" even among leftists in Alabama, because "there was a lot of male domination among some of the working class men in the mines and steel mills," but

> we had some incredible men, like Louis and Ed and James Jackson, who considered themselves revolutionaries. They believed in what Engels said about the family and respect for women. They would urge us not to just do office work—to speak, go to the wives of the miners and steel workers. In a sense they were "purists"—they were just totally dedicated revolutionaries.[25]

In 1943, four months after the birth of her first daughter, Harriet Dolores (named for Harriet Tubman and Dolores Ibarruri, a Communist heroine of the Spanish Civil War), Esther Cooper became executive director of SNYC. The change came as Jack Jackson, Ed Strong, and several other SNYC members left for service in the army during World War II. Jackson served in a segregated unit, the 823rd Aviation Engineer Battalion, in India, Burma, and South China. During his absence Esther continued to live in the housing project in Birmingham and was fortunate, she thought, to have help from her mother, her mother-in-law, and her close friend Dorothy Burnham, who all pitched in to care for Harriet while her mother traveled for SNYC.[26]

Like the Communist Party, SNYC kept victory against fascism at the top of its agenda during the war. Before he left for Burma, James Jackson attacked Nazis and the Klan with equal vigor in a two-act play called *Don't*

Play Hitler's Game, published in the Communist newspaper *Southern News Almanac*. Three years later, in her introductory greeting to delegates to the Sixth All-Southern Negro Youth Conference, Esther rejoiced that the Allied advance "in west and east in Europe is strangling the life out of the world's greatest purveyor of white supremacy. . . . The common people of the world (whose century is at hand) gird themselves for a last final effort." She spoke glowingly of the youth of China "and all the far East, and India, and Africa" and pledged American youth's support "to end the vestiges of imperialism." But throughout the war years SNYC also supported the "Double V" campaign touted by black newspapers, and local and regional civil rights issues remained Cooper's and Organizational Secretary Louis Burnham's daily concern. They led several delegations to Washington to speak with members of the Fair Employment Practices Committee (FEPC) about discrimination in defense hiring in the South. On one trip Esther reported that she "had tea" at the White House with Eleanor Roosevelt "to try to get her interested in the Southern Negro Youth Congress." Unfortunately Mrs. Roosevelt just said, "'Well, I'll discuss it with Mrs. Bethune,' and that was the last I heard of it." Another delegation met with the members of Truman's Civil Rights Committee, urging them to recommend new federal protections for black southerners at the voting booth. Robin Kelley says that in the years when Esther served as its executive secretary SNYC "fought racial discrimination in the armed forces, expanded the voter registration drive, continued to investigate police brutality cases and civil liberties violations, collected a mountain of data on discrimination for the FEPC in 1943, and even waged a campaign to end segregation on buses." At the same time, SNYC's leaders strengthened ties to mainstream organizations like local NAACP chapters, and continued to have wide support from leaders in the broader civil rights community.[27]

As Esther Cooper approached her twenty-eighth birthday in 1945, SNYC seemed solid, despite intense opposition from the white supremacist majority, and was poised on the brink of new and wider campaigns in the postwar years. But threatening clouds loomed on the horizon. In 1940 the Dies (House Un-American Activities) Committee had listed SNYC as a Communist front and an agent of a foreign power, and J. Edgar Hoover cast the first of many official aspersions on SNYC, calling it "the most active Communist front organization among Negro Youth in the Southland." The same year the Federal Bureau of Investigation began routine surveillance of the Birmingham office that continued through its demise in 1949, with "technical and microphone" eavesdropping beginning in 1943.

Agents fanned out across the South, not only following SNYC activists but interviewing participants in SNYC conferences throughout the 1940s. The tone and bias of FBI reports on the Youth Congress is evident in a 1944 memo that mentions "Esther V. Cooper, Negress, who is the Executive Director of the Southern Negro Youth Congress, a Communist front." Other reports use the word "girl" to describe black women rather than the offensive term from slavery days, *Negress*. Pressure increased after the war; the organization would be listed by the attorney general as a "subversive agency" in 1947 and lose its tax-exempt status in 1948.[28]

Problems arose on a local level as well. During the U.S. Senate Democratic primary campaign of 1944, white supremacist candidate James Simpson littered Birmingham with flyers suggesting violence against SNYC, which, in the wake of the Supreme Court's decision that year ending all-white primaries, was pushing to register more black voters. She remembered "an editorial in the main Birmingham paper calling me all kinds of names," and one Simpson campaign flyer urged his constituents to "get" Esther Cooper using especially despicable and offensive racist language. At least Simpson lost in the end to the incumbent Roosevelt loyalist, Lister Hill.[29]

Right after V-E Day, Esther accepted an invitation to attend the founding meeting of the World Youth Conference in London, a convocation of young people from Europe, Africa, India, China, and the Americas. Leaving Harriet in the loving arms of her mother and her husband's parents in Virginia, she departed for what would turn out to be a journey of several months. Because she had to wait for Atlantic transport as soldiers came home, in a reverse of the normal soldier's homecoming story, Sergeant Jack Jackson returned from the Pacific before his wife returned from Europe, and he met her at the boat in New York. In any case, Esther found the conference of "437 young delegates from 62 countries" exhilarating. The U.S. delegation recommended internationalizing atomic weapons under United Nations control, and the conference passed many other resolutions urging the end of racial discrimination and imperialism, most of them introduced by youth delegations from the European colonies in Africa and Asia. Esther became one of the six U.S. members of the permanent council of the World Federation of Democratic Youth.[30]

Equally important, while in London she met W.E.B. Du Bois for the first time. After attending the Fifth Pan African Conference in Manchester, England, Du Bois traveled down to London to meet the American delegates at the Youth Conference and to introduce them to some African leaders, including Kwame Nkrumah of Ghana. Esther asked Du Bois to a small dinner with some of the SNYC members in attendance, a dinner she cooked herself. Before this meeting the African American scholar had been only vaguely acquainted with SNYC, but his report to the NAACP after the meeting "spoke of the SNYC as a major social force in the making and of Esther Jackson's organizational aptitude and remarkable political intelligence." Since Du Bois declined even to mention the NAACP's own "more conservative" delegate to the conference, his report caused consternation at home, where NAACP leaders commented that they had suspected from the beginning that the American delegation was "a Communist front group."[31]

At the end of the World Youth Conference, young volunteers enlisted to help to rebuild war-ravaged Stalingrad. Esther gathered her courage and called her mother "to say I had a chance to go to Russia. And she said Harriet's doing fine, and so I went."

> I worked with an all-women's brigade bringing cement and bricks to rebuild this building. There was nobody in Stalingrad at that time except German war prisoners, and everything was just totally devastated, like the area is now around the twin towers [in New York], just rubble. I thought—why are they even going to try to rebuild it? We lived in the basement of the one non-bombed-out building.[32]

She remembers several Americans with whom she lived in Stalingrad—a YMCA delegate, a Baptist woman, a Jewish man—although representatives to the conference from the NAACP and the Urban League declined the invitation. Twenty years later she returned to the Russian city with her husband and saw "the building they claimed I had helped to build." While there she gave the Museum of the Revolution "a little book that I got for working there signed by [Soviet foreign minister V. M.] Moletov [sic]—and they put it in a little case and took pictures of me in front of it."[33]

When Jack and Esther Jackson returned to Birmingham, she began planning SNYC's 1946 Youth Legislature, at which Du Bois would deliver his stirring "Behold the Land" speech, and they both participated in SNYC's first order of business after the war: a South-wide voter registration campaign aimed at returning black veterans. The organization joined the NAACP, the CIO Political Action Committee, and state committees of the Southern Conference for Human Welfare in "a loose regional confederation to promote the democratization of southern politics." When it began work in Mississippi, SNYC's drive to increase the vote joined a simultaneous national campaign to defeat Theodore G. Bilbo, the ranting racist senator from Mississippi. James Jackson and others went into Mississippi to work in the registration drive among black veterans, and to assist in documentation of discrimination in the 1944 democratic primary that might lead to Bilbo's censure in the Senate. Mississippi police arrested Jack when he brought a group of veterans to a precinct polling place located, beyond all reason, on the front porch of Senator Bilbo's house.[34]

By this time Jack Jackson had decided to devote himself full-time to party work. He remained active in SNYC's activities in 1946 as he prepared to take up residence as the state chairman of the Communist Party of Louisiana. Soon after Jackson's arrival in the Crescent City, however, the party sponsored a celebration on the anniversary of the Russian Revolution. The new chairman spoke eloquently, but "a bunch of thugs from the Seaman's Union" broke up the meeting, and when police arrived they arrested Jackson, not the mob. Out on bond, he hid in a compatriot's home in Baton Rouge until his trial and departure from the state. Expecting to move to New Orleans, Esther had relinquished her SNYC position to Louis Burnham; in 1947 she followed Jack to Detroit, instead, where he began work as an organizer for the Communist Party in the Ford plant. Esther remembered well the day the family received a Detroit visit from their dear SNYC friends the Burnhams, because it was also the day of Jack's next arrest, during a strike against the "speed up" at Ford. Louis Burnham had waited with Jack during Harriet's birth in Birmingham; just recently close new friends, Coleman, later to become the city's mayor, and Marion Young, had sat with him during the birth of his second daughter, Kathryn Alice. While Jack sat in jail as result of the strike arrest, Esther and the little girls continued to live in a two-apartment building with the Youngs. She worked for the Progressive Party, under whose banner former vice president Henry Wallace ran for the presidency in 1948, and for the Detroit branch of the Civil Rights Congress, a civil rights and legal defense organization with close ties to the party and roots in both the National Negro Congress and the International Legal Defense.[35]

In 1952 the family moved to New York, eventually setting in Brooklyn. The postwar wave of anti-Communism peaked just as the party named James Jackson its southern director. He soon faced indictment under the Smith Act as part of the "second round" of trials of party leaders, and in what David L. Lewis calls "an utterly self-defeating gesture of contempt for capitalist justice" went into hiding while under bond, on party orders.

His family did not see him for five years, until he emerged in 1957 for "an eleven-month show trial" involving several party leaders. W.E.B. Du Bois and H. D. Coke, editor of the *Birmingham World* in the 1930s, testified as to Jackson's good character, as did his own father and mother. Despite her normal reserve and five years of FBI intimidation during his "underground" period, Clara Kersey Jackson delivered a strong statement in her son's behalf, her first public speech, during the trial's sentencing phase. Sentenced to two years, Jackson was saved from prison when the Supreme Court, in the *Yates* decision, almost simultaneously declared the Smith Act unenforceable.[36]

During the five years of separation, Esther held her small family together but faced difficulties finding jobs and, even worse, endured the agony of living in the constant presence of FBI surveillance. She worked in the office of a "sympathetic left wing doctor" and for the National Committee to Defend Negro Leadership, which published her pamphlet "This Is My Husband: Fighter for His People, Political Refugee" in 1953. Even after her husband returned, employers felt pressured by the Jacksons' politics. The Urban League, for whom she worked in 1957 and 1958, and the National Board of the Girl Scouts, which hired her in 1959 and 1960, both released her for political reasons. Esther described government surveillance in the 1950s as "a method of intimidation. Every single day . . . walking behind [my daughters] to school, visiting all their teachers; standing in front of the school. [At] movies and they would be a few aisles behind us; I would go to a meeting at night and turn a corner and there would be two FBI agents."[37]

Although FBI harassment did not go away, a new challenge centered Esther's mind on more congenial matters when she accepted a position as editor of *Freedomways: A Quarterly Review of the Freedom Movement*, in 1961. Louis Burnham had been the main force behind planning the magazine, which had the support of Du Bois. After Burnham's untimely death in 1960, backers recruited Esther as founding coeditor of the publication, along with Du Bois's wife, Shirley Graham Du Bois. A journal of radical and liberal thought and a narrative of the international civil rights struggle, *Freedomways* published writers, poets, and commentators as diverse as Martin Luther King, Jr., Paul Robeson, Alice Walker, Langston Hughes, Kwame Nkrumah, Du Bois, Harry Belafonte, and Angela Davis. Soon after publication began the Du Boises left for Ghana, where he would die in 1963.[38] Although Graham Du Bois stayed active in *Freedom-*

ways from long distance for some time, Esther Jackson remained the managing editor until the journal ceased publication in 1986. Circulation reached about 10,000 at its peak, but averaged around 6,500 annual subscriptions. Through the years invaluable assistance came from loyal associates and contributors like Jack O'Dell, a former SNYC activist and former member of King's Southern Christian Leadership Conference staff, Esther's old friend Augusta Jackson Strong, scholars W. Alphaeus Hunton and John Henrik Clarke, novelist John Oliver Killens, and playwright Lorraine Hansberry. These talented people and many others, Esther said, "either worked for [next to] nothing or expenses. It was just a small group of dedicated people." *Freedomways* sponsors also included Ernest Kaiser of the New York Public Library's Schomburg Center for Research in Black Culture, whose wife served as office manager for the journal, and, for the entire life of the project, entertainers Ossie Davis and Ruby Dee. Julian Bond remembered how important each issue became to civil rights workers of his generation: "Each issue was eagerly awaited and its contents roundly debated. . . . That the central problem was race, no one doubted. But *Freedomways* also argued that race was immensely complicated by greed, that prejudice and poverty were necessarily linked, and that it would take organized mass action to carry the day for freedom." Bond's analysis of the journal's message echoes the philosophy of the experienced activist and observer of American society Esther Cooper Jackson.[39]

By 1984 the staff, facing exhaustion, began trying, unsuccessfully, to find replacements for themselves. When forced by debt and declining circulation to close down the publication in 1986, *Freedomways'* leaders decided to "have a big party to pay off all the debts" and closed down publication. "*Freedomways* passed from the scene," one admirer wrote, "leaving a vacuum in its wake. It had been, in some ways, the finest intellectual product of the Popular Front, speaking with a distinctive voice about matters that concerned African Americans."[40]

By the 1970s, in the wake of Stalinism, the Cold War, U.S. anti-Communism, de-Stalinization during the Khrushchev years, and the rise of the diverse, less doctrinaire "New Left" of the 1960s, the Communist Party had lost most of its American members. But James Jackson remained a faithful party leader until the 1980s, serving for some time as International Affairs secretary. During part of that time, his wife accompanied him to conferences in London, Paris, Cuba, Canada, and the U.S.S.R. She met Communist leaders from all over the world, and some of the leaders of the African National Congress, as well, "long before victory."[41]

The Jacksons took another trip, less exciting perhaps but more evocative of their own contributions to their native land, in the late 1980s. They toured the South, from Virginia down through Georgia, Alabama, and Tennessee; for Esther, it was the first trip south of Virginia since the move to Detroit in 1947. They visited with Frank and Sallye Davis in Birmingham, looked up old friends in Nashville, and, because she'd given them all away, had copies of Esther's thesis made at Fisk.

> So we had a wonderful time, and in Birmingham, the Davis' took us all around—we insisted on going to all the big hotels to eat lunch. My children don't understand [why we wanted to do this]. It was like a revolution—they "yes sired" us and "yes mamed" us in places we could only go in the back door. Even some of the young black waiters couldn't understand why we were so excited. If you tell them about going through a separate door they say "I don't know why you put up with it."[42]

But Esther had not "put up with it," ever; she fought against racism from the day she walked across the Washington bridge to avoid Jim Crow streetcars to her days at *Freedomways*. She knew that segregation and disfranchisement had been an exercise of control by a powerful majority, a much more complicated situation than young critics supposed. Her understanding of Jim Crow has always transcended the apartheid that ordered southern race relations before the civil rights laws of the 1960s; her whole working life seems to center on the question of American priorities. Do we value property or persons? Why is there poverty in the midst of our plenty? Why are race and class so inextricably linked in America? How can we organize to make government more responsive to people's issues? Now in her mid-eighties, Jackson is hopeful but still vitally concerned about the future of African American life and culture. Answering a 1998 question about contemporary civil rights problems, she said, "the struggle continues. After the struggle of the sixties, we're redefining in what direction we go, what organizations we build." Architects of the civil rights movement of the 1930s and '40s, the generation of Esther Cooper and James Jackson cheered, supported, and sometimes participated in the movement of the 1950s and 1960s. Now, ever pushing forward, ever vigilant, they offer examples, encouragement—and warnings of dangers ahead—for new leaders of a twenty-first-century progressive movement.[43]

Notes

1. David Levering Lewis, *W.E.B. Du Bois: The Fight for Equality and the American Century, 1919–1963* (New York, 2000), 524; W.E.B. Du Bois, "Behold the Land," in Esther Cooper Jackson with Constance Pohl, eds. *Freedomways Reader: Prophets in Their Own Land* (Boulder, CO: 2000), 10.

2. The Smith Act of 1940, the first peacetime sedition act since 1798, made it a crime to join, endorse, organize, publish, or use the mails to distribute material supporting "any society, group or assembly of persons who teach, advocate or encourage . . . overthrow of the government of the United States." It provided for ten-year sentences and fines up to $10,000 for those so convicted. Earlier espionage acts condemned verbal attacks on the American form of government, but the Smith Act bans only advocacy of acts of violence or force to overthrow the government. *Digest of the Public Record of Communism in the United States* (1955; reprint, New York, 1977), 188–205; Augusta Strong, "Southern Youth's Proud Heritage," *Freedomways Reader*, 18; Esther Cooper Jackson, telephone interview by author, tape recording, October 23, 2001.

3. Esther Cooper Jackson, telephone interview by author, tape recording, October 23, 2001; Paulina Cooper Moss, "At Home and At War, 1917–1919," *The Negro History Bulletin* 45, no. 2 (April, May, June, 1982): 42–5 (published by the Association for the Study of Negro Life and Culture, Washington, D.C.); untitled notes for article (page begins "when a woman whose interests. . ."), box 4, Esther Irving Cooper Papers, Moorland-Springarn Research Center, Howard University, Washington, D.C. (hereafter cited as E. I. Cooper Papers).

4. Jackson interview, October 23, 2001.

5. Ibid.

6. "Family Paper: Mrs Esther Irving Cooper," box 4, E. I. Cooper Papers; Louis E. Burnham, foreword to Esther Cooper Jackson, *This Is My Husband* (Brooklyn, N.Y., 1953), 3; Della Scott, "An Interview with Esther Cooper Jackson," *Abafazi: The Simmons College Journal of Women of African Descent* 9, no. 1 (fall/winter 1998): 2.

7. "Family Paper," box 4, E. I. Cooper Papers; Jackson interview, October 23, 2001; Scott, "An Interview," 2; Constance E. H. Daniel, "Two North Carolina Families— The Harrises and the Richardsons," *The Negro History Bulletin* 13, no. 1 (October 1949): 3–14.

8. Jackson interview, October 23, 2001.

9. Ibid.; Harriet Dolores Jackson, "Biographical Sketch of Esther Cooper Jackson," unpublished paper in possession of the author; "Dunbar High School," in "Duke Ellington's Washington: Virtual Tour of Shaw," <*http://www.pbs.org/ellingtonsdc/vtSchools.htm*>.

10. Jackson interview, October 23, 2001; Daniel, "Two North Carolina Families," 11–4.

11. Jackson interview, October 23, 2001; Moss, "At Home and At War," 45.

12. Scott, "An Interview," 4; Jackson interview, October 23, 2001.

13. Scott, "An Interview," 4; Ella Baker and Marvel Cooke, "The Bronx Slave Market," *The Crisis* 42 (November 1935): 331.

14. Jackson interviews, October 23, 25, 2001.

15. Ibid; John Patrick Diggins, *The Rise and Fall of the American Left* (New York, 1992), 150–1; Ellen Schrecker, *Many Are the Crimes: McCarthyism in America* (Princeton, 1998), 15.

16. For a revealing interpretation of leftist—especially Du Boisian—analysis of *American Dilemma*, see Lewis, *W.E.B. Du Bois, 1919–1963*, 450–3, 518, 523. Lewis calls Jackson's father a "pharmacist well invested in real estate . . . [who] reared his children on a steady diet" of Du Bois's *Crisis* columns, and adds: "Like many Talented Tenth children, Jackson bore an indelible memory as a ten year old of Du Bois's visit to his parents' home on Du Bois Avenue in Frederick Douglass Court, a tree lined enclave for affluent colored families. Mrs. Jackson had emerged from frenzied preparation of her finest cooking, to be told by the distinguished, perverse guest, 'Madam, I will have a slice of cheese on toast and a glass of milk, thank you.'" Jackson interview, January 5, 2001; James E. Jackson, quoted in Robert Cohen, *When the Old Left Was Young: Student Radicals and America's First Mass Student Movement, 1929–1941* (New York, 1993), 222.

17. Jackson interview, January 5, 2001; E. C. Jackson, *This Is My Husband*.

18. The National Negro Congress emerged from a 1935 conference on the status of the Negro at Howard University and had wide Popular Front support from the black community and leaders as diverse as Ralph Bunche of Howard, A. Philip Randolph of the Brotherhood of Sleeping Car Porters, John P. Davis of the Joint Committee on National Recovery, and James Ford of the Communist Party. Bunche and later Randolph (and others) left the Congress concerned about increasing Communist influence in the late 1930s and early 1940s, and the organization was always internally divided over this issue, but for a while it made an important contribution. It built nineteen state organizations, sponsored conferences, published newsletters and magazines, and fought Jim Crow and other evils in local venues alongside groups like the Southern Conference for Human Welfare and the NAACP. In 1946 the NNC merged into the new Civil Rights Congress, a civil rights and civil liberties legal defense organization with close ties to the Communist Party. Scott, "An Interview," 5; Robin D. G. Kelley, *Hammer and Hoe: Alabama Communists During the Great Depression* (Chapel Hill, 1990), 200–1; Johnetta Richards, "The Southern Negro Youth Congress: A History" (Ph.D. diss., University of Cincinnati, 1987), 32–42; "Tentative Conference Program," box 167–3, folder 29, Edward E. Strong Papers, Moorland-Springarn Research Center, Howard University, Washington, D.C. (hereafter Strong Papers).

19. H. D. Jackson, "Biographical Sketch," 2; Jackson interview, October 23, 2001.

20. Kelley, *Hammer and Hoe*, 213; Jackson interview, January 5, 2001.

21. Jackson interview, October 23, 2001.

22. As cited in Kelley, *Hammer and Hoe*, 25, 69, 213.

23. Cohen, *When the Old Left Was Young,* 221; Kelley, *Hammer and Hoe,* 213; Jackson interview, January 5, 2001.

24. Ibid.

25.   Jackson interview, January 5, 2001.

26. Jackson interview, October 23, 2001.

27. Ibid.; "Proceedings: Sixth All-Southern Negro Youth Conference," Atlanta, Ga., November 30–December 3, 1944, 7, Strong Papers; "Don't Play Hitler's Game," cited in Kelley, *Hammer and Hoe,* 219, 221–2.

28. Richards, "The Southern Negro Youth Congress," 130–77, quotes on 142, 145, 154.

29. Ibid., 104; Diane McWhorter, *Carry Me Home: Birmingham, Alabama, The Climatic Battle of the Civil Rights Movement* (New York, 2001), 65.

30. Jackson interview, October 23, 2001; Esther Cooper Jackson, "Historic London Conference Unites Youth of World," box 167, folder 18, Strong Papers.

231. Jackson interview, October 23, 2001; Lewis, *W.E.B. Du Bois, 1919–1963,* 518–9.

32. Jackson interview, October 23, 2001.

33. Ibid.

34. Patricia Sullivan, *Days of Hope: Race and Democracy in the New Deal Era* (Chapel Hill, 1996), 22, 56, 294; Jackson interview, January 5, 2001.

35. Ibid.; Kelley, *Hammer and Hoe,* 224–8.

36. H. D. Jackson, "Biographical Sketch," 2; Lewis, *W.E.B. Du Bois, 1919–1963,* 555; McWhorter, *Carry Me Home,* 107n.

37. H. D. Jackson, "Biographical Sketch," 2; Jackson interview, October 25, 2001.

38. Esther and Jack Jackson arranged the 1961 press conference at which Du Bois announced his membership in the Communist Party and his intention to become a Ghanian citizen. They were standing in the crowd at the 1963 March on Washington when they heard the announcement of Du Bois's death. Jackson interview, October 25, 2001.

39. Ibid.; Mari Jo Buhle, Paul Buhle, and Dan Georgakas, eds., *Encyclopedia of the American Left* (Urbana, 1992), 244; H. D. Jackson, "Biographical Sketch," 3; E. C. Jackson, ed., *Freedomways Reader,* xi–xxx.

40. Jackson interview, October 25, 2001; Buhle et al., *Encyclopedia of the American Left,* 245.

41. Jackson interview, October 25, 2001; H. D. Jackson, "Biographical Sketch," 3–4.

42. Ibid.

43. Scott, "An Interview," 4.

11

From Sharecropper to Schoolteacher

Thelma McGee's Mississippi Girlhood

Kathi Kern

The first time I met Thelma McGee, a public school teacher in Yazoo City, Mississippi, she told me a story that might have come right out of the pages of Anne Moody's classic memoir *Coming of Age in Mississippi*. As small children, Thelma and her brothers and sisters, the children of share-cropping parents, were attacked on their walk home from school. Taking their usual path across Dunn plantation en route to their home on Hammond Plantation, the children were run off the dirt road by a man in a red-and-white pickup truck. For over twenty minutes this man—no stranger to the McGee children for he was the notorious overseer at the Dunn plantation—kept Thelma and her brothers and sisters held hostage at gunpoint. Thelma cried and wondered "what they had done." Much later she had an answer: They had broken an unwritten law of the Missis-sippi Delta. These young children had dared to attend school during "cotton picking" season.[1]

Thelma McGee's story resonated with what little I knew about the Mis-sissippi Delta of the 1950s, which was based almost entirely on Moody's account. From her I had learned of the poverty of black Mississippians, of the often savage violence of white Mississippians, of the frustrating pas-sivity of black people too scared to protest, of the courage of those few young people like Anne Moody who fought to challenge the generations-old system of economic and political apartheid. Moody's account remains a powerful memoir, a scathing indictment of Mississippi's past. But as much as it illuminates the past, the autobiography also obscures important ele-ments in the recent history of black Mississippi women. As my friendship with Thelma McGee deepened, I saw less of her story nested in Anne Moody's. Instead, Thelma McGee's stories deepened Moody's portrait of rural black women in the Delta.

When I first read Anne Moody's autobiography as a student, I assumed it to be generally representative of her generation, a cohort the historian John Dittmer has tagged the "Emmett Till generation."[2] Yet, as I read her now, after spending several summers working with schoolteachers in the Delta, I am struck more by how exceptional Moody's life was. What stands out for me are the ways in which Moody was let down by the bonds of family, church, school, and community that kept so many southern blacks safe and alive in this period.

As I came to know Thelma McGee, her family, and her colleagues, I also wondered about how exceptional her life has been. Coming-of-age stories in Mississippi are almost synonymous with stories of migration. As one daughter of the Delta put it as she plotted her escape to the North: "I'm gonna be Somebody."[3] But Thelma McGee's story is about staying in Mississippi and being somebody: that somebody who puts off college to chop cotton; who cares for aging parents; whose schoolteaching wages allow the family's history of landowning to continue; and who welcomes family members back, one by one, as they begin the most recent migration from the North back to Mississippi.

Thelma McGee's story is not about moving North, neither is it primarily about the civil rights movement. The movement is a factor in Thelma's life, but it did not shape her in the way it did some other women and men of the Emmett Till generation. Rather, Thelma's life as a child and as a young adult was molded by her commitments to family, work, and church. Her struggles "to be somebody" are rooted in the aspirations of rural black people who stayed in the Delta. Thelma navigated the challenges of this era not just as an individual seeking her own path, but as a family member intent on holding onto the land her family has owned for generations. Thelma struggled with the stigma of being a sharecropper, ridiculed by town children and discriminated against by town schoolteachers. It is in the context of this childhood—where Thelma confronted violence for attending school when there was cotton to pick, and discrimination for picking cotton when she did attend school—that makes her journey and her triumph in becoming a schoolteacher all the more inspiring.

Thelma McGee grew up on the edge of the Delta, moving among the cotton plantations in the rural area outside of Yazoo City, Mississippi. Yazoo City—as the chamber of commerce puts it: "where the Delta meets the hills"—is best known for producing the white writer Willie Morris, whose books *North Toward Home* and *Yazoo* chronicled life in his segregated hometown. But Thelma McGee was not a town person. And that distinction is crucial. She was born in 1945 on Dunn Plantation to Mary Woods McGee and the Reverend Ollie McGee, the sixth daughter and tenth child in a line that would reach fourteen. For the first two years of her life, the family sharecropped on Dunn's plantation, a site that now houses a federal prison, she points out. And then it seemed their luck was changing. The McGees moved back to the homeplace.[4]

Thelma's maternal grandfather, Alonzo Woods, had owned his own 180–acre farm on Stewart's Ridge since 1918. Woods acquired his property in an era when black landownership in Mississippi was in decline. Although African Americans operated over half of the farms in the state (and three-quarters of the tenant farms), in three out of four cases the farms themselves were white-owned. In the period 1910–40 Yazoo County, with its black majority, had, according to Neil R. McMillen, "an appreciable black ownership class" with three hundred or more black farm owners. But this land on the periphery was not as valuable as that in the heart of the Delta, the area that dominated the region's cotton production. Quite a few of Alonzo's acres were wooded, land that provided its owners "with the satisfaction of proprietorship and little more." Still, in an era when most black farmers never realized the dream of ownership, Alonzo Woods's achievement stood out.[5]

McMillen has pointed out that for a black farmer to buy land, a relationship with an influential white man was a "frequent requirement." For Alonzo Woods that white man, Frank Hammond, was Jewish. To this day, Frank Hammond is remembered in the Woods-McGee family as simply a "nice man." But family members also concede that his Jewish background set him apart from the dominant white Protestant culture of Yazoo City. "They [Hammond and his family] were not accepted very well in Mississippi either," Thelma explained. "But they were wealthy people and they didn't care what other people thought." Frank Hammond's son Francis would continue his father's legacy of selling property to African Americans. Francis Hammond was not only set apart for being Jewish, he was also unusual because he was unmarried, a status that generated speculation in the community about his sexuality. "I don't know . . . I know he was interested in blacks obtaining land," Thelma concluded, "and he made it possible for people to pay in installments."[6]

For a black man to buy land in this era was rare; keeping that land free of debt and mounting taxes proved nearly impossible. McMillen contends that "whatever their relationship to whites, black farmers who would buy property usually had to pay premium prices at exorbitant interest for land that was less desirable to whites."[7] As the land passed in Thelma's family from her grandfather to her uncle, the financial problems facing all small cotton farmers in the Delta multiplied. According to Pete Daniel, the policies of the U.S. Department of Agriculture (USDA) in the years after World War II consciously created the conditions that caused small farms to fail. Following in the mold of the New Deal's Agricultural Adjustment Act, the USDA's policies of the 1940s and 1950s "drastically cut allotments to raise prices and reduce surplus." With their acreage allotments cut, small farmers tried to produce more with the land they were permitted to cultivate, and increased their use of (and consequently their expenditures on) fertilizer and chemicals. These federal policies took on a distinctively local character. Allotment policies were decided on the county level and routinely favored white farmers.[8]

In this climate of economic crisis, Thelma's uncle, Lucious "Shug" Woods, who was farming the family land, fell ill. In 1947, Thelma's parents decided to uproot from Dunn plantation and to apply their greatest asset—their large family's labor—to the economic crisis at hand. It was a family decision, Mary Woods McGee, Thelma's mother, explained, "to save the place for EVERYBODY."[9] Mary McGee's brother Gaston Woods came home from Chicago to assess the situation. He was reluctant to give up a lucrative job in the North to try to work the property out of debt, especially when his sister Mary's family was barely getting by as sharecroppers. So in 1947 Ollie and Mary McGee, along with their ten children, relocated to work the family land on Stewart Ridge. With Shug ailing, Thelma's parents took over the cotton production and had a successful season. But her uncle recovered in time for the settlement.[10] Mary McGee recalled: "We picked all that cotton and everything, and I said, 'Shug, now all that cotton you have made, you should be able . . . to pay this place out of debt.'" But her brother betrayed her and told her that the land was legally his and his alone. "He called me a darn fool. I reckon I was a fool for not seeking into everything. I just trusted my brother and I was working to get the place out of debt." Shug offered Mary and Ollie $150 for the year of their family's labor. "I told my husband, 'I dare you to take it!' We had done all this work and he was going to give us $150!"[11]

Bitterly disappointed, the McGee family returned to sharecropping at Dunn plantation from 1948 to 1950. But the climate had changed. The sale of the property had brought a new, detested overseer with a reputation for "beating his workers into submission." Thelma was only five years old in 1950, but she remembers her mother arming all of the McGee children with "skillets, pots and pans." They received strict instructions that if the overseer came into the house seeking their father, to immobilize him with these makeshift weapons. "I waited for [the overseer] to come to our door to get our father, but he never came."[12] Francis Hammond, whose father had sold Thelma's grandfather property in 1918, intervened and convinced Ollie and Mary McGee to come work his land on a neighboring plantation.

From 1950 to 1956, the McGee family sharecropped on Hammond plantation. The move brought one disadvantage, however; it placed the McGees at a farther distance from the rural churches that dotted the plantations outside of Yazoo City. Thelma's father adjusted to the move by holding Sunday School on the front porch of their new home on Hammond. The McGee children got up early on Sunday mornings to line up the homemade benches on the front porch before all the children and their parents from the plantation arrived for the morning class. Although Reverend McGee had no transportation of his own, he arranged to use two of Hammond's trucks to carry the makeshift Sunday School class on to church for the afternoon. When church let out around three o'clock, the trucks returned the children and their parents to Hammond. The plantation children always stayed to play with the McGee children, and Thelma's mother began a Sunday dinner tradition that lasted thirty years. "My mama would cook and feed basically anybody that would come by her house. . . . These children knew they were going to get a decent meal on Sunday because my mama would have cooked for us and the community."[13]

On Hammond plantation, Ollie and Mary McGee exercised considerable autonomy, especially in educating their children. As Thelma's story of being held hostage illustrates, however, the move to Hammond did not entirely safeguard the children from their former overseer. Thelma started school at age five, a year earlier than was the custom. When her sister Evelyn, who was a year older, prepared to go to school, Thelma cried to go along. Her parents relented. The school, a former sharecropper's cabin on the Wiseton plantation, was adapted for use as a one-room schoolhouse. Reverend McGee and several other men built tables and benches for the students, grades 1–8, to use. The student body was composed of African American sharecropping children from the three surrounding plantations: Wiseton, Dunn, and Hammond. Like other plantation schools, Wise School operated according to the rhythms of cotton production, which meant the children never attended school for a full school year as the children in town frequently did. The teacher, Miss Johnnie W. Clark, taught all grades and even risked opening the school during cotton-picking season for those children too young to go to the fields.

One day in early September 1955, when the town children had already started school, Thelma was working with her sisters at the end of a row of cotton. She saw her father approaching the field with the *Chicago Defender* in hand; her older siblings eagerly snatched it up and began poring over it. This was a regular family tradition, a highlight of the week. Ollie McGee routinely brought home the *Defender*, *Jet*, and *Ebony* magazines from his part-time job moonlighting at a black barbershop in town. The older children in the McGee family would read to the younger children, "even during picking cotton time." But something was different. Thelma could see horror in the faces of her sisters and brothers as they read the *Defender*. Feeling suddenly trapped inside the wire mesh of the trailer, Thelma began to shout, "I want to see it, I want to see it!" "You don't need to see this," her oldest sister replied protectively. "But I want to see it," Thelma insisted. Reluctantly, her sister tossed the newspaper up over the side and into the trailer. As the paper floated and landed softly on the bales of stomped cotton, Thelma saw the photograph of the mutilated corpse of Emmett Till. "It was a shock. It was a fear. It was a sadness that went through my body . . . and it still does something to me right now to see that picture."[14] Thelma was ten years old when Emmett Till, a fourteen-year-old boy from Chicago, was murdered by Roy Bryant and J. W. Milam in Money, Mississippi. Till was beaten, shot, and deposited in the Tallahatchie River, but not before his body was weighted down with a fan from a cotton gin, attached to his neck with barbed wire.[15] That Sunday at Pleasant Green Missionary Baptist Church, Reverend Frazier spoke of the murder, but nothing he said could calm Thelma's fears. "At the time I had young brothers. And I just thought all young black boys were going to be killed, that was just my fear."[16]

Later that fall, Thelma and her family witnessed another incident that would indelibly shape their local history. In response to the Supreme Court decision *Brown vs. the Board of Education, Topeka, Kansas*, the NAACP launched a petition drive in Mississippi communities. The organization asked black parents to sign a petition requesting that their children be admitted to white schools. Ollie McGee was approached by an NAACP canvasser one day when he was visiting a friend in town, but he declined to sign. Fifty-three parents in Yazoo City did sign, however, and the retribution was swift. Still known among blacks in Yazoo City as the "Great White Boycott," the economic reprisals against those parents proved financially devastating. James Wright was a plumbing contractor with a very successful business that included contracts with schools and hospitals, but his signature cost him his livelihood. Suddenly he was unable to buy even a rubber washer in town. Thelma's childhood friends James and John Wallace had a step-grandfather who could not read or write. He placed his mark on the petition and was fired from his job at the cotton seed mill, along with ten or twelve other workers. James Wallace recalls the predicament of black storeowners like Blue Stewart who owned a grocery on Lamar Street. "I seen him out there trying to flag a bread man down and the bread man just kept on going, wouldn't even stop to sell him a loaf of bread to stock his store." When Stewart was forced out of business, he turned his grocery into a dry cleaning plant, but this business failed too when no supplier would sell him cleaning fluid.[17] Thelma's family was well acquainted with the parents who had signed the petition. Most of those who signed were not just put out of business, they were forced out of town.[18]

For several years after, whites in Yazoo continued to document the success of their economic strategy. A report of a meeting of the White Citizens Council detailed the endeavor:

> [W]hen a petition was circulated among the Negroes seeking admission to the white schools . . . the names of these Negroes signing the petition were printed on the first page of the local newspaper, and no further action was taken, other than to bring these names to the attention of the people without any suggestions. The result was an economic boycott on the part of the white citizens of Yazoo County, and caused practically all of the Negro signers of the petition to request that their names be taken off . . .[19]

The list of fifty-three names was posted even in the cotton fields. The success of the white strategy in Yazoo City became a statewide symbol and, as one newspaper put it two years later, "with the awful spectre of Yazoo City before them, few Mississippi Negroes would sign a desegregation petition today."[20]

Owing both to its size and the long reach of its elite leadership, the White Citizens Council of Yazoo City was able to undermine the petition drive. By September 1955, the Council claimed a membership of 1,500 in a town of 11,000.[21] The executive committee of the Council, a veritable "Who's Who" of Yazoo City, met for lunch every Friday. A physician, Dr. R. J. Moorehead, served as the president of the Citizens Council; other executive committee members included attorney Tom Campbell and Albert S. Gardner, a member of the House of Representatives and the editor of the local newspaper.[22] The members of the executive committee were often joined by A. C. Russell, chief of police; Sheriff J. H. Moore; and Zack Van Landingham, investigator for the Mississippi State Sovereignty Commission. The Citizens Council had been so effective, Sheriff Moore reported with satisfaction to the Sovereignty Commission investigator in 1959, that the number of registered black voters in the county had dropped from 300 to 28.[23]

The connecting ties extending from the White Citizens Council to the Sovereignty Commission and back again intricately linked community and state power structures in a finely spun web that entrapped African Americans. Sovereignty Commission investigators, for example, silently documented license-plate numbers of cars parked outside of suspected NAACP meetings. The commission ran tag numbers through the state motor vehicle records to establish ownership and then relayed that information to the county sheriff or the White Citizens Council.[24] The council then took the following action against the "Negro agitator": "[A] committee will go to the Negro's boss and discuss the situation with him. Usually the boss will fire the Negro. That will end the matter without the Citizens Council ever being outwardly involved."[25]

While the Sovereignty Commission operated surreptitiously in the county, the Citizens Council was visible to blacks in Yazoo City in the 1950s. Thelma McGee remembers the moment in her childhood when she first became aware of it. Attending the Yazoo City Christmas parade in December 1959, Thelma recalled the end of the parade, when Santa Claus made his way down Main Street tossing candy onto the street. Children quickly scattered in all directions to gather it up. Suddenly, a crop duster—an increasingly familiar sight over the fields surrounding Yazoo City—flew over the length of Main Street, dropping leaflets. Black and white children rushed onto the street again, this time to retrieve the bounty from the biplane. "As children we wanted to see what was on the leaflets. . . . I personally thought the [leaflets] were going to say 'Merry Christmas,'" Thelma sighed. But the sheets of paper advertised a meeting of the White Citizens Council.[26]

The tradition of the Christmas parade was thus ruined for Thelma. Earlier, the beginning of 1956 had brought renewed hope to her family. The death of Thelma's uncle from a heart attack once again raised the issue of the availability of the family's land. And in this go-round, Thelma's mother was determined not to be a "darn fool."[27] She and her husband retained the "best lawyers in Yazoo City" and asserted their claim to the family farm. Thelma's parents won the case and paid off her siblings who asserted competing claims, only to discover that her dead brother had never paid the back taxes on the property. Once again, Francis Hammond offered his assistance and fronted the money for the back taxes. He told them "if they made the money to pay him back he would accept it, if they didn't, he would never tell them they owed him." They repaid the loan.[28]

Living on and working their own land on Stewart Ridge from 1956 to 1973, the McGee family became a highly disciplined economic unit. As Thelma put it, "You know it was a sense of accomplishment for us, for me. And we enjoyed it. However, on Stewart Ridge we were basically isolationists because we were far apart from [other] people." By necessity, the family turned inward, became "close-knit," and organized their work and leisure around each other. The eldest sister, Marian, sewed all the clothing for the younger children until she left for Chicago in 1958.[29] Other sisters took charge of cooking, in addition to their field work. With so many children, Mary Woods McGee established a child care system in which each of the older girls was assigned a younger one to look after. By 1956 the youngest daughter, Veronia, was six years old and, consequently, more of the siblings' labor could be directed at the family's cotton production and needs. The availability of the older children to do field work, however, coincided with the implementation of acreage allotment reductions. Ollie McGee annually did battle with the local white surveyor, Jack Duncan, who never failed to determine that the McGees had overplanted their allotment. "I remember my daddy used to have to plow up acres of his cotton after Jack Duncan came through," Thelma recalled. The McGees had better luck with the county's black surveyor, Arthur Claiborne.[30]

Coupled with their reduced acreage allotments, the introduction of the family's first tractor and the increased use of a chemical fertilizer created an unlikely labor surplus for the McGee family. Thelma and her older siblings began to hire out as day laborers during cotton season. But Ollie McGee was protective about where and for whom his children would work. "My father used to say 'We will eat nails before a daughter of mine works in a white man's kitchen.'"[31] From his contacts in the community, especially his work at the barber shop, McGee no doubt understood that working in a "white man's kitchen" rendered black girls sexually vulnerable. Endesha Ida Mae Holland has written that there was a silent recognition of the risks involved among girls who worked in white people's homes. Their conversation focused on the superficial details of white people's décor, but Holland and her friends did not fool each other: "Our eyes met in the mirror and we both knew; I knew she had been upstairs, and she knew I had been upstairs. It brought us together and kept us apart." Part of Holland was proud of the money she earned; "My other half was raging jealous of the girls who had daddies who knew the score about white men and kept their daughters safe by refusing to let them work in white households."[32]

Working in a "white man's kitchen" was off-limits to the McGee sisters, but field work for certain white farmers was more attractive. The McGee children had strength in numbers, and brothers and sisters were able to protect one another. Ed Able, a white tenant farmer who lived close to Stewart Ridge, approached Ollie McGee with an interest in hiring his children to work in his fields. He agreed, with the stipulation that Able treat his children fairly. Thelma and her siblings worked in Able's cotton fields alongside his own children. This, she recalled, was her first real contact with white people.

The infusion of cash from day labor—each child earned $2.00 to $2.50 a day—augmented a family economy that had already improved with the move to Stewart Ridge. McGee continued his part-time barbering in town at a rate of a quarter a cut, but he never turned down a man who could not pay. Men in need of a haircut found their way to the Ridge, where Thelma's father would barber for free. His children teased him that when men actually had a quarter, they went to a "real" barber.[33] On the Ridge, Mary Woods McGee cultivated a large truck patch. "People would name my garden the Red Cross garden," she explained. The Red Cross garden kept the family rich in produce and allowed them to spread the wealth among the surrounding plantations. Thelma's mother remembers the day her midwife confessed to coming by the house while everyone was in the fields. She helped herself to a whole ham and reported: "You all didn't even miss it."[34]

The abundance of food was one of the important distinctions between rural and town life for many black Mississippians in the 1950s. The memoirs of town children are full of painful memories of hunger and malnutrition. In *Coming of Age in Mississippi*, Anne Moody writes of her relentless efforts to help provide food for her younger siblings. She swept a lady's porch for two gallons of milk a week, until she witnessed the woman's cats drinking from the same milk supply. Anne's three dollars a week from domestic labor enabled her mother to buy bread and peanut butter, the mainstay of their family diet. Anne gathered leftover hot dogs from the Friday night football games at the white school in her town. "The wieners and the three dollars a week that I earned kept us from being hungry at school and at home," she writes.[35] Government policies exacerbated the problem. When Thelma's friends James and John Wallace, whose mother worked as a domestic, moved into Yazoo City's first public housing project for African Americans in 1955, it was "a giant step up," except where food was concerned. The regulations for the housing project stipulated that residents could not maintain gardens, animals, or for that matter, even walk on the grass.[36] As town children who were nevertheless accustomed to keeping hogs, the occasional cow, as well as their own vegetable patch, the Wallace brothers found the new restrictions forced them to rely exclusively on their wage earning abilities to help provide food for their family.

The McGee children were more fortunate. Not only was there an abundance of food, the children's day wages were their own to spend. "Our little money was our little money," Thelma explained. "We just had to get our school clothes out of it." As teenagers, Thelma and her siblings delighted in the Saturday ritual of going to town. Stewart Ridge was four to five miles outside of Yazoo City, so the McGee children would start the journey on foot. But before long someone in a truck would come by and offer them a ride. The ride was not free, however, "you would give them a dime, twenty-five cents, whatever. They didn't put a price on it, but they would just come around and pick people up." The infusion of people from the countryside into the town on Saturday afternoons was a special time for rural and town young people alike. John Wallace explained, "It was like being at the state fair, only you didn't have no [amusement] rides." Shopping was the ostensible purpose of the gathering and the stores stayed open late on Saturday night to accommodate the crowds. But going to town was about more than shopping. It was time to catch up on the news from each plantation; it was time to see friends from school. It was a time to buy new clothes, or show off a new pair of Converse All-Stars or Edwin Claps. As John Wallace put it, "Saturday was your time. You spent Sunday in church, so you didn't do it then."[37]

The lower end (the black section) of Main Street would swell with people. Across the tracks, Water Street, with its all-black Rien Theatre and nineteen cafés, would come alive. "We had an expression on Saturday morning—it should have been recorded by Webster and defined somewhere—it was: 'show fare,'" James Wallace explained. If someone asked to hire a young person to do an odd job, "show fare" was the going rate. "Show fare, that was a quarter, everybody knew that Saturday morning, it was common." Thelma McGee too spent many a Saturday in the Rien Theatre. Especially as a small child Thelma and her younger sisters were deposited at the Rien by the older ones who went on to shop on Main Street. A cousin of the McGees was employed by the theater and kept an eye out on "Ollie's children." "I would see a movie sometimes twenty times, just sitting there. When it would go off, we would change seats."[38]

As Thelma got older, she too joined her sisters in the parade of shoppers walking up and down Main Street. "We would go in the store . . . sometimes thirty times to look at different things." Thelma's sister Eudora remembered that even if she intended to buy several items, she would not buy them all at once. Rather, she would savor each purchase. The Black and White Department Store on Main Street was a favorite. Here the McGee sisters purchased fabric for their school clothes and experienced their first thrills at spending their hard-earned cash. Although the Black and White had a reputation for being friendly, the transactions were not always free of confrontation. In a case of mistaken identity, one of Thelma's brothers was accused of shoplifting, an incident that still angers the family. "We were always poor, but we had pride. We were not rogues. We were hardworking people," Thelma explained. On another occasion, Thelma's mother was challenged by a cashier when she went to write a check. "'Well, where do you have money?'" the clerk snapped officiously. Yet, despite these incidents, McGee family members continue to make annual pilgrimages to the Black and White Department Store. Thelma recently drew the line with a nephew who had traveled by bus from Flint, Michigan, to Jackson, Mississippi. He was in Jackson only long enough to watch a football game between Jackson State and Grambling University. But when he insisted that his aunt Thelma drive him thirty-six miles to Yazoo City (and back again to catch his bus) to purchase something at the Black and White, she replied: "If you want anything out of Black and White, you're gonna get it out of Metro Mall.'"[39]

The McGee family's devotion to the Black and White Department Store goes deeper than nostalgia. It underscores a central theme in the scholarship on black consumer culture of this era. As Ted Ownby, Grace Elizabeth Hale, and others have argued, consumer culture was a contested terrain for African Americans. Ownby has demonstrated that black consumers "saw shopping as a potentially democratic experience and hoped to find pleasure and dignity in the experience."[40] In the case of the McGees, the occasional insult, or enforced act of deference, did not override the powerful surge of independence that came from purchasing something desirable. As Grace Hale has pointed out, "African American southerners could not vote, but despite white efforts to keep them down they could spend." In Hale's analysis, "the potentially more subversive consuming practices" of life in southern towns undercut the power of segregation. It was difficult, if not impossible, to maintain strict segregation on a Main Street crowded with people moving in and out of shops. Indeed, the effort to do so produced awkward business practices that only maintained segregation in the most superficial sense. Thelma described the process of buying a hamburger at The Exchange, a shop on the end of Main Street. "You would go in the same door . . . but the black customers would go to the left and the white customers would go to the right." After waiting in separate lines and ordering burgers, black and white patrons would sit facing each other on opposing sides of the tiny restaurant eating them.[41]

Shopping, however, was as much about challenging and reinforcing class distinctions as racial ones. African Americans eroded segregation with the expenditure of their hard-earned wages. But they met with white resistance when they seemed to purchase above their station. Hale asserts that segregation could not "reattach racial and class identities, could not make middle-class blacks poorly clothed . . . and thus more easily identified by whites of all classes as inferior." Instead, the patterns of segregation marked the spaces of African Americans as "inferior," and whites could judge them according to the racial geography they were forced to inhabit.[42] But in the 1950s, as these complex processes of race and class were performed in the everyday acts of buying and selling, class distinctions were routinely reinforced, sometimes subtly, sometimes with a vengeance. As Charles McDew, a Student Nonviolent Coordinating Committee protestor, was instructed by a Mississippi policeman, "Down here, niggas don't wear white shirts during the week unless they teachers or preachers." White shirts were off-limits to black agricultural workers, but so too was something as simple as a beverage: Coca-Cola. As James Wallace explained, "You could buy an R.C., but only certain Blacks could buy Coca-Cola, those with clout. . . . Just anybody couldn't buy a Coca-Cola."[43]

Cars were perhaps the clearest signifier of social status, and black men in the Delta had to select them with care. The McGee family cars were so old they were a source of embarrassment. Thelma tells the story of her brother Winfield, who in the late 1950s acquired a used car, a 1938 Chevrolet that required a crank to start the engine. While they desperately wanted a ride to town, they forced their brother to park the vehicle on the periphery of Yazoo City and they walked the rest of the way. The sisters were not going to be seen entering town in that old car. But such was not the case with John and James Wallace's father, who owned a successful trucking firm. A light-skinned African American, Henry Wallace operated with considerable latitude in Yazoo City. But he instinctively understood the racial limits. He owned a new Cadillac, but only drove it at night. By day, he drove an old Chrysler. When his sons questioned him about this, he explained that one of his white clients owned the same kind of fancy car. "If he sees me driving a car just like his, I never will haul another [cotton] seed." According to the Wallace brothers, only one black in Yazoo City was "permitted" to drive a luxury car by day: T. J. Huddleston, the founder of a black hospital. As James puts it: "He was well to do and he stayed out of their way and they let him alone, but he had twenty-five funeral homes and two hospitals. He could drive a Cadillac."[44]

Consumer culture held out the possibility of a more democratic social order and instilled in young Mississippians like Thelma McGee a sense of power and economic independence. Yet that feeling was constantly checked by a culture that insisted on racial deference and the articulation of class hierarchies. For Thelma McGee, the city schools would prove to be more of the same. From the time she can remember, Thelma loved going to school, made good grades, and played at being a schoolteacher. In ninth grade, she began to attend the city school for blacks, Yazoo City Training School. The transition from a rural one-room school to the city high school was difficult. First of all, the city students started the school year earlier. Rural children were forbidden to attend school during September, the height of cotton picking season. City school buses began to run rural routes on the Monday after the fourth Sunday in September. An enterprising rural youngster attempting to attend school in September had a rude awakening. One of Eudora McGee's friends tried walking into town to attend school, but was caught by a plantation overseer who "put a pistol on her and made her go back to the field."[45] School simply started without the rural students, who began every school year a month behind the city students. In contrast, football season did not start without the rural students. As John Wallace remembers, "Half of the football team was still picking cotton. They were the larger boys . . . and coach would wait on them." The field truck would deliver young men from the cotton field to the football field. They began their practice after picking two or three hundred pounds of cotton during the day.[46]

But for Thelma, rarely a day passed in the city schools in which she did not feel stigmatized by her teachers for picking cotton. In the rural schools, the eager young girl had grown accustomed to sitting in the front row. When she took a seat in the front row at the Yazoo City Training School, however, Thelma was humiliated by the teacher, who promptly moved her to the back of the room. James and John Wallace, boys from town, remember the same custom of teachers using the classroom to stratify students according to skin color. In their grade school in town (with the absence of rural children), the teacher placed the light-skinned children in the first two rows, James Wallace recalls, "just like a segregated classroom, white and black."

The curriculum was also adjusted to reflect the common prejudice against rural children. "They taught the city children algebra," Thelma explains, "because they were teachers' children and they were supposed to go to college, but you were nobody's child and you weren't going anyplace." When Thelma was a senior, the school held a "career day" in the library to introduce students to different career possibilities, but Thelma's teacher kept her behind. "You don't need to go up there, that's for the students who are going to college," her teacher told her. Despite the changing rural economy and the massive migrations of rural blacks to the North, the teachers never questioned the status quo. As Thelma recalled, "It was just a given that you were going to return to the farm and high school would be the end of your educational endeavor." James and John Wallace suffered a similar prejudice, not because they were rural, but because they were the sons of a domestic, a "shadow family" of their successful father. John, who like Thelma was an excellent student, bore the brunt, the stigma of being poor. The teachers knew the score, he remembers: "'I know this guy, I know his mother can't afford to send him to college.' So instead of teaching to John Wallace they would teach to Nathaniel Johnson because [he] was definitely going to Jackson State." Wallace earned a college degree much later through the G.I. Bill, but his experience in high school was much like Thelma's; the teachers taught classes "that you knew were not meant for you."[47]

The fact that the McGee family worked the land they owned did not make an impression on city schoolteachers. Thelma's status was seemingly fixed by the labor she performed. The rhythms of cotton production structured every aspect of the lives of Thelma and her siblings: their work, leisure, education, and prospects for the future. Even their salvation was timed according to King Cotton. The summer weeks that fell between the chopping of the cotton and the picking of the crop were earmarked for religious revivals. A group of Missionary Baptist churches, both rural and in town, took turns holding a revival every week. A local man, Doug Coleman, used his overseer's truck to make the rounds of the plantations and carry parishioners to the weekly revival. Because the McGees were such a large family, their potential conversion was perceived to be a coup for any revival preacher. But the McGees had a reputation for being "hard-hearted." Week after week each summer, Thelma and her sisters dutifully attended revival and took their place among the unconverted, on the mourning bench. Thelma's sister Eudora admitted to being the easy mark in the family. One minister claimed "If he could get me off the mourning bench, he would get all the McGees." The moment of reckoning came in the summer of 1957 at Holly Green Missionary Baptist Church. A preacher boasted he was going to "clear the bench" of McGees. But he made a tactical error in thinking Thelma could be so easily swayed by his "silly" methods. Preaching from the tenth chapter of Romans, the minister took faith as his topic. Verse twenty-one quotes Moses: "'All day long I have held out my hands to a disobedient and contrary people.'"[48] Such was the frustration of this revival preacher who despite his "screaming and hollering" made no inroads among the unbaptized McGee sisters. In frustration, he turned to Thelma. Placing a chair in the front of the sanctuary, he asked her: "Do you believe this chair would hold you?" "Yes," she answered. "You didn't know," he continued, "but you had faith that the chair would hold you. So take it," he gestured toward the chair. "No," Thelma replied emphatically. "Take the chair," the preacher thundered back. "No!" Thelma replied again, refusing to be converted. At that moment, the preacher grabbed her off the mourning bench and attempted to forcibly place her on the chair. But Thelma—at twelve years old and well on her way to her adult height of 5'10"—towered over the preacher. "He snatched me and I snatched him back." Sisters Charlene and Helen fell out laughing. "She was about to whup that little preacher," Eudora observed. Pandemonium ensued and the revival was suspended. "They had to turn out the church," Thelma remembered, "and I became the girl who broke up revival."[49]

Although she and her sisters had grown up in the church under the careful watch of their preacher father, Thelma did not see conversion as automatic. But her father had no objection. "He wanted you to believe in what you believed in. You didn't have to do things his way. He would try to direct you on the right path, but he also gave you a sense of independence."

It was precisely that lack of independence that caused another young Mississippian, Anne Moody, to disparage the rural black church.[50]

For her, it was at the root of the problem of racial injustice. "We've been praying too long," she told a colleague in the wake of the Birmingham bombing in 1963. "Yes, as a race all we've got is a lot of religion. And the white man's got everything else, including all the dynamite."[51] Much has been written about the importance of the black church in this era that would seem to contradict Anne Moody's harsh critique, however. According to many of her contemporaries, the black church was a safe haven; it was a buffer. For Endesha Ida Mae Holland, who spent more time in juke joints than in church, "It was a place where black people could behave with dignity and fill responsible roles we could usually only dream about. Outside we might be laborers or mammies or drunks, but inside God's house we were deacons and choristers and Mothers of the Church."[52] In Thelma McGee's experience, the church was also a sacred place for the assertion of individual conscience. She converted when she was ready, when she was moved. In contrast to the cotton fields where her body was carefully monitored at all times, or the city school, where she was sent to the back of the room, the church provided Thelma a certain freedom. Within the church, her body and soul were her own. Thelma experienced a quiet conversion at age seventeen in 1962. She was baptized, dressed in white, by immersion in the Yazoo River. It was the same place her mother had been baptized in 1918.[53]

By the mid-1960s, the McGee family's ability to stay put in the Delta was in itself an accomplishment. When mechanization and chemicals made it possible to work the land with fewer laborers, and federal subsidies made it profitable to not work the land at all, white Mississippians promoted black migration with relish. James Cobb, in *The Most Southern Place on Earth*, identifies a virtual conspiracy among whites to eliminate African Americans from the Delta altogether. "Delta whites looked upon a black exodus as their 'final solution,'" Cobb writes.[54] Most of the McGee children joined the exodus. Some of Thelma's sisters desperately wanted to get as far as possible from picking cotton. But for others, particularly Thelma's brothers, migration was the only viable economic choice. Municipal jobs were not opened to African Americans until a successful black boycott of downtown stores in 1969.

Thelma graduated from high school in 1963, and she too left (briefly) to join her sister Helen in Pontiac, Michigan. She and her sister Evelyn traveled by Greyhound bus. It was her first time to leave the South. But she could not stay. By September, her mother called the girls back home to pick cotton: "So we just gave up and came back. We stayed there from June to the first of September. It was very short but it was like in heaven for us." When Thelma and Evelyn returned to Stewart Ridge, even the Mississippi heat seemed oppressive. For the next three years, Thelma alternately worked her family's land on Stewart Ridge and hired out as a day laborer to Ed Able. But her older sister Eudora had a different plan in mind. She wanted to send Thelma to college. Eudora had put herself through Piney Woods Country Life School and by 1966 was set to graduate with a teaching degree from Jackson State. Eudora was determined that "if I ever get out, I'm going to help put [my brothers and sisters] through college." But Thelma, according to Eudora, was "hard-headed." She felt obligated to stay with her parents and help them maintain their farm. But Eudora persisted: "Twenty years from now you'll be an old person and you'll have nothing." As a last resort, Eudora threatened to send Thelma's girlfriend, "Baby Ruth," to college in her stead.[55]

That summer of 1966, Thelma was moved to change her mind. Since 1963, when her father purchased the family's first television, Thelma and her sisters had followed the civil rights movement. "We were glued to the TV." When the three civil rights workers disappeared in Philadelphia, Mississippi, in 1964, Thelma and her sisters watched with a mixture of horror and sympathy: "We KNEW those boys were dead." And in 1966, when James Meredith launched his March against Fear and was subsequently shot, the television cameras of the nation once again focused on Mississippi. The Reverend Martin Luther King, Jr., picked up Meredith's torch and marched through the state. He was coming to Yazoo City. Thelma's mother begged her daughters not to go to the rally. She feared reprisals to her family. But the McGee sisters were determined. They were chopping cotton for Ed Able and requested that they be allowed to leave early. Able appeared to comply, but as he drove them back from the fields, he made repeated stops. At one point, he stopped at one of his gardens and announced, "'You all need to pick your mama some tomatoes.'" Then instead of driving them directly home, he took another detour: "'I got some okra for your mother and I need to go by the house and pick them up.'" Thelma and her sisters concluded that "Ed Able didn't want us to go either."[56]

That night at Campinella Field, Thelma and her sister met Dr. King. "When he finished speaking, we rushed forward to shake his hand," Thelma recalled. King's entourage talked with the McGee sisters and all the people "of different status" who were in the football field that night.

"They emphasized, they said: 'you all go to school.'" One of the civil rights workers pointedly asked Thelma: "What are you doing?" She replied: "I'm just a farm girl." "Go to school!" he replied. Coupled with Eudora's threats to send Baby Ruth, the encouragement from the civil rights workers compelled Thelma to go to college.

Thelma McGee's story does not end there; indeed, college was only the first step in her long road to becoming a schoolteacher. Like every other chapter of her life, Thelma's college years were shaped by her ongoing commitments to her family economy, her parents and siblings, and her church. Although historians have suggested that the family economy was all but dead by this time in Mississippi's history, Thelma's family story suggests otherwise. Thelma never positioned herself as a lone individual. While earning her bachelor's degree, she worked her education around her family's needs. During the week, she read *The Autobiography of Malcolm X*, rallied in opposition to the war in Vietnam, signed petitions to free Angela Davis, and hurled herself under a bed when her Jackson State dormitory was fired on by the Mississippi State Highway Patrol in May 1970. Virtually every weekend, however, she returned to Stewart Ridge to work her family's land and attend her rural church. Sister Evelyn sported an Afro, but Thelma could not go that far. She compromised her worlds by donning an Afro wig on campus and wearing her long hair straightened on her return trips home.[57]

Thelma McGee's life story is full of both struggle and triumph. In an era when black Mississippians lost land at an alarming rate, the McGee family managed to hold onto Stewart Ridge. At a time when teachers discouraged rural children from attending college, Thelma McGee was inspired to go anyway and was enabled by her sister Eudora to do so. At a moment in history when the only option for many African Americans was to leave the Delta, Thelma found a way to stay. As rich as the memoirs are of young people "coming of age" in Jim Crow Mississippi, Thelma McGee's life suggests that the stories have not all been told.

Notes

Research for this project was supported by the Louisville Institute for the Study of Religion in American Culture and the Freshman Discovery Program at the University of Kentucky. I offer my thanks to Kate Black, Bruce Clayton, and John Salmond for their helpful comments, and my deepest gratitude to Thelma McGee, her family, and her friends for allowing me to tell a part of their story.

1. Anne Moody, *Coming of Age in Mississippi* (New York, 1976); Thelma Dolores McGee, interview with author, Yazoo City, Miss., August 18, 2001, Oral History Collection, Special Collections and Archives, University of Kentucky, Lexington (hereafter, Thelma McGee interview).

2. John Dittmer, *Local People: The Struggle for Civil Rights in Mississippi* (Urbana, 1994), 58. The Emmett Till lynching is discussed later in this essay.

3. Endesha Ida Mae Holland, *From the Mississippi Delta* (New York, 1997), 136.

4. Willie Morris, *North Toward Home* (Oxford, Miss., 1982); Willie Morris, *Yazoo: Integration in a Deep-South Town* (New York, 1971). Most memoirs of black Mississippians who grew up in the era of segregation chronicle the experience of living in town. See, for example, Moody, *Coming of Age Mississippi* [Centreville]; Holland, *From the Mississippi Delta* [Greenwood]; Clifton Taulbert, *The Last Train North* [Glen Allan] (Tulsa, 1992). For an exception to this, see Chalmers Archer, Jr., *Growing Up Black in Rural Mississippi: Memories of Family, Heritage of a Place* (New York, 1992).

5. These figures are from Neil R. McMillen's study *Dark Journey: Black Mississippians in the Age of Jim Crow* (Urbana, 1990), 112–3.

6. Thelma McGee interview.

7. McMillen, *Dark Journey*, 119.

8. Pete Daniel, *Lost Revolutions: The South in the 1950s* (Chapel Hill, 2000), 41–42.

9. Mary Woods McGee, interview with author, Yazoo City, Miss., August 20, 2001, Oral History Collection, Special Collections and Archives, University of Kentucky, Lexington (hereafter, Mary Woods McGee interview).

10. The "settlement" referred to the financial settlement between sharecroppers and landowners after the cotton had been harvested and weighed. See James C. Cobb, *The Most Southern Place on Earth: The Mississippi Delta and the Roots of Regional Identity* (New York, 1992), 99.

11. Mary Woods McGee interview.

12. Thelma McGee interview.

13. Ibid.

14. Ibid.

15. Emmett Till's murder has been the subject of a great deal of historical analysis. See, for example, Ruth Feldstein, "'I Wanted the Whole World to See': Race, Gender, and Constructions of Motherhood in the Death of Emmett Till," in *Not June Cleaver: Women and Gender in Postwar America, 1945–1960*, ed. Joanne Meyerowitz (Philadelphia, 1994), 263–303; Stephen J. Whitfield, *A Death in the Delta: The Story of Emmett Till* (New York, 1988). Bryant and Milam were exonerated from murder charges, but later confessed (for a fee) to journalist William Bradford Huie. They murdered Till in retaliation for allegedly whistling at Bryant's wife.

16. Thelma McGee interview.

17. James and John Wallace interview with author, Yazoo City, August 18, 2001,

Oral History Collection, Special Collections Archives, University of Kentucky, Lexington (hereafter, James and John Wallace interview).

18. Thelma McGee interview.

19. Zack J. Van Landingham to Director, State Sovereignty Commission, November 26, 1958, State of Mississippi Sovereignty Commission Files, Yazoo County, Document 2-13-0-3-1-1-1. The Sovereignty Commission papers indicate that most of the petitioners were forced to leave Yazoo City, a trend noted in my interviews as well.

20. *Delta Democrat-Times*, January 31, 1957, as quoted in Neil R. McMillen, *The Citizens' Council: Organized Resistance to the Second Reconstruction, 1954–64* (Urbana, 1971), 211.

21. McMillen, *The Citizens' Council*, 211.

22. Van Landingham to Director, November 26, 1958.

23. As reported in Zack J. Van Landingham to Director, State Sovereignty Commission, January 13, 1959, Mississippi State Sovereignty Commission Papers (MSSCP), Yazoo County, Document 2-13-0-10-1-1-1.

24. See, for example, Tom Scarbrough, "Yazoo County-Emma Johnson, Negro female," Investigation, March 17, 1961, MSSCP, Yazoo County, Document 2-13-0-25-1-1-1. In this investigation, the Sovereignty Commission sought information on Emma Johnson, the wife of James Johnson, a teacher in the black public schools in Yazoo City. According to the investigator, the Johnsons' 1955 Pontiac was tagged outside an NAACP meeting in Jackson on March 28, 1961.

25. Van Landingham to Director, MSSCP, November 26, 1958.

26. Thelma McGee interview.

27. Mary Woods McGee interview.

28. Thelma McGee interview.

29. The historian Ted Ownby has written that the economic savings from homemade clothing was a point of emphasis among home demonstration workers in the Delta. See his discussion of the Mississippi agriculture extension service in Ted Ownby, *American Dreams in Mississippi: Consumers, Poverty and Culture, 1830–1998* (Chapel Hill, 1999), 99–101.

30. Thelma McGee telephone interview with author, March 16, 2002 (hereafter Thelma McGee telephone interview).

31. Ownby has argued that the decline in agricultural labor reshaped the family's relationship to the economy. The family unit was displaced by the individual as "the primary component of the economy." But in the case of the McGees, the family as an economic unit persisted, despite wage labor, despite migration. To cite only one example, Thelma's sister Helen, who migrated to Pontiac, Michigan, provided the family with their first automobile. See Ownby, *American Dreams in Mississippi*, 111; Thelma McGee telephone interview.

32. Holland, *From the Mississippi Delta*, 90.

33. Thelma McGee telephone interview.

34. Mary Woods McGee interview.

35. Moody, *Coming of Age in Mississippi*, 43–5. See also Holland, *From the Mississippi Delta*, 55–6.

36. James and John Wallace interview. This rural/town dichotomy was not absolute, however. Some landowners did not permit sharecroppers to maintain gardens, and in those cases, sharecroppers had to spend a greater portion of their earnings on food. For a discussion of this issue, see Ownby, *American Dreams in Mississippi*, 106.

37. Thelma McGee interview; James and John Wallace interview.

38. Thelma McGee interview

39. Eudora McGee Horton, telephone interview with author, March 16, 2002 (hereafter, Eudora McGee Horton interview); Thelma McGee interview.

40. Ownby, *American Dreams in Mississippi*, 154.

41. Grace Elizabeth Hale, *Making Whiteness: The Culture of Segregation in the South, 1890–1940* (New York, 1998), 125, 185, 186, 193. Thelma McGee interview.

42. Hale, *Making Whiteness*, 131. Hale maintains (on p. 137) that "Consumer culture made the disjuncture of race and class in the figure of the middle-class black more visible at a time when southern whites already felt threatened."

43. Charles McDew, quoted in National Civil Rights Museum, "Honoring the Struggle of a Generation," 5–11, as quoted in Ownby, *American Dreams in Mississippi*, 151. James and John Wallace interview.

44. Thelma McGee interview; James and John Wallace interview.

45. Eudora McGee Horton interview.

46. James and John Wallace interview.

47. Thelma McGee interview; James and John Wallace interview. Recent studies of African American schools during segregation tend to be more celebratory than my interviews in Yazoo City seem to warrant. See, for example, Vanessa Siddle Walker, *Their Highest Potential: An African American School Community in the Segregated South* (Chapel Hill, 1996), 135–6.

48. Romans 10:21.

49. Eudora McGee Horton interview; Thelma Dolores McGee telephone interview.

50. Moody, *Coming of Age in Mississippi*, 70, 74, 79.

51. Moody, *Coming of Age in Mississippi*, 319.

52. Holland, *From the Mississippi Delta*, 110.

53. Thelma Dolores McGee, telephone interview; Mary Woods McGee interview.

54. Cobb, *The Most Southern Place on Earth*, 267. Pete Daniel writes that Mississippi lost more than 376,000 farmers in the 1950s. See Daniel, *Lost Revolutions*, 44.

55. Eudora McGee Horton interview; Thelma McGee interview.

56. Thelma McGee interview.

57. Thelma McGee interview.

12

"Bridges Burned to a Privileged Past"

Anne Braden and the Southern Freedom Movement

CATHERINE FOSL

On the September 27, 1963, episode of the nationally televised *Today* show, instead of promising justice in the murders of four little girls in a Birmingham church bombing, Alabama governor George Wallace fiercely defended segregation and excoriated the civil rights movement as communist-led. As proof he waved a photograph of the Reverend Martin Luther King, Jr., with a white southern activist named Anne McCarty Braden.[1]

Petite, well-dressed, almost demure in appearance, and descended from among the first white settlers to her native Kentucky, Anne Braden looked the part of and had the proper pedigree for a modern version of the "southern lady" of whom Anne Firor Scott has written. But Braden had so thoroughly transgressed the region's racial boundaries in her radical calls for dismantling segregation that the mere mention of her name pumped adrenaline into the veins of segregationists in the Cold War South. Her presence, Wallace suggested, and a handful of other whites like her had precipitated the black civil rights protests and subsequent violence of white reaction that had swept his state.[2]

Hyperbolic displacement like that espoused by Wallace had governed the South for quite a while by the time he lambasted Anne Braden on national television. Earlier, in the New Deal–World War II years, a broad-based, left-liberal Popular Front coalition had promoted a variety of southern reforms and had begun to chip away at white supremacy, but that popular upsurge was decimated by the hysterical fear of internal Communist subversion that engulfed American culture in the post–World War II period. The fearful Cold War crusade against Communism found special resonance in the South, where officials linked any hint of civil rights agitation to the threat of a Red conspiracy emanating from Moscow. "Red-baiting" was not new to segregationist zealots in the postwar years, but cultural anticommunism gave new legitimacy to their crusade to defend seg-regation as it came under increasing assault and as the Red Scare infected labor unions and other liberal reform organizations. Among them were civil right groups such as the NAACP and the Congress of Racial Equality, who purged suspected Communist Party (CP) members from their ranks even as they fought off charges of being communists or communist fronts themselves.[3]

In the years following the Supreme Court's 1954 announcement of the controversial *Brown* school desegregation decision, a generation of south-ern politicians adopted the histrionic anticommunism that had catapulted Wisconsin Senator Joseph McCarthy to fame four years earlier. After 1954 (the year of McCarthy's censure by the U.S. Senate), the anxious ideology we know today as McCarthyism found new life in the South even as it waned elsewhere in the nation. The result was a modern-day witch hunt that drove out or silenced liberals who had once advocated southern social and racial reforms. By the 1960s, though southern anticommunist cru-sades could not halt the march of civil rights advances, they slowed or kept them modest by marginalizing pro-integrationist voices, especially those who—like Anne Braden—saw an end to segregation as only the first step in a wider social and economic justice agenda. Wallace was neither the first nor the last to invoke the specter of communism in order to discredit her in a desperate attempt to uphold a racial order that was crumbling around him.[4]

Braden's unabashed alliances with causes labeled "communistic" made her a convenient target of embattled southern political authorities during the 1950s and 1960s, and she and her equally activist husband, Carl Braden, somehow came across as even more threatening as a pair. Though less confrontational than Carl, Anne was more outspoken and more left-leaning than most of her white southern counterparts in the postwar era in her denunciations of segregation. As events of the past half-century have shown, she was also far more resilient than most white southern dissent-ers, a quality that enabled her and Carl to become among the relatively few survivors rather than casualties of the phenomenon the writer John Egerton has called "anticommunism, southern-style."[5]

Braden's persistent campaigning against racial hierarchy continued (and continues at this writing) long after George Wallace's defiant embrace of it had been discredited. With her antiracist activism encompassing more than half of the twentieth century and now reaching into today, very few figures in southern history—male or female, African American or white—

have matched Braden's relentless service to the cause of racial justice. That stamina is especially remarkable in light of the unrelenting opposition she faced for much of her adult life, not only from notorious white supremacists such as Wallace and his ilk, but from moderate civil rights supporters as well, who often shied away from associating with her or even joined the attacks on her because of the utter demonization with which the wider postwar southern political culture had endowed her.[6]

It was only with the end of the Cold War and the fall of the Soviet Union in 1990 that Braden's contributions to the cause of civil rights could be fully evaluated. Yet no examination of modern southern women's activism is complete without placing Anne Braden in that history. Her life has intersected on some level with the great social movements of her lifetime, and she has participated in most of them, self-consciously identifying herself as a white southern woman and reminding coworkers of the importance of racial justice in any and all social reforms. Born in 1924, she is one of the few slender threads tying southern protest movements of the thirties and forties to the new nonviolent movement that spawned a decade of social change in the 1960s and to the continuation of civil rights campaigns in the last quarter of the twentieth century. Her tempestuous efforts to break through the barriers against racial dissent in the twentieth-century South—especially among whites, of whom the culture demanded a kind of racist solidarity—has, as Angela Davis has written, "helped to reconfigure the very terrain on which social movements are organized." Once very nearly a "police state" (as Braden herself has often referred to it) that forbade dissent, the South today is no more segregated than the rest of the United States and only marginally—if any—less sympathetic to social protest.[7]

This essay reflects on Braden's importance in modern southern women's history and locates her as a connecting figure between consciousness about race and also class and gender, and as a bridge of sorts between generations; between blacks and whites; and between liberals and the left. What were the influences from Braden's southern youth that caused her to go against the grain of white southern culture and turn her life in the direction of racial justice? What supports allowed her to persist—even to thrive—through years of stormy opposition that was not merely political, but had serious reverberations in all of her closest relationships and her standing in the community?

Anne Braden is far from representative of her generation, but neither is she an aberration—and certainly not the "outside agitator" Wallace and other southern image-makers accused her of being. Instead, her experiences and choices are firmly rooted in the culture of her upbringing, and her enormous social conscience was informed by a selective absorption from the lessons of her privileged white southern girlhood. Braden's dissenting voice in southern history has been raised mostly in service of recruiting other whites in the region to act against racial injustice, but her radicalism threatened the postwar southern status quo not only on the basis of its racial arrangements. In the Cold War South, that threat (including class and gender) could not be ignored. But neither could it be extinguished.[8]

Anne Braden is part of a transitional generation that came after both the women's rights/Progressive reform of the earlier part of the century and the more broadly based social protest provoked by the urgency of the Great Depression, but before the activism of the 1960s, when a generation of youth launched the student civil rights protests and later the antiwar and women's liberation movements. Braden's generation of women is best known as the progenitors of the post–World War II glorification of female domesticity that journalist Betty Friedan called the "feminine mystique"—a cultural phenomenon that, while widespread, fails to capture the range of experiences Anne Braden lived as a young adult.[9]

During a middle-class childhood spent mostly in Anniston, Alabama, Braden (then Anne McCarty) was troubled but not directly affected by Depression-era inequities. One of the most profound influences on her as a young, academically gifted girl was the encouragement she received from her mother for developing a career as a writer. Another was the social-gospel strain of southern Episcopalianism provided by her childhood minister, who emphasized the value of human engagement to improve social conditions. Braden came of age in the post–World War II era, attending college during the same four years the United States fought in World War II. In the close-knit women's community she found at two exclusive Virginia women's colleges (Stratford Junior College and Randolph-Macon Woman's College), her political transformation began as an intellectual awakening born when she encountered for the first time New Dealers critical of segregation and met independent female professors who became her mentors. She caught what she has called the "spillover" from early-twentieth-century feminism and graduated from college in 1945 with an expansive sense of what was possible for women and a vague notion that "as women we had something special to give to the world."[10]

Her critique of social conventions sharpened when, as a young reporter in 1946 Birmingham covering the courthouse, she saw the ugly underbelly of racial hierarchy. But her response as an ambitious, individualistic career woman was to flee the Deep South. When Braden's newspaper career took her back to her native Louisville, however, she came to know African Americans personally for the first time as she began covering desegregation campaigns in higher education. Doing so made her take stock of the region's broader racial conventions, and her political consciousness took shape once she began meeting Communists and other radical thinkers and activists in that city's beleaguered but vigorous postwar labor and civil rights movements. Although the threat of communism was in the headlines nearly every day by the time Braden moved to Louisville in 1947, the flowering social movements spawned by Popular Front organizing were still wide open, and they beckoned to her as a spiritual home after she began to perceive glaring inequalities in the culture that had produced her.[11]

Braden was more an inheritor than a full participant in the reform drives that swept the South and nation during the 1940s after the upheaval wrought by the Great Depression. The postwar movement she found was in eclipse, but it was enormously vital, offering her an alternative world view and a set of convictions with which she could identify, and the political transformation she experienced that year was one not just of racial but also of class allegiance. ("Otherwise," she later reflected of her change in priorities, "I would've become another white liberal.") The young journalist's most dramatic break with the path set for her by familial and regional norms came in the spring of 1948, when she fell in love with Carl Braden, a fellow reporter and a Marxist, working-class reformer ten years her senior. They married that June and left mainstream journalism, dedicating their lives jointly to revolutionary social change but not sure how to accomplish it in the increasingly narrow climate for dissent amidst a hardening domestic cold war. Over the next few years they worked in the beleaguered left wing of Louisville's labor movement and in various campaigns for modest local racial and economic reforms. Opposing segregation became a form of obsession to Anne because she felt that it so diminished the lives of all who lived with it, black and white. The Bradens worked with liberal groups like the NAACP and with more left-leaning ones such as the Civil Rights Congress (CRC) (once pronounced by the historian Gerald Horne as "the most successful Communist front of all time").[12]

Contrary to the national trend, Braden came to know CP members such as CRC director William Patterson not as abstract menaces to society, but

as simply people who were outstanding organizers and role models of idealism, especially in their steadfast defense of racial equality. Through her
work with the CRC, Braden received two significant pieces of advice from
Patterson, an African American. One offered her a new way of maintaining the regional identity and deep sense of place that went hand in hand
with the southern racial traditions to which she no longer adhered. She has
reiterated the relevance of Patterson's suggestion many times throughout
subsequent decades; over the years, it became her mandate for linking up a
variety of people and causes.

> The culture I grew up in was fascist: I couldn't have my roots there.
> But he told me I had a choice: I could be a part of the world of the
> lynchers, or I could join the "other America"—the whole lineage of
> people who had opposed slavery and injustice. That's what I joined
> ... it gave me a connection to a past and a future to be part of a long
> chain of struggle that was here before [me] and will be here when
> [I'm] gone. That became a very real concept to me all my life; it still
> is.[13]

That "other America" became a major source of Braden's resilience in the
face of intense, sustained repression that followed critics of the postwar
southern racial order. She soon realized that there was also an "other
South"—however small and besieged—which she learned about from a
new interest in undercurrents of southern history—from the slave resister
Denmark Vesey to white southern liberals who sought interracial regional
reforms through the New Deal. In embracing a new community, she became part of a small but tenacious network of resisters who refused to be
silenced by the oppressive social climate and—in her case—by the powerful cultural prescriptions surrounding white southern womanhood. Over
the coming half-century and more, she would reinforce that small tradition of southern resistance to race, class, and gender injustices by recount-
ing the radical currents of southern history to her contemporaries and to
younger generations of southern activists.[14]

The other lesson Anne Braden drew from William Patterson has also
informed her lifelong approach to racial justice activism. Like many young
radicals of later generations, she initially surrounded herself with African
American friends and causes, where she found political sympathy and the
excitement of cultural diversity. But when she began a 1951 series of
speaking engagements in black churches in Louisville and reported on her
activities to Patterson, he gently admonished her that it was white people

whom she needed to convince, not blacks. Braden took his words to heart, and that perspective predisposed her later not to take personally blacks' migration into all-black organizing (and their suggestion that whites also organize among their own color) in the mid-1960s.[15]

Even in the border South, white civil rights supporters were so few in the early 1950s that they "stood out like sore thumbs," she wrote later. Still, the Bradens were rather ordinary local activists and might have remained so had it not been for one fateful step taken in the spring of 1954 in the tense weeks surrounding the *Brown* decision. In May 1954, the pair acceded to a friend's request for help and bought a suburban house on behalf of Andrew Wade, an African American World War II veteran unable to buy it himself because of Jim Crow housing restrictions. As misfortune would have it, the Wade family moved into their new home the weekend before the announcement of *Brown*, and they were greeted by shots, vandalism, and a burning cross—the recipients, perhaps, of local white backlash against more fundamental racial changes on the horizon. Six weeks later—after a barrage of threats—the house was partially destroyed by dynamite, and the Bradens made national headlines that fall when they and five other white supporters of the Wades were charged with sedition on grounds that the dummy purchase and subsequent violence had actually been a Communist plot engineered to stir racial discontent.[16]

On December 13, 1954, after a lengthy and highly sensationalized trial and despite Andrew Wade's repeated assertions that the purchase was entirely his idea, Carl Braden was convicted of sedition and sentenced to fifteen years imprisonment. Though no hint of evidence linked any of the defendants to the dynamiting, Anne and the others charged awaited a similar fate. Unlike most victims of local McCarthy-style harassments, however, the Bradens would not go down without a fight. They employed their journalistic and organizing skills in an ambitious campaign to publicize the raw injustices in the case: rarely had an anticommunist prosecution so blatantly relied on pro-segregationist sentiments. In her first real effort at organizing without her partner, Anne Braden raised the $40,000 bond needed to free him on appeal, and together the couple traveled the nation and the region to win support. Though the real bombers were never prosecuted and the Wades were never again able to live in the home they had wanted, Carl Braden's conviction was thrown out in 1956 after a Supreme Court ruling invalidating state sedition laws.[17]

More than any one thing, it was the 1954 Louisville sedition case that alerted southern politicians to the threat posed to regional conventions by "the Bradens." But the other irksome feature of the activist pair was their refusal to be silenced. The sedition ordeal left the couple (who had two children) jobless, deeply in debt, and pariahs in Louisville among both blacks and whites because of their having been publicly denounced as Communists. They were on the verge of leaving the South for a new life in Chicago, but Anne remained troubled by that prospect. She felt a sort of urgency, as a white southerner, to stand with blacks in the struggles waged in the aftermath of *Brown*, especially since the 1955 Montgomery bus boycott. As she later recalled,

> One of the things that I came away [from that case] with was a passion to play a part in changing the patterns of people's thinking here. From the little bit of traveling we had done around the case, the disturbing thing [we saw] was that there seemed to be so few white people . . . openly supporting the new black movement.[18]

Anne's wishes carried the day. By 1957 the pair had regrouped and found jobs as field organizers with the Southern Conference Educational Fund (SCEF), an organization that was a carryover from Depression-era southern reforms, now focused solely on recruiting whites and blacks to work together to topple segregation. SCEF's origins lay in the "Old Left"—specifically in an interracial though white-led Popular Front coalition with an agenda of economic reform and composed of trade unionists, liberals, New Dealers, and Socialists, with a handful of Communist Party members on its front lines. Like its predecessor—the Southern Conference for Human Welfare (SCHW), established in 1938—SCEF retained a Popular Front style of politics. Although there were no known CP members in SCEF by the time the Bradens joined its staff, its failure to ban communists from its ranks made it an ongoing subject of highly sensationalized congressional and southern legislative hearings to investigate its supposed "Red" connections. SCEF's militant leadership, while focusing the organization's minuscule resources on racial integration, also cherished a broader vision of economic reform. The Bradens and SCEF were a companionable fit. Yet—already pariahs in white southern culture for their Marxist perspectives and dramatic challenge to segregation—the couple almost guaranteed themselves further harassment by joining an organization as suspect as SCEF.[19]

In the fall of 1957, Anne Braden took over the editorship of the *Southern Patriot*, SCEF's monthly newsletter that circulated to about 2,200 readers in and outside the South. Over the following few years she expanded the *Patriot* into a more widely read tabloid newspaper that became one of the few outlets for sympathetic reporting of the region's halting moves toward racial integration. Though the couple continued to be red-baited in the southern press and highly controversial among whites generally, they provided support and media attention to a new generation of African American civil rights leaders, sustaining through SCEF a small network of southern whites and blacks working together to counter the larger sentiments in the region. The two used press contacts from their years in journalism—and from their most recent effort to mobilize public opinion against their sedition indictments—to encourage greater news coverage of southern anti-black violence. They also designed brochures to raise public awareness—such as their 1959 *They Challenge Segregation at Its Core*, which brought the beleaguered Birmingham movement its first media attention. Through such efforts, they proved themselves among the staunchest of white allies to blacks in their battle against segregation.[20]

As a southern white woman of genteel background, Anne Braden, in particular, seemed almost exotic to liberals, leftists, and other civil rights supporters who were her peers and elders. Her Alabama upbringing had left her with a wide drawl, and she possessed an impassioned eloquence in conveying her narrative of white racial transformation both orally and in writing. Reverend Martin Luther King, Jr., upon meeting Braden in 1958 and hearing about her odyssey into civil rights activism, reportedly told his wife, Coretta, he "could not believe such a white woman existed." That same year Anne wrote a memoir of the Louisville sedition case, entitled *The Wall Between*, which became another organizing vehicle for her and Carl as they tried to reach over the racial barriers that hobbled most southern whites. Her narrative and her convictions became the basis upon which King later named her in his now-legendary "Letter from a Birmingham Jail" as one of five white southern publicists who truly understood the need for nonviolent resistance to Jim Crow laws.[21]

Throughout the late 1950s, the Bradens became among the relatively few whites to lay the groundwork for the new mass movement that burst forth in 1960, working closely with Birmingham's Fred Shuttlesworth, Ella Baker (then director of the Southern Christian Leadership Conference), and others who would become the sung and unsung heroes of the civil rights era. Yet despite the heightened push for better treatment, when southern students sat down en masse in lunch counters and restaurants in early 1960, they did so in a regional climate intensely hostile to racial reform. Anne Braden became one of the first writers to offer analytical but sympathetic coverage of the new student upsurge in the pages of the *Patriot* and one of the few adult white southerners to lead by example. Her media know-how and adamant commitment to racial justice—along with a level of outspokenness and leadership that was, to many, all too rare in a woman—won her the respect of young student activists and began to break through the miasma of Cold War anti-Communism that had hampered her effectiveness.[22]

Braden was enthusiastic about the new wave of student activism, but she continued to emphasize the role William Patterson had impressed on her as a young crusader: to bring whites in to the cause of racial reform. She once wrote to James Forman, who by 1961 directed the new students' organization the Student Nonviolent Coordinating Committee (SNCC), "I know how hard this movement is for the buried white southerner to find—even though it is geographically all around him. Everything is pulling at him to continue . . . life in its old ditches and ruts. Something has to open the way." One of Braden's most significant contributions to the new student movement was to advance a "white student project" that resulted in the 1961 hiring of Bob Zellner, an Alabamian and recent college graduate, to find new SNCC recruits on white southern campuses. Braden originated that idea, built support for it within SNCC and SCEF, secured funding for it, and kept searching until she found a white southerner willing to take on such an intimidating job.[23]

Because their names were frequently employed by segregationists attempting to smear the movement as "communistic," the Bradens remained controversial all through the 1960s even within the civil rights community itself, especially in its older, more moderate-to-liberal wings such as the NAACP and the Southern Regional Council (SRC), a regional think tank of liberal white southerners founded in 1944. To those who worked closely with them, the fear of their alleged subversiveness in relation to taking over SNCC was almost laughable, considering how intently Anne in particular strove to honor the autonomy of SNCC youth, who were more concerned at that point with fighting adults than with CP interference. Her willingness to offer political insights and material assistance without trying to dominate student activists made them respect her in turn and, ultimately, to begin grappling with the divisive and limiting effect Cold War anti-Communism was having on civil rights reforms. Her message regarding the importance of civil rights not only to blacks but to whites as well was a liberating one in the narrow confines of majority southern culture. For many young women in SNCC, especially, she also became a sort of role model whose overt championing of women's equality was something radically new.[24]

As the 1960s unfolded and student sit-ins spawned wider social movements against the Vietnam War and for liberation of blacks, women, and other oppressed groups, Braden's voice sought persistently to link together the new peace and justice movements and to emphasize points of unity among them. She continued to stress to younger southern activists her vision of a radical interracialism that was also anticapitalist, inherited from her early exposure to the "Old Left." To whites in particular, she and Carl continued to proclaim the need for black leadership and close black-white consultation in an effort to counter the growing divide between the races even in the movement. But in the wake of the sustained violence of the 1964 Mississippi Freedom Summer and elected officials' unwillingness to enact meaningful racial changes toward racial equality, the "beloved community" vision of the early sixties splintered at mid-decade. By 1968 social movements themselves were nearly as segregated as the larger society they had first criticized. Black activists—though they frequently opposed the Vietnam War and other injustices—kept their sights on racial freedom in any social movement of which they became a part, while whites flocked into campus organizing and new causes like the anti-Vietnam and women's liberation movements, with many leaving behind the antiracist impulse that had first ignited 1960s social action.[25]

Anne Braden spent years attempting to stem that trend. She and Carl continued with the same radical interracialism that had long characterized their organizing efforts—until his unanticipated death of a heart attack in 1975. Anne reacted to her wrenching loss with even greater immersion in social change efforts. As she confronted a resurgence of racism and the Ku Klux Klan around the South in the mid-seventies, Braden also began to consider more seriously the psychology of white racism and its persistent power even among social justice crusaders themselves. Getting whites to confront their personal and institutional racism became the focal points of her political philosophy and her rhetorical and organizing strategy. As she wrote in a 1999 essay, "[N]o white people in a society founded on racism can ever totally free themselves from this prison."[26]

A widow at age 51 in 1975, Braden brought her influence and increasing seniority to bear on the women's and antinuclear movements of the 1970s and eighties, delivering to a variety of social justice activists around the South her message of white responsibility to oppose racism and her appeal for a broader social vision of interconnectedness. She spoke always from the vantage point of a white southern woman, and that social identity gave her a way to be heard, even though her "communistic" reputation continued to shadow her, especially in her hometown of Louisville.

In the women's liberation movement, for instance, Braden became one of a relatively few white women whose impassioned, sometimes uncomfortable calls for a more multicultural feminism echoed those of radical women of color. Her *Letter to White Southern Women*, for example, was originally published as a 1972 pamphlet, then revised and strengthened for a 1977 essay in *Southern Exposure* magazine. Aimed at feminists active in the antirape movement, these "open letters" cautioned women to remember the history of black-male-on-white-female rape in the South, suggesting that they challenge rape cases in which there was racial injustice and make sure their sisterhood extended to black women too. She wrote that

> I am aware that my appeal to you . . . comes at a time when the women's movement . . . is struggling to make our society . . . deal with the crime of rape. My position is not at odds with this struggle; it is simply another dimension. For the fact is that rape has traditionally been considered a crime in the South—if the woman was white and the accused Black. But it has not been seen as a crime—and is not now—if the woman is Black. . . . we who are white will overcome our oppression as women only when we reject once and for all the privileges conferred on us by our white skin.[27]

Braden took her message of white privilege into the new antinuclear campaigns in the 1980s, and her efforts contributed to the development of new crusades against environmental racism—the locating of polluting and environmentally degrading industries in poor and minority southern communities.

Since the 1990s, Braden has continued to work unrelentingly—mostly in community efforts in Louisville—to enlist white involvement in antiracist causes, her leadership in a half-century of regional civil rights campaigns understood by only a portion of those who know her local work. The ostracism of bygone days, together with a lifelong humility, gave her the habit of staying in the background in movement activities, but over the years she has also, like many organizers, found that an effective tactic for cultivating new leadership. Although her radicalism made her seem menacing and subversive in earlier decades, her voice has consistently been one of unity and peacemaking within the spectrum of liberal to left-leaning activism, and her embrace of identity politics has sought connections rather than divisions.

Such dedication has had its costs, of course. Braden entered her senior years with little in the way of financial security or material possessions. An independent woman attached to nothing so much as her own enormous social conscience, she never remarried after the 1975 death of Carl Braden (it was impossible, she felt, ever to find such a political and personal camaraderie again). She has expressed real regrets at having allowed relationships with beloved family members and old friends to erode due to the press of work obligations, and a Louisville news weekly affectionately referred to her a few years back as a "rebel without a pause." Most of her personal goals and interests were absorbed long ago by what became her consuming passion—pursuit of a more just region and nation.[28]

In the post–Cold War South of the late twentieth century and early twenty-first, however, Anne Braden has finally evolved from a pariah into a heroine of sorts, becoming the recipient of numerous human service awards. In December 1992, the Southern Regional Council (SRC) convened for its annual meeting in Atlanta. Established in 1944 as successor to the older Commission on Interracial Cooperation, the SRC remains today as the region's longest-lasting racial reform organization. After a dinner featuring hearty southern fare, Braden—white-haired now and slightly bent over from age—found herself nodding off as the speeches began. She did not nap long, however: what was said jerked her suddenly back to full consciousness. Her first thought about the words she heard was: "They're apologizing for 50 years of history!"[29]

The SRC paid tribute that night to Anne Braden's half-century of persistent dedication to racial justice by bestowing on her the organization's highest award as a Life Fellow. But it was not always so. While the Cold War abroad may have given the U.S. government some impetus for curbing racial inequalities, the cold war at home wracked the modern civil rights movement with internal divisions and kept it fairly modest in its reach, as Braden's difficulties illustrate. For nearly half a century, she has written and spoken of the "silencing of a generation." While her own case defies that conclusion, her observation is acute regarding regional and national moves toward greater democracy.[30]

Braden's reputation in Louisville and the South has improved, but her "subversiveness" remains in her continued calls for a reinvigorated white response to racism as part of a twenty-first-century movement toward broader social justice. With a focus on whiteness that prefigured the outpouring of social science literature on the subject in the 1990s, her identity is still deeply bound up with "southern-ness." Her claim to a social identity as a white southerner, informed by her generation's experiences, has consistently foregrounded the subversive elements of that identity, insisting that to be southern means that one must fight racism. Her life's work illustrates an important point of connection between generations, between liberals and the left in southern history, and between the civil rights movement and other social movements it spawned. In that bridge-building process, Anne Braden has unwittingly become a sort of "conscience" for the white South, who has kept alive—and continues to do so—an inclusive vision of racial and social justice both through her work and her legacy.[31]

Notes

1. *Today* program transcript, September 27, 1963, in box 56, folder 10, Carl and Anne Braden papers, mss. 6, Civil Rights Collection, State Historical Society of Wisconsin, Madison (hereafter referred to as Braden Papers SHSW). [Note: I capitalize the word "Communist" and "Communism" throughout this essay only when it refers unmistakably to the Communist Party-USA (CP). Wallace's use of the word in the *Today* program, for instance, seems to me generic enough to refer only to beliefs of a certain sort, which may or may not have entailed membership in the CP.]

2. Ibid.: see especially p. 4 of transcript.

3. On the origins of the Popular Front uniting Communist Party members and supporters with liberals, socialists, and other Marxists, see Harvey Klehr, *Heyday of American Communism: The Depression Decade* (New York, 1984). Patricia Sullivan's *Days of Hope: Race and Democracy in the New Deal Era* (Chapel Hill, 1996) is possibly the best survey of southern reforms during this period, and its epilogue explores the eclipsing of popular protest with the onset of the domestic cold war; on southern anticommunism, see also John Egerton, *Speak Now Against the Day: The Generation Before the Civil Rights Movement* (New York, 1994), 448–60; purges among racial reform organizations are discussed in Ellen Schrecker, *Many Are the Crimes: McCarthyism in America* (New York, 1998); Alabama's anticommunist banning of the NAACP, for example, is discussed in Howell Raines, *My Soul Is Rested: The Story of the Civil Rights Movement in the Deep South* (New York, 1977), 134–5.

4. This thesis has been advanced by a number of scholars: most informative for me was the work of Anthony Dunbar, *Against the Grain: Southern Radicals and Prophets, 1929–1959* (Charlottesville, 1981).

5. Even the most cursory glance at manuscript collections such as those of the Mississippi Sovereignty Commission or other southern state anticommunist legislative committees reveals a plethora of references to "the Bradens," as do various insertions into the *Congressional Record* by southern segregationists. For details, see my dissertation, "Once Comes the Moment to Decide": Anne Braden and the

Civil Rights Movement," Emory University, May 2000, esp. chaps. 10–11; Egerton, *Speak Now,* 448; this point does not imply that Braden was the only or the most radical white southern integrationist of the era, but she was one of only a few dozen whose work was regional and not just local. Others included her husband, Carl; James Dombrowski; Virginia and Clifford Durr; and Aubrey Williams: All of these named and most others were affiliated with the Southern Conference Educational Fund (SCEF).

6. Wallace's true views on race are the subject of much debate: see, for instance, Dan T. Carter's *Politics of Rage: George Wallace, The Origins of the New Conservatism, and the Transformation of American Politics* (New York, 1995), especially the preface and epilogue.

7. This passage is taken from Davis's foreword to my biography of Braden, entitled *Subversive Southerner: Anne Braden and the Struggle for Racial Justice in the Cold War South* (New York, 2002).

8. Wallace remarks in *Today* transcript, p. 5.

9. I have borrowed the notion of Anne's generation as transitional from Susan Hartmann, "Women's Employment and the Domestic Ideal in the Early Cold War Years," in *Not June Cleaver: Women and Gender in the Post-War America, 1945–1960,* ed. Joanne Meyerowitz (Philadelphia, 1994), 84. Meyerowitz's own essay in that same volume informed my thinking on the incompleteness of the "feminine mystique" trope in depicting postwar women's lives: see "Beyond the Feminine Mystique: A Reassessment of Postwar Mass Culture, 1946–1950," 229–62.

10. Braden to author, "Feminism and My Relation to It," January 3, 2002, typescript in author's possession. Activist women like Braden often adopted an essentialist, maternalist kind of feminism in these years. For a fuller exploration of this ideology, see Ruth Rosen, "The Day They Buried Traditional Womanhood," in *The Legacy: Vietnam in the American Imagination,* ed. Peter Shafer (Boston, 1990), 233–62.

11. Braden correspondence with author, June 11, 1997, in author's possession; Anne Braden, interview with Sue Thrasher, Louisville, Kentucky (tapes and transcripts held in Highland Center library, New Market, Tennessee), April 18, 1981, tape 6, side 2, 179; the sort of ideology that influenced Braden in post–World War II Louisville is examined most thoroughly in Bob Korstad and Nelson Lichtenstein, "Opportunities Lost and Found: Labor, Radicals, and the Early Civil Rights Movement," *Journal of American History* 75, no. 3 (December 1988): 786–811.

12. Anne Braden, interview with author, Louisville, Kentucky, October 21, 2001; Gerald Horne, "Civil Rights Congress" entry, in *Encyclopedia of the American Left,* ed. Mary Jo Buehle, Paul Buehle, and Dan Georgakas (Urbana, 1992), 134.

13. Anne Braden, interview with author, Louisville, Kentucky, June 17, 1999.

14. For more on Braden's role as a mentor in bringing radical southern history to life, see, for example, Sue Thrasher, "Oral History," *Southern Exposure* 12, no. 6 (November/ December 1984): 80–1.

15. Anne Braden, interview with author, Louisville, March 8–9, 1989 (tape 3).

16. A thorough accounting of the Wade purchase can be found in Anne Braden's memoir *The Wall Between* (New York, 1958); the quoted material is from her epilogue to the book's re-released edition (Knoxville, 1999), 335.

17. Ibid.

18. Anne Braden's comments are from her interview with Sue Thrasher, tape 9, side 1, pp. 268–9, and tape 10, side 1, p. 287.

19. For more on the contiguity between SCHW and SCEF, see Linda Reed, *Simple Decency and Common Sense: The Southern Conference Movement, 1938–1963* (Bloomington, Ind., 1991); the importance of these two groups to broader southern social changes is most compellingly evoked in Sullivan's *Days of Hope*, 169; on Communists in SCEF, see Anne Braden to Virginia Durr, August 9, 1959, in box 31, folder 9, Braden Papers, SHSW.

20. Circulation figures are taken from Reed, *Simple Decency*, 241 n. 36; there are numerous examples of the negative press coverage the Bradens received for their participation in civil rights crusades; for one, see "Tuskegee Group Makes Mistake," *Birmingham News*, November 26, 1959; n.a., *They Challenge Segregation at Its Core* (SCEF Publications, 1959), copy in author's possession; for more on the Birmingham media campaign, see Anne Braden to Fred Shuttlesworth, July 18, 1959, in box 47, folder 14, Braden Papers, SHSW; Fred Shuttlesworth comments at some length on the assistance the Bradens provided in Aldon Morris, *The Origins of the Civil Rights Movement: Black Communities Organizing for Change* (New York, 1984), 171.

21. This observation comes from a number of interviews I have conducted with others active in social reforms of the 1950s: see, for example, Fred Shuttlesworth, interview with author, Cincinnati, Ohio, December 6, 1997, privately held by author; the story of King's comment is in Anne Braden interview with Thrasher, tape 11, side 1, 345–8; King's letter has been widely reprinted: find it in full, for example, in Clayborne Carson, ed., *The Autobiography of Martin Luther King, Jr.* (New York, 1998), 187–204.

22. Julian Bond, interview with author, Charlottesville, Virginia, September 17, 1997; Joan Browning, e-mail interview with author, September 26, 1999; Constance Curry, interview with author, Atlanta, Georgia, August 8, 1997; Sue Thrasher, telephone interview with author, November 16, 1999.

23. Anne Braden to Jim [Forman], October 11, 1962, in box 20, folder 13 (1), Papers of the Student Nonviolent Coordinating Committee, Martin Luther King Center for Nonviolent Social Change, Atlanta; the white student project is discussed in Clayborne Carson, *In Struggle: SNCC and the Black Awakening of the 1960s* (Cambridge, Mass., 1981), 52–3.

24. The history of the SRC is told in Morton Sosna, *In Search of the Silent South: Southern Liberals and the Race Issue* (New York, 1977); Bond interview; Browning e-mail interview; Thrasher telephone interview; on Braden's respect for the students' autonomy, see, for example, her correspondence in box 33, folders 1–3, Braden Papers, SHSW.

25. Anne Braden to author, January 4, 2002, personal correspondence in author's possession; see, for example, Maurice Isserman, *If I Had a Hammer: The Death of the Old Left and the Birth of the New Left* (New York, 1997). This history of the evolution of 1960s social movements is outlined more fully in Howard Zinn, *A People's History of the United States* (New York, 1990); examples of white women's disillusionment with movements of later in the 1960s are evidenced in several narratives (see especially Penny Patch and Emmie Schrader Adams) contained in Constance Curry et al., *Deep in Our Hearts: Nine White Women in the Southern Freedom Movement* (Athens, Ga., 2000).

26. Braden interview with author, November 23, 2001; Braden quoted in *Wall Between* (1999 edition), 339. Note: when Anne re-capped this passage to me in 2001, she added the word "totally."

27. Quoted material is from Anne Braden, *Free Thomas Wansley: A Letter to White Southern Women* (Louisville, 1972), pamphlet in author's possession; see also Anne Braden, "A Second Open Letter to Southern White Women," *Southern Exposure* 4, no. 4 (July 1977): 50–3.

28. Braden interview with author, June 17, 1999; cover, *Louisville Eccentric Observer*, November 24, 1999.

29. The SRC award was only one of many such awards: among the first (and most prestigious and, in some ways, surprising) was Braden's receipt of the American Civil Liberties Union's first Annual Roger Baldwin Medal of Liberty in January 1990. For full coverage of the December 1992 SRC conference, see *Southern Changes* 15, no. 1 (spring 1993): esp. 13–6; Anne Braden, interview with author, Mt. St. Francis, Indiana, December 28, 2001.

30. On the relationship of the Cold War to the civil rights movement, see, for instance, Timothy Tyson, "Robert Williams, Black Power, and the Roots of the African-American Freedom Struggle," *Journal of American History* 85, no. 2 (September 1998): 540–70. I first came across this particular concept of Braden's in her 1961 speech delivered at the Freedom and the First Amendment Conference, Chapel Hill, North Carolina (transcript in author's possession); the quotation is from Braden interview with author, March 8, 1989 (tape 2).

31. The literature on whiteness as a social construction seems to have grown up at least partly in reaction to Toni Morrison's *Playing in the Dark: Whiteness and the Literary Imagination* (Cambridge, Mass., 1992). During the 1990s that literature has expanded enormously, ranging from Ruth Frankenberg's *White Women, Race Matters: The Social Construction of Whiteness* (Minneapolis, 1993) to the periodical *Race Traitor: Journal of the New Abolitionism*. One of the studies most relevant to southern historians of the post–World War II period is Becky Thompson's recent book *A Promise and a Way of Life: White Anti-Racist Activism* (Minneapolis, 2001).

13

Vivion Brewer of Arkansas

A Ladylike Assault on the "Southern Way of Life"

Elizabeth Jacoway

In the fall of 1957 the world watched in horror, on newly acquired televisions, as events unfolded at Little Rock Central High School that would change the course of twentieth-century American life. As nine courageous black children climbed the steps of Central High and then continued their ascent toward the American dream of equality, citizens of Little Rock and ultimately of the nation came face-to-face with the reality of American racism. In that moment of recognition, and in the ensuing two-year process of resolution, much of America's innocence fell away. Out of crisis, however, came opportunity, and the working through of the clash of interests in Little Rock, although flawed, gave birth to new patterns of racial and gender relations in the South.

Central to resolving the Little Rock crisis was the role of a band of dedicated women who, when faced with the humiliation of having the governor close their schools, significantly modified traditional southern gender roles by creating the Women's Emergency Committee to Open Our Schools (WEC). As their leader, the esteemed Adolphine Fletcher Terry, remarked to *Arkansas Gazette* editor Harry Ashmore: "I see the men have failed again; it's time to call out the ladies."[1]

Starting with three women and ultimately numbering over two thousand, the Women's Emergency Committee became the moral and political force by which Little Rock was brought to its collective senses. Over a five-year period the women of the WEC worked tirelessly and mostly anonymously, organizing the city into elaborate networks of access, producing dozens of newsletters and memos in an effort to shape public opinion. They gathered figures and information for an extensive financial report documenting the devastating impact of the crisis on Little Rock's economy, interviewed candidates for political office, studied proposed measures, and lobbied for the passage of bills in the Arkansas legislature. For these women the WEC offered their first tastes of political action and organizing skill; for their city it presented a clear choice between a just future or financial ruin. Little known, this is a story that needs to be told.[2]

Vivion Lenon Brewer was president of the Women's Emergency Committee from its inception in September 1958 until the close of the crisis phase of Little Rock's school situation in 1960. A lifelong resident of Little Rock and the daughter of a former mayor and leading businessman as well as a graduate of Smith College, Vivion Brewer felt shocked and shamed by the upheaval in her hometown. "In short," as she wrote in her memoir, "I was sick with it all." And so when the call came through on September 12, 1958 (when the Supreme Court handed down *Cooper v. Aaron* and Governor Orval E. Faubus responded by closing the high schools), and Terry's voice came across the line asking: "Are you ready to do something about Little Rock, Vivion?" Brewer replied: "I certainly am."[3]

Through the ensuring months and years of unremitting effort, harassment, and alienation from old friends, as Vivion Brewer's days swirled by her in purposeful activity, this southern lady orchestrated a movement that resolved the racial crisis in her city and that also struck to the heart of the patriarchal scheme of which "The Southern Lady" was the centerpiece. By challenging time-honored patterns of interaction and propriety, by withstanding the assaults of frightened defenders of the old order, and especially by demonstrating the financial folly of clinging to the chimera of massive resistance, Vivion Brewer and the WEC relentlessly prodded the heretofore silent "leadership" of their city. Ultimately, working under cover of traditional patterns of female behavior, these women played a central role in toppling ancient constructions of both race and gender in Little Rock.[4]

Until six weeks before Orval Faubus surrounded Central High School with the Arkansas National Guard, almost no one in Little Rock expected trouble. Virgil Blossom, superintendent of schools for the Little Rock district, had developed a plan for gradual school desegregation, and in hundreds of speeches throughout the city, he thought he had prepared school patrons and city fathers for the minimal amount of compliance with nebulous federal guidelines. Governor Faubus had said repeatedly, and had demonstrated at Hoxie the year before, that he intended to leave local affairs in the hands of local officials. As a former member of the liberal Sid McMath administration as well as a lifelong resident of a practically all-white county, he could have been expected to hold progressive views with regard to race; and he had, in fact, offered no real opposition to the Little Rock School Board's efforts to comply with the *Brown* decision.[5]

The NAACP had filed a lawsuit against the Little Rock School District in February 1956 (*Aaron v. Cooper*), arguing that the district was not moving fast enough in its desegregation efforts. The federal judge in the case ruled in favor of the school district; he also retained jurisdiction in the case, thus removing the voluntary aspect of the Blossom Plan. The Capitol Citizens Council, the Little Rock chapter of the Citizens Council of America, had mounted a campaign in the school board elections in March 1956; although they had been repudiated at the polls, they had begun to attract a growing following from the blue-collar neighborhoods around Central High School.[6]

In the November 1956 general election, the people of Arkansas had approved by wide margins several measures designed to preserve segregation; furthermore, in February 1957 the Arkansas General Assembly had passed four laws to maintain racial segregation in the public schools. In Little Rock, however, two segregationist, blue-collar candidates for the school board had met defeat in March 1957, losing to candidates of the businessmen's lobby who ran on a platform of compliance with federal mandates. Little Rock's traditional leaders, the civic elite of downtown business and professional men, had also succeeded in winning approval for a new city manager–council form of government, thereby leaving a lame-duck, discredited mayor until the November 1957 elections.[7]

A key element of the Blossom Plan would enable the civic elite to send their children to whites-only Hall High, slated to open in the fall of 1957. As a "man of the people" of humble origins, and with few social pretensions, Orval Faubus felt a natural kinship with the working-class families whose children would attend Central High; and as the pressures mounted on him from all sides to intervene in local affairs, the governor remained true to his populist heritage.[8]

In public statements, Faubus suggested repeatedly that he had no intention of taking a stand either for or against integration in Little Rock. Believing his involvement in the desegregation process would be politically costly, no matter what position he took, his primary interest was in improving the economic and social conditions of the average Arkansan. Midway through the summer of 1957, however, Faubus began to receive reports of impending violence at Central High, many of these reports coming directly from Superintendent Blossom himself. He may also have made promises to key political operatives in eastern Arkansas that he would oppose integration in return for their support of his legislative agenda. Whatever the source, it is clear that by early August, Faubus had concluded that he could not avoid playing a role in the upcoming drama in Little Rock.[9]

Faubus appealed first to the Justice Department, calling Assistant Attorney General William Rogers to ask what assistance the federal government might be able to provide in the event of an emergency in Little Rock. Rogers sent a member of his staff, Arkansas native Arthur B. Caldwell, to Little Rock to meet with Faubus, but the governor was able to draw little comfort from Caldwell's position that the government could not intervene in the absence of a dead body.[10]

Faubus and Blossom both realized that Little Rock's lame-duck mayor, Woodrow Wilson Mann, would not be able to command the loyalty of the city's service personnel. Increasingly it became apparent that state authority would be the only force strong enough to control or contain an emergency situation if one were to arise. Faubus briefly considered using the state police, but apparently about this time he settled on the use of the Arkansas National Guard. Blossom and various members of his school board appealed to Faubus repeatedly, as did his director of the Arkansas Industrial Development Commission, Winthrop Rockefeller, to make a statement to the effect that he would not tolerate violence at Central High. Faubus demurred.[11]

Through August Little Rock saw a flurry of legal activity, as various lawsuits sprang up in chancery court in an effort to block desegregation. At one point, in response to a suit filed by the newly formed Mother's League of Central High School (an auxiliary of the Citizens Council), Chancellor Murray Reed issued an injunction against the Blossom Plan. Within a matter of days, however, visiting federal judge Ronald Davies, of Fargo, North Dakota, overruled the chancery court decision and suspended the injunction, demanding that desegregation proceed as scheduled.[12]

Into this charged atmosphere stepped Governor Marvin Griffin of Georgia. The invited guest of the Capitol Citizens Council, Griffin spoke to a large and enthusiastic audience at the civic auditorium about his handling of desegregation in Georgia. Assuring the crowd that Georgia's schools would remain segregated under his tenure, he left his audience with the question: "Why do you have to have integration here?" Why, indeed? That was the question on everyone's lips as the day for school opening drew near.[13]

A part of the conventional wisdom about the Little Rock crisis holds that Orval Faubus manufactured a crisis at Central High School to win election to a highly unusual third term. Faubus said at the time, and maintained ever after, that he acted to prevent violence and bloodshed in Little Rock. Whatever his motivation, Governor Faubus placed the Arkansas National Guard around Little Rock Central High School on September 2, 1957, thereby precipitating a major constitutional crisis over the extent of state authority.[14]

Three weeks of inconclusive maneuvering ensued, in the local courts, at the White House, and behind the scenes from Little Rock to Washington. After two weeks Arkansas congressman Brooks Hays proposed that the governor and President Dwight Eisenhower meet face-to-face in an effort to resolve the crisis. Arranging the meeting through his friend Sherman Adams, administrative assistant to the president, Hays persuaded Faubus to fly with him to Newport, Rhode Island, to meet with the president at a favorite golfing retreat. Faubus and Eisenhower both believed that during their private meeting they arrived at a workable solution. Because, however, Faubus failed to take along a lawyer, he had to yield to Attorney General Herbert Brownell's insistence that the proposed agreement was unacceptable. The governor returned to Arkansas empty-handed to face a court date with Judge Davies, who enjoined him from interfering further with the desegregation of Central High. Faubus then removed the soldiers from their posts around the school and flew off to the Southern Governor's Conference at Sea Island, Georgia. The city of Little Rock settled in for an anxious weekend.[15]

On Monday, September 23, the nine black children slipped into a side entrance of Central High School, precipitating rioting among the angry crowd gathered outside. The Little Rock police were no match for the emotional protesters, and by noon Assistant Police Chief Gene Smith removed the nine from the school for their own safety. At the urging of a group of concerned citizens including former governor Sid McMath, his law partner Henry Woods, Congressman Brooks Hays, *Arkansas Gazette* editor Harry Ashmore, and School Superintendent Virgil Blossom, Mayor Woodrow Mann called President Eisenhower and requested that he send troops to restore order. Wednesday morning Little Rock awakened to the eerie spectacle of seeing U.S. army paratroopers in full battle gear stationed around Central High. The "Little Rock Nine" entered school this day through the front door, with a full military escort, and desegregation was under way.[16]

Confusion reigned among the traditional leadership of the city, the downtown businessmen. These were the same men who had worked for a decade to reverse the fortunes of the pre–World War II economy in Arkansas. They had lobbied successfully for industrial development and an improved image for their city and state, and had just launched a movement toward cleaning up city government and making it more amenable to the needs of the business community. These men now feared that all they had worked for would soon vanish before their eyes. As one of them lamented, "we *knew* that we were more progressive in the beginnings of racial integration than most of the South, and most *all* of the North, so our feelings were: Why us?"[17]

The twenty-five former presidents of the chamber of commerce began meeting daily, as an ad hoc committee, in an effort to ascertain what steps could be taken to resolve the crisis. All came to naught, however, as opinion was too divided within the group to arrive at any commonly shared understanding. Some among the businessmen resented the fact that Eisenhower had sent troops; others were relieved that he had; most felt dismayed that the familiar pattern of segregation was now coming forcibly to an end in their city, but not everywhere else in America. In this situation of high emotion, embarrassment, and outrage, a vacuum in local leadership became readily apparent. The few voices raised in favor of compliance, such as that of *Arkansas Gazette* editor Harry Ashmore, became suspect as agents of the "enemy" forces, and increasingly Governor Faubus moved center stage.[18]

The October 5 launching of the Soviet spaceship *Sputnik* took Little Rock off the front pages of the world's newspapers, but as the weeks wore on with little abatement of the tension in Arkansas' capital city, Virgil Blossom and his school board found themselves under mounting local criticism for continuing to work to implement the Blossom Plan. In the face of proliferating Citizens Council activity and visibility, the chamber of commerce group eventually decided that the most feasible means of ending the tension would be to persuade the school board to appeal to the federal court for relief. Surely in this situation of high emotion and the continuing threat of violence, they reasoned, the court would allow a "cooling off" period to permit the school board to devise a more workable plan. A former football coach and a large man in will and size, Virgil Blossom refused to consider retreat. His decision to hold out against both the downtown leadership and the governor predictably pushed him and his board into an isolated, lonely position. Harassing phone calls and even threats became routine for members of the school board, and especially for Blossom and his family.[19]

Harassment extended as well to the nine courageous children, who faced a hostile environment every day inside Central High School. At the outset of the school year some white students had made overtures of welcome and friendliness, but as the segregationist forces became more organized and more emboldened by the governor's support, the black children found themselves increasingly isolated at school. They had made their way into a fortress; now they were under siege from within.[20]

A pall descended upon Little Rock. High hopes had been dashed on all sides: The black community now saw the limited extent of their city's commitment to desegregation; the business community despaired over the damage to their city's image; the school board realized belatedly that their carefully crafted plan was woefully inadequate; thinking elements in the white community began to encounter their own racism. Two generations of segregation had blinded the races to seeing each other whole, but few understood the impairment or thought in terms of remedy. Anger and resentment prevailed.[21]

At length the chamber of commerce committee persuaded the school board to seek relief through the federal courts. Support for the school board position had evaporated, leaving the individual members under siege and the community viewing integration as "their problem." Only the *Arkansas Gazette* spoke out publicly in favor of supporting the board; Harry Ashmore's courageous editorials would win him a Pulitzer Prize but cost his paper millions of dollars in lost subscribers and advertisers.[22]

In February 1958 the school board's attorneys petitioned the federal district court for a postponement of integration in Little Rock. The petition described the school board as "standing alone, the victim of extraordinary opposition on the part of the state government and apathy on the part of the federal government." In this context the board asked for a delay until the courts clarified the concept of "all deliberate speed," the nebulous terminology employed in the *Brown* decision.[23]

In June 1958 Judge Harry J. Lemley of Hope, Arkansas, found in favor of the school board and granted the requested two-and-a-half-year delay of integration. The NAACP immediately appealed this decision to the Eighth Circuit Court of Appeals in St. Louis, which overturned the Lemley decision in August. While the school board appealed its case to the United States Supreme Court, Governor Faubus called a special session of the Arkansas General Assembly, which quickly passed a series of stridently anti-integration bills. One of these empowered the governor to close the schools in the event of integration and then hold an election within thirty days to determine whether voters wanted them to stay closed or to be reopened on a desegregated basis.[24]

On September 15, the United States Supreme Court, meeting in an unusual summer session, handed down *Cooper v. Aaron*, which instructed the Little Rock School Board to proceed immediately with the Blossom Plan. Faubus responded by closing the city's four high schools. Not far from the capital, Adolphine Terry picked up the telephone to call Vivion Brewer.[25]

Vivion Lenon Brewer was, to all outward appearances, the embodiment of the southern lady. Refined, dignified, demure in speech and appearance, she had been reared and educated in Little Rock and had returned there after college to work in her father's bank, join the Junior League, and look for a suitable mate. At the Democratic National Convention in 1928 she met and fell in love with Joe Robinson Brewer, the nephew and administrative aide of Arkansas' senior senator, Joseph T. Robinson, at that time the Democratic Party's candidate for vice president of the United States. Vivion Lenon and Joe Brewer married in 1930 and spent the next fifteen years living in Washington, D.C., surrounded by the excitement of being insiders in Democratic politics. They returned to Arkansas in 1947, when Joe took a position as personnel director of the Veterans' Administration Hospital at Fort Roots in North Little Rock.[26]

The Brewers made the unconventional decision to live about fifteen miles outside Little Rock at Scott, where Vivion's father owned a summer home on Bearskin Lake. Vivion loved the wild beauty and peacefulness of their lakeside cottage, and she may have wanted to escape the social demands of the country club set in Little Rock. Certainly she refused to join the plantation society of the Scott community, where the women centered their lives around the bridge table, the luncheon, and the church. Having no formal religious affiliation and no children, having lost their only child as an infant, Vivion threw herself into restoring and winterizing the old cabin, gardening, and in her words, "taking care of Joe." Soon after her return to Arkansas she became aware of the appalling living conditions of her plantation Negro neighbors. Brooding over the inequities of the plantation system, she eventually began to teach some of the children to read.[27]

As unremarkable as Vivion's privileged background was in some respects, it was extraordinary, for a southern woman, in others. Not only had her parents sent her to Smith College in Northampton, Massachusetts, too far away even to come home for Christmas, they allowed her to travel in Europe with a Smith friend for fourteen months after college. Furthermore, when she returned to Little Rock to work for her father's bank, he encouraged her to get a law degree. She did, and when she became the first female vice president of her father's Peoples' Bank and Trust Company, even the *New York Times* found this departure from tradition worthy of note. In Washington Vivion seems not to have challenged traditional roles and expectations, although in a long illness there she developed a genuine friendship with a black woman who nursed her; with this came a glimpse beyond the veil of segregation.[28]

By the time she returned to Arkansas at thirty-seven, Brewer had known career, glamour, motherhood, and sorrow. Vivion Brewer had the confidence, and the status, to be her own person. Trusting her instincts and perceptions, she showed no hesitation in challenging the norms of plantation society when her moral compass and her sense of honor pointed her in that direction. And so when disaster struck in her native city, Brewer despaired increasingly as the male "leadership" failed to take control.[29]

Brewer and Adolphine Terry had worked together closely in a number of enterprises, most notably the American Association for University Women and the hugely successful dinner in honor of Harry Ashmore's Pulitzer Prize. Terry was the age of Vivion's mother, and she had been involved in every conceivable project for the public good since her graduation from Vassar fifty years before. Wife of a former congressman, sister of renowned poet John Gould Fletcher, she possessed a level of respectability and a moral leadership unparalleled in Little Rock. And so when Adolphine Fletcher Terry sounded the trumpet for a group of women to follow the example of the Association of Southern Women for the Prevention of Lynching by working to put an end to the ongoing crisis in their city, fifty-eight intrepid women defied husbands, social mores, and the likelihood of public opprobrium to form the Women's Emergency Committee to Open Our Schools.[30]

Vivion Brewer told the story of the WEC in a remarkable memoir she called *The Embattled Ladies of Little Rock*. It is significant that she chose the term *ladies*, thereby unselfconsciously placing her heroines in the upper strata of southern society. Black women at that time and place were never called ladies, at least not in polite white society; they were called women. Nor were lower-class white women called ladies; they were referred to by proper southern girls' grandmothers as "common," and they, too, were called women. In referring to her protagonists as ladies, Vivion Brewer revealed her understanding of them as emerging from (and perhaps in her mind remaining within) the South's traditional range of expectations for proper female behavior; and yet while Brewer never set out to subvert traditional southern gender norms, it is nonetheless certain that under her leadership, such subversion is precisely what the Women's Emergency Committee accomplished.[31]

In *The Embattled Ladies of Little Rock* Brewer captured the drama and the frustration of her cohorts' efforts to galvanize Little Rock's male elite into action. Beginning in September 1958 with the closing of the schools, she discussed the excitement of political organizing in the election "for integration" (reopening the schools) or "against integration" (keeping them closed). She described the crisis of electing a new school board when the Blossom board resigned in despair, the development of an extensive organizational structure and membership, and the production of a proliferating amount of newsletters, memos, and advertising. She told of the emergence of the men, finally, in a campaign to recall the segregationist half of the new school board, and of the development of a report documenting the devastating impact of massive resistance on Little Rock's economy. She welcomed the reopening of the schools and grieved over the splintering of the WEC as its members become involved in diverse political campaigns. She mourned the destruction of Joe Brewer's career as a result of her opposition to Faubus. Throughout, Brewer's resoluteness and her energy in the face of unrelenting harassment and outright attack were striking. She never wavered under assault; it was only when a key WEC operative questioned her leadership and her distraught husband was forced into retirement that she passed the presidency of the organization to a younger colleague.[32]

However much Vivion Brewer may have looked the part of a southern lady, she never fully bought into that construct. Attractive, soft-spoken, witty, and charming, she seemed to all appearances to be the perfect complement for her handsome and dapper southern husband. They both loved to dance, and they reveled in being called "The Duke and Duchess of Little Rock" during their early years back in Arkansas. They were, by all accounts, quite the toast of the town. Despite her upbringing in a proper Little Rock home, however, Vivion did not learn from her Iowa-born parents the necessary emotional and intellectual habits of the southern lady.[33]

The southern lady was the centerpiece of the South's patriarchal scheme of race, class, and gender arrangements. As described by Anne

Firor Scott in *The Southern Lady,* in the antebellum era the lady was supposed to be:

> a submissive wife whose reason for being was to love, honor, obey and occasionally amuse her husband, to bring up his children and manage his household. Physically weak, and "formed for the less laborious occupations," she depended upon male protection. To secure this protection she was endowed with the capacity to "create a magic spell" over any men in her vicinity. She was timid and modest, beautiful and graceful, "the most fascinating being in creation . . . the delight and charm of every circle she moves in."

Of course the demands of submissiveness and perfection were unattainable, but Scott argues that from earliest childhood, southern girls learned to strive toward these ideals, and "by the time they arrived at their teens most girls had absorbed the injunctions of the myth." In return for male protection, the lady became the arbiter of morality, the custodian of conscience—within the sphere of her household.[34]

Scott suggests that the ideal of the southern lady was a necessary adjunct to the system of plantation slavery. "Any tendency," she writes, "on the part of any members of the system to assert themselves against the master threatened the whole, and therefore slavery itself." Furthermore, "It was no accident that the most articulate spokesman [*sic*] for slavery were also eloquent exponents of the subordinate role of women."[35]

One has to wonder what these southern men feared. What haunted these "would-be patriarchs" who endeavored so earnestly to inculcate impossible ideals in their wives and daughters, ideals that they had no intention of imposing on themselves? Scott suggests that perhaps the southern masters feared that the women "to whom they had granted the custody of conscience and morality" might turn that bequest to an examination of male behavior—"to sharp trading in the market place, to inordinate addiction to alcohol, to nocturnal visits to the slave quarters." Clearly this would not do, and so the lady obtained the reward, or the bribe, of being revered and extolled in every southern forum, even going so far, as W. J. Cash claimed, as to become the banner under which "the ranks of the Confederacy went rolling into battle in the misty conviction that it was wholly for her that they fought."[36]

Although the mythology of the lady developed under the conditions of plantation slavery, it did not fade away with the uprooting of the South's "peculiar institution." Of course the harsh conditions of life in the postwar

South, coupled with the arrival in the region of the industrial revolution, combined to undercut the traditional ideology, but the construct of "the lady" remained as characteristic and unifying an element of the "southern way of life" as Democratic politics, evangelical religion, and segregated society. Even the arrival of the "New Woman" in the early twentieth-century South did not signal her demise. While she now could hope to be educated and to move beyond the home into restricted roles in public life and the workplace, the proper southern woman continued to aspire to elevated standards of "ladylike" behavior, admonished by fathers and husbands to cultivate a deferential attitude and to function in subordinate roles. Occasionally a willful or intelligent "belle" defied male domination, but usually not for long, and almost certainly not without negative consequences.[37]

In short, the southern lady was for over a hundred years the ultimate bulwark of elite white male dominance of southern society. She was the key to the maintenance of patriarchal control of southern life, and even as the South industrialized and urbanized, a patriarchal, hierarchical mindset continued to characterize regional thought. Buttressed by evangelical religion, this pattern of thought imposed a maximum of control on elite women while it gave maximum freedom to their men. At the heart of the arrangement was the lady's absolute protection against sexual advances by black men; as the guarantor of the purity of white bloodlines, she bore the ultimate responsibility for the preservation of white civilization. This was the source of male reverence for her, the explanation for all the care and delicacy surrounding her estate. It was only in her sphere of domesticity and morality that she dared to challenge male leadership; but in her sanctioned role of conscience she was in time to find the means of her escape from a system that was in some ways as oppressive for her as it was for the people of color it was designed to control.[38]

Vivion Brewer was born into a world in which the lady was the ideal for women of her status and expectations. The daughter of a prominent banker, mayor, and key player in Little Rock's physical development, Brewer spent her girlhood surrounded by the softening influences of a prosperous urban life. While she imbibed much of the southern ideology of racism, the Baptist Sunday School, and the code of ladylike behavior, however, she was not socialized properly to function as a true southern lady, because her parents were not southerners.[39]

But rather than encourage her submission to male leadership, Vivion's parents rejoiced in her keen intellect and encouraged her to think, to read, and to pursue the education they never had. Rather than insist that she spend her postgraduate year making her social debut in Little Rock, as was the custom, they allowed her to spend that year traveling about Europe unsupervised, a most unladylike pursuit. And rather than insisting that she stay at home learning domestic virtues from her mother, or even steering her toward more acceptable voluntary pursuits, they sent her to law school and made her a vice president of the bank. In all these ways Warren and Clara Lenon cultivated independence of thought and confidence in their daughter, rendering her quite unsuitable to serve in any capacities of submission to or intimidation in the face of male authority. Not understanding, or perhaps not accepting, the southern patriarchal system and the need for female complicity in maintaining social control over a threatening black population, the Lenons cultivated an independent woman within their otherwise bourgeois household.[40]

When the time came for Vivion Lenon Brewer to challenge male authority in her world she was relentless in her assault, if ladylike in her demeanor. She infuriated many of the men among Little Rock's civic elite because, never having mastered the indirection of the southern lady, she asked embarrassing questions, and she said exactly what she thought. Throughout, one can trace an undercurrent of impatience and frustration with male temporizing, an irritation that probably showed through in her one-on-one dealings with these male "leaders." Utterly fearless in her righteousness, she pounded out letters on her overworked Smith-Corona to such recipients as J. William Fulbright, senator from Arkansas, that minced no words:

> We are proud that you, Bill, a fellow Arkansan, have the chance to be a leader in solving the imperative problem of World Peace. We want to help. We offer you our help, even though we have been deeply disappointed and dismayed that you have not tried to help us.[41]

Surely the southern gentlemen who found themselves the beneficiaries of such criticism found their encounters with Vivion Brewer to be unsettling, even irritating.

Adolphine Terry came home from Vassar vowing that she was *not* going to be a southern lady and then spent the rest of her life being one. Quite as principled and as honorable as Vivion Brewer, Terry was the daughter of a Confederate veteran and had mastered the high art of manipulating southern men without directly challenging their prerogatives.

As a recent student of her behavior has described her, "when the WEC needed the cooperation of men for one of its early projects, Terry insisted that they have the men over for dinner, arguing that 'southern gentlemen have been taught to be courteous to their hostess, so when you give men food to eat they cannot be impolite to you and they must do a favor in return.'" Vivion Brewer understood this approach, but it did not come naturally to her. She was much more inclined to confront a businessman directly, in his office when she could get in, and it is not surprising that the men whose leadership she sought to inspire found her a trial.[42]

Anne Scott has suggested that antebellum southern society closed ranks around the ideology of the lady as a means of securing internal stability when the institution of slavery faced increasing attack from outside the region. It may be true that Vivion Brewer and the WEC—and the women of Help Our Public Education (HOPE) in Atlanta, Save Our Schools (SOS) in New Orleans, and other similar organizations throughout the South—succeeded in their assault on the "southern way of life," namely its gender relations as well as its racial arrangements, because the revolutionary processes of the mechanization of agriculture had already removed the economic underpinnings of racism. In other words, it was no longer an economic necessity to keep women and blacks "in their place," although the force of habit mandated these racial and gender relations, and they were certainly convenient arrangements for elite white males.[43]

As the arbiters of conscience and morality in the South, white women had society's permission to have and to voice opinions on moral issues, especially those bearing on the welfare of children. Although many of the women of the WEC undoubtedly did not share their leaders' racial liberalism initially, they did know that they needed schools for their children. They could speak to this need without undermining any of the South's cherished traditions or significantly challenging Little Rock's racial mores.

As their work for open schools led them into daily contact with other like-minded women and daily discussions of the issues surrounding desegregation, many in the WEC examined southern racial customs in ways that they had never before been called upon to do. Many also discovered a sense of purpose and of camaraderie that was unusual in the southern female experience, and this gratification and support emboldened them to follow to their logical conclusions many of the arguments they were learning to make.[44] By 1960, 82 percent of the WEC members responding to a group survey could answer "No" to the question "Do you believe that desegregation will permanently damage public education?" Southern society's sanctioning of female moral leadership had led these women, at last, to challenge the central feature of the southern social structure.[45]

Vivion Brewer's and the WEC's fierce dedication to freeing black Arkansans from the inequitable racial practices in their city had the unexpected consequence of freeing white women as well. While it is doubtful that these women made the connection between the two patterns of oppression, it is nonetheless clear that in giving Little Rock's elite women their voice, in teaching them to think in terms of organizational skill and political action, and in leading them into the unaccustomed forums of shaping public opinion, the WEC opened doors that Little Rock's women had not known were there, and through which they escaped in growing numbers. In the years after the WEC shut down its operations, the women Brewer had "trained" remained active in a broad range of public pursuits in Little Rock and elsewhere.[46]

Although the great majority of the active workers in the WEC were "outsiders" in the sense that they did not grow up in Little Rock, or they were from the North, or they were Jewish (in a very WASPish community), in the wake of the WEC experience a younger generation of elite Little Rock women employed the critical skills this remarkable organization had fostered. For example, there can be little doubt that the WEC legacy of questioning old certainties had a direct bearing on the decision of eleven women to resign from the Junior League of Little Rock in 1967 and 1968, in protest over that organization's refusal to admit to membership a prominent and popular Jewish woman. The absolute summit of respectability in Little Rock, the Junior League had long been the unquestioned preserve of the civic elite. Its dictates took precedence over all other commitments, and its control over proper female behavior was the final word. But when elite women in Little Rock began to decline membership in the Junior League because of its refusal to admit Jewish members, a new day had at last arrived. Little Rock's women were looking out at the world through new eyes, as were many other residents of their city.[47]

The ancient Chinese symbol for crisis bears within itself the equal and opposite symbol for opportunity. This wisdom drawn from countless ages of experience would seem to be a fitting commentary on the "Little Rock crisis," for out of what seemed to be a crisis in one southern community came unnumbered opportunities. However falteringly, black children began to receive an equal education in Little Rock; other local people of color began to see that as the walls of separation came down, new opportunities for dignity and economic advancement awaited them. Other cities learned from Little Rock's experience and allowed desegregation to proceed without incident to the benefit of all; white women found their voices and began to speak out on issues far removed from their traditional spheres of influence. Black people and white people began to see beyond the veil of segregation and began the laborious process of learning to see each other whole.

Crisis and opportunity are intertwined in the human experience, but it is only through human agency that the mechanisms of the process of interaction are set in motion. Vivion Brewer died without comprehending the full dimensions of her contributions and without being recognized for them. But through her dedication to principle, her unrelenting effort, and her sacrifices of time, friends, security, and comfort, she rose to the challenge and helped to open the way toward a new era of opportunity in her region and in her nation.

Notes

The author would like to thank the University of Arkansas Press for permission to quote portions of her *Understanding the Little Rock Crisis: An Exercise in Remembrance and Reconciliation* (Fayetteville, 1999); and also the *Arkansas Historical Quarterly* for permission to quote portions of her "Down from the Pedestal: Gender and Regional Culture in a Ladylike Assault on the Southern Way of Life" (fall 1997), 345–52. The author also wishes to thank four friends for reading and commenting on an early draft of this paper: Andrea Hollander Budy, Virginia Jeans Laas, Elizabeth Payne, and Virginia Wray.

1. Harry Ashmore speech, June 14, 1966, Fletcher-Terry Family Papers, Archives and Special Collections, University of Arkansas at Little Rock. In an interview with Sara Alderman Murphy on June 13, 1994, Ashmore remembered that "Miss Adolphine" came to his office to deliver this news wearing a hat and white gloves. Sara Alderman Murphy, *Breaking the Silence: How Little Rock Women Reopened the Schools* (Fayetteville, 1997).

2. The papers of the Women's Emergency Committee to Open Our Schools are housed at the Arkansas History Commission in Little Rock, Arkansas.

3. For biographical information about Adolphine Fletcher Terry, see Murphy, *Breaking the Silence*, chap. 1, and Lorraine Gates, "Power from the Pedestal: The Women's Emergency Committee and the Little Rock School Crisis," *Arkansas Historical Quarterly*, spring, 1996, 45. Gates writes of Terry: "There was perhaps no other person in Little Rock who could have organized the first stand against the segregationists and made such opposition legitimate." Gates, "Power from the Pedestal," 32. The second president of the Women's Emergency Committee reflected on

Terry's significance as follows: "Mrs. Terry . . . was wealthy but always she had used her wealth not for herself or her family but for the community. . . . she was the kind of person whom no one could attack. No one could threaten her with loss of money. No one could threaten her with loss of her reputation. She was unassailable. . . . She was completely morally upright. She had done everything for the church. So she could not be attacked there. She'd done everything for education, not there, every-thing for business, not there, everything for the arts, not there. There was no area." John Luter interview with Mrs. Pat House, August 22, 1971, Eisenhower Adminis-tration Project, Columbia University Oral History Program, New York.

4. For the full story of the development of the Women's Emergency Committee, see Vivion Lenon Brewer, *The Embattled Ladies of Little Rock: 1958–1963: The Struggle to Save Public Education at Central High* (Fort Bragg, Calif., 1999).

5. Virgil Blossom, *It Has Happened Here* (New York, 1959); and Roy Reed, *Faubus: The Life and Times of an American Prodigal* (Fayetteville, 1997).

6. For an excellent brief overview of the activities of the Capitol Citizens' Coun-cil, see Neil R. McMillen, *The Citizens' Council: Organized Resistance to the Second Reconstruction, 1954–64* (Urbana, 1971), 267–85.

7. Elizabeth Jacoway, "Taken by Surprise: Little Rock Businessmen and Desegre-gation," in *Southern Businessmen and Desegregation*, ed. Elizabeth Jacoway and David R. Colburn (Baton Rouge, 1982), 15–41.

8. Harry S. Ashmore, *Arkansas: A History* (New York, 1978), 153–4.

9. Reed, *Faubus.*

10. Orval Eugene Faubus, *Down from the Hills* (Little Rock, 1980), 197–8.

11. John Luter interview with Orval Faubus, August 18, 1971, Eisenhower Ad-ministration Project, Columbia University Oral History Program, New York.

12. J. W. Peltason, *Fifty-Eight Lonely Men: Southern Federal Judges and School Desegregation* (New York, 1961), 161–207. For an interesting treatment of the Cen-tral High Mothers' League, see Graeme Cope, "'A Thorn in the Side?' The Mothers' League of Central High School and the Little Rock Desegregation Crisis of 1957," *Arkansas Historical Quarterly,* summer 1998, 160–70.

13. Peltason, *Fifty-Eight Lonely Men,* 163–4.

14. For the theory of a "manufactured crisis" see ibid., especially 165.

15. Brooks Hays, *A Southern Moderate Speaks* (Chapel Hill, 1959).

16. Jacoway, "Taken by Surprise," 24–8.

17. Ibid., 25.

18. Ibid.

19. Blossom, *It Has Happened Here,* 147–75.

20. Melba Patillo Beals, *Warriors Don't Cry* (New York, 1994); Daisy Bates, *The Long Shadow of Little Rock* (New York, 1962; reprint, Fayetteville, 1987); Elizabeth Huckaby, *Crisis at Central High: Little Rock, 1957–58* (Baton Rouge, 1980). Virgil Blossom estimated the number of white tormentors to be fewer than fifty; Blossom, *It Has Happened Here,* 156.

21. Jacoway, "Taken by Surprise."

22. Harry S. Ashmore, *Civil Rights and Wrongs: A Memoir of Race and Politics, 1944–1994* (New York, 1994).

23. Tony Freyer, *The Little Rock Crisis: A Constitutional Interpretation* (Westport, Conn., 1984), 145–6.

24. Irving Spitzberg, *Racial Politics in Little Rock, 1954–64* (New York, 1982).

25. Freyer, *Little Rock Crisis*, 145–54; see also Peter Irons and Stephanie Guitton, eds., *May It Please the Court: Transcripts of Twenty-Three Live Recordings of Landmark Cases as Argued before the Supreme Court* (New York, 1993), 249–61.

26. Elizabeth Jacoway interview with Vivion Lenon Brewer, October 15, 1976, for the Southern Oral History Program, now deposited in the Southern Historical Collection, University of North Carolina, Chapel Hill, North Carolina; see also John Luter interview with Mrs. Joe Brewer, August 20, 1971, Eisenhower Administration Project, Columbia University Oral History Program, New York.

27. Jacoway interview with Vivion Lenon Brewer.

28. Ibid.

29. Ibid.

30. Murphy, *Breaking the Silence*, 67–90.

31. Brewer, "Embattled Ladies of Little Rock"; the observations about terminology are drawn from the author's experience as a Little Rock native. For an enlightening article about Atlanta's HOPE see Paul Mertz, "'Mind Changing Time All Over Georgia': HOPE, Inc. and School Desegregation, 1958–1961," *Georgia Historical Quarterly*, spring 1993, 41–61.

32. Brewer, *Embattled Ladies of Little Rock*.

33. Elizabeth Jacoway interviews with Patricia Rostker (Vivion Brewer's niece), August 1996, Scott, Arkansas; Mimi Dortch, August 1996, Little Rock, Arkansas; Pat House, August 1996, Little Rock, Arkansas; Fred Poe, September 1996, by telephone from Little Rock, Arkansas; Louise Vinson, September 1996, Exeter, New Hampshire. See also Jacoway interview with Brewer, and Luter interview with Brewer.

34. Scott, *The Southern Lady*, 4, 7.

35. Ibid., 17.

36. Ibid.; Wilbur J. Cash, *The Mind of the South* (New York, 1941), 89; see also Elizabeth Jacoway, "The South's Palladium: The Southern Woman and the Cash Construct," in *W. J. Cash and the Minds of the South*, ed. Paul D. Escott (Baton Rouge, 1992), 112–33.

37. For excellent treatments of the persistence of the lady ideal into the twentieth century see Jacquelyn Dowd Hall, *Revolt Against Chivalry: Jesse Daniel Ames and the Women's Campaign Against Lynching* (New York, 1979); Marjorie Spruill Wheeler, *New Women of the New South: The Leaders of the Woman Suffrage Movement in the Southern States* (New York, 1993); Gilmore, *Gender and Jim Crow;* and Pamela Tyler, *Silk Stockings and Ballot Boxes: Women and Politics in New Orleans, 1920–1965* (Athens, Ga., 1996). For a clear-sighted view of the hazards of the belle role, see Virginia Jeans Laas, *Love and Power in the Nineteenth Century: The Marriage of Violet Blair* (Fayetteville, 1998).

38. For a classic interpretation of the connections between race and gender in the South, see Lillian Smith, *Killers of the Dream* (New York, 1949). For an elegant elaboration of "the moral economy of gender" see Drew Gilpin Faust, *Mothers of Invention: Women of the Slaveholding South in the American Civil War* (Chapel Hill, 1996). For a later period see Jean Friedman, *The Enclosed Garden: Women and Community in the Evangelical South, 1830–1900* (Chapel Hill, 1985).

39. Information about Vivion Brewer's ancestry, girlhood, and adulthood may be gleaned from the Vivion Lenon Brewer Papers, Sophia Smith Collection, Smith College, Northampton, Massachusetts, and from the Vivion Lenon Brewer Papers, Archives and Special Collections, University of Arkansas at Little Rock.

40. Ibid.

41. Brewer, *Embattled Ladies*, 89.

42. Gates, "Power from the Pedestal," 45. Pat House assessed Terry's tactics somewhat differently: "She called in every I.O.U. that she had put out all through the years, and naturally a woman who has been this active and this intelligent and this much of a leader has many I.O.U.'s because she doesn't need to gather them in . . . she had no children in public school either, see, and nothing to gain. Nothing to gain at all. She didn't need anything. There was no profit, nothing anywhere. She didn't even need any accolades. She didn't need another star in her crown. So she gathered all these people, and if any of us were discouraged or if we got tired—how can you say to an eighty year old woman, you know, 'I'm tired'? Or 'I can't do this,'" Luter interview with House.

43. Scott, *The Southern Lady*, 21.

44. Charlotte Gadberry interview with Kathryn Wittenberg Lambright, November 27, 1978, Little Rock Women Project, Oral History Program, University of Arkansas at Little Rock.

45. Brewer, *Embattled Ladies*, 282–6.

46. Ibid. In 1971 Vivion Brewer remarked in an interview that "one of the most wonderful parts of the committee . . . is that it alerted so many woman to civic problems, and they have remained active in all sorts of good organizations, working for the betterment of the city." Luter interview with Brewer.

47. Although the Women's Emergency Committee always maintained that it did not have a formal membership, a membership list is included in the Vivion Lenon Brewer Papers at the University of Arkansas at Little Rock. For an interesting treatment of the Junior League imbroglio, see Paula Barnes, "The Junior League Eleven: Elite Women of Little Rock Struggle for Social Justice," *Arkansas Historical Quarterly*, spring 1998, 46–61. For insight into the changing attitudes of Little Rock women on many other topics, see interviews in the Little Rock Women Project at the University of Arkansas at Little Rock, especially those with Kathryn Wittenberg Lambright, Peg Newton Smith, and Mary Fletcher Worthen.

14

After the Wives Went to Work

Organizing Women in the Southern Apparel Industry

MICHELLE HABERLAND

In 1939, a small town in south central Alabama experienced a momentous event. Vanity Fair, a large lingerie manufacturer from Reading, Pennsylvania, opened the doors to its new factory in Jackson, Alabama. The opening of the factory was the culmination of years of work by the community to attract industry to their rural town. Local businessmen had dedicated themselves to courting industry, presenting Jackson as a small town with a large number of docile, inexpensive laborers.[1] And when a chance meeting between the mayor of Jackson and the vice president of Vanity Fair occurred, the community had found its industry. Businessmen then launched a fund-raising campaign and urged residents of Clarke County to buy bonds to build the factory. The response was extraordinary, especially considering the difficult economic times. Clarke County raised $55,000 from its mostly impoverished residents and hired local workers to build the factory to Vanity Fair's specifications. And while the men in Clarke County were busy raising bond money and constructing the building for Vanity Fair, their wives and daughters prepared to become factory workers. Thus, when the factory finally opened its doors, one employee recalled, "Vanity Fair put the ladies to work and the men stayed home and kept house."

Soon after the company was up and running, organizers from the International Ladies Garment Workers Union (ILGWU) arrived. They distributed pro-union leaflets, standing just beyond the company's property boundary. Many decades later, a sewing machine operator recalled that day with particular clarity. Before the sewing room workers finished their shift, the managers at Vanity Fair called a meeting. The message of that meeting was clear: Managers told the employees that "they wouldn't operate under a union." The sewing room workers left the factory and walked right past the union organizers.[2] In a poor rural county like Clarke County there were few other jobs for white women, who had two choices for employment, the fields or Vanity Fair. Besides, everyone understood what the factory had meant to Jackson and the surrounding towns. It had been the savior of an area that, at the time, was trapped by its dependence on a dying livelihood.[3] Prices for cotton had hit rock bottom in the latter years of the Great Depression, and the market showed no signs of improvement. Families lived for generations in ramshackle unpainted structures. There was little electricity or reason for getting it because few could afford the utility bill that would come with it. Describing the situation of Clarke County residents before the arrival of the clothing factory, one woman remarked, "We had nothing."[4]

Vanity Fair, and the money the company brought into the local economy, transformed the county into a series of small towns that seemed to have a bright future. But it was a future that depended on Vanity Fair. Jackson was not quite a company town, but it relied heavily on the income the plant brought in. There were sawmills and a few public utility projects, but they employed mostly male workers. As Arcola McLean put it, "there wasn't any jobs for women." Even as late as 1986, fully two decades after the U.S. clothing industry's decline, Vanity Fair was the largest employer in the state, underscoring the importance of the clothing industry to Alabama's economy. The impact of the clothing industry on a local level was even more striking, with Vanity Fair dominating the manufacturing occupations available in Clarke County in 1997.[5]

In the mid-1970s, the ILGWU tried once again to organize Vanity Fair. By this time, the once all-white factory counted African Americans among its workers. Indeed, black women were central to the success of the 1970s organizing campaign. The introduction of African Americans seemed to signal, at least to some white workers at Vanity Fair, the arrival of the ILGWU. They believed that African Americans would organize and seek collective action as they had done in earlier civil rights actions in Alabama and throughout the South. A history of the southern apparel industry in the post–World War II era exposes interrelated systems of segregation that simultaneously functioned along lines of race and gender.[6] The civil rights movement and the women's movement provide an important context for labor organizing in the postwar southern apparel industry. By including the dynamics of race and gender, the complicated relationships between the ILGWU and the civil rights and women's movements at a local level become clearer.

In the 1950s and early 1960s, connections between race and the new challenges facing the two primary garment unions, the ILGWU and the Amalgamated Clothing Workers of America (ACWA), were real and substantial. Although the needle trade unions organized within a racially segregated environment in the South, the efforts of both the ILGWU and the ACWA to organize southern clothing workers often focused on an alignment with civil rights organizations and the targeting of African Americans. This was the context in which southern apparel factories opened their doors to blacks in the mid-1960s. And, as they did so, the apparel unions took on new challenges, new potential unionists. The work force became ethnically more diverse as African Americans and, in smaller numbers, Latinas came to replace a generation of predominantly white women stitchers. Reflecting that increase in ethnic diversity among the needle trades labor force, the union membership also grew increasingly diverse. As the ILGWU and ACWA recruited African Americans and Latinas as members, the apparel unions also suffered when anti-unionists drew connections between desegregation and unionism. The "race card" became a fixture of anti-union practices. The apparel unions' connections to established civil rights organizations were extensive and reinforced the association of unionism with blacks.

With the establishment of the Equal Employment Opportunity Commission (EEOC) in 1964 mandating nondiscrimination in employment, African Americans slowly made their way into the apparel industry, and the racial exclusivity of the industry declined.[7] For the nation as a whole, the number of black workers in the industry increased from 51,000 workers in 1966 to nearly 100,000 workers in 1980, an increase of around 100 percent. As a percentage of U.S. apparel workers, the increase of African Americans in the clothing industry was also notable, from 8.6 percent in 1966 to 15.6 percent in 1980. This increase in the apparel industrial labor force coincided with a decline in the industry's presence in New York City and surrounding areas as it became more southern.[8] In addition, the number of apparel workers in the nation suffered a substantial decline during the same period. The *Economic Census* reported that the number of U.S. apparel workers fell from 1.35 million workers in 1966 to 1.18 million workers in 1982. Thus the increase in African American employment in the needle trades coincided with an overall 13 percent decline in apparel industry employment. Although the clothing industry became more ethnically and racially diverse as a whole, at the individual plant level in the South, white, black, and Latina workers found the integration to be incomplete. In 1965 Burl C. Robinson, an ILGWU organizer, noted that one South Carolina plant was racially integrated, but he also recognized a system of occupational segregation. The Capital City clothing manufacturer of Columbia, South Carolina, employed "50 to 175 employees. There are approximately 60 to 70 colored operators and 24 to 30 pressers (colored). Supervisor [sic] are all white."[9] The plant was racially integrated, but at the floor level, the categorization of occupations reinforced racial segregation. At Vanity Fair's factory in Jackson, Alabama, a black woman hired shortly after desegregation remembered that not all jobs were open to black women. Vevelyn "Queenie" Gilchrist believed that she was unable to get certain jobs because she was black. Nick Bonanno, president of the ILGWU's southern office, pointed out that in a typical factory, "black girls were pressers."[10] Pressers received less pay than the white women sewers or the male mechanics who fixed the sewing machines. Although desegregation challenged apparel companies to relax their ban on hiring all-white or all-black in the mid-1960s, it did little to challenge the pattern of race-based occupational segregation within individual factories.

Both black and white workers in the southern apparel industry believed that federal legislation was responsible for opening the factories to large numbers of African American women. Vivian Long, the white personnel secretary at Vanity Fair's Jackson plant, explained that desegregation occurred "When the government required you to hire them." Unable to ask questions regarding race on applications, Long placed the "blame" for desegregation of Vanity Fair directly at the feet of the federal government. Black women at Vanity Fair also credited the federal government, specifically the EEOC, with desegregation.[11] Similarly, the only published study of African American apparel workers points to 1964 as the beginning of the racial desegregation of the industry. Elaine Gale Wrong attributes this beginning to a combination of factors including the enfranchisement of increasing numbers of black southerners and a shrinking supply of white labor. As African Americans gained access to voting booths, they could demand that the numerous apparel factories, built or subsidized with local tax dollars, employ blacks as well as whites.[12] The traditional explanation for the transition to African American factory employment focused on a shortage of white labor during the 1960s, while newer scholarship emphasizes the role of litigation and federal antidiscrimination legislation in the desegregation of the southern textile labor force. Federal legislation caused the southern apparel industry to integrate its work force, as evidenced by the many comments about and frequent emphasis on the role of the federal government and its policies.[13]

The precise moment of desegregation in each of the factories is best conveyed by the memories of a whole spectrum of sewing machine operators and factory personnel. While white sewing machine operators frequently complained about the introduction of African American workers, other observers saw a potential alliance of black and white. In 1981 Paula McClendon described the desegregation of the Jackson Vanity Fair factory in the late 1960s as the uniting of African American and disgruntled white workers. In the early years of the factory white women were grateful to have jobs, happy to escape the fields. But as time passed, some white women stitchers, many of whom had been with the company for decades, resented their low wages and minimal benefits.[14] But there were other women, especially among the older generation of white women employees, who felt personally connected to and obligated to the company. As one of the original members of the Vanity Fair's ILGWU organizing committee put it, "A lot of the women in there have been there for years and years and years and they were under the impression that if it wasn't for Vanity Fair they'd just dry up and blow away and never be seen again." The white women who began working in the factory in the years surrounding World War II felt a strong loyalty to and identification with the company that saved them from agricultural work. Moreover, they felt their whiteness entitled them to work there, an advantage that African American women obviously could not claim.[15]

Eager to attract industry from the North, boosters sought to preserve the racial divisions of women's work. Arcola McLean, a sewing machine operator at the Jackson Vanity Fair plant for twenty-three years, explained that the nature of the work helped determine the whiteness and racial exclusivity of sewing machine operators. Sewing at Vanity Fair was a team effort and individual operators, in order to make decent wages, relied on the quick, accurate work of other stitchers on the line. A slower worker would mean that the whole line of sewers would fall short of the standard, a minimum piece rate required in order to achieve incentive pay. Explaining why she left Vanity Fair after African American women were hired as operators in the 1960s, Arcola said, "If you sewed next to [one of the coloreds], you just had to wait for work. . . . You couldn't make nothin,' you just made the day, that's all." The interdependence of a sewing line helps to explain the racial and gender exclusivity of southern apparel factories. In most of the southern apparel industry, prior to the late 1960s white women workers wanted to work with other whites. This preference not only fostered a better relationship and cooperation among workers who depended on one another for their wages, but it also ensured the availability of black women's labor for domestic and agricultural work. As Vivian Long explained, "We had some [blacks] apply ... We didn't hire any until ... that [federal] legislation came [in the 1960s] because most of the blacks were doing domestic work. They were maids and things." Labor surveys of Greenville, Mississippi, similarly revealed that local boosters envisioned only white women workers in garment factories.[16]

Later, in the 1960s and 1970s, black women were newcomers to Vanity Fair and they felt much less grateful toward the corporation than an earlier generation of whites. One African American sewing machine operator complained that supervisors ordered the women workers to "keep their heads down," and "no talking." Another woman recalled, "[T]here were so many people there I would see crying—just crying to no end ... I don't like to see people mistreated." But it was not simply a case of difficult supervisors and insensitive management. Sewing was difficult work, as were other positions in the factory. Packing garments into boxes required skill. And the ever-changing styles of the women's fashion industry resulted in many complaints among sewing machine operators—as styles changed, sewers would be forced to change jobs and machines.[17]

There was also substantial resistance to federally mandated desegregation in the middle of the 1960s. Some white workers resented the demise of their once largely segregated and racially exclusive workplace community. Arcola McLean, who worked at the Vanity Fair plant in Jackson almost since its beginning in 1939, eventually quit because of desegregation, saying, "It wasn't a nice place to work anymore."[18] Vivian Long complained about African Americans' work ethic, claiming that the quality of production had been better when only white women operated the sewing machines.[19] The reluctance of white workers to work alongside African Americans had a long history in the apparel industry. Nearly a decade before integration this feeling was so strong among the workers at a North Carolina plant that an ILGWU campaign virtually evaporated. The organizer reported that "supervisors [told employees] that if [a] union came in, they would have to work with Negroes. This stopped the [ILGWU's] campaign dead in its tracks."[20]

But after 1964 interracial workplaces and unions became more common in the southern apparel industry. And eventually the opposition to racially integrated workplaces in the southern garment industry came to be associated with anti-union sentiment and activities. That connection developed only after the southern apparel industry had begun to integrate and after the international offices of the clothing unions sought to facilitate their organizing efforts by targeting African Americans. The experience of white and black workers at Vanity Fair underscores these national trends on a local and personal level.[21]

In 1975 Sarah Boykin, an African American sewing machine operator, initiated the request for union representation at Vanity Fair. Sarah described how she came to see unionization as the solution to the way the company mistreated workers. Richard Boykin, her husband, had been an activist in the local civil rights struggle. One evening he asked her, "Why are you crying?" She replied, "If you had seen [what I saw at the factory] you would cry." And then, the suggestion: "Well, don't cry. What you need to do is get a union."[22] In addition to his civil rights work, Richard was also an active member of the formidable International Brotherhood of the Teamsters. Another black woman on the Vanity Fair organizing committee, "Queenie" Gilchrist, remembered that after she heard about the union's organizing campaign she sought the advice of her father, who, as a minister and long-time activist, had experience in collective and political organizing. It was only with his endorsement that Gilchrist joined the Vanity Fair in-plant organizing committee and helped lead the ILGWU to victory there in 1976. From the very inception of the campaign to organize Vanity Fair, civil rights and labor organizing were connected concerns.[23]

The ILGWU itself was proud of its opposition to the "race card." Nick Bonanno, union leader, boasted often that the "ILGWU never had segregated locals." In some instances, the apparel union targeted African American workers by hiring African American organizers. As early as 1956, the ILGWU asked southern organizers to assess the effectiveness of organizing black workers through black union organizers, while an emphasis on African American organizing continued through the civil rights era.[24] The ILGWU's southeastern regional office was particularly concerned with the racial composition of their locals. From December through the early months of 1974, the regional office, led by Bonanno, received dozens of reports on the racial composition of ILGWU locals. The reports frequently listed not only African American unionists and their occupations, but also the names of any black officers in each local.[25]

Some unionists contended that African American workers were easier to organize. In a 1963 interview with a business professor from Mississippi State University, Claude Ramsay argued that firms with a large number of African Americans were more receptive to unionism than those that were all-white. A few years later, one union leader emphasized that a sleepwear plant in Greensboro, North Carolina, employed a substantial percentage of

African American workers, further suggesting that their presence in the plant was a benefit to organizing. Textile union organizers made similar statements.[26]

The ILGWU was unable to penetrate Vanity Fair's plant in Jackson until African American women began working there. Arcola McLean and Vivian Long, both white, drew clear connections between the arrival of the union and the desegregation of the sewing room. Long complained the ILGWU's organizing strategy was one that targeted African Americans, as the ILGWU organizers cunningly linked "gullible" black workers with disgruntled white workers. "You could take a black worker [and] much of them around here don't have too much intelligence. And [the organizers] could motivate them. And if they could find one white person that was dissatisfied, they stuck with that one." To her mind, the combination of black and white workers in a labor organization "festered" like a wound within the Vanity Fair community.[27]

The ILGWU sought the help of African Americans in organizing apparel plants and as officeholders in local unions. Organizers reported a number of African Americans on the executive boards of their locals. In 1972 an ILGWU organizer in Spartanburg, South Carolina, reported that while only one of the seven executive board members was African American, nearly half of the locals' shop stewards and committee members were black.[28] Especially at the local level, organizers and officers were aware of the need to promote better race relations. After Vanity Fair workers requested union assistance, the ILGWU sent two women organizers to Jackson, one black, one white.[29] And the Vanity Fair employees themselves made their commitment to interracial unionism clear. By careful design, the original in-plant organizing and negotiation committee contained equal numbers of black and white women. When they traveled together to the regional offices of the ILGWU in Atlanta, the new unionists arranged to share hotel rooms. In an effort to combat the "race card" and the "black versus white" perception of anti-unionists, the organizing committee conveyed an image of racial harmony.[30]

The ILGWU made no secret of its many affiliations with southern civil rights organizations and causes. In 1965 the director of the ILGWU's Southeast Region, Martin Morand, commented, "The Negro organizations in the South are much closer to the labor movement than in the North."[31] Morand, who would later became the civil rights director for the AFL-CIO, maintained close relations with many civil rights organizations. Early in 1965 a colleague from Pennsylvania wrote complimenting his dedication to the civil rights movement: "I must add a special word of appreciation for your consistent work in the anti-discrimination field. . . . Atlanta is doubly fortunate in now having two Martins who share the same ideals in civil rights. Martin Luther King does have a bit of an edge on you with his Nobel Prize recognition but that gives you something to work for."

He specifically referred to the ways in which Morand's leadership entitled him to expert status on race relations in the South.[32] Other members of the ILGWU's Atlanta office also received and accepted invitations to functions hosted by civil rights organizations. The previous director of the Southeast Region, E. T. "Al" Kehrer, was dedicated to civil rights action. After Kehrer left the ILGWU he went on to work in the AFL-CIO's Civil Rights Department and to teach at the Southern Staff Training Institutes. Jack Handler, regional counsel for the ILGWU's Southeastern Region, offered his services to a Southern Christian Leadership Conference meeting in 1966.[33]

The ILGWU's commitment to civil rights in the South went far beyond mere words and participation on a handful of committees. In 1963 an ILGWU business agent from Atlanta wrote Kehrer about his participation in a meeting of the Negro Baptist Ministers Union. Local and regional labor officials were notable attendees. The president of the Atlanta Labor Council attended and other unions, including the ILGWU, sent representatives. At the meeting, a leader of the Atlanta Voters League praised the "Great International Ladies' Garment Workers' Union" for its donation of "one million dollars for the use of the Atlanta Negro Community in acquiring housing."[34]

But relations between civil rights organizations and the ILGWU were hardly trouble-free. While the ILGWU never officially accommodated segregated unions in the region, the union countenanced informal segregation among its southern union members. Bonanno argued that white unionists generally accepted the union's commitment to racial integration, yet admitted that there was a "certain amount of self-segregation" of blacks and whites in the southern locals. And then there were concerns in the post-1964 period about the financial irresponsibility of some of the civil rights organizations to which the ILGWU had contributed. Bonanno reported that some of the black ministers who received funds from the ILGWU were corrupt. Although most of the tensions between the union and the civil rights movement arose out of such financial concerns, the relationship between the ILGWU and a number of local civil rights organizations remained strong.[35]

The 1960s and 1970s proved to be a critical era for the southern apparel industry. It was only after the enactment of the Civil Rights Act in 1964 that southern clothing factories began to hire African American women in any great numbers.[36] But it was also during these years that the ILGWU secured an important victory, winning the National Labor Relations Board election at Vanity Fair. While the unions made it clear that they were committed to ending race-based discrimination, they made few promises about gender. African American women entered clothing factories like Vanity Fair and brought a notion of social justice inspired by the civil rights movement. But gender, the tie that bound them to an earlier generation of white women apparel workers, was not a primary concern of either the unions or the industry.

The apparel industry was, for the most part, racially segregated since its very beginnings in the first half of the twentieth century. In this way, the apparel and textile industries are quite similar. With respect to issues of gender-based segregation, however, the apparel and textile industries should not be confused. Textiles employed nearly equal numbers of men and women throughout the second half of the twentieth century, while women apparel workers generally outnumbered men workers four to one. With the exception of a few positions such as mechanics, bundlers, and managers, the southern clothing industry was a feminine one. Even today, the position of sewing machine operator remains one of the most segregated by sex of all occupations in the United States.[37]

After World War II, clothing manufacturers looking to relocate to the South frequently cited their desire for female labor. Similarly, southern counties looking to attract factories would boast of a pliant female work force in addition to the community's anti-unionism. Vivian Long worked in Vanity Fair's personnel office from 1946 to 1983. She pointed out that in the 1930s, the men in the community worked to sell bonds so the women could get jobs. "Employment for ladies in this part of the country was very limited." Of course, the "ladies" to which Long referred were white women. Ken Hundley, a plant manager at the same factory, explained that Vanity Fair's proclivity for women sewing machine operators was based on a belief that women were simply "more dextrous."[38] Assumptions about women's essential characteristics explain the persistence of the craft's identification as women's work, and the focus on low-wage labor made the choice of women employees seem natural. These conclusions reflected a gender-specific contradiction. Though women were believed to be naturally more "dextrous" than men, this dexterity was not regarded as a skill worth high wages. The apparel industry was (and continues to be) notorious for seeking the lowest wage level possible, and female employment became synonymous with low-wage labor.[39]

In colonial times, women sewed clothes for their families; some contributed significantly to the household earnings by selling their products. It is not surprising, then, that the apparel industry that developed in the centuries that followed would seek to hire women workers. Sewing and spinning were essentially domestic crafts that evolved into women's outside work. The fact that sewing and garment manufacturing came from a craft that symbolized domesticity throughout the eighteenth and nineteenth centuries is not without significance. In the decades just prior to World War II, southern white women joined the ranks of the nation's apparel workers as garment factories opened from North Carolina to Texas.[40]

Domesticity, however, honored in rhetoric, afforded little protection to women workers. Eula McGill, a clothing worker who later became the first woman business agent for the ACWA, recalled that women workers were often sexually assaulted on the job. "Right there in the mill . . . the bosses took girls back there." At the Fulton Bag and Cotton Mill in Atlanta, women workers endured a whole range of sexual harassment and objectification ranging from obscene language to sexual assault. It was this kind of experience that cried out for remedy at the hands of organized labor.[41]

Even ILGWU officials were sometimes guilty of similar behavior. Nick Bonanno claimed that the former director of the region, E. T. "Al" Kehrer, "was a womanizer" and that his long list of sexual indiscretions hurt the movement. Kehrer was regional director of the southern branch of the ILGWU from 1954 to 1964. According to Bonanno, another regional director "used to bring in these country girls from small towns for sensitivity sessions. They'd sit around holding hands . . . and, you know." Bonanno's own perspective on these activities is also revealing. As he discussed the sexual indiscretions of his male colleagues, he remarked, "I'm not opposed to womanizing to a certain extent, don't get me wrong. I'm not a saint." This sexualized perspective created an environment that was not especially conducive to addressing working women's concerns or to organizing in an industry that was overwhelmingly female.[42]

Even within the union, women agreed that union activism was more difficult for women to achieve. As a result of women's dual commitments to work and to family, men simply had more time to devote to such matters. Interestingly, many women union activists in the clothing industry did not have children of their own and reported difficult relations with men. Eula McGill felt mismatched with her husband and lived with him only briefly. While she was on the job, organizing and negotiating, her parents raised their only son. Similarly Evelyn Dubrow, who became one of the first women lobbyists for the ACWA's political department, suffered "a bad experience with a very brief marriage" when she was young. On family and children, Dubrow remarked, "[W]hile I love children . . . I never felt that necessity. There's some of us who are domestically inclined and some of us who aren't." The clothing unions attracted women who had some freedom to become activists, often women who did not have husbands or children. Having a family was not, of course, an insurmountable barrier to union activism; it simply made activism more difficult.[43]

On a local level, the story was different and yet the same. After a few years of experience organizing and representing her fellow Vanity Fair employees, Emily Woodyard felt that "Women are at a disadvantage. They put in their eight hours a day. . . . They go home. They cook supper. They tend to the kids. And they get ready for another day at the plant." Woodyard went on to say that as a result of women's double duty, union activism was more of a sacrifice for women than for men. In 1979 the women on Vanity Fair's organizing committee remembered how exhausted they were from their labors for their jobs, the union, and their families. And yet, somehow, they managed to spread the word and win at Vanity Fair.[44]

Yet the ILGWU itself seemed to betray these women's sacrifices as it accommodated an industry that valued men's work over women's. After the failed 1963 Oneita strike in Andrews, South Carolina, the union offered loans to striking members who were not reemployed after the strike. The loans varied according to gender. The Southeast Regional Office reported to the ILGWU's headquarters in New York that women could borrow twenty-five dollars while men could get thirty dollars per week. While it is certainly true that men, who typically held positions as mechanics and cutters, tended to earn higher wages than women, the union did nothing to challenge that gender-based occupational segregation of the clothing industry.[45]

In the political arena, women unionists could be very valuable to the apparel unions' agenda. The ILGWU persistently sought the active support of women members at the polls. As early as 1957, a bulletin emphasizing the many reasons women should vote in an upcoming election was distributed in Alabama. Women were asked, "How well is your house being kept?" The bulletin urged women to "keep politics clean." With a strong emphasis on the metaphor of cleaning house, the Alabama Labor

Council's Committee on Political Education (COPE) synthesized domestic and political images. One item reminded women that "Voting is as much a woman's job as it is a man's. . . . When I hear a woman say . . . 'My husband doesn't want me to vote,' then I begin to think, 'Poor thing, what kind of man is she married to?' I feel sorry for any woman married to a man who thinks his wife should not vote."[46] In this bulletin, Alabama's COPE challenged the de-politicization of women's roles. An accompanying memo explained how the leaflet would attract women to the polls by discussing political matters "in the everyday terms of housekeeping which every woman will understand." COPE went on to state that this handout "will be particularly effective in those Locals which have a substantial number of women." Labor specifically targeted the women of the ILGWU.[47]

Given organized labor's ambitions to have women flock to the polls, the union's reluctance to affiliate with the Equal Rights Amendment (ERA) activists seems contradictory. Certainly this was a political crusade that sought equity in the workplace. Workers from Vanity Fair and organizers for the ILGWU and ACWA reported that the ERA had not stirred up much controversy or support among southern clothing workers. Even Nick Bonanno, president of the Southeast Region during the fight for the ERA, remarked that the women's movement had little effect on his union. Anti-unionists and labor leaders at Vanity Fair alike remarked that they were largely unimpressed with the fight for the ERA or the women's movement in general.[48]

Perhaps there was no place for equal work and equal pay, the primary principles of the ERA, in the clothing industry.[49] Positions there were rigidly separated by sex and the unions had done little to change that by the time of the ERA. Evelyn Dubrow argued that organized labor's reluctance to support the ERA stemmed from the Women's Trade Union League's efforts to pass protective legislation for women workers, restricting the number of hours women could work and improving working and safety conditions.[50] Although the validity of this popularly held position has been challenged quite effectively, to many activists the ERA seemed to threaten hard-earned protections for women in the workplace. And sex-specific protective legislation seemed to have greater relevance to the clothing industry because of its mostly single-sex composition. The perception that organized labor was opposed to an amendment that would erode protective legislation for women may have been more important than the truth.[51]

Moreover, advocates of working people sometimes viewed the women's movement as dominated by elite women. Dubrow commented that the

ERA supported professional women against organized labor's rank-and-file women unionists. Although Dubrow eventually became active in support of the women's movement (and not the ERA), initially she was unconvinced of the movement's sincerity toward working women, saying that the movement "was started by women who were not working in the garment plants. . . . Mostly they were professional women." By initially focusing on what Dubrow saw as "frivolous" cases rather than on important issues like "equal pay for equal work . . . equal opportunity for jobs and promotions," the movement had to earn Dubrow's support.[52]

Although the clothing unions' support of the ERA was virtually nonexistent at the local level, and the position of sewing machine operator remains one of the most feminine occupations in the United States, the degree of gender segregation eased over time. Vivian Long believed the women's movement resulted in the promotion of a few women to managerial positions and cited this as the only effect it had had on Vanity Fair.[53]

In many ways the organizers, officials, and local members of the ILGWU cannot be blamed for their reluctance to join in the fight for the Equal Rights Amendment. Garment workers at Vanity Fair and presumably throughout the South experienced greater connections with union activism and the civil rights movement than they did with the women's movement. Segregation occurs at many levels and in many different forms. Racial segregation may have eased in response to the civil rights movement and federal legislation, but the gender desegregation of the southern apparel industry remains incomplete.

Finally, by the 1980s the southern communities that had once welcomed apparel factories and their promises of jobs and economic salvation began to notice a change. Apparel factories across the South closed their doors forever, leaving more and more black, white, and Latina women stitchers unemployed. Meanwhile, communities in Mexico and other Latin American countries welcomed the apparel industry and looked forward to the fulfillment of the same promises of jobs and economic salvation that had once brightened the South's future. The apparel industry has continued its long-standing reliance on female labor in Latin America, just as it did in the 1930s when the industry moved from northeastern states to southern states. It remains to be seen just how much of the industry's history will repeat itself.

Notes

1. For a discussion of the ways in which southern communities attracted runaway industry, see James Cobb, *The Selling of the South: The Southern Crusade for Industrial Development, 1936–1980* (Baton Rouge, 1982). See also Bruce J. Schulman, *From Cotton Belt to Sunbelt: Federal Policy, Economic Development, and the Transformation of the South, 1938–1980* (Durham, N.C., 1994); Joan M. Jensen and Sue Davidson, eds., *A Needle, a Bobbin, a Strike: Women Needleworkers in America* (Philadelphia, 1984), xii–xv; Tami J. Friedman, "Fashioning a Favorable Business Climate: The Industrialization of Greenville, Mississippi," paper presented at the 63rd Annual Meeting of the Southern Historical Association, Atlanta, Georgia, November 5–8, 1997.

2. Mike Breedlove, "Jacksonians Raised Plant Funds," *The South Alabamian,* June 8, 1989, sec. C, 16; Vivian Long, interview by author, August 9, 1998, Jackson, Alabama, tape recording in author's possession. Arcola McLean recalled, "They tried to get in, but the Vanity Fair people, they told us, they made a speech and they told us that they wouldn't operate under a union. So we all voted against it." Arcola McLean, interview by author, Jackson, Alabama, August 8, 1998, tape recording in author's possession.

3. Long, interview.

4. Long, interview.

5. McLean, interview; Max McAliley, "Monroeville's Vanity Fair Boasts Many Firsts in Four-Year History," *Mobile Register,* August 11, 1986, sec. B, 2. Over a decade later, despite Vanity Fair's relocation of much of its sewing operations to Mexico, the *1997 Economic Census* listed the apparel industry as a primary employer, perhaps the largest manufacturing employer, in Clarke County. U.S. Census Bureau, *1997 Economic Census.* County data available from <http://www.census.gov/e~cd/ec97/al/AL025 31.HTM>.

6. On the intersection and interrelationships between race and gender, Evelyn Brooks Higginbotham's 1992 essay is particularly useful. Evelyn Brooks Higginbotham, "African American Women's History and the Metalanguage of Race," *Signs* 17 (1992): 251–74.

7. In the only substantial study of African Americans in the apparel industry, Elaine Gale Wrong argues that federal civil rights legislation such as the Fair Employment Practices Commission was ineffectual and did little to alter the racial composition of the industry. However, that pattern changed with the Civil Rights Act of 1964. Wrong states that the provisions of the Civil Rights Act initiated change and opened occupations in apparel factories to African American women. The Civil Rights Act combined with a labor shortage compelled apparel employers to redefine occupations in terms of race. Again and again employers told Wrong, "In order to obtain a labor supply, apparel employers had no choice but to abandon the discriminatory hiring policies of the 1950s and early 1960s." Elaine Gail Wrong, *The Negro in the Apparel Industry* (Philadelphia, 1974), 122–4.

8. Wrong, *The Negro in the Apparel Industry*, 35, 46–7, 104.

9. For the racial composition of Capital City see Burl C. Robinson to Martin J. Morand, January 29, 1965, box 3051, folder 8: "Organizing Activities, 1961–1965," International Ladies Garment Workers Union, Southeast Regional Office (hereafter, ILGWU-SERO) Records, 1945–1978, Southern Labor Archives (SLA), Special Collections, Pullen Library, Georgia State University, Atlanta, Georgia.

10. Vevelyn "Queenie" Gilchrist, interview by the author, tape recording, Atlanta, Georgia, August 21, 1998; Nick Bonanno, interview by the author.

11. Long, interview; Gilchrist, interview.

12. Wrong also argues that southern governments built more manufacturing facilities as an incentive for relocating for garment companies than for any other industry. Wrong, *The Negro in the Apparel Industry*, 43. Cobb, *The Selling of the South*, 9–10, 22–4, 31, 54, 61, 69, 97–116.

13. Herbert R. Northrup and Richard R. Rowan's 1970 study of African Americans' participation in southern industry emphasized a shortage of white labor in the 1960s as the impetus behind the entrance of African Americans into manufacturing positions. Timothy Minchin's more recent work challenges the emphasis on a labor shortage through a careful study of federal court records and suggests that federal legislation played a more important role in decreasing the racial exclusivity of southern textile factories. Herbert R. Northrup and Richard L. Rowan, *Negro Employment in Southern Industry* (Philadelphia, 1970); James J. Heckman and Brook S. Payner, "Determining the Impact of Federal Antidiscrimination Policy on the Economic Status of Blacks: A Study of South Carolina," *The American Economic Review* 79 (March 1989): 138–77; Timothy J. Minchin, *Hiring the Black Worker: The Racial Integration of the Southern Textile Industry, 1960–1980* (Chapel Hill, 1999); Timothy J. Minchin, "Color Means Something: Black Pioneers, White Resistance, and Interracial Unionism in the Southern Textile Industry, 1957–1980," *Labor History* 39 (May 1998): 109, 116.

14. Paula McLendon, "Union Turns Loners into Leaders," *Anniston [Alabama] Star*, n.d., n.p., reprint among Paula McLendon's personal clipping file in author's possession.

15. Rebecca Blackmon and Emily Woodyard, interview by Paula McLendon (selected transcription), Leroy, Alabama, December 16, 1979, original among Paula McLendon's personal clipping file in author's possession. Michelle Brattain explores many facets of whiteness in southern politics and labor throughout her important new book on textile workers in North Georgia: Michelle Brattain, *The Politics of Whiteness: Race, Workers, and Culture in the Modern South* (Princeton, 2001), 277.

16. Tami J. Friedman, "'What Price Industry?': Southern Organizing and the Runaway Shop, 1946–1966," paper presented at the annual Southern Labor Studies Conference, Williamsburg, Virginia, September 1997, 6–7; McLean, interview; Long, interview.

17. Vevelyn "Queenie" Gilchrist, interview by Paula McLendon (tape summary), Frankville, Alabama, November 1979, original among Paula McLendon's personal

clipping file in author's possession. Quoted in Paula McLendon, "Time and Time Again: The Women, the Union and the Vanity Factory," *Southern Changes*, October/November 1984, 10–11.

18. McLean, interview.

19. Long, interview.

20. Based on World War II–era Gallup Poll research, Robert H. Zieger notes that "In general, workers held to positions on a wide range of issues considerably to the right of their leaderships, that of race being the most dramatic example." At Vanity Fair, one white worker argued against racial desegregation, stating that she made more money working alongside other white women than she did with African American women. Robert H. Zieger, *The CIO: 1935–1955* (Chapel Hill, 1995), 162, 422–3n; McLean, interview; "Organizing Drive Questionnaire," box 3105, folder 2: "Ahoskie Manufacturing Company: Organizing, 1956," ILGWU-SERO Records, SLA.

21. In an essay on changes in the textile industry, Mary Frederickson argues, "After black workers entered the [southern textile] mills in . . . larger numbers in the mid-1960s, their initial response to unionization was so overwhelmingly positive that the unions tended to take that firm commitment for granted." Clyde Bush, a Textile Workers Union of America (TWUA) organizer during the Oneita Knitting Mills strike of 1973, commented, "Back in the late 1960s, whenever you went into one plant the first thing that you looked to was how many blacks are working in there. And if there were forty blacks you could count on forty votes." Timothy Minchin concludes that the presence of African Americans in the textile factories resulted in easier union victories. He finds that organizers were able to build on the infrastructure that the civil rights movement developed within African American communities. Mary Frederickson, "Four Decades of Change: Black Workers in Southern Textiles, 1941–1981," in *Workers' Struggles, Past and Present: A "Radical America" Reader*, ed. James Green (Philadelphia, 1983), 77; Carolyn Ashbaugh and Dan McCurry, "On the Line at Oneita," in *Working Lives: The Southern Exposure History of Labor in the South*, ed. Marc S. Miller (New York, 1980), 210; Minchin, *Hiring the Black Worker*, 247–54.

22. McLendon, "Time and Time Again," 9–11.

23. Gilchrist, interview by the author; see also Gilchrist, interview by Paula McLendon (tape summary).

24. Nicholas Bonanno, interview by the author, tape recording, Atlanta, Georgia, March 27, 1998. See also Nick Bonanno, interview by Chris Lutz, September 13, 1995, Voices of Labor Oral History Project, SLA. "Organizing Drive Questionnaire," box 3105, folder 2: "Ahoskie Manufacturing Company: Organizing, 1956," ILGWU-SERO Records, SLA.

25. See total contents of box 3049, folder 6: "Membership: African-Americans in Locals, 1973–1974," ILGWU-SERO, SLA.

26. Donald C. Mosley, "The Labor Union Movement," in *A History of Mississippi*, vol. 2, ed. Richard Aubrey McLemore (Hattiesburg, 1973), 270–1. As early as

the 1930s, the ACWA also reported successes in organizing African American work-ers. In Baltimore, Maryland, one unionist asserted that "colored workers in Balti-more are eager to organize." Quoted in Jo Ann E. Argersinger, *Making the Amal-gamated: Gender, Ethnicity, and Class in the Baltimore Clothing Industry, 1899–1939* (Baltimore, 1999), 165. For a discussion of the impact of race on the ILGWU's efforts to organize the Greensboro plant, see Morton Shapiro to Martin Morand, Atlanta, Georgia, January 10, 1965, box 3051, folder 8: "Organizing Activi-ties, 1961–1965," ILGWU-SERO, SLA. Minchin, *Hiring the Black Worker*, 246–9.

27. Long, interview; McLean, interview.

28. In 1973 and 1974, locals and business agents sent in rosters of African Ameri-can members in southern ILGWU locals. Several included a special mention of a number of "colored" and white union members and officers. See various documents in box 3049, folder 6: "Membership: African-Americans in Locals, 1973–1974," ILGWU-SERO, Records, 1945–1978, SLA.

29. Gilchrist, interview.

30. McLendon, "Time and Time Again," 14. See also Wilda Blackmon, interview by Paula McLendon (tape summary), Jackson, Alabama, November 1979, original among Paula McLendon's personal clipping file in author's possession.

31. Martin Morand to Eliott M. Shirk, n.d., ca. January 1965, box 3029, folder 6: "Morand, Martin J., Regional Director: Personal Correspondence, 1965," ILGWU-SERO, SLA. Timothy J. Minchin similarly concludes that for African American tex-tile workers, union work was an extension of civil rights work: Timothy J. Minchin, "Color Means Something," 128–9.

32. Southern Christian Leadership Coalition to Martin Morand, July 28, 1966, box 3024, folder 7: "Handler, Jack G. Regional Counsel: Personal Correspondence, 1966"; Elliot M. Shirk to Martin Morand, January 8, 1965, box 3029, folder 6: "Morand, Martin J., Regional Director: Personal Correspondence, 1965," all in ILGWU-SERO, SLA.

33. E. T. "Al" Kehrer was assistant to the director of the Southeast Region from 1953 to 1954. He spent the next ten years as the director of the Southeast Region. For a discussion of the AFL-CIO's Southern Staff Institutes, see "Staff Training with a Southern Accent," *AFL-CIO Federationist*, September 1965, 19–22.

34. Albert I. Gross to E. T. "Al" Kehrer, June 19, 1963, box 3029, folder 5: "Kehrer, 'Al' ET., Regional Director: Personal Correspondence, 1963," ILGWU-SERO, SLA.

35. Bonanno, interview by author; Bonanno, interview by Chris Lutz.

36. In 1966 the Equal Employment Opportunity Commission (EEOC) published its first report on patterns of employment by race and sex, and these reports con-tinue to be an invaluable source for tracing the occupational history of several differ-ent groups in American history. Still, the data presented in them are somewhat problematic. From the very beginning employers were only required to submit data to the EEOC if they employed 100 or more persons. The U.S. garment industry is composed mostly of smaller establishments and thus many of these firms are not (and were not) required to submit data to the EEOC. The average number of em-ployees in an apparel industry firm is less than fifty. U.S. Equal Employment Oppor-

tunity Commission, *Equal Employment Opportunity Report No. 1: Job Patterns for Minorities and Women in Private Industry, 1966* (Washington, D.C., 1966), 1, 19–129; U.S. Equal Employment Opportunity Commission, *1978 Report: Minorities and Women in Private Industry* (Washington, D.C., 1980), 23–5. Elaine Wrong discusses the shortcomings of EEOC data in Wrong, *The Negro in the Apparel Industry*, 2.

37. From 1966 to 1980, the percentage of men and women in the U.S. apparel industry remained relatively constant, with men accounting for roughly 19 to 21 percent and women accounting for 79 to 81 percent of the industry's work force. These figures are derived from reports issued by the EEOC.

38. The secretary of the Georgia Department of Commerce sent a memo to "ILGWU Organizers" that explained that several companies expressed interest in locating in Georgia. The memo details the requirements of two blouse manufacturers. Both firms requested information on "available female labor pools" and both operations (or their agents) were currently located in New York City. Nelson M Shipp, "Memo: Industrial Prospects," September 13, 1954, box 3051, folder 6: "Organizing Activities, 1954," ILGWU-SERO, SLA; Long, interview; Ken Hundley, Jr., interview by author, Jackson, Alabama, August 9, 1998.

39. Bruce Raynor, the current secretary-treasurer of the Union of Needletrades, Industrial and Textile Employees (UNITE!), commented that apparel companies have always sought the lowest wage level possible. This explains, in part, the motivations behind the industry's move to the U.S. South and, later, to Mexico. Bruce Raynor, comments, session on "Victory at Kannapolis and the Significance for Southern Labor History," 1999 Southern Labor Studies Conference, Atlanta, Georgia, October 2, 1999 (Haberland notes); Bonanno, interview with author.

40. Sue Davidson makes a similar point in her co-edited volume of essays on the textile and garment industries. See Sue Davidson, introduction to Jensen and Davidson, *A Needle, a Bobbin, a Strike*, xii. See Joan M. Jensen, "Inside and Outside the Unions, 1920–1980," in *A Needle, A Bobbin, A Strike: Women Needleworkers in America*, eds. Joan M. Jensen and Sue Davidson (Philadelphia, 1981), 189.

41. *The Uprising of 1934*, documentary film produced by George Stoney and Judith Helfand, Point of View Series, PBS, 1995. Gary M. Fink, "Efficiency and Control: Labor Espionage in Southern Textiles," in *Organized Labor in the Twentieth-Century South*, ed. Robert H. Zieger (Knoxville, 1991), 25.

42. Nicholas Bonanno, interview by author.

43. Eula McGill, interview by the author, Irondale, Alabama, July 10, 1998; Lydia Kleiner, *Oral History Interview with Evelyn Dubrow, International Ladies Garment Workers' Union*, The 20th Century Trade Union Woman: Vehicle for Social Change Oral History Project (Ann Arbor, 1978), 30–1; Eileene Brown, interview by the author, Oxford, Alabama, July 24, 1998. The Vanity Fair original organizing committee members were both married and divorced, and most had children.

44. Rebecca Blackmon and Emily Woodyard, interview by Paula McLendon; McLendon, "Time and Time Again," 14.

45. The terms of the loan included any unemployment insurance payments as

part of the figures of the twenty-five-dollar limit for women and the thirty-dollar limit for men; Nick Bonanno to Mitchell Yager, March 2, 1964, box 3162, folder 12: "Oneita Knitting Mills, Inc.: Correspondence, 1963–1964," ILGWU-SERO, SLA.

46. Alabama Labor Council Committee on Political Education, "She Said: Politics Is Such a Dirty Business," n.d., "The Story of Jim and Anna," nd., both in box 3043, folder 11: "Committee on Political Education (COPE), 1957," ILGWU-SERO, SLA.

47. E. J. Barnett, Barney Weeks, and Leroy Lindsey to All Alabama Local Unions, AFL-CIO, December 4, 1957, box 3043, folder 11: "Committee on Public Education (COPE), 1957," ILGWU-SERO, SLA.

48. The absence of documents supporting or even mentioning the Equal Rights Amendment in the records of the ILGWU's Southeastern Regional Office is striking, especially in comparison to the boxes of documents relating to the union's support for local civil rights organizations and initiatives. Long, interview; Arcola McLean, interview; Brown, interview; Eula McGill, interview; Bonanno, interview by author.

49. Donald G. Mathews and Jane Sherron DeHart have written the only book-length study on the ERA and the South. In addition to offering an important account of the political history of the amendment, they also argue that "The politics of gender was stained with racism." Opposition to the ERA often coincided, especially in the South, with opposition to federally mandated desegregation. Donald G. Mathews and Jane Sherron DeHart, *Sex, Gender, and the Politics of the ERA: A State and Nation* (New York, 1990). See also Sara Evans, *Personal Politics: The Roots of Women's Liberation in the Civil Rights Movement and the New Left* (New York, 1979).

50. Nancy Gabin, *Feminism in the Labor Movement: Women and the United Auto Workers, 1935–1975* (Ithaca, N.Y., 1990).

51. Nancy Schrom Dye's 1980 study argues that "There is little historical evidence to suggest that labor was the main force behind most protective labor efforts." Moreover, the Women's Trade Union League only "casually endorsed protective legislation for women." Nancy Schrom Dye, *As Equals and As Sisters: Feminism, the Labor Movement, and the Women's Trade Union League of New York* (Columbia, 1980) 140–66, n.182. See also Dennis A. Deslippe, *"Rights, Not Roses": Unions and the Rise of Working-Class Feminism* (Urbana, 2000), 137–8.

52. Lydia Kleiner, *Oral History Interview with Evelyn Dubrow*, 7–8, 45–6. Myra Wolfgang, vice president of the Hotel and Restaurant Workers (HERE), felt much the same way. She argued that elite women were the driving force behind the ERA and she feared that their appeals to working-class women were insincere. Deslippe, *Rights, Not Roses*, 137–8.

53. Long, interview by author.

Notes on the Contributors

Sarah Hart Brown is an associate professor of history at Florida Atlantic University. She specializes in twentieth-century America with an emphasis on the American South. Her research interests include southern radicalism and liberalism and civil rights law. Her book *Standing Against Dragons: Three Southern Lawyers in the Era of Fear, 1945–1965* was published in 1999. She received the E. Merton Coulter Award of the Georgia Historical Association and the Leroy Collins Prize of the Georgia Historical Association for earlier articles.

Orville Vernon Burton was born in Royston, Georgia, reared in Ninety Six, South Carolina, graduated from Furman University, and received his Ph.D. in American history from Princeton University in 1976. Since 1974 he has been in the History Department at the University of Illinois, Urbana-Champaign, where he is currently professor of history and sociology and a senior research scientist at the National Center for Supercomputing Applications, where he heads the initiative for Humanities and Social Science projects. He is the author of more than a hundred articles and the author or editor of seven books, including *In My Father's House Are Many Mansions: Family and Community in Edgefield, South Carolina* (1985), and with Judy McArthur, *"A Gentleman and an Officer": A Social and Military History of James B. Griffin's Civil War* (1996).

Bruce L. Clayton holds the Harry A. Logan Sr. Chair in History at Allegheny College. A graduate of the University of Missouri and of Duke University, he has published widely in the fields of southern history and intellectual history. These twin interests conjoined in his acclaimed biography of the southern writer W. J. Cash. His most recent book, *Praying for Base Hits*, is a memoir of his boyhood in Kansas City.

Karen L. Cox is a senior writer with The History Factory in northern Virginia. She earned a Ph.D. in U.S. history from the University of Southern

Mississippi, and her book on the United Daughters of the Confederacy, entitled *Dixie's Daughters: Women, the Lost Cause, and the New South,* will be published by the University Press of Florida.

Warren Ellem did his undergraduate studies at the University of New England in Australia (1964–68) and his graduate studies at Yale University (1969–73). He teaches history at La Trobe University in Melbourne and has a particular interest in nineteenth-century America. His publications on southern and Civil War and Reconstruction history, as well as on Australian sporting history, have appeared in American and Australian journals and as book chapters. He coedited with William J. Breen *Irish and German Immigration to the United States of American in the Mid-Nineteenth Century* (1993). He is currently completing a biography of Adelbert Ames (1835–1933).

Glenn Feldman is an assistant professor in the Center for Labor Education and Research at the University of Alabama at Birmingham. He is the author of *Politics, Society, and the Klan in Alabama, 1915–1949* (1999) as well as *From Demagogue to Dixiecrat: Horace Wilkinson and the Politics of Race* (1995). Feldman is the editor of *Reading Southern History: Essays on Interpreters and Interpretations* (2001). He holds five degrees, including a Ph.D. in History from Auburn University (1996).

Catherine Fosl is a teaching scholar at the Commonwealth Humanities Center of the University of Louisville. Her biography of Anne Braden, *Subversive Southerner: Anne Braden and the Struggle for Racial Justice in the Cold War South,* was published in 2002. Dr. Fosl's earlier book, *Women for All Seasons: The Story of the Women's International League for Peace and Freedom,* appeared in 1989.

Michelle Haberland received her B.A. in 1990 and her M.A. in 1993 from the University of Florida in Gainesville. She received her Ph.D. from Tulane University in 2001. Her dissertation, "Women Workers: The Apparel Industry in the United States South, 1937–1980," is a full-length study of the race, gender, and class dynamics of the southern clothing industry and its workers. She is currently an assistant professor at Georgia Southern University.

Anya Jabour received her Ph.D. in history from Rice University in 1995. She is currently an associate professor of history at the University of

Montana, where she teaches courses in U.S. women's history, family history, and the history of the American South. Professor Jabour's first book, *Marriage in the Early Republic: Elizabeth and William Wirt and the Companionate Ideal*, was published in 1998. Her essays, articles, and conference papers have explored such themes as gender and adolescence, same-sex friendship, and women's education. She is presently at work on two book manuscripts, including *Daughters of the South: Coming of Age in the Nineteenth Century*, an in-depth study of girlhood, adolescence, and young womanhood in the Victorian South.

Elizabeth Jacoway, an independent scholar, lives in Newport, Arkansas. She received her Ph.D. from the University of North Carolina, where she worked under George Brown Tindall. She is the author of *Yankee Missionaries in the South: The Penn School Experiment* (1980) and ten articles. She is also the editor or coeditor of four other books. She is currently at work on a history of the Little Rock desegregation crisis of 1957. Her books include *Southern Businessmen and Desegregation* (1981); *"Behold, Our Works Were Good": A Handbook of Arkansas Women's History* (1986); *The Adaptable South: Essays in Honor of George Brown Tindall* (1990); and *Understanding the Little Rock Crisis: An Exercise in Remembrance and Reconciliation* (1998).

Kathi Kern did her undergraduate work at Allegheny College, where she studied American history with Bruce Clayton. She went on to earn a Ph.D. from the University of Pennsylvania. Currently an associate professor of history at the University of Kentucky, Kern is the author of *Mrs. Stanton's Bible* (2001). From 1993 to 1999, she spent a portion of every summer working with public school teachers in the Mississippi and Arkansas Delta under the auspices of the National Faculty.

Barbara E. Mattick is a doctoral candidate in American history at Florida State University, focusing on the South and women's history. Her dissertation will be on the work of the Sisters of Mercy and the Sisters of St. Joseph in St. Augustine, Florida. She earned a bachelor's degree in American history from Emory University in 1972, and has master's degrees from Florida State University in American history (1976), library science (1985), and anthropology (1995). Previous publications include "Tallahassee and the 1841 Yellow Fever Epidemic," *Apalachee*, 1971–1979; and "Cotton Technology in Antebellum Leon County, Middle Florida," *Apalachee*, 1991–1996. Since 1988, she has worked for the Florida Department of

State, Bureau of Historic Preservation, and is currently the deputy state historic preservation officer for Survey and Registration, overseeing the National Register of Historic Places Program in Florida.

Giselle Roberts is honorary research associate in history at LaTrobe University, Melbourne, Australia, where she earned her Ph.D. She specializes in southern American history and women's history, and has published articles in the *Journal of Mississippi History* and *Louisiana History*. She is currently editing the courtship correspondence of Sarah Morgan and Francis Warrington Dawson.

John A. Salmond has held the chair of American history at La Trobe University, Melbourne, Australia, since 1970. A graduate of the University of Otago in Dunedin, New Zealand, and of Duke University, he has published widely in the field of southern history. His most recent book, *The General Textile Strike of 1934: "From Maine to Alabama,"* appeared in 2002.

Anne Firor Scott is William K. Boyd Professor Emerita of history at Duke University, Durham, North Carolina. One of the first historians to do serious research in women's history, her 1970 book *The Southern Lady: From Pedestal to Politics, 1830–1930* is regarded as a classic in the field. Since then a steady stream of articles and books has enhanced her reputation. The title of a 1992 festschrift in her honor, *Making the Invisible Woman Visible,* neatly encapsulates her importance to women's history.

Paula A. Treckel graduated from Kent State University and received her M.A. and Ph.D. degrees from Syracuse University. She has been a member of the Department of History at Allegheny College in Meadville, Pennsylvania, since 1981. A specialist in the field of early American women's history, she is the author of *To Comfort the Heart: Women in Seventeenth Century America* (1996), and has written extensively on Allegheny College graduate "Lady Muckraker" Ida Tarbell. Treckel is currently at work on "'Dearly Beloved . . .': The Romance and Rituals of American Weddings."

Pamela Tyler earned a Ph.D. in American history from Tulane University and is the author of *Silk Stockings and Ballot Boxes: Women and Politics in New Orleans, 1920–1963* (1996). Now an associate professor of history at North Carolina State University, she teaches U.S. women's history and the history of the New South, and is currently researching a book on the complicated relationship between Eleanor Roosevelt and the American South.

Index